FAITH & PHILOSOPHY
OF
SIKHISM

INDIAN RELIGIONS SERIES: 4

FAITH & PHILOSOPHY
OF
SIKHISM

Sardar Harjeet Singh

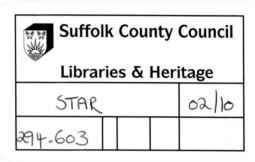
Faith & Philosophy of Sikhism

Rs. 675

© Sardar Harjeet Singh

ISBN: 978-81-7835-721-8

Published in 2009 in India by
Kalpaz Publications
C - 30, Satyawati Nagar,
Delhi - 110052
E-mail: kalpaz@hotmail.com
Phone: 9212729499

Printed at: Singhal Print Media, Delhi

Contents

Preface

It may be said that the Guru Nanak is one of the most revolutionary thinkers and the holiest persons ever lived on the earth. He has been a bright light not only for India but for the entire world. His advocacy of pursuit of salvation and practice of *Ahmisa*, his vision of equality and avid longing for obliteration of suffering of others as one's own cross all barriers of race, creed, country and even humanity. His benevolent teachings of universal compassion and cosmic goodwill, his emphasis on the noble virtues of *Japji (prayer)*, Nam Simran (Think about God), Kirt Kaara (do good), Wand Chhako (Share with the needy), all these have a significant message for the present-day distracted humankind suffering from exhaustion of spirit and languishing in the narrow and rigid confinements of materialistic consumerism.

This book deals with almost every aspect of Sikh philosophy from personality to doctrine of Guru Nanak, Ten Gurus, fundamental character, nature, and spirit of philosophy and the development of Sikhism. The book covers the subject of Sikhism thoroughly in a manner which makes it interesting to read and easy to understand. A special care has been taken to put the principles of Sikhism philosophy in proper order so that the reader finds the book very useful and enjoyable.

The chapters in this volume have been well-weaved and the events connected with them are mentioned in a comprehensive way. Efforts have been made to mention about the religious customs and ceremonies from birth to death, including religious verses which are recited daily at the Gurudwaras. Indeed the information given in this volume is fairly comprehensive in contents so that all the readers should feel benefited with the text of the religion which they follow, preach, and profess.

A productive bibliography, along with references is provided to prove the authenticity of the work and in order to guide the scholars and readers for further studies. Hopefully, this volume would be able to satisfy the urge of all those who desire to know about real Sikhism and also to create a new awareness regarding this religion.

1

Sikhism: An Introduction

Sikhism is the fifth greatest organized religious faith in the world based on the teachings of Nanak and nine successive Gurus. This organization of religious doctrine and aspect has been commonly known as the Gurmat or the Sikh Dharma. Sikhism developed from the word Sikh, which in turn arrives from the Sanskrit word sishya meaning "disciple" or "learner", or siksha meaning" teaching.

The chief belief of Sikhism is faith in Vahe Guru; made up of using the sanctified symbol of Ek Onkar, the Universal God. Sikhism recommends the pursuit of salvation through trained, personal meditation on the name and content of God. A key distinctive feature of Sikhism is a non-anthropomorphic concept of God, to the degree that one can understand God as the Universe itself. The followers of Sikhism are ordained to follow the instructions of the ten Sikh Gurus, or enlightened leaders, as well as the Holy Scripture entitled the Guru Granth Sahib, which includes selected works of many devotees from several socio-economic and religious backgrounds. The religious text was decreed by Gobind Singh, the tenth Guru, as the final Guru of the Khalsa Panth. Sikhism's customs and teachings are distinctively linked with the history, society and tradition of the Punjab. Disciples of Sikhism are known as Sikhs and number over twenty-three million across the world. Most Sikhs live in the Punjab in India and, prior to the country's partition, thousands of Sikhs lived in what is at present known as the Punjab state of Pakistan.

A mode of life and philosophy well ahead of its time when it was founded over five hundred years ago, The Sikh religious faith at present has a following of over twenty-three million people worldwide. Sikhism preaches a message of devotion and commemoration of God at all times, truthful living, equality of mankind, social justice and marks superstitions and blind rituals. Sikhism is assailable to all through the teachings of its ten Gurus and Sikh Holy Book and Living Guru, Shri Guru Granth Sahib.

Definition of Sikh

The word 'Sikh' in the Punjabi language means 'disciple', Sikhs are the disciples of God who adopt the writings and teachings of the Ten Sikh Gurus. The wiseness of these teachings in Shri Guru Granth Sahib is hardheaded and universal in their appeal to all humankind.

Guru Nanak's Hindu and Muslim followers started to be called Sikhs.He instructed them to bow down only before God, and to associate themselves to the Guru, the Light of Truth, who lives ever in directly awareness of God, experiencing no separation. Through words and example, the Guru teaches to followers how to experience God within themselves, contributing them from darkness into light. Guru Nanak was a humble bearer of this Light of Truth. He opposed superstition, rituals, social inequality and injustice, apostasy and hypocrisy and inspired searchers by singing divine songs which touched the hearts of the most callous listeners. These songs were memorialized, and formed the originations of the Sikhs' holy writings, later to turn the "Siri Guru Granth Sahib".

The Sikhs constitute about two percent of India's billion populations. The groovier Punjab region is the historic homeland of Sikhism. Most Sikhs are from the Punjabi people and now come from the Punjab region of India, although substantial communities live around the world.

Basics of Sikhism

Sikhism is the youngest of all World's religions. Its history goes back to 1469. Its beginner Guru Nanak Dev was born in a village called Talwandi, now known as Nankana Sahib in Pakistan, in 1469. The Sikhs have ten Gurus. It is thought that they all had same soul though they had unlike bodies, and that it was Guru Nanak Dev's teachings which passed on into his nine heirs. The Sikhs call God as 'Wahe-Guru', meaning that God is great.

Guru Granth Sahib is the holy book of the Sikhs. It is thought that the tenth Guru, Guru Gobind Singh imparted upon the Granth the title of the Guru. The Sikhs pray to only one Almighty God in his nonobjective form. They are not admitted to worship any idols, images or photographs. According to the Sikh belief, God is the eternal truth; he is beyond fear, enmity and death. He is unborn and is self illuminated. He himself is the creator, preserver and destroyer. The Sikhs conceive that all creation is assured by one almighty, ubiquitous and omniscient Lord called by different names: Ishwar, Jehovah, Allah and WaheGuru.

Sikhism is the fifth greatest world religious faith. Among all world, regional, and atheistical customs, Sikhism is the ninth largest religion. Sikhs presently number more or less 25 million across the globe, placing Sikhism below Buddhism and over Judaism in terms of size.

Sikhs consider men and women as being completely equal. Women are expected to take part in daily and religious life in the same way as men. Blocking or discouraging women from any activity or position based on sex is against the rules of Sikhism.

In Sikhism, every person is fully in charge for leading a lesson life. Sikhs do not conceive an intermediator can request on one's behalf to God. Hence, Sikhs have no priestly class. Those educated in religious matters or with a special perceptiveness on God are free to teach or guide others, but they cannot claim to have a market on access to God. Religious services are usually conducted by a Giani, literally, one who is educated in religious affairs. However, members of the congregation are also asked to be active players.

Sikhs do not consider God as a man in the clouds or any other form of human being, male or female. The commencement of God in Sikhism is of unity with the entire universe and its spirit. God is firm not by searching in far-off places, but by eradicating ego, which is said to allow a more mysterious, more accurate position on the nature of reality.

Sikhs believe that upon death one blends back into the universal nature, just as a drop of rain merges back into the ocean. Individualism is lost. Sikhs do not believe in heaven or hell. Heaven can be felt by being in tune with God while still alive. Conversely, the suffering and pain caused by ego is seen as hell on earth. Sikhism views religious pursuits as positive experiences in and of themselves that transcend death, not as sacrifices made in order to collect a honor that is waiting until after death.

The only documented religious text of the Sikhs is Shri Guru Granth Sahib Ji, a 1430-page religious text comprising hymns written directly by Guru Nanak Dev Ji and later Gurus. This religious text was signed by Guru Gobind Singh Ji as the final assurance on Sikh spiritual doctrine. Later, other religious texts such as Dasam Granth were integrated into Sikhism's exercise, but these textual matter are of much less grandness and their genuineness has been challenged.

Sikhs conceive they have no right to enforce their impressions on others or even to wheedle members of other religions to change over. Such practices are rigorously forbidden in Sikhism. Sikhs are compulsory to fight the freedom of adoration of other religions just as they would their own. Sikhs do not consider that followers of other religions are doomed in the eyes of God regardless of their personal character and behaviour, nor does turning into a Sikh family guarantee redemption. However, this does not mean Sikhs view all religions as being comparable. The philosophy, practice, and history of Sikhism are exclusive and seen as undoubtedly distinct from any other religious faith.

All people, regardless of race, gender, or nationality, are free to turn Sikhs. Young children who are not yet capable of concord the doctrine of Sikhism and making their own decisions are not suitable to be initiated into the trust until they have grown older. One does not have to be a Sikh to take part in Sikh religious services and actions. Members of other religions are received.

Like the Jewish religious belief which has been subject to crowning historical ill-treatment, Sikhs have faced extreme stress from a variety of groups. Being a small minority, they were nearly decimated by Muslim invaders on multiple occasions and again later by the British Raj during the settlement of India. More recently, they have endured a great deal from attacks by Hindu fundamentalists. However, they have always seemed to repercussion strongly and overcome such horrors. Sikhs played the leading role in ending both the Mughal majestic rule and the British Raj of India. Sikhs now are flourishing and remain one of the fastest developing religions in the world. Practicians of Sikhism can at present be found in every major city in the world.

Gurus

Guru Nanak: Nanak Dev, founding father of the Sikh religious faith was born in 1469, in Rai Bhoi di Talvandi (now Nankana Sahib), 65 kilometres from Lahore (now in Pakistan). He started intermingling with holy men of both Hindu and Islamic impressions at a very early age. Thus, he was determined by both religions in his conceptualization of Sikhism. For some time, Nanak worked as an accountant of Nawab Daulat Khan Lodhi, the Afghan chief at Sultanpur. There he started linking with Mardana, a Muslim family servant. Mardana was a rebec player. Nanak started composing hymns and Mardana gave them the soul of music and the two started community hymn singing. They organized a kitchen wherein both Hindus and Muslims ate together as if belonging to the same community.

At Sultanpur he had his first imagination of "The One God Whose Name Is True", in which he was ordered to preach to human race. He went around preaching in different towns of Punjab and finally rooted with his family at Kartarpur (Abode of His Creator), a township on the banks of the river Ravi.

Guru Angad: Guru Nanak Dev at the time of his death appointed Angad as the second Guru of the Sikhs. He stayed the religious head for thirteen years from 1539 to 1552. On the proposal of Nanak, Angad left Kartarpur and lit the Guru's lamp in Khadur. Angad spread the message of Guru Nanak. He started a regular system of accumulating offerings to meet their expenses including that of ' Langar ' (distribution of food). He made replicates of the Guru Nanak's hymns and circularized one to each centre. These scripts had no precise alphabets of their own. Angad took the 35 letters of the poems and hymns compiled by Nanak, selected the appropriate letters from other scripts of northern India and devised the Gurumukhi (from the mouth of the Guru) script. Angad's compilings became the centre point of the holy writings of the Sikhs. He was a keen admirer of physical fitness. He dictated to his disciples to take part in practice and competitive games after the morning service. At the time of his death, he nominated a seventy-three year old disciple, Amar Das, to follow him as the third Guru.

Guru Amar Das: Amar Das was born in 1479 and belonged to the Bhalla sub-caste. A Khatri, he demonstrated great exuberance in spreading the work of Nanak and Angad. He made ' Langar ' an inherent institution of the Sikh church by insisting that anyone who wanted to meet him should first accept his hospitality by eating with all the disciples. He made more replicates of the works of Nanak and Angad and added his own hymns and that of other Hindu Bhaktas whose teachings were in compliance with the Guru's words. He lived to the age of 95 and chose his son-in-law, Ram Das to follow him as the fourth Guru.

Guru Ram Das: Soon after his appointment as the fourth Guru, Ram Das built a religious capital of the Sikhs known as Guru-ka-Chak or Chak-Ram-Das. He promoted tradesmen and merchants to set up business in the town and with revenues thus gathered, spread his activities to different parts of the country. One of the most imposing disciples of Ram Das was Bhai (brother) Gurdas, who prophesied for some years in Agra.

Like his predecessors, Ram Das wrote hymns, which were later integrated into the Adi Granth, holy book of the Sikhs.

Guru Arjun Dev: Guru Arjan Dev born in 1563, was the fifth Guru. He was made a Guru, by Guru Ramdas Ji in 1581. Guru Arjan was a holy person and scholarly person of the highest order. He gathered the hymns and compositions of Guru Nanak, and his predecessors selected the holy scriptures of some Hindu and Muslim saints, wrote his own hymns and thus composed the Adi Granth. The accomplishments and the works of Guru Arjan upset the reigning Emperor, Jahangir who concerned him and tortured him. The Guru endured quietly and bravely and set to the whole world an example of self-sacrifice and peaceful suffering. In spite of being made to sit in simmering water, and on a red hot iron plate while stinging sand was poured over his body, he chanted cheerfully and softly "Sweet is Thy Will, My Lord; Thy grace solely I Beseech". He passed off in 1606.

Guru Hargobind Sahib: The sixth Guru, Guru Hargobind Sahib, was born in 1595. He became Guru in 1606. He built many religious shrines and was responsible for contributing the spirit of warriorship to the Sikhs. He recommended them to be well intimate in the art of using sword and other arms for self-defence and self-preservation. He himself wore two swords, Miri, constituting political reign and Piri, signifying spiritual sovereignty; a balance of material and religious life in the world.

Guru Har Rai: The seventh Guru, Siri Har Rai, born in 1630, spent most of his life in divine service, meditation and advocating the teachings of Guru Nanak. He also extended the enforcing task of nation-building initiated by Guru Hargobind.

Har Krishan: The eighth Guru, Siri Har Krishan, was born in 1656. He got nirvana in 1661. He personified service, purity and truth. The Guru gave his life while processing and curing the epidemic-stricken people in Delhi. Anyone who raises Him with a pure heart has no difficulties whatsoever in life.

Guru Tegh Bahadur: The ninth Guru, Siri Guru Tegh Bahadur, was born in 1621 in Amritsar and became Guru in 1664. He preached in the town of Anandpur. The Guru laid down his life for the auspices of Tilak (devotional mark painted on the forehead) and their hallowed thread of Hindus. He recommended the right to the freedom of worship. He gave up his life for the case of down-trodden Hindus.

Guru Gobind Singh: The tenth Guru, Siri Guru Gobind Singh, was born in 1666 and became Guru after the calvary of his father Guru Tegh Bahadur. He produced the Khalsa (The Pure Ones) in 1699, altering the Sikhs into a saint-soldier order with special symbols and sacraments for defending themselves. He fought many wars against oppression. His four sons also gave their lives in defence of their faith. He died in 1708.

Guru Gobind Singh, at the time of his death empowered the 'Guru Granth Sahib' as the sovereign head of the Sikhs, thus bringing the practice of proposing a religious head to a grinding halt. He lauded this in his 'Dasam Granth'. His military career could not arrive at any glorious heights. In fact, he lost all four of his sons in a clash with the Mughals. After his death Mughal governors invariably persecuted the Sikhs. The invasion of Persian and Afghan rulers brought them some relief as the Mughals thus had to defend their empires, and the Sikhs formed themselves under twelve different Misls or militias. Maharaja Ranjit Singh (1780-1839) amalgamated all the misls (groups) and demonstrated a homeland of the Sikhs after numerous bloody battles. The Sikhs were often under fire by several invaders which they successfully repulsed and released control of the Punjab only to the British after Ranjit Singh's death.

Sri Guru Granth Sahib: Sri Guru Granth Sahib is the eleventh and timeless Guru of the Sikhs. Guru Gobind Singh, the tenth Guru in Sikh custom, confirmed the religious text Adi Granth as his heir, ending the line of human Gurus, and lifting the text to Guru Granth Sahib. From that time, the text remained not only the Book of the Sikhs, but is also viewed by them as the living incarnation of the Ten Gurus. The role of Guru Granth Sahib, as a source or guide of prayer, is central in worship in Sikhism. The Adi Granth was first composed by the fifth Sikh Guru, Guru Arjan Dev (1563-1606), from hymns of the first five Sikh Gurus and other great holy men of the Hindu and Muslim customs.

The original author of the Adi Granth was Bhai Gurdas and later Bhai Mani Singh. After the death of the tenth Sikh Guru many written copies were prepared for circulation by Baba Deep Singh. The 'Guru Granth Sahib' is a big text of 1430 pages, collected and composed during the period of time of Sikh Gurus, from 1469 to 1708. It is composed in the form of hymns written in praise of God, which describe what God is like and the right way to live. Written in the Gurmukhi script, it is written mostly in Punjabi but includes casual use of other languages including Braj, Old Punjabi, Khariboli (Hindi), and Persian.

REFERENCES

Attar Singh: *Socio-Cultural Impact of Islam on India.* Chandigarh: Punjab University, 1976.

Avtar Singh: *Ethics of the Sikhs.* Patiala: Punjabi University, 1983.

Brown, Kerry: *Sikh Art and Literature.* New York: Routledge, 1999.

Callewaert, Winand M. and Pater G. Friedlander: *The Life and Works of Raidas*. New Delhi: Manohar, 1992.

Chandar, Satish: "Jizayah and the State in India during the 17th Century. " *Journal of the Economic and Social History of the Orient* 12. 1969.

Cole, W. Owen: *Sikhism and Its Indian Context 1469–1708*. New Delhi: D. K. Agencies, 1984.

Cole, W. Owen, and Piara Singh Sambhi: *The Sikhs: Their Religious Beliefs and Practices*. Brighton: Sussex Academic Press, 1995.

Coward, Harold: *Sacred Word and Sacred Text: Scripture in World Religion*. New York: Orbis Books, 1988.

Coward, Harold, and David Goa: *Mantra: Hearing the Divine in India* Chambersburg, Pa.: Anima Books, 1991.

Cunningham, Joseph Davey: *A History of the Sikhs*. Delhi: S. Chand and Company, 1985.

Grewal, J. S.: *Sikh Ideology Polity and Social Order*. New Delhi: Manohar, 1996.

Grewal, J. S.: *Contesting Interpretations of the Sikh Tradition*. New Delhi: Manohar, 1998.

Grewal, J. S. and S. S. Bal.: *Guru Gobind Singh*. Chandigarh: Punjab University, 1987.

Griffin, Lepel H., and Charles Francis Massy: *Chiefs and Families of Note in the Punjab*. Lahore: Punjab Government Press, 1939.

McLeod, W. H.: *The Sikhs: History, Religion and Society*. New York: Columbia University Press, 1989.

McLeod, W. H.: *Historical Dictionary of Sikhism*. Lanham: The Scarecrow Press, 1995.

McLeod, W. H.: *Sikhism*. New York: Penguin, 1997.

Nripinder Singh: *The Sikh Moral Tradition*. Columbia, Mo.: South Asia Publications, 1990.

O'Connell, Joseph T., et al.: *Sikh History and Religion in the Twentieth Century*. Toronto: University of Toronto, 1988.

Pashaura Singh: "Scriptural Adaptation in the Adi Granth. " *Journal of American Academy of Religion*, 1996.

2

History

Guru Nanak the founding father of Sikhism, was born in the village of Rai Bhoi di Talvandi, now known as Nankana Sahib, near Lahore. His father, Mehta Kalu was a Patwari. Nanak's mother was Tripta Devi and he had one older sister, Nanaki. His parents were Khatri Hindus of the Bedi clan. As a boy, Nanak was fascinated by religion, and his desire to explore the mysteries of life eventually led him to leave home.

Sikh culture states that at the age of thirty, Nanak went dropping and was presumed to have submerged after going for one of his morning baths to a local stream called the Kali Bein. Three days later he reappeared and would give the same answer to any question posed to him: "There is no Hindu, there is no Muslim". It was from this moment that Nanak would begin to spread the commandments of what was then the beginning of Sikhism. Although the exact chronicle of his itinerary is disputed, he is widely recognized to have made four major journeys, spanning thousands of kilometres.

ORIGIN

In India Hinduism has been a religion for ages. All Vedas demonstrate this point and later when Buddhism and Jainism arrived the Hindu religious faith carried on side by side with the population acting concording to their likes. By the Seventh century AD, Hinduism had once again become the main religious faith of the Country.

Bhakti movement in Medieval India is accountable for the many rites and rituals linked with the worship of God by Hindus, Muslims and Sikhs of Indian subcontinent. "The word bhakti is deduced from Bhakta meaning to serve, honour, revere, love and adore. In the religious idiom, it is fastening or fervent devotion to God and is defined as "that particular affection which is mothered by the knowledge of the attributes of the Adorable One."

Bhakti movement yielded into several different movements all across North and South India. In North India, Bhakti movement is nonexempt not differentiable by a Sufi movement of Shia Muslims of Chisti fame. People of Muslim faith adopted it as a Sufis while Hindus as Vaisanava Bhakti. Sufi saints of Chisti order developed first Punjabi sufi saint named Baba Sheikh Farid Shakarganj, who paved the way for the Punjabi patriotism as well as brought peace among Hindus and Muslims.

In the north the cult was basically Vaisnava-based, but rather of being focussed on Vishnu, it chose to focus itself on Vishnu's human embodiments, Rāma and Krishna, the respective avatars or deities central to the two epics Ramayana and Mahabharata. For bhakti now Vishnu's personifications (Rama and Krishna) were the direct objects of devotion. Adoration of the devotees was focussed on them in association with their respective accords. Followers of Bhakti movement in twelveth and thirteenth Century admitted the saints such as Bhagat Namdev, and Saint Kabir. Sikhism doubtless accepted some of the faces of radicalized bhakti, and admitted some of its practices into its own enacted set. It did lay down religious love as the way to the deity, but the deity to be idolized was neither Shiva nor Vishnu.

By the Tenth century there was a steady influx of the Muslims from the West. Soon they demonstrated their empire in the country and being the ruling class they started disseminating their religious faith. Conversions, at times, took red form and this lead to tension and distrustfulness between the Hindus and the Muslims. Over a period the two communities grew far apart and there was a category division between the rulers and the ruled. The Northern part of the Country was always in agitation with ever flowing Muslim encroachments from the North-West. The constant Hindu-Muslim fights and mistrust gave rise to a movement of angelical persons by the Fifteenth century. They were both Hindus and Muslims and their effort was to bring the two together and make them earn that there was only one God though we concerned to Him by different names.

One such person was born in the area of the present Pakistan and he was called Nanak. Born in a Hindu family he denied to under-go Hindu rituals and prophesied that there was but one God and that He was the only Truth. He took two persons, one each from the two communities, and contracted journeys through the length and breadth of the country including a trip to Ceylon, Tibet and in West to Mecca and Baghdad. Through out these travels Nanak prophesied that he was neither a Hindu nor a Muslim but a follower of the "Truth" and that his knowledge came from the "Word", meaning that the God could only be agnized by meditation and self improvement. He betrayed the rigid rituals of the Hindus and blind following of the systems of fasting, visiting spiritual places, and undergoing several forms of self-abasement etc lead by the dogmatic Hindu priests. He snitched the Muslims for their maltreatment of the Hindus and also their oppressive means of convincing people to their faith which was being led by their fundamentalist mullahas.

Nanak's preaching of the middle path and his denouncing the drawbacks of both the communities soon led to his having a large following. Nanak asked his Disciples to earn their living by honest means and insisted they have a proper family life. His idea was that man could be living a normal life yet he could be a true follower of God by binding the word 'Truth'. No priests were demanded nor was there a need of a particular place or time for one to convey with one's God. Nanak's followers were called 'Sikhs' meaning in Sanskrit 'shishya' a student-one who is learning. People from both the faiths became his adherents in multitudes.

Nanak became the first Chief of the Sikhs and was followed by three others before the Mughal rulers at Delhi took notice of the fast developing sect. The Fifth Master, Arjun Dev, was put to death on instructions of the Mughal court. This ensued in the sect taking up arms to protect itself. The changeless friction between Delhi court and the new community lead to the Tenth Master, Gobind Rai, convincing the members to a warrior class and calling them 'Khalsas' the ' pure ones'-those who are pure in the heart and pure in their actions. This changeover leads the male members adding the word 'Singh' and the females 'Kaurs' to their name which means a loin and lioness respectively. The community has thenceforth been always at the head of the struggle against repressiveness of any kind.

Babar, founding father of the Mughal dynasty in India, had a force of 12,000 men, mostly undisciplined group of men who wanted to plunder the riches of India. Guru Nanak in his famous epos named Babarvani identifies the barbarities of Babar and his men in Punjab. Babarvani (Babar's command or sway) is how the four verses by Guru Nanak mentioning to the intrusions by Babar (1483-1530), are jointly known in Sikh literature.

In his first intrusion, Babar came as far as Peshawar. The following year he crossed the Indus and, inhibiting Sialkot without resistance, marched on Saidpur (now Eminabad, 15 km southeast of Gujranwala in Pakistan) which suffered the worst ferocity of the invading host. The town was taken by assail, the garrison put to the sword and the inhabitants carried into captivity. During his next invasion in 1524, Babar ransacked Lahore. His final intrusion was launched during the winter of 1525-26 and he became master of Delhi after his Victory at Panipat on 21 April 1526.

Guru Nanak was an eye-spectator to the mayhem created during these invasions. Janam Sakhis mention that he himself became prisoner at Saidpur. A little of his, outside of Babarwani hymns, indicates that he may have been present in Lahore when the city was given up to plunder. In six sententious words this line conveys, "For a pahar and a quarter, i.e. for nearly four hours, the city of Lahore stayed subject to death and fury" The mention in one of the Babalvani sayings of the use of guns by the Mughals against the Afghan defence desiring mainly upon their elephants may well be a address to the historical battle of Panipat which decided the fate of the Afghan king, Ibrahim Lodhi.

The Sikh culture powerfully subscribes to an encounter in 1520 between Guru Nanak and Babar during the latter's intrusion of Saidpur, now called Eminabad, in Pakistan. The town was taken by outrage, the garrison put to the sword and the habitants carried into captivity. According to the Puratan Janam Sakhi, Guru Nanak and Mardana, also among the captives, were ordered to be taken to prison as slaves. The Guru was given a load to carry and Mardana a horse to lead. But Mir Khan, says the Janam Sakhi, saw that the Guru's bundle was carried without any support and Mardana's horse followed him without the reins. He accounted this to Sultan Babar who remarked, "If there was such a holy man here, the town should not have been demolished." The Janam Sakhi continues, "Babar kissed (Guru Nanak's) feet. He said, 'On the face of this fair one sees God himself.' Then all the people, Hindus and Musalmans, began to make their greetings. The king spoke again, 'O dervish, accept something'. The Guru responded, 'I take nothing, but you must release all the captives of Saidpur and restore their property to them'. King Babar ordered, 'Those who are in detainment be released and their property be returned to them'. All the captives of Saidpur were set at liberty.

Babarvani verses are not a narrative of diachronic events like Guru Gobind Singh's Bachitra Natak, nor are they an indictment of Babar as his Zafarnamah was that of Aurangzab. They are the bombardments of a pity soul touched by scenes of human miserableness and by the cruelty committed by the invaders. The distresses of the people are delivered here in accents of intense power and protest. The events are placed in the larger social and historical position decline in moral standards must lead to chaos. A corrupt political system must end in adjournment. Bait of power divides men and violence unreserved tends to flourish It could not be wished away by magic or necromancy Guru Nanak reiterated his faith in the Almighty and in His justice. Yet so intense was his recognition of the suffering of the people that he could not withstand making a complaint.

The people for Guru Nanak were the people as a whole, the Hindus and the Muslims, the high-caste and the low-caste, soldiers and civilians, men and women. These verses are noteworthy for their moral structures and poetical persuasiveness.

In spite of his damaging role Babar is seen by Guru Nanak to have been an ignorant instrument of the divine Will. Because the Lodhi's had desecrated God's laws, they had to pay the punishment. Babar descended from Kabul as God's chosen broker, demonstrating the absolute authority of God and the payback which must follow rebelliousness of His laws. Guru Nanak's commentary on the events which he actually witnessed thus becomes a part of the same universal message. God is infrangible and no man may disobey. His commands with impunity. Obey Him and experience freedom. Disobey him and the result must inescapably be vengeance, a dire calculating which brings suffering in this present life and continued reincarnation in the hereafter. The clash between Sikh and Islamic tradition was destined and resulted in first small antagonisms between Guru's followers starting with the Sixth Guru Guru Hargobind and later into full scale with Tenth Guru Guru Gobind Singh.

EARLY HISTORY

After the end of Guru Nanak there were several followers who followed the fundamental principle layed by him or more exactly Sikhism.The successors of Guru Nanak were ten in all starting from Guru Angad dev to Guru Granth Sahib.

Guru Angad

Guru Angad was born in 1504. Guru Angad prepared and presented the Gurmukhi script and made it known to all Sikhs. The Holy Scripture of Guru Granth Sahib is written in Gurmukhi. This scripture is also the foundation of the Punjabi language. It turned into the script of the masses very soon. Guru Angad was an example of self-less service to his Sikhs and demonstrated them the way to religious service prayers. He took great concern in the education of the children by curtain raising many schools for their instruction and thus greatly altered literacy. For the youth he commenced the culture of Mall Akhara, where physical as well as religious exercises were held. He gathered the facts about Guru Nanak Sahib's life from Bhai Bala Ji and wrote the first life history of Guru Nanak Sahib. He popularized and elaborated the institution of 'Guru Ka Langar' commenced by Guru Nanak Sahib earlier.

Guru Amar Das

He was born in 1479. He took up the courage of spiritualism to fight against caste confinements, caste preconceptions and the curse of untouchability. He reinforced the culture of the free kitchen, Guru Ka Langar and made his Disciples, whether rich or poor, whether high born or low born have their meals together attending one place. He thus demonstrated social equality amongst the people.

Guru Amar Das brought in the Anand Karaj marriage ceremony for the Sikhs, substituting the Hindu form. He also completely abolished amongst the Sikhs, the custom of Sati, in which a married woman was pushed to burn herself to death in the pyre of her husband. The custom of Paradah (Purda), in which a woman covered her face with a caul, was also done away with.

Guru Ram Das

He was born in 1534. He founded the city of Amritsar and started the building of the famous Golden Temple at Amritsar, the Celestial City of the Sikhs. He requested the Muslim Sufi, Mian Mir to lay the foundation of the Harmandir. The temple remains open on all sides and at all times to every one. This indicates that the Sikhs believe in One God who has no fondness for any particular place, direction or time. The touchstone of Sikh marriage ceremony known as the Anand Karaj is focused on the Lawan, a four stanza hymn compiled by Guru Ram Das Ji. The marriage couples confine to the Guru Granth Sahib as each stanza is read. The first round is the Divine consent for beginning the householder's life through marriage. The second round states that the union of the couple has been brought about by God. In the third round the couple is depicted as the rosiest as they have sung the praises of the Lord in the party of saints. In the fourth round the impression of the couple that they have met their hearts desire and are being congratulated is described.

Guru Arjan Dev

He was born in 1563. He was the third son of Guru Ram Das Ji. Guru Arjan was a paragon of virtue and scholarly person of the highest quality and repute. He composed the Adi Granth, the Holy Scripture of the Sikhs, and wrote the Sukhmani Sahib. To make it a worldwide teaching,

Guru Ji included in it hymns of Muslim saints as well those of low-caste pariah canonizes who were never allowed to enter several temples.

Guru Arjan Dev completed building of Shri Darbar Sahib also known as Golden Temple in Amritsar. Shri Darbar Sahib welcomes all without secernment, which is represented by the four doors that are open in four directions. Guru Ji became the first great sufferer in Sikh history when Emperor Jahangir ordered his murder.

Guru Har Gobind

He was born in 1595. He was the lad of Guru Arjan Dev and was known as a "soldier saint," Guru Hargobind coordinated a small army, explicating that extreme non-violence and passivism would only encourage evil and so the rationales of Miri-Piri were demonstrated. Guru Ji taught that it was necessary to take up the sword in order to protect the weak and the suppressed. Guru Ji was first Gurus to take up arms to fight the faith. At that time it was only emperors who were permitted to sit on a raised platform, called a takhat or throne. At the age of 13, Guru Hargobind raised Shri Akal Takhat Sahib, ten feet over the ground and decorated two swords, Miri and Piri, instituting temporal and spiritual power.

Guru Har Rai

He was born in 1630 and spent most of his life in divine service, meditation and advocating the instructions of Guru Nanak. Although, Guru Har Rai was a man of peace, he never dissolved the armed Sikh Warriors, who earlier were exerted by his grandfather, Guru Hargobind. He always encouraged the military spirit of the Sikhs, but he never himself indulged in any direct political and armed controversy with the Mughal Empire. Guru Ji carefully annulled conflict with Emperor Aurangzeb and committed his efforts to missionary work.

Guru Har Kishan

He was born in 1656. Guru Har Kishan was the most youthful of the Gurus. Established as Guru at the age of five, Guru Ji astonished the Brahmin Pundits with his knowledge and religious powers. To the Sikhs he established to be the very symbol of service, purity and truth. The Guru yielded his life while serving and curing the epidemic-stricken people in Delhi. The young Guru began to assist the martyrs regardless of cast and creed. Particularly, the local Muslim population was much impressed with the purely humanistic deeds of the Guru Sahib and dubbed him Bala Pir (child prophet). Even Aurangzeb did not try to disturb Guru Harkrishan Sahib sensing the sensitivity of the state of affairs but on the other hand never brushed off the claim of Ram Rai also.

Guru Tegh Bahadur

He was born in 1621 in Amritsar and founded the town of Anandpur. The Guru laid down his life for the aegis of the Hindu religious faith. He was a loyal believer in the right of people to the freedom of worship. It was for this cause that he confronted martyrdom for the defence of the down-trodden Hindus. So miserable was the torture of Guru Tegh Bahadur that his body had to be burned surreptitiously at Delhi while his severed head was secretly taken four hundred kilometres away to Anandpur Sahib for incineration.

MEDIEVAL HISTORY

Guru Gobind Singh

He was born in 1666 and turned Guru after the execution of his father Guru Tegh Bahadur. He founded the Khalsa in 1699, modifying the Sikhs into a saint-soldier order with special symbols and religious ritual for protecting themselves. After the Guru had allotted Amrit to his Five Beloved Ones, he stood up in invocation and with folded hands, begged them to christen him in the same way as he had baptized them. He himself became their adherent. The Five Beloved Ones were amazed at such astonished at such proposition and represented their own unworthiness, and the grandness of the Guru, whom they viewed as God's angel upon earth.

He handed the Sikhs the name Singh (lion) or Kaur (princess). He fought many fights against the armies of Aurangzeb and his friends. He had lost his father, his mother, four sons, finally, after his famous letter (the zafarnama) to Aurangzeb, in which he charged the Grand mughal with his betrayal and Godliness, the attacks against the Guru and his Sikhs were called off. Aurangzeb died soon after reading the letter. Soon, the true heir to the Mughal throne searched the Gurus' assistance in winning his kingdom. It was the envie and fear of the growing friendship between the new Emperor and the Guru which lead to the fink attack of the Pathan assasins of Wasir Khan who imposed the wound which later caused the Guru's death. Thus the tree, whose seed was established by Guru Nanak, came to realization when Guru Gobind Singh created the Khalsa, and on 3 October 1708, nominated Guru Granth Sahib as the Guru.

Guru Granth Sahib

Guru Granth Sahib also known as the Adi Granth, is the Holy Scripture of the Sikhs. No Sikh observance is regarded as complete unless it is executed in the presence of Guru Granth Sahib. The Granth was written in Gurmukhi script and it comprises the actual words and verses as emitted by the Sikh Gurus. It is considered the Supreme Spiritual Authority and Head of the Sikh religious faith, rather than any living person. It is also the only Holy Scripture of its kind which not only carries the works of its own religious founders but also the writings of people of other faiths. The living Guru of the Sikhs, the book is held in great reverence by Sikhs and covered with the utmost respect. Guru Granth Sahib is a book of Revelation. It carries the Word of the Master through His messengers on earth. It is worldwide in its scope. The grandness of Guru Granth Sahib lies not only in its being the Holy Scripture of the Sikhs but also in it being a universal Holy Scripture available to humankind, meant for everybody, everywhere.

Just before his death, Gobind Singh ordered that the Guru Granth Sahib (the Sikh Holy Scripture), would be the final religious authority for the Sikhs and secular authority would be vested in the Khalsa Panth; The Sikh Nation or Community. The first scripture was composed and edited by the fifth Guru, Arjan Dev, in 1604. After the Guru's death, Banda Bahadur became the leader of the Sikh army and was responsible for several onslaughts on the Mughal kingdom. He was put to death by the emperor Jahandar Shah after rejecting the offer of a pardon if he changed over to Islam.

The Sikh community's embracement of military and political organization made it a respectable regional force in medieval India and it continued to build up after the death of the Gurus. After the death of Banda Bahadur, a loose federation of Sikh warrior bands known as misls took shape. With the decline of the Mughal empire, a Sikh empire developed in the Punjab under Maharaja Ranjit Singh, with its centre in Lahore and limits extending to the Khyber Pass and the borders of China. The order, cultures and field developed over centuries culminated at the time of Ranjit Singh to give rise to the religious and social individuality that the term "Sikhism" describes.

After the death of Ranjit Singh, the Sikh kingdom fell under disorder and was finally took over by Britain after the tough Anglo-Sikh Wars. This brought the Punjab under British rule. Sikhs founded the Shiromani Gurdwara Prabandhak Committee and the Shiromani Akali Dal to preserve Sikhs spiritual and political system.

Misldari

Misldari or Misaldari, was an organization of political relationship which led to the rise of Sikh power in the eighteenth century Punjab. The

Sikh individuals who, since the death of Banda Singh Bahadur in 1716, had lived frugally as small irregular bands, had by the middle of the century sorted themselves into eleven main parts and started developing territories as Misls. This was the origin of the Sikh misls which established their sway in the Punjab. Under the misl system of land tenure which now prevailed, the chief or sardar of each misl could allot land to a member of his own misl, or even to an outsider, not as a grant jagir, but as a share of the territory in the conquest of which the latter was an equal partner.

Sometimes the subordinate misldars or commanders occupied territory on their own, but continued to accept the sardar of the misls their chief. The misldars were freelance in the direction of their respective territories. They could alienate it to a member of the parent misl, but not to an outsider. Their relationship with the sardar of the parent misl remained that of subordinates, but only for the purpose of the offence and defence against outsiders. Again, business of territory only entitled them to a share in the produce. The misldars, like the jagirdars, could not interfere with the cultureal proprietorship or occupancy rights of the tillers of the land. Misaldari was a transient development. With the emergence of the Sikh kingdom under Maharaja Ranjit Singh in the early decades of the nineteenth century engaging most of the misls, the organization became non entity.

Start of Rakhi System

The rakhi arrangement was one of the most essential developments which happened during the period of Misls which laid the seeds of the Sikh political agency in the land. In the early stages, the rakhi or protection was looked for by the people from the Sikhs and later, in order to bring more districts under the rakhi system, the offer of rakhi was made to the people of the towns and villages of the Punjab and was actively engaged by the Sikhs, as a regular characteristic of their activities. The word rake literally means 'protection' and in practice, it was a tribute experienced by the Sikhs for the auspices provided or guaranteed by them against external hostility to the people paying it. The circumstances which led to the introduction of this system were correlative with the rise of the Sikhs power.

During the three years that came after Mir Mannu's death, there were nine swift modifications in the governorship of the Punjab that ensued in chaotic circumstances in the state. The Punjab was thrown into the turmoil of such political confusion and contradictory political claims that peace was completely tattered and the stability of this land wracked. On Mir Mannu's death, Emperor Ahmad Shah appointed his three year old son, Mahmud Khan, viceroy of the two states of Lahore and Multan, on the 13th November 1753, and, interesting enough, the baby viceroy was allowed a two-year old deputy in the person of Muhammad Amin Khan, son of late Mir Mannu.

It was a charade of administration. Between the ineffective administration of Mir Mannu's widow, Mughalani Begum, and the schemes of Adeena Beg, the land of the Punjab became a prize for which the hereditary claim of the political authority at Delhi competed with the military genius at Kabul. The people of Punjab were suffering from the evils of a dual autarchy, not knowing whether the state was a part of Indian Empire to be controlled in its government from Delhi or from Kandhar or Kabul. During these years the state political apparatus had literally collapsed and, as such, the protection of law and life could not be given to the people by the titular governments professing to be holding charge of the state. Trade had practically come to an impasse as the highways and seaways were not safe.

Under these considerations, the dire need of the people was an introduction that should protect them from internal anarchy and external danger which constantly loomed large before the people. The state was divided into a number of princedoms, their jurisdictions conflicted and the different agencies squeezed the poor barbarians of their hard-earned money without any expectation of law and security. Economically, the people were being ruined, and politically, there was no hope of peace or justice.

This was a long-sought chance for the Sikhs from which they drew full vantage. As sons ofthe soil, the Sikhs knew how the individuals of the Punjab had suffered because of unsafe and unstable conditions under the Mughals. Besides other circumstances if any, they genuinely felt the need of providing refuge to their follow-beings in the Punjab. The Dal Khalsa, being a well formed body of the Sikhs, devised the institution of rakhi. They regarded themselves adequate to extend their protection to the people where they required it.

Under this System the auspices was granted to the people against foreign encroachment and internal victimization of zamindars and government officials and against the ravages of the local adventurers. It meant that the entire safety of their persons and property was to be assumed. Generally, in return they received one fifth of their income twice a year after every harvest, that is, harhi and sauni or rabi and kharif, but the value of rakhi seems to be one-fifth of the receipts.

When even a Sardar of ten cavalrymen placed an area under his rakhi even one of the largest Sardars having five hundred or more cavalrymen under him could not interfere in that area. On the other hand the defrayment of chauth merely saved a place from the unwished presence of the Maratha soldiers and civil subsidiaries, but did not impose on Shivaji any corresponding duty to guard the district from foreign invasion or internal disorder. The Marathas awaited only to their own acquire and not to the fate of their prey after they had left. The chauth was only a means of buying off one thief; and not a subsidiary system for the sustainment of peace and order against all enemies. The lands subject area to the chauth cannot, therefore, be rightly called spheres of influence.

Thus rakhi system was surely a betterment upon chauth as the Sardar bidding rakhi to a village or an area conceived himself under obligation to give protection to the people from subjugation and attack from whichever quarter it came, as against the pattern of chauth. Secondly, the areas under rakhi could rightly be called the spheres of influence and these areas formed the basis of the future Misals.

This pattern worked successfully, partially for the reason that the separation between the successive invasions of the Abdali gave the Khalsa leaders time adequate to organize their territorial acquisitions, and partly for the reason that most of the central Punjab territories soon elected to come under the new 'Protective System' of the Khalsa. Having thus assured a habitat and a more or less regular source of income from the raked strategy and a wider field for enlisting to its ranks, the day was in a better perspective to contest with the Abdali this change of their home-land.

This protection was extended equally to the Hindu and Muslim zamindars and individuals belonging to both the communities gained from it. The Mughals and Muslim Rajputs, who refused this offer on account of religious fanatism and opposed the Sikhs otherwise, were forced out to find homes elsewhere in fact, these Muslims who were expelled included most of those people who had seized the lands of the Sikhs, when they had, under government pressure, left their homes to seek protection in jungles and deserts. Waving reclaimed the possession of their lands and having entrenched themselves in their respective areas, the Sikhs began to coordinate some sort of government which became the basis of the organization known as the Misaldari system.

When the interpreters of the Dal Khalsa came to collect the specified portion of the produce of the village due to them as protectors, they experienced the welcome due to the deliverer and not the glares meant for the tax collector. In a short time four out of the five Doabs of the Punjab came under the auspices of the Dal Khalsa. To make the system function successfully one or more units of the day could combine to take charge of a big piece of district that came under their protection. To meet a situation in emergency a substitute force was placed at Amritsar in addition to the acting units.

Amritsar began to be defended by Nishanwalias and Dallewalias. The district, south-west of Lahore, fell under the auspices of Nakais; the Chaj and Rachna Doab territories came under the protective cover of Hari Singh Bhangi and Charhat Singh Sukarchakia. Some districts north of Amritsar also fell under the rake of Jassa Singh Ramgarhia and Jai Singh Kanaihya. The southern bank of the Satisfise came under the protection of Deep Singh and Karora Singh, while the Ahluwalias and the Singhpurias concerned some territories on both banks of the Satluj. To reward and humour the Sikhs for their help, Adeena Beg paid them a lakh and a quarter of rupees as rake or security money for the Jalandhar Doab. To manipulate and identify himself further with them, he acknowledged or styled himself to be a sort of round-head Sikh and brought karat prasad worth a thousand rupees on festive affairs to he distributed among them. Thus, rakhi proved as a boon both for those who benefitted from it and for those who gave it. The former decided to their peaceful pursuits and the latter laid bases of their independent princedoms in the Punjab.

MODERN HISTORY

Shiromani Gurdwara Prabandhak Committee

SGPC is the body constituting of the elected representatives of the Sikhs related primarily with the management of holy Sikh enshrines under its control. SGPC originated with the Gurdwara Reform or Akali cause of the early 1920's, which lasted until the 1925 when the Gurdwara bill was placed on the statute book. The administration of Darbar Sahib (the Golden Temple) complex had been, since the appropriation of the Punjab to the British territory in 1849, controlled by the British government through a commission of Sikh patricians and a manager appointed by the British deputy commissioner of Amritsar district. The committee and the sarbarah, a retired risaldar major and honorary captain of the Indian army, Arur Singh, were accursed among Sikhs for their association with the Jallianvala Bagh tragedy.

On 12 October 1920, the Khalsa Baradari, an organization of Sikhs from backward classes, held a meeting in Jallianvala Bagh at which some teachers and students of the Khalsa College were also present. A large number of new fledglings were initiated into the Khalsa Brotherhood by distributing to them the rites of the Khalsa. As the ceremony resolved, the entire sangat went to the Golden Temple to offer karah prasad and urdns. The priesthood at first refused to accept the oblations from the so called Harijan/but later agreed when on a reference being made to the holy book, a Hymn which was read out instantly favoured the reformists' views. The sangat then went to the Akal Takhat, esteemed as the highest seat of religious authority for the Sikhs, to pay their homage. The priests on seeing the sangat coming fled leaving the holy Takht Sahib Unatended. The reformers occupied the Akal Bunga and nominated Teja Singh Bhuchchar as Jathedar of the Akal Takhat, with 25 volunteers to safeguard and serve it.

The deputy commissioner, on 13 October 1920, had a meeting with the priests, the sarbarah, and some notable citizens for consultation. The priests did not appear at the meeting, and the deputy commissioner nominated a fresh committee under the chairmanship of the sarbarah. The crusaders on the other hand summoned, under the authority of the Akal Takhat, a general assembly of the Sikhs to meet in front of the Akal Takht on 15 November 1920 to consider the question. The government held hasty audiences with the Maharaja of Patiala and, on 13 November, appointed a committee of 36 Sikh notables for the direction of the Golden Temple and other Gurdwaras admitting the Darbar Sahib at Tarn Taran.

The Sikh assembly held on 15 and 16 November elected a commission of 175 members constituting all the districts, Sikh states of the Punjab, other Indian states, and Sikh organizations in Burma, Malaya, China and North America. It also included the 36 government nominees in the committee which it named the Shiromani Gurdwara Parbandhak Committee, SGPC for short. The first meeting of the SGPC was held at the Akal Takht on 12 December 1920. It constituted a subcommittee to draft the Committee's constitution. It elected Sardar Sundar Singh Majithia as president, Harbans Singh, of Atari, as vicepresident and Sundar Singh Ramgarhia as secretary.

The Majithia Sardar quitted early in 1921 to join the ministry set up under the Government of India Act, 1919, and Baba Kharak Singh was elected, in his place, president of the SGPC. The Committee was filed under the Societies Registration Act, 1860, on 30 April 1921. Under its constitution, 80 per cent of the 175 member Committee were to be elected from different constituencies in the Punjab and outside including the princely states and the left over seats were to be nominated by the elected members. In the committee, there was to be president, a vicepresident, a secretary, an executive committee of thirty-five members of whom nineteen could form a majority and a seven member acting committee.

In addition, local commissions with paid secretaries were to be made for the management of important enshrines or groups of shrines. Circumstances of membership of the SGPC admitted conformity to the teachings of the Gurus, adhesion to the injunction regarding five K's, and a subscription of Re. 1.25 per month. The main functions of the Committee were to handle all Gurdwaras under its control, to regularize consumption and to utilize all income appropriately for purposes such as expension of religious faith and education, upkeep and betterment of buildings and the running of communal Kitchen.

Sikh Gurdwaras Act 1925: Government started recognizing the prerogative of the Sikhs to handle their own religious shrines. Sikh Gurdwaras Act, 1925, passed by the provincial legislative assembly on 9 July 1925 and enforced with effect from 1 November 1925 created a "Board", nominated Shiromani Gurdwara Parbandhak Committee soon after to provide for the better administration of sure Sikh Gurdwaras and for inquiries into matters and settlement of disputes linked therewith. This covered Gurdwaras listed in Schedules I and II annexed to the Act, located within the then state of Punjab. Later after the fusion of the Patiala and East Punjab States Union (PEPSU) with the Punjab in 1956, Gurdwaras falling in that were also included in the several schedules vide the improving Act I of 1959, while Gurdwaras lying in parts separated under the Reorganization Act of 1966 extended to remain under SGPC's jurisdiction. The Committee's check over Gurdwaras in Pakistan ceased on 15 August 1947.

The inaugural meeting of a freshly elected committee must be applied not afterwards than one month later the government notification concerning its constitution, and thereafter a general meeting must be held at least once in a year. The gathering will consist of thirty-one members. The executive to be elected in general meeting every year comprises of the president, two vice president; (one senior and one junior) and a general secretary, and between five and eleven members. The executive exerts, on behalf of the committee, all powers conferred on the latter which are not expressly allowed in the Act for the general meeting. All decisions in the executive as well as in the general meeting will be decided by majority vote, the president possessing a casting vote in the case of equivalence of votes for and against, furnished that the head; ministers are not entitled to vote during the election of the officeholders and members of the executive committee.

To judge any disputes concerning recognition of any enshrines as being Sikh Gurdwara beneath the Act or on charges with respect to the SGPC or its commissions or against any of its office bearer or member past or present, a Judicial Commission comprising of three members is contituted under the Act. Its members must be Sikh lawyers or existing of not fewer than 10 years standing. Appointments to it are made by the government provided that two of them must be took out of a panel of seven names submitted by the SGPC. The expenses of the Commission are divided by SGPC and the government in the ratio of two to one. The Commission is not a court in the legal sense but ajudicial body which considerably controls the functioning and procedure of Gurdwara management. Cases before it are looked upon as complaints and not as cases. It is permanently located in a building owned by the SGPC, close to territory courts in Amritsar.

Functions of the SGPC: Although incorporated as a purely spiritual body for the directions of Gurdwaras, the Shiromani Gurdwara Parbandhak Committee with its huge resources (its yearly budget now is around a thousand million rupees) performs miscellaneous functions. Besides generation of religious faith including running of free kitchens, it runs a large number of schools and colleges, conducts agricultural farms on Gurdwara lands, encourages research, printing and issue of works on Sikh religious faith and history, and helps victims of political repression as well as of natural calamities. It arranges visits of Sikh pilgrims to Gurdwaras exited in Pakistan and maintains liaison with Sikh establishments in other Indian states and abroad. It takes up with the government matters of Sikh interests or grudges. In this it collabourates with the Shiromani Akali Dal, a political party representing the Sikh masses. The perspective of the Shiromani Gurdwara Parbandhak Committee vis-a-vis the Shiromani Akali Dal changed soon after the drawing of the Sikh Gurdwaras Act, 1925.

REFERENCES

Blunt, E. H. H.: *The Caste Systems of Northern India.*

Crooke, W.: *The North-Western Provinces of India: Their History, Ethnology and Administration,* 1994.

Cunningham, Joseph Davey: *A History of the Sikhs.* Delhi: S. Chand and Company, 1985.

Daljeet Singh: *Sikhism.* Chandigarh, 1979.

Daljeet Singh: *Essay on the Authenticity of Kartarpuri Bi[and the Integrated Logic and Unity of Sikhism.* Patiala: Punjabi University, 1987.

Dewana, Mohan Singh: *A History of Punjabi Literature.* Jalandhar: Bharat Prakashan, 1971.

Ibbetson Sir Denzil: *Punjab Castes.* Patiala, 1970.

Jagjit Singh: *The Sikh Revolution.* Delhi, 1981.

Jogendra Singh: *Sikh Ceremonies.* Chandigarh, 1968.

Kanwaljit Kaur: *Sikh Women, Fundamental Issues in Sikh Studies,* Institute of Sikh Studies, Chandigarh, 1992.

Levering, Miriam: ed. *Rethinking Scripture: Essays from a Comparative Perspective.* Albany: State University of New York Press, 1989.

Mann, Gurinder Singh: *The Goindval Pothis: The Earliest Extant Source of the Sikh Canon.* Harvard Oriental Series 51. Cambridge: Harvard University Press, 1996.

Marenco, E. K.: *The Transformation of Sikh Society.* Portland, Oregon, 1974.

Mohammed Marmaduke Pickthall, translator: *The Meaning of Glorious Koran,* Mentor Book, New American Library, New York and Scarborough, Ontario, 1924.

Prinsep, H. T.: *Origin of the Sikh Power in the Punjab and Political Life of Maharaja Ranjit Singh.* Calcutta, 1834.

Randhawa, Harveen Kaur: *"Early Printing History of Guru Granth Sahib. "* M. Phil. term paper, Guru Nanak Dev University, 1985.

Randhir Singh: ed., *Prem Sumarag Granth.*Jalandhar, 1965.

Robert O. Ballou: *The Portable World Bible,* Penguin Books, 1976.

Schomer, Karine, and W. H. McLeod: eds. *The Sants: Studies in a Devotional Tradition of India.* Delhi: Motilal Banarasidass, 1987.

3

Philosophy

The Sikh religious faith is monotheistic, believing in One Supreme God. Absolute yet all-penetrating, the Eternal, the Creator, the Cause of Causes, without antagonism, without hate, both Subjective in His creation and beyond it. It is no longer the God of one nation, but the God of Grace. That being so, He creates human not to punish them for their sins, but for the actualization of their true purpose in the cosmos and to merge themselves into Him. The basic postulate of Sikhism is that life is not extraordinary in its origin, but having emanated from a Pure Source, the True One endures in it. Not only the whole of Sikh Doctrine, but the whole of Sikh history and character is due 'this principle'. The Sikhs do not recognize the caste system nor do they believe in Idol-worship, rituals or superstitions. The Gods and Goddesses are conceived as nonentities.

This religious faith consists of practical living, in depicting service to humanity and engendering tolerance and brotherly love towards all. The Sikh Gurus did not believer retirement from the world in order to attaining redemption. It can be attained by any one who makes an honest living and leads a normal life and shares his earnings with the impoverished.

Sikhism does not assume the mythos of pessimism. It recommends self-confidence, temperament and hope. The maxim, "Resist not evil but whosoever shall smite thee onto the right cheek, turn to him the other also", does not find any position in Sikh way of life. On the other hand it orders its followers to practice self-rule, self-respect, and self-defence. Viewpoint of Sikhism is characterized by logic, comprehensiveness and its "without frills" approach to spiritual and material world. Its theology is marked by simplicity. In Sikh ethics there is no conflict between individual's duty to the self and that towards society (sangat).

Sikhism is the youngest world religious faith. Sikhism was founded by Guru Nanak some 500 years ago. It emphasizes the belief in One

Supreme Being and the Creator (WaheGuru) of the universe. It offers a simple straight path to eternal bliss and spreads a message of love and universal brotherhood. Sikhism is strictly a monotheistic faith and recognizes God as the only One who is not subject to limits of time or space.

Sikhism believes that there is only one God, who is the Creator, Sustainer, Destroyer and does not take human form. The theory of Avtarvad (incarnation) has no place in Sikhism. It does not give any value to Gods and Goddesses and other divinities.

In Sikhism the ethics and religious faith go together. One must instill moral qualities and practice virtues in everyday life in order to step towards spiritual development. Qualities such as honesty, compassion, generosity, patience and humility can only be built up by efforts and perseverance. The lives of our Great Gurus are a source of inspiration in this direction. The Sikh religious faith teaches that the goal of human life is to break the cycle of birth and death and merge with God. This can be accomplished by following the teachings of the Guru, meditation on the Holy Name (Nam) and performance of acts of service and charity. Nam Marg emphasizes daily devotion to the remembrance of God. One has to control the five feelings, viz., Kam (lust), Krodh (anger), Lobh (greed), Moh (worldly attachment) and Ahankar (pride) to achieve salvation.

The rituals and routine practices like fasting and pilgrimage, omens and austerities are rejected in Sikh religious faith. The goal of human life is to merge with God and this is accomplished by following the teachings of Guru Granth Sahib. Sikhism emphasizes Bhakti Marg or the path of devotion. It does, however, recognize the importance of Gian Marg (Path of Knowledge) and Karam Marg (Path of Action). It lays greatest stress on the need for earning God's Grace in order to reach the spiritual goal.

Sikhism is a modernistic, coherent, and pragmatic religious faith. It believes that normal household-life (Grahasth) is no block to salvation. Celibacy or renunciation of the world is not necessary to achieve salvation.

It is possible to live detached in the midst of worldly ills and temptations. A devotee must live in the world and yet keep his head above the usual tension and turmoil. He must be a scholarly soldier, and saint for God.

Sikhism is a universal and a secular religious faith and thus disapproves all differentiations based on class, creed, race or sex.

It believes all human beings are equal in the eyes of God. The Gurus stressed on equality of women and rejected female infanticide and Sati (widow burning) practice. They also actively propagated widow remarriage and rejected purdah system (women wearing veils). In order to keep mind focussed on Him one must meditate on the holy Name (Nam) and perform the acts of service and charity. It is considered honorable to earn one's daily bread through honest labour and work (Kirat Karna) and not by begging or dishonest means. Vand Chhakna, sharing with others, is also a social responsibility. The individual is expected to help those in need, through the Dasvandh (ten percent of his earnings).

Seva, community service is also an integral part of Sikhism. The free community kitchen (langar) found at every Gurdwara and open to people of all religions is one expression of this community service. Sikh religious faith advocates optimism and hope. It does not accept the ideology of pessimism.

The Gurus considered that this life has a purpose and a goal. It offers an opportunity for self and God realization. Moreover man is responsible for his own actions. He cannot claim immunity from the results of his actions. He must therefore be very vigilant in what he does. The Sikh Scripture, Guru Granth Sahib, is the Eternal Guru. This is sole religious faith which has given the Holy Book the position of a religious Guru. There is no place for a living human Guru in Sikh religion.

BASIC PHILOSOPHY

Humans has been intellectually attempting since long time to understand and translate the philosophy of ultimate Realism. Religion and philosophy are two different approaches to find out its nature. Philosophy intellectually studies the religion and its problems that arise in all forms including the problems concerning the nature of God, Grace, freedom, immortality, creation of universe, and ways of life in that particular religious faith. The understanding of religious philosophy may not help directly to deepen the spiritual life but it helps in understanding the intellectual gifts of a person. Philosophy is deduced from Greek word which means study of the Ultimate Reality, reasons, and rationales underlying being and thinking.

Sikh religious faith has its own religious theory, doctrine, notions and practices. Sikh doctrine is enshrined in Shri Guru Granth Sahib. It is Divine wisdom. The Sikh religious faith is based on rationalized faith than on reason but the faith is not blind and ritualistic. It deals with the way in which life is to be lived. It has its own theory of Ultimate Reality which is spiritual in nature. The religious doctrine of Sikhism manifests itself through the hymns of the Gurus and saints enshrined in Shri Guru Granth Sahib. Sikh doctrine means religion in action. It is called Gurmat. It is thought, view, belief, doctrine and religion of the Gurus. It is Gurmat Marg or Gurmat Rah. The religious school of thought of Sikhism is evident in Gurbani and is spread through Gurbani Shabads of passion and veneration.

Guru Nanak's philosophy starts with inquiry of Ik (One God) who is all Penetrating, the Everlasting, the Creator, the Cause of causes, without enmity, without jealousy and who can be attained with His Grace. Adi Granth which covers the span of six centuries, is concerned primarily with the nature of Reality. Sikh religion is strictly monotheistic, believing in One Supreme God. Absolute yet All-pervading, the Eternal, the Creator, the Cause of Causes, without enmity, without hate, both Immanent in His creation and beyond it. One God is no longer the God of one country, one nation, but the God of Grace. He is Omnipotent, Omnipresent and Omniscient. He creates man not to punish him for his sins, but for the realisation of his true purpose in the cosmos and to merge in from where he emanated. So Sikh faith and philosophical system centres on one God, His mystery and cognition of self as told above.

God is One (non-dualism) and second to none. He is called by different names by people of different religions. He is Nirgun (unmanifest-impersonal) and Sargun (Manifest-personal). Manifest world according to Sikhism is real. Reality is unity. The unity concept may either be personal or impersonal. God has metaphysical, ethical, aesthetical, logical, epistemology and indescribable attributes as appear in Mul Mantar and Shri Guru Granth Sahib. God is Omnipotent, Omniscient and Omnipresent. He is Karta Purkh. He is the parent of all. His Creation is limitless. There are countless universes. God created countless species of diverse forms. God enjoys His sport after creation of universe. God is devoid of fear and enmity. He is eternal. He is Adi Guru (Beginning)and Jugadi Guru (Primal age). He does not take birth and never he dies. He can be attained with His Grace.

Jiva is divinity. It is constituent of Supreme Soul but it is not Brahma in itself. However it carries the attributes of Supreme Soul. Because of Jiva's actions involving with Maya, It goes through cycle of births and deaths in human form till it merges with the Supreme Soul. Body dies but not soul. Soul never dies, it is like Brahma. It carries on for ever but it acts under the will of Brahma.

The world appears to be of two varieties; one is the conception of God and other is the trap. If man comprehends that all that is created is the revelation of God and it is his sole motive to attain the Creator, then the mortal can head towards union with God. If the mortal, on the other hand perceives that materialism or Moh-Maya is end of every thing, then he gets into the web of Haumai and would remain in the cycle of births and deaths. So it depends on, how the response is made by the mortal.

Sikhism believes that the world is not mere delusion or fantasy, it is rather reality seen in a distorted fashion. God is its Creator. What God created is real in the obvious sense. So it cannot be illusory. It is a stage for the practice of righteousness. Nature is portrayed as beauty and wonder created by God. This colourful earth is a garden of flowers. It has kith and kin relationship with humanity in Sikhism. According to Sikhism, God created every thing. His creation is real and limitless like Him. He created numerous nethers and earths. He created countless species of different forms and colours. God is Creator of the universe. No body knows the exact time when the universe was created. It is God only who knows all this, not the human being.

Truth is fundamental concept in Sikhism. It has different meanings. Literally, Truth means Sach, Sat, Reality, veracity, honesty, justice and righteousness. Importantly, in Sikhism, Truth (Sach) stands for God who is Ultimate Reality. God is Satya. God is Sojourner Truth and Truth is God. Truth is blissfulness. Truth is always refreshing and sweet.

DIVINE LAWS

Sikhism contains many dissimilar beliefs than other faiths. At its conception it was unique due to, the abolishment of any caste system, the denunciation of empty ritualistic practices, the prohibition of any persecution of individuals, and the promotion of equality rights. A Sikhs goal in human life is to develop the three parts of their body, which is the body, the mind, and the soul. The development of the body is achieved by earning a livelihood and by following the laws of health. The cultivation of the mind integrates study and education to create a better intellect to interpret the mysteries of nature and life. Their soul must follow a strict moral discipline. The soul of a human is the product of many cycles of birth and death and the human form is the final stage before the soul can return to its source. The body is very important to Sikhs for the body is the "House of Soul" and is therefore a temple of God. This is because God and the individual's soul are one and the same and humans only think that God and their soul are different because of egotism. The God is Inviolable yet All-penetrating, the Ageless, the Maker, the Cause of

Causes, without ill will, without hatred, both Subjective in His creation and beyond it.

When one breaks off their self-importance then one will find their individuality with God. The aim of human life is to try, to integrate the individual dimension with God and also to fully develop their soul to reach true spirituality. The Guru's roll is to spread the word and to help teach the way to develop the soul. The Guru does not have to be human either, for many years the Guru was human, but now the Guru for all time is the Guru Granth, which presides over all Sikh ceremonies. The relationship between the Sikh and the Guru is one of learning. The word "Sikh" means a student or learner whereas "Guru" means teacher and also means light. The Guru teaches the Sikhs the ways of life and the Sikh takes in the Guru and starts to become the "Guru". Sikhs also believe in Karma, as a law of cause and effect. One's future is determined by their past Karma and their present Karma; the laws of Karma do not stop when someone dies either it continues on with a person's soul. The act of doing good or bad things will make a person feel better or worse and will make them turn into a good or bad character. However, destiny can be altered in two ways; the first being the individual trying to become a better person and the second is to improve through supplication or by the grace of God. Karma discontinues to survive when one accedes to God's will and serves only Him.

There are also five main Chastities and five Vices that Sikhs abide by. The five Merits are Trueness, Happiness, Patience, Trust, and Daya (compassionateness), these Virtues set by the Gurus are followed by Sikhs to become one with the Ultimate Reality. The five Vices are Kam (Lust), Krodh (Anger), Lobh (Greed), Moh (Worldly attachment), Ahankar (Pride). These are comparable to Christianity's seven deadly sins and they are avoided by Sikhs as much as they can so they can advance in their spirituality. The one true evil of Sikhism is egotism, which creates a wall between man and God, and only through the submission to one's will can egotism be taken down. There is one group of Sikhs who are there to protect their beliefs; these people belong to the Khalsa. The Khalsas were created by the last human Guru to be the holy warriors to protect Sikhism for all time. The Khalsas have five symbolic representations, which are Hair (kesh), the comb (Kanga), underwear (Kachh), sword (Kirpan), and the steel wristband (Kara). All Khalsa have these five symbols on them at all times. All male Sikhs do not cut their hair and put on turbans to hold their hair. These are the main notions of the Sikhs nevertheless there are many more beliefs that they have that cover all parts of a person's life.

PRIMARY BELIEFS

The Sikh faith has several laid down beliefs and values that are constitutional in the basic philosophical system of the faith. A Sikh believes in only one God, This God is the same for all peoples of the Cosmos and is neutral in gender. So when we refer to God, we can call God masculine or feminine. So God can be referred to as 'He' or 'She'. This one God is the God of the Sikhs, Hindus, Muslims, Christians, Jews, etc – of all the peoples. He is formless, fearless, without enemies, self-created, etc. The Sikh Holy Scriptures, called the Shri Guru Granth Sahib explain the several facets of God in substantial detail. This principle leads to the concept of equality amount all human races, sects, gender, social classes, etc. There is an accepted belief that people of other faiths can also reunify with God provided they adopt the true path of their own religion. So the Sikh does not think that they have dominance on God or are the 'preferred' people.

The Sikhs believe in the development of the Soul and the precept of rebirth. The soul is believed to be a tiny spark of God's illumination separated from the Lord. This spark is separated from God and wants to become pure so that it can reunify with God. For this to happen, the Soul has to evolve and purify itself so that this reunification with the Supreme Soul can take place. The law of Karma is another concept central to this faith. Ones actions in this life will have a direct influence on the type of life in your next existence! So to adhere to these principles, the dedicated follower must lead a disciplined personal life and must uphold the moral and ethnical rights of all the peoples of the world. So it is a must to conduct a spiritual correct life at all times and to be ready to be subjected to personal sacrifices if the autonomy of any feeble person is at stake.

Another fundamental tenet of Sikhism is the concept of Chardi kala, Positivist attitude to life at all times. Gracefully and with humbleness to accept the will of God at all times. Always to lead ones life unattached and untangled with the material world. Not to come under the charm of Maya – the illusional and short-lived world around us. To remain isolated from this world but to acknowledge ones duties to God and his conception.

One God

Sikhs consider there is only one God, who has non-finite characters and names. He is the same for all religions. God is the Almighty, Maintainer and Destroyer. All that you see around you is God's creation. He is everywhere, in everything. He is fearless and without enmity. His form is indestructible. He doesn't need to revolve into any living form. God is is neither born nor die. He is illuminated with his own light. He has and will live eternally.

Reincarnation

According to Sikhism beliefs, every animate being has a psyche. In demise, the soul passes from one body to another until last release. The travel of the soul is regularized by the deeds and actions we execute during our lives. A pure existence of 'good deeds' (i.e., working honestly to earn our living, remembering the Creator, helping those who are less fortunate, being kind) is rewarded with happiness and joy in the next life, while wrongful actions and sinful deeds lead only to incarceration and fitting consequences in the next life. As the intent of God is found in all life and thing, a soul can be passed onto other life forms, such as plants and insects; not just human bodies. An individual who has developed to accomplish spiritual flawlessness in his lifetimes attains salvation.

Brotherhood

Sikhs consider that all human beings are equal. "We are progenies of WaheGuru, the Almighty." Sikhs are taught to treat all people of the world the same. No gender, racist, social or other favouritism is allowed. This is the substance of Guru Nanak's message as taught by the ten Sikh Gurus.

Disciplined Life

Upon induction, a Sikh must wear the Sikhs Five Ks (five Ks), execute strict recitation of the five prayers, Banis, etc. Sikh baptism is not generally performed at birth, but is a decision made by individuals who choose to dedicate themselves completely to the mandates of the Sikh religion. The majority of Sikhs are not baptized, although many wear some of the Five K's. As a part of a trained life, Sikhs are required to obey certain bans.

ETHICS

It is hard to define virtuousness or ethics. Dictionary definitions cannot possibly cover its full attributes, but they all agree on Righteous action and honorable conduct. In the Sikh credo, virtue in its essence is love. That universal love which finds expression in the brotherhood of man and in respecting the common man. This love is the source of selfless service and charitable work. It drives out ego, which is the root of conceit and exploitation. In its real sense, virtue means the love of God and His creation.

Sikhism believes in providential justice and the morality of the world order. Evil will ultimately fail, though it may often seem to succeed for a while. God alone is the Perfect Judge; He cannot be deceived by hypocritical acts or any cunning of man. He reads all hearts and knows every person's innermost motivation. Goodness is to be rewarded and wickedness punished. Ultimately Truth alone will prevail.

Sikhism does not regard selfless acts or beneficial behaviour as ends in themselves. These are means to achieve the end. Man's divine spark is dimmed only by his ignorance or indifference to the force and suddenness of the temptations that constantly beset him; it is this inbuilt weakness that leads to his surrender to such forces and pressures. It is only by affiliation with good and pure people that he will feel encouraged to face the challenge of life.

Sikhs consider that the objective of life is to love God, and to use self-will to replace greed, desire, angriness, and pridefulness, with happiness, humbleness, and pardon. Sikhs emphasize the importance of work with hands, head, and heart in the service of themselves, their family, and the social community. In adopting God's will, Sikhs hope to lose their sense of the grandness of themselves and their day-to-day concerns, and to feel a sense of harmoniousness with God.

For a Sikh, God is non-finite and ageless, and the Maker of all. He cares equally for all people, regardless of their religion, and God is within everyone. Sikhs believe that God is the source of love, and that people should act with love to God, to one other, and to the world. Musing on God's name is one of the key spiritual actions of Sikhs.

There is no priesthood in Sikhism, because it exercises equivalence of all, both men and women. Women read from the Guru Granth Sahib (holy book) in services in the Gurdwara, and can join the Khalsa (order or community of Sikhs). On joining the Khalsa, men are given the name Singh (lion), and women are called Kaur (princess). In practice, women have total spiritual equality with men, but the roles of men and women differ. Men are more active in society at large, and women have more responsibilities in the home. Restrictions placed upon women are of social rather than religious origin. Sikhs disapprove the caste system and do not believe in irrational practices, consulting astrologers, ancestor worship, or wearing the sanctified thread. This reflects the circumstances, views, and practices of the founding Gurus, in their oppositeness of aspects of the tradition of Hinduism and Islam.

METAPHYSICS

Metaphysics is the analyze of who and what we are, why we are here, what encounters to us when we die. These questions can only be replied by our inner Guru, the inner master, our more eminent selves. Answers are found through meditation, direct experience, service, cultism, prayer, and life's lessons. Each of us must answer these questions for ourselves. Our visit on earth school facilitates this process. We are Divine energy encased in time and space based on the rationale of causation or the Law of Karma.

Destiny means action to include our thoughts, feelings, and physical activities. The Law of Karma orders for every action there are consequences which in turn turns the causal factor for yet another effect. These effects (Samskaras) can bind us to restate the cycles of birth and death, until we can free ourselves from the effects we have created while alive. However, we individual expressions of our Divine Source (Mother-Father God). As such, we are already endless and immortal beings of Light and Love. We simply need to awaken to this Truth by raising our consciousness. Thus, our purpose in life is to raise our awareness, to free ourselves from the Law of Karma, or the cycles of birth and death, to express the God in us here and now. Our intention is the be God realized, to bring Heaven on Earth. When we die, our gross energy draws back from our physical being. Our more pernicious energies (i.e. thoughts, emotions and memories) which constitute our true nature are clumped together.

This pernicious energy unit may permanently or temporarily occupy on a higher plain hinging upon it's attachments and any disconfirming Karma remaining to be worked off. Thus, we become our own judge, reexamining our past life's events, the effects of our accomplishes, our purpose, etc. as part of the process of deciding our next path. If that path entails rebirth, we may choose our new life's considerations and the type of parents we need to be born to that would best afford us a chance for spiritual growth and for getting rid of any negative Karma (Samskaras) we produced in our many past lives.

Prophets of religion, like other men, are as well travelled in time and place. The educations of a prophet may amount to unique contributions of abiding value to the regarded as their age and they may say that it is a class by itself, without a harbinger, without a successor, logical untraceable to ancestors, yet thereby a prophet does not cease to belong to his age; just as he is going up most above it, he is truly bedded in it. This is true of Sikhism also.

He instructs that it is not the cerebral formula or verbal bow down to it that releases man, but the act and his character of living. Truth is mellower than everything but higher still is true living. Self-estrangement is the most fundamental affliction, not only of the modern man but it has been so ever afterwards man began to look within. In the most ancient recorded thought of man—the Veda— this ego-alienation, kilvis, the primal fission where the One became many, is pinpointed as the basic problem of the human psyche, and the ritual proficiency of yajna is recommended for re-gaining this lost unity, and this is the beginning of the honored Hindu contribution of the techniques and systems of Yoga to the insights into the psychologies and religious patterns of mankind. Religion always proceeds from an existential duality between man and the world, between man and God, and man longs to overcome this dichotomy to achieve a wholeness which appears to him as necessary for a meeting and authentic living. Pascal describes the point well by observing that "all man's troubles bow from the fact that he cannot bear to stay in a room alone with himself". Each one of us, more or less, encounters a sense of despair, when he is forced to via media his inner vision with the worlds of a world he must part with others.

It is one of the conditions of a social being as it is the plight of a lonely person and, therefore, part of adult life, in particular of the intellect, whom Albert Camus describes as "someone whose mind watches itself", and in whom this disease of self-estrangement is apt to run rampant. In the whole of the Sikh scripture, as in the revelations of Guru Nanak himself, there are repeated acknowledgments to this great wrench in human psyche and the cure is declared as a spiritual system and discipline based on the fundamental mental insights of the Yoga and its adaptation to a secular, social life, thus discarding the requirement of turning one's back on the world, and full social participation in it in search for annulment of man's self-alienation. This system and way of life is the Nam-Yoga of Sikhism that establishes the greatest donation of Guru Nanak to the Religion wherein the secular and the religious are indissolubly married. This Yoga of the Name is the core of the 'Religion of the Name' which Religion is and which God dominated Guru Nanak to exercise and prophesy to the world.

The third Fundamental teaching of Guru Nanak is that the fully incorporated person, the released individual, the deified man, must return to the world and society to take part in its activities to guide and aid it in striving for achieving a position in which human mind is free, hymn psyche is made whole, authentic living is facilitated and individuals may evolve into "deified men." When Guru Nanak moved deep into the Inner Himalayas crossing Nepal and some portions of Western Tibet, reaching the fabled Kailash Mountain and the celestial Mansarovar lake, the snowy and inaccessible abode of the honed yogis who were amazed to see a mere mortal reach there, "How does the news go with the world of the mortals?," they asked Guru Nanak. "The society is rotted to its core", replied Guru Nanak, and then raised an accusing finger at these yogis adding," And sires, you are shamefaced ones, for, it is men of high tradition and sensitivity who alone can guide and confirm society, but you have chosen to be self-indulgent escapees. When asked as to what power and competency there was for lifting society out of its incurable morass, Guru Nanak has gone on record as saying: "The two levers, that of organized opposition with and opposition to evil and the right idea that must inspire it."

REFERENCES

Archer, John Calrk: *"The Bible of the Sikhs. "Punjab Past and Present,* 1977.

Bachittar Singh, Giani: ed. *Planned Attack on Aad Shri Guru Granth Sahib.* Chandigarh: International Centre of Sikh Studies, 1994.

Banerjee, A. C.: *Guru Nanak to Guru Gobind Singh.* Patiala, 1978

Barth, A.: *Religions of India.* Delhi, 1963.

Blunt, E. H. H.: *The Caste Systems of Northern India.*

Crooke, W.: *The North-Western Provinces of India: Their History, Ethnology and Administration,* 1994.

Cunningham, Joseph Davey: *A History of the Sikhs.* Delhi: S. Chand and Company, 1985.

Daljeet Singh: *Sikhism.* Chandigarh, 1979.

Daljeet Singh: *Essay on the Authenticity of Kartarpuri Bi[and the Integrated Logic and Unity of Sikhism.* Patiala: Punjabi University, 1987.

Dewana, Mohan Singh: *A History of Punjabi Literature.* Jalandhar: Bharat Prakashan, 1971.

Ghurye, G. S.: *Caste and Race in India.* 1986.

Hutton, J. H.: *Caste in India.* 1980.

Ibbetson Sir Denzil: *Punjab Castes.* Patiala, 1970.

Jagjit Singh: *The Sikh Revolution.* Delhi, 1981.

Jogendra Singh: *'Sikh Ceremonies.* Chandigarh, 1968.

Kanwaljit Kaur: *Sikh Women, Fundamental Issues in Sikh Studies,* Institute of Sikh Studies, Chandigarh, 1992.

Ketkar, S. V: *History of Caste System in India.* 1979.

Mann, Gurinder Singh: *The Goindval Pothis: The Earliest Extant Source of the Sikh Canon.* Harvard Oriental Series 51. Cambridge: Harvard University Press, 1996.

Marenco, E. K.: *The Transformation of Sikh Society.* Portland, Oregon, 1974.

Mohammed Marmaduke Pickthall, translator: *The Meaning of Glorious Koran,* Mentor Book, New American Library, New York and Scarborough, Ontario, 1924.

Narang, G. C.: *Transformation of Sikhism.* Delhi, 1956.

Prinsep, H. T.: *Origin of the Sikh Power in the Punjab and Political Life of Maharaja Ranjit Singh.* Calcutta, 1834.

Randhawa, Harveen Kaur: *"Early Printing History of Guru Granth Sahib.* " M. Phil. term paper, Guru Nanak Dev University, 1985.

Randhir Singh: ed., *Prem Sumarag Granth.*Jalandhar, 1965.

Robert O. Ballou: *The Portable World Bible*, Penguin Books, 1976.

Schomer, Karine, and W. H. McLeod: eds. *The Sants: Studies in a Devotional Tradition of India.* Delhi: Motilal Banarasidass, 1987.

Shackle, Christopher: *Catalogue of the Punjabi and Sindhi Manuscripts in the India Office Library.* London: India Office Library and Records, 1977.

Singh, G.B.: *Gandhi: Behind the Mask of Divinity.* Prometheus Books, 2004.

Teja Singh, Sikhism: *Its Ideals and Institutions.* Bombay, 1938.

Weber, Max: *The Religions of India,* 1960.

4

Concept of God

Shri Guru Granth sahib, the holy book of Sikhs covers most of the spiritual doctrine about Sikhism. Detailed guidance is given on how to carry on their life so that redemption can be obtained. The holy text abstracts the convinced actions that one must take to make progress in the evolution of the person. One must remember the Creator at all times, it reminds the person that the soul is on loan from God, who is ever merciful and that the follower must commit their life to all good causes, to help make this life worthier. Given below is the message of the God in Sikhism:

- One God: There is only one God who has countless qualities and names. This God is the same for all religions. God is Creator and Sustainer. This God is all over, in everything. This God is audacious and with no enemies. Only God is without birth or death, and has lived and will exist forever.

- Remember God: Love God, but have concern of Him as well. Only by keeping the Creator in your mind at all times will you make advancement in your religious evolution.

- Reincarnation, karma and salvation: Every creature has a soul. Upon death, the soul is communicated from one body to another until dismission The journey of the soul is governed by the deeds and actions that we execute during our lives.

- Uphold moral values: Defend, protect and crusade for the rights of all creatures, in particular your fellow human beings.

- Personal sacrifice: Be groomed to give your life for all supreme principles.

- Humanity: All human beings are equal. We are cubs and daughters of WaheGuru, the Almighty.

- Positive attitude toward life: Always have a positive, affirmative and buoyant view of life. God is there, He will help.

- Many paths lead to God: Sikhs are not special; they are not the people of God. Simply calling yourself a Sikh does not bring you redemption. Members of all faiths have the same human right as Sikhs.

- Disciplined life: Upon sacrament, a Sikh must wear the 5Ks and execute exacting recital of the five prayers Banis.

- No special worship days: Sikhs do not consider that any particular day is holier than any other.

- Conquer the five Sins: It is every Sikh's duty to overcome these five sins: Pride, Anger, Greed, Attachment, and Lust.

- Five Ways to conquer Sins: Through Happiness, Charity, Kindness, Positive Energy, Humility.

- Equality: All humans are equal before God. No secernment is allowed on the basis of caste, race, gender, creed, origin, colour, education, status, wealth, et cetera. The teachings of universal equality and union are important pillars of Sikhism.

- God's spirit: Although all living beings including plants, minerals and animals have been produced by God, only the human being comprises God's Spirit which is capable of becoming a Gurmukh.

- Personal right: Every person has a right to life but this right is limited and has attached certain duties (simple living) are necessity. A Sikh is expected to rise early, meditate and pray, consume simple food, perform an honest day's work, execute duties for his or her family, enjoy life and always be positive, be large-hearted and support the needy, et cetera.

- One's actions: Salvation is received by one's actions, good deeds, commemoration of God (Naam Simran) and Kirtan.

- Family life: Encouraged to live as a family unit to allow for and raise children for the perpetual benefit of creation.

- Sharing: It is promoted to share and give to charity 10 percent of one's net earnings.

- Accept God's will: Develop your attribute so that you recognize happy event and deplorable events as one – the will of God causes them.

- The four fruits of life: Truth, happiness, contemplation and Naam.

- Material obsession: Accumulation of materials has no meaning in Sikhism. Wealth such as gold, portfolio, stocks, goods, properties, et cetera, will all be left here on Earth when you go. Do not get attached to them.

- Non-family oriented living: A Sikh is promoted not to live as a recluse, beggar, monk, Nun, celibate, or in any similar vein.

- Intoxication: The usage of alcohol, drugs, tobacco, or other intoxicants is disallowed.

- No priestly class: Sikhs do not have to depend on a priest for any of the functions that need to be performed.

- Naam: Ponder upon God's name (WaheGuru in the Sikh religion) through spoken repetition. This is done so that the mind is calmed and cleansed in order to become one with God. The technique taught by the Guru Granth Sahib is "Urd Uhrd". This means to inspire with the "Wahe" syllable and exhale on the "Guru" syllable. This is the most important part of the religion.

- Kirat Karni: Earning an honorable living while remembering the Lord.

- Wand kay Shakna: Share with others who are deserving, as during langar.

DEFINING GOD

The key belief of Sikhism is that God exists, not merely as an idea or design, but as a Real Entity, unspeakable yet knowable and perceivable to anyone who is prepared to dedicate the time and energy to become perceptive to His persona. The Gurus never spoke about validations of the existence of God: For them He is too literal and evident to need any logical proof.

In any case, knowledge of the ultimate Reality is not an affair for reason; it comes by revealing of the ultimate reality through "nadir" or decorate and by "anubhava" or mystical experience. Sikhism as a faith is uncompromising monotheistic. The Gurus have described God in legion ways in their hymns included in the Guru Granth Sahib, but the unity of the deity is consistently emphasized throughout.

God is Karta Purakh, the Maker-Being. He created the spatial-secular universe not from some pre-existing forcible element, but from His owns self. Universe is His own emission. It is not "maya" or illusion but is real (sat) because, as say Guru Arjan, "True is He and true is His creation because all has exhaled from God Himself". But God is not identical with the universe. The latter exists and is contained in Him and not vice versa.

God is subjective in the produced world, but is not limited by it. "Many a times He extends Himself into such worlds but He ever remains the same One Ekankar". Yet at one time "there are hundreds of thousands of skies and realms". Admitted in Sach Khand (Realm of Truth), the nonliteral abode of God, there is countless regions and universes". Creation is "His sport which He witnesses, and when He rolls up the sport, He is His sole Self again". He is the Creator, Maintainer and the Destroyer.

The main aim of the ceartor to create the world is not for man to investigate or judge the purpose of His Creator. Purakh increased Karta in the Mool Mantar is the Punjabi form of Sanskrit purusa, which literally means, besides man, male or person, "the aboriginal man as the soul and original source of the universe; the personal and inspiring principle; the supreme Being or Soul of the universe." Purakh in Mool Mantar is, therefore, none other than God the Creator. The term has zero to do with the purusa of the Sankhya school of Indian doctrine where it is the spirit as a peaceful viewer of prakriti or creative force.

That God is "nirbhay" (without fear) and "nirvair" (without rancour or enemy) is apparent enough as He has no "sarik" (rival). But the terms have other intensions, too. Nirbhay not only indicates bravery but also the absence of fearfulness. It also implies reign and unchallenged exercise of Will. Similarly, nirvair implies, besides absence seizure of enmity, the positive attributes of compassionateness and impartiality.

God is Akal Murat, the Eternal Being. The eternity involved in the damaging name akal has made it popular in Sikh culture as one of the names of God, the Timeless One, as in Akal Purakh or in the slogan Sat Shri Akal (Satya Shri Akal). One of the most consecrated shrines of the Sikhs is the Akal Takhat, the Eternal Throne, at Amritsar. Murat here does not mean form, figure, image or idol. Sikhism express forbids idolatry or image-adoration in any form. God is called "Nirankar", the Formless One, although it is admittedly that all forms are the expressions of Nirankar.

Bhai Gurdas, the earliest expositor and the copyist of the original recension of Guru Granth Sahib, says: "Nirankar akaru hari joti sarup anup dikhaia (The Formless One having created form manifested His wondrous refulgence". Murat in the Mool Mantra, therefore, means verity or expression of the Timeless and Formless One. God is Ajuni, Unembodied, and Saibhan (Sanskrit svayambhu), Self-existent. The Primal Creator Himself had no creator. He merely is, has ever been and shall ever be by Himself. Ajuni also affirms the Sikh act of the theory of divine personification.

God in Sikhism is thus described in three distinct aspects, viz. God in Himself, God's relation to creation, and God's relation to man. God by himself is the one Ultimate, Surpassing Reality, Nirgun i.e. without attributes, Timeless, Boundless, Formless, Ever-existent, Immutable, Ineffable, All-by Himself and even Transcendent in His entirety. The only nomenclatures that can rightly be applied to Him in this state of sunn (Sanskrit, sunya or void) are Brahman and Parbrahman (Sanskrit, Parbrahman) or the pronouns He and Thou. During a discourse with Siddhas, Hindu solitaries, Guru Nanak in reply to a question as to where the Surpassing God was before the stage of creation replies, "To think of the Transcendent Lord in that state is to enter the kingdom of wonder. Even at that stage, he permeated all that Void". This is the state of God's samadhi, self-involved trance.

When it suits God, He becomes sarguna (with attributes) and bears witness to Himself in conception. He becomes subjective in His created universe, which is His own emission, an aspect of Himself. As says Guru Amar Das, Nanak III, "This (so-called) poison, the world, that you see is God's picture; it is God's outline that we see". Most names of God are His prenominal, action-related signifiers, kirtam nam or karam nam (Dasam Granth, Jaap Sahib). God in the Sikh Holy Scripture has been referred to by several names, picked from Indian and Semitic customs. He is called in terms of human relations as father, mother, brother, relation, friend, lover, beloved, husband. Other names, expressive of His domination, are Thakur, Prabhu, Svami, Sah, Patsah, Sahib, Sain (Lord, Master).

Some conventional names are Ram, Narayan, Govind, Gopal, Allah, Khuda. Even the blackball terms such as nirankar, niranjan et al. are as much related to assigns as are the positive terms like data, datar, karta, kartar, dayal, kripal, qadir, karim, etc. Some terms particular to Sikhism are naam (literally name), sabad (literally word) and VaheGuru (literally Wondrous Master). While nam and sabad comprise mystical terms standing for the inspired manifestation and are used as exchange terms for the Supreme Being, VaheGuru is an explainatery phrase expressing awe, wonder and enraptured joy of the worshipper as he covers the greatness and nobleness of the Lord and His Creation.

Immanence or All-pervasiveness of God, however, does not limit or in any way affect His transcendency. He is Transcendent and Immanent at the same time. The Creation is His Lila or cosmic play. He enjoys it, pervades it, yet Himself remains uncommitted. Guru Arjan describes Him in several hymns as "Unattached and Unentangled in the midst of all"; and "Amidst all, yet outside of all, free from love and hate". Creation is His manifestation, but, being specified by space and time, it provides only a partial and frail glimpse of the Timeless and Boundless Supreme Being.

The Creator also sustains His Creation compassionately and benevolent. "My Lord is ever fresh and ever Bountiful"; "He is the exterminator of the pain and sorrow of the humble". The universe is created, sustained and moved according to His hukam or Divine Will, and Divine purpose. "The mysterious hukam is the source of all forms, all creatures. All are within the ambit of hukam; there is nothing beyond of it." Another principle that determines the created beings is destiny (actions, deeds).

The created cosmos though real is not endless. Whenever God desires, it merges back into His Timeless and Formless Self. Guru Gobind Singh calls this procedure of creation and dissipation udkarkh (Sanskrit, utkarsana) and akarkh (Sanskrit, akarsana), respectively: "Whenever you, O Creator, cause udkarkh (increase, expansion), the creation presumes the boundless body; whenever you effect akarkh (attraction, contraction), all bodily existence merges in you" (Benati Chaupai). This process of foundation and adjournment has been repeated God alone knows for how many times.

Man, although an minute part of God's creation, yet bears apart from it insofar as it is the only species blessed with reflection, moral sense and potential for understanding matters theoretical. In Sikhism, human birth is both a special perquisite for the soul and a rare chance for the actualization of union with God. Man is lord of earth, as Guru Arjan says, "Of all the eight million and four hundred thousand species, God conferred superiority on man", and "All other species are your (man's) water-bearers; you have form of government over this earth". But Guru also reminds that "now that you (the soul) have got a human body, this is your turn to unite with God". Guru Nanak had warned, "Listen, listen to my advice, O my mind! Only good deed shall endure, and there may not be some other chance". So, realization of God and a reunion of atma (soul) with paramatma (Supreme Soul, God) are the quality goals of human life. The accomplishment in the end rests on nadar (God's grace), but man has to strain in order to deserve His grace. As a first step, he should have religious belief in and craving for the Lord. He should believe that God is near him, rather within his self, and not far away. He is to see him in his self.

DIMENSIONS OF GOD

Below are the main characters that Sikhism assigns to God:

- Only God is suitable of worship and meditation at all times.
- He is the Creator,Upholder and also the Destroyer.
- God is Kind.
- With His Grace, He comes to inhabit the mind and body.
- He is kind and wise.
- He is the ultimate Shielder of all beings.
- Only with His will can pain, poverty, disease and rigorousnesses be removed from one's life.
- God is everywhere.

Concept of Sahaj

The idea of sahaj relates to the most eminent religious state humanly attainable and has thus most mystical intensions attached to it. In other words, it is a simple human suggestion, that a man should become a man par excellence; a real man; no adherences, no defaults, no accretions, no deviations. But this self-contradictory word Sahaj does not go with mere 'saying' orverbal formula. It is an actuality, a real human state, a palpable, workable human achievement. Bearing in mind the bewildering nature of this term, it can safely be said that the concept of Sahaj belongs to the realm of 'Esoteric-mysticism', in as much as the meaning of Sahaj is constantly associated with its manifold aspect or its expressive quality which, in nonliteral terms, we call Anhad Sabad.

It is only the experienced who can comprehend these two unitive states within his soul, without being capable to express them because these are exclusively unspeakable realizations. Guru Nanak himself, having received directly the blissful union with God and the accompanying divine manifestations attending such Beatitude, has mystically conveyed these visions in symbolical language, incorporating and using esoteric terms already current in Bedanta or Yoga mysticism and in higher Buddhism, endowing them with new meanings.

The junction of an experience which was fundamentally a mystical one and hence, according to Guru Nanak himself, constituted incapable of constituting translated in communicable terms, was indeed beyond human expression, had necessarily to be in cultural mystical terms made current and somewhat apprehensible by his predecessors belonging to several mystic orders of sants and sadhus, and in well-known cultural symbols and images that had some meaning, however faint and generalized, to those whom his words were addressed to." In order to conceive the concept of Sahaj in its mystical intension, it would be useful first to study its etymological meaning.

Sahaj is in the first place a Sanskrit word meaning having been born together and thus something inside perceived or comprehended along with one's birth as a human being - a sort of in-dwelling mystical principle of divine perception given to man as his birthright and therefore, a natural and effortless heritage of divinity ingrained in humanity. Strictly speaking, Sahaj is the very 'mysticality' of religion. It is the adoption of core and 'philosophical doctrine' as the true basis of religion, to the denial of all ritualism externalities.

In Guru Nanak's thought, Sahaj comes to imply the acceptance of Hukam as the first cardinal principle of Sikhism. Sahaj in this meaning would be the mystical state of a man who has accepted the divine will (Hukam, Bhana, Raza). Sahaj, thus, is the highest spiritual state attainable in Sikhism. It is the highest bliss. In the meaning expressed above Sahaj connotes a natural slowness and steadiness required for perfect action. Haste makes waste, has been truly said, Sahaj is the opposite of inordinate haste. Sahaj is compactness and self -sufficiency, while haste is flippancy and inner weakness. A sure man is the 'poised' man.

In this anthropomorphic sense, Sahaj would mean equipoise, equanimity and equilibrium. It may be called "balanced perspicacity" or sambuddhata, in the psychological sense. All true balance and true actions engender aesthetic as well as spiritual pleasure, while spiritual fulfilment produces infinite bliss. Sahaj which is "the state of enlightenment.achieved through self-discipline" has been generally accepted to be "the ultimate goal which is the religious and spiritual disciplinelaid down by Guru Nanak was supposed to leadto." Hence this term has been used to denote the ineffable union with God.

Several expressions have been current as synonymous with Sahaj, such as Sunn-samadh, turia-avastha, chautha pad, amar pad, param pad, maha-sukh, param anand, dasam duar, Anhad and, sach Khand, Jiwan-mukti and so on. The term sahaj samadh has also been used by Kabir and the Sikh Gurus.All this terminology connected with Sahaj was commonly used by all the Nirgun-Sampradaya saints, Kabir, Namdev, Dadu, and others, along with Guru Nanak, having borrowed it from the Sahajayani Buddhist and also from Tantrie Hathayoga and the Nathpanthi-Kanphata Yogis with whom Guru Nanak came into direct and close contact. TheSahajiya Vaishnavas and Bauls of Bengal also adopted this esoteric terminology.

The patent meaning of Sahaj has been the abnegation of duality and the perception of unityin God as well as the creation. Devoidness, is also the primordial state of the Nirgun BrahmHimself. Mohan Dingh Uberoi describes theSikh Sahaja Yoga as "unification with Selfthrough cultivation of a state of natural, easySelf-Hold, Self-Rest." Again: "Sunn is a state inwhich there is no movement, in the receptacle,of any type, no sound, no wind, no object orobjectivity, the subject God, is there as thecontainer, the presence."

Guru Nanak has copiously used esoteric termsand expressions such as sunn, shiv-shakti,trikuti, unman, sas-ghar-sur, bajar-kapat, ira-pingla-sukhmana, ajapa-jap, dasamduar,dhundhukar-niralam, sache amerapur, sachinagari, bij-mandar, sunn kala, satsar, panch-sabad, akul niranjan, purakh-arit, gagnantar dhanakh, sunn-samadh, bis-ikis, dubmue-vinpani, surat-dhun, nijghar, guptibani, anhat sunnand surat-sabad in all his compositions, specially in Ragas, Ramkali and Maru. These are purely mystical terms common to all Indian religions.

Guru Nanak's use of these tantric and yogic terms does not logically follow that he actually practiced or inculcated their practice among his followers, since he has used them only as figures of speech or technical esoteric terms which were current and handy for use and were generally understood among advanced mystical orders of his time. He had actually many discussions during his travels and at Kartarpur with Yogis, Sadhus and ascetics of several mystical cults and denominations.

Guru Nanak, in fact, had his own mystical message to convey to humanity and it was original with him and had no conceptual reference to the mystical philosophies of saivites, vaishnavites, yogies and even to Kabir, Dadu, Namdev and others, though many of them were accepted as allied co-mystics and their compositions included in the Adi-Granth more with a view to illustration and elabouration than to identification and syncretism.

The achievement of Sahaj-avastha in the form of maha-sukha or Jiwan-mukti which was the ultimate goal of all the mystical cults using esoteric terms concurrently during Guru Nanak's times was to Guru Nanak a matter of inner discipline and direct experiential contact with divine Reality. Mere esoteric niceties or intricacies, especially of Tantric Yoga were quite alien to his mystic temperament which was fundamentally Dynic, ethical and synthetic.

Guru Nanak's mystic thought is easily distinguishable from the Natha-panthi and Kanphata Yogi cult, as also from Tantrism, Vaishnavism and Shaivism, though a general fallacy exists to equate or identify it with Kabir's mysticism. But as Mcleod has lucidly discussed, much of Kabir's mystical jargon remains obscure and personal whereas Guru Nanak's postulation especially of the mystic path and discipline is clearer and more cogent than that of Kabir. There is much inconsistency and incoherence in Kabir's thought from which Guru Nanak's mysticism is absolutely free, with the result that whereas it is difficult if not impossible to construct a theology.

Sikh Cosmology

Origin and the structure of the universe is one of the major topic about which man is always curious to know from the beginning. To locate the stable base of this universe and to fix his own place in it have been the subjects of his constant search and speculation for man. The Gurus brought their own mystical and philosophical powers for solving the riddle. In their poetry in the Guru Granth Sahib, they have expressed their sense of wonder and sung paeans of praise for the Almighty. A minute observation of the phenomenon of nature forms an important part of the Sikh metaphysical insight. It brings into view a palpable vision of the Creator and His creation. The medium used is poetry of far reaching import. It is at the same time poetry of elemental beauty as well as of grandeur.

The Gurus have unequivocally and forcefully stressed the unicity of the Godhead. There is no room in it for any dualisitic or polytheistic doctrines. The deities of the Hindu mythology, for instance, have no place in their belief as the objects of worship; nor was anyone of them regarded coeternal with God. The matter out of which forms are shaped and the selves that inhabit them are eternal in Him but not with Him. Again, the God of Sikh teaching is not a mere concept or principle; He is the Ultimate Reality. True and eternal, He is the Power that has existed for ever and will continue to exist when everything else has ceased. This power is endowed with will and supported by a conscious intelligence, which serves as the chief instrument for the fulfilment of His designs and purposes.

With this will He comes out of His transcendental state of absorption in the Self and becomes the all powerful immanent Creator. When He so wills, He draws it back, which is its dissolution. The world for the Gurus is a creation, and owes its existence to the will of the Divine. It is the Creator's sporting gesture, lila. He Himself is its material as well as efficient cause. There was a time when the world had not yet appeared and there will be a time when the world will again disappear. The Gurus have called the precreation state suna, meaning 'empty void', 'negative abyss,' 'nothingness.' Describing this stage, Guru Nanak says For countless ages utter darkness prevailed There was neither earth nor heaven, The will of the Infinite Lord reigned everywhere. There was neither day nor night, Nor sun nor moon, Only Sunya stayed in solitary meditation. Again, for a good many ages Utter darkness filled everywhere. The Creator was wholly absorbed in deep meditation. There existed only His true nàm, His glory, And the lustre of His eternal throne.

Many schools of thought have put forth the view that the world was born out of nothingness. However, the Sunya of the Gurus does not correspond to the Buddhistic concept, nor the absolute nothingness, the 'exnihilo' of other schools. The "nothingness" of the Gurus refers to absence of creation, and not to the absence of the Creator or His essence or potency. The Gurus have used "Sunya" in conjunction with terms like samadhi, tan or Sahaj or sach (holy truth). These terms describe the state of complete tranquillity and oneness of the Absolute Self, and refer to that latent form in which every aspect of creation lies dormant in Him, waiting for the operation of the Divine urge for its unfoldment. With this urge, from apparent nothingness, the Formless assumes form, "The unattributed becomes the Attributed "nirgun te sargunu thia" and thus this world of a myriad colours takes shape.

The Gurus do not subscribe to the view that the world suddenly appeared in its finished form. It has passed through a gradual process of evolution. They also reject the view that it has been 'produced' or 'manufactured' mechanically as an artisan might produce an article out of a given substance. God and His creation are one the creation was merged in Him. God raised the creation out of Himself. It is a gradual unfoldment of what lay folded within the Ultimate cause the Absolute Self. From the stale of Sunya, The latent form became active. The elements of air and water were evolved out of Sunya. Within the fire Water and living beings is His Light, And the power of Creation lies within Sunya. From Sunya came out the moon The sun and the firmament. The earth and heaven have been evolved out of Sunya. Guru Nanak mentions three stages in the process of cosmic evolution.

The first is the atmosphere when there was only all pervasive air. The second stage was that of water; the third was lithosphere when the crust of the earth took form. Situated in the midst of the elements, the self has to evolve its potentialities to merge into the Absolute, which is the state of liberation. Thus, a theory of spiritual evolution is implicit in this process. The source and origin of Creation is Shabad, sabda, (sound), nam, nad, barn or anahad sabad. The will of God (Hukam) becomes synonymous with the word of God. The creative power of sabad (Word) is a concept common to most religious cultures; Sabad has been referred to as nad, van or vak in Vedic and Upanisadic literature. There are clear references to it in the Zoroastrian sroasha, the Word or Logos of the Christians, and Kun or Kalima of the Muslims.

The poets of the Nirgnna School like Kabir and Dadu also equate the sabad (Word) with the Creator. Sabad (sound manifested) produces the subtle element akash (ether), from which the other four subtle elements emerge, which in turn give rise to the five gross elements. Air evolves from ether, fire from air, water from fire, and earth from water. The Gurus regard these five elements as the basic constituents of the whole creation.The evolution of the world from sabad (Word) indicates that the Gurus do not accept the cultural division of the world into matter and spirit. Since the light of the Lord (sabad) pervades the entire universe, what has sprung from Him cannot be lifeless or inert. Lifeless matter can neither respond to outer and inner influences, nor can it be translated into an evolutionary process. There is no such thing as pure matter in the entire universe. Forms may be with or without a self or soul.

The ensouled forms have been called Jivas. In and through them the conscious luminous spirit, a spark of the Divine Flame, gains vital expression. While Jivas have been divided into four broad categories (khanis) eggborn, wombborn, earthborn and sweatborn references are also made to the Gods, ghosts and the like. Creation cannot be limited to any fixed number of categories. The Gurus have given vivid accounts of the visible and invisible worlds. They refer to countless kinds of creation. They speak of innumerable mountains, oceans, countries, continents, galaxies and universes. Guru Nanak's composition "Japu" which is considered to be the epitome of the entire Sikh doctrine, gives a highly imaginative account of the gross and subtle worlds in the stanzas known as "khands" (regions). Metaphorical references to the three worlds (tribhavan), the nine divisions (nav khand), the fourteen regions (chaudah bhavan or lok) of Hindu and Muslim belief are also referred to, but the Gurus repeatedly say that like the Lord, His creation is also limitless.

The Gurus believe that there are many solar systems like that of ours and each solar system have its own Brahma, Vishnu and Mahesa (gods of creation, sustenance and dissolution). So great is the lord and so boundless in His creation that countless planets and worlds are being created and dissolved in it in the twinkling of an eye. Time and space are two very significant factors in the process of creation. The whole creation is under their influence and sway. It is, therefore, subject to growth and decay. Only the Creator, the Transcendental One, is beyond the influence of time and space. In fact time and space exist only as part of the creatior not only is creation in time and space, it can only be understood in relation to them. When creation itself dissolves at the time of pralaya (dissolution),time and space also merge into Eternity. Therefore, the Gurus do not accept the independent existence of time and space.

Time has been dealt with in Sikh teaching in detail. While the Creator has been called Akal (Timeless), which is a central concept in the Sikh philosophical thought, the universe is governed by the element of time. There is a continuing process of creation and dissolution. Says Guru Arjan in Sukhmanr. 'Kai barpasario pasar, sada sada iku ekankar' Numerous times has the visible Universal expanse been manifested; only the Supreme Being is eternal, In Gurbani, temporality and eternity are constant opposites. Time itself is immeasurable, beyond human conception. During it the universe has appeared and disappeared through endless ages. Occasionally the kaliyuga era too is mentioned. In the sum, for most practical purposes the prevalent Indian computation of time has been adopted. The Gurus regard man as the crown of creation.

The human body is the model of the whole creation, we, each one of us, are the complete universe. Man is the microcosm of the cosmos which is the macrocosm. The study of this macrocosm can reveal all the secrets contained in the macrocosm. Our body is the epitome of all creation and we have only to turn within to seek the truth. There is a complete parallel system between the physical processes of the universe and the biological processes in the body of man. Above and beyond the nine visible "gates" (eyes, ears, nostrils, mouth and the two lower apertures) of the body there lies the invisible "tenth door"(dasam duar) where the true sabda, in all its resplendent glory and bliss, keeps ceaselessly resounding.

This unstruck music (akhand sabad), the stream of perennial life, the true Nectar is incessantly in operation in the "tenth door" from where man can travel back to his true Home (sach khand) on the ship of the Word (sabda). He can then merge his individual self in the universal self to obtain lasting release from the cycle of birth and death. In fact, the human body is a precious gift, the golden opportunity which the great Lord mercifully grants to creation so that it may realize its true self and become one with the transcendent. To utilize the body for this purpose is the real goal and end of life, and the only justification for man's sojourn in this world.

The concept of cosmology advanced by the Gurus is not merely theological or speculative. It is the outcome of their own spiritual and mystical experience. The Gurus were unmatched spiritual teachers who in their own spiritual ascent beheld the splendid vision of the entire creation. They described what they themselves saw vividly revealed within their personal mystical experience is the real base and authority of their revelation. They founded a living communion with God and possessed firsthand experience of all the secrets of creation. However, in their humility the Gurus time and again have proclaimed that the mystery of creation is known to the Creator alone. Unlike those creeds which have set dates for the origin of creation, the Gurus have visioned it as wrapped in the mystery and infinity of the Creator. As stated in the Japu, none can claim knowledge of this mystery which the Creator alone beholds

Philosophy of God

The superiority of human life is such that even heavenly Gods and Goddesses yearn for it for their salvation. Man is the crown creation of the universe; his body is God's temple" as well as & replica of the universe. It should, therefore, be sustained and maintained properly, and not abused by intoxication or tortured by penances, and it should not be wasted in futile pursuit.

Naam mainly implies God, but has several other connotations such as word (shabad). Guru, Gurbani, divine order and formulae to meditate upon the Reality. All these terms are one and the same. Naam, like God, is eternal, great, absolute and formless. Naam is panacea for all the fulfilment of desires, whilst forgetting God is the source of all diseases and distress. Naam is the most potent detergent to cleanse the mind of its impurities. God pervades everywhere and in everything. Man alone is blessed with this awareness which can be rekindled by recitation of Naam. Naam is the harbinger of peace and tranquillity. Naam inculcates in us all the Godly qualities.

Naam Sadhana is the interaction of gur-shabad and the soul consciousness for which no intermediary is required as the gur-shabad is Guru by itself. All the ten Gurus, during their earthly life, have stressed that Gubani or shabad is the True Guru, and not their bodies. During his discourse, Guru Nanak said that God is his Guru. Guru Gobind Singh, also confirmed it when he enthroned Shri Guru Granth Sahib as the eternal Guru.

Sadhana is primarily co-ordination of the sense organs — tongue, ears and eyes, with the love and devotion provided by the heart). Whilst the tongue redtes or sings, the ears hear, and the eyes visualize the presence of God. Our soul-consciousness (surti or mind) absorbed in the sound of the words, gets in contact with the Greater Consciousness. Our mind is thus the disciple and the soul-sound of the word is the gur-shabad in this state, our attention remains absorbed to the presence and love of God.

The most difficult part of Naam Sadhana is the control of mind. The mind is likened to a donkey that stops kicking only when burdened with a load. The mind's burden is Naam, the more we stress it with Naam, the quieter it becomes." Naam Sadhana is primarily intended to awaken the mind, God-realisation comes out from within and then widens out to embrace other spheres of human activity.

There is a school of thought and practice, which prescribes focussing of attention on a picture of a Guru, pir, saiat, an idol or any one of the energy points in the body such as the forehead, heart and navel during Naam Sadhana. This is a fruitless exercise as a lifeless entity cannot bestow any favour. Besides, the all-pervading God, whom we want to cultivate, is formless or Nirankar. Our firm belief in God's Reality should be the focus of concentration. The realisation of His existence is the essence of meditation." Guru Gobind Singh is said to have gone in samadhi for many days together uttering the word Tuhi Tuhi "Thou art Thou art", and to have written a number of lengthy pages just repeating Tuhi Tuhi without a pause.

Guru Ram Das, the fourth Nanak, in his shabad quoted below prescribes the routine of a Sikh.

"He who calls himself a Sikh of the True Guru should rise early everyday, take bath and meditate on God's name, according to the Guru's instructions. This will remove his pain and even suffering of his past life. At sunrise, he should recite and sing Gurbani. During the rest of the day, he should remember God whilst doing his normal work and with every breath and morsel.

A Sikh moulds his life, both in form and spirit, according to the tenets of Gurbani. Gurbani teaches us to keep the company of God-inspired souls, to seek spiritual guidance, and to take part in congregational prayers (Kirtan). This is the highest and the noblest deed. The other aspect of meditation is service (sewa), particularly of the poor, needy and invalids to cultivate ' humility.

The famous Sikh disciple, Bhai Gurdas has stated in his ode that when God asked Guru Nanak for a boon, he requested Him for Naam and humility. Guru Nanak in his 'Asa Di Var' the morning chant, has stated that sweetness (of talk and behaviour) and humility are the essence of all Godly qualities'.

MESSENGERS OF GOD

In Sikhism, messengers of God are represented by Gurus. Guru is often used for a Brahman, a teacher or a guide. The term Guru in Sikhism is not used for a teacher or a guide or an expert or even a human body. In Sikhism the word Guru is defined as the Light that dispels all darkness, and that is called Jot (Divine Light). Guru Nanak was, therefore, the Embodiment of Divine Light. The Guru in Sikhism is a perfect Prophet or Messenger of God in whom the Light of God shines fully, visibly and completely. Guru is in union with Divine. Thus he ushers the devotees, the seekers of Truth into a spiritual birth. Through him the Glory of the Lord is transmitted to humanity. On account of his Divine prerogatives, the Guru, though human in form, is Divine in Spirit.

When Guru Nanak conferred Guruship on Guru Angad, the Jot was passed on and Guru Angad too became the embodiment of Divine Light. In the same way all the nine Gurus were the embodiments of Gur Nanak Jot. The tenth Master, Guru Gobind Singh then conferred the Guruship on Guru Granth Sahib, which too became the embodiment of Divine Light.

NIRVANA

Nirvana, Mukti or moksha means release, deliverance, liberation, release, freedom and emancipation. Although translated as salvation', mukti is different from the Christian salvation. The latter is a composite concept personifying salvation. Redemption is the change in man's relation to God by the removal of guilt and sin.

Mukti essentially implies a bonded state from which man must be freed, be it ignorance, ignorance, mortality, suffering, passion, desire, attachment, superstition, physical body or the wheel of life and death. All these spell only a perilous existence for man. Mukti, however, is not to be construed as escapism. It is not that man is removed to a safe quarter in existence where no perils overtake him. He, rather, discovers within himself an unexpected power to withstand and not be shaken by any threat or danger. The security and integrity experienced are spiritual and ultimate; neither ephemeral nor circumstantial.

On the positive side, mukti signifies the fullest and truest realization of the self. The saved life is a fully human self, open and unhindered. It embodies the realization that there is no other than the self. Separation and ego-consciousness stand decimated. Everlasting peace of the eternal and infinite self transcend the make-believe world of weal and woe, good and evil, gaiety and sorrow, wisdom and folly.

The basic concept underlying mukti is that human life is in bondage on account of its own works (karma). Schools of Indian philosophy conceive of an emancipated soul which, after exhausting the effects of all karmas, attains the liberated state. However, what exactly is conceived as bondage, and what as liberation varies from school to school. The Sankhya view characterizes mukti as the cessation of the three types of pain. The self is able to attain such a state only by transcending the adjuncts of material nature (Prakrti). Happiness and misery are the handicraft of the qualities. The liberated soul having transcended the gunas goes beyond pleasure and pain.

In Vedanta, mukti stands for the removal of duality (dvaita) and the merger of the self (Jivatman) with the Absolute (Brahman). The self then becomes resplendent as existent, intelligent and blissful (sat, cit, and ananda). Nirvana is the name for mukti in the Buddhist vocabulary, the two being considered mutually comparable in the same Thought category. Nirvana literally means extinction, and implies the extinction of the five'— viz, rupa (form), sanjna (name), sanskara (impression), vijnana (knowledge) and vedana (pleasure-pain). According to Bhakti schools, mukti is attained through upasna (worship) and consists in finding an abode in the spiritual realm of the upasya (worshipped deity).

REFERENCES

Barque, A. M.: *Eminent Sikhs of Today*. Lahore: Barque and Company, 1942.

Bhandari, Sujan Rai: *Khulastut Tvarikh*. Trans. Ranjit Singh Gill, ed. Fauja Singh. Patiala: Punjabi University, 1972.

Chaupa Singh: *The Chaupa Singh Rahit-nama*. Ed. W. H. McLeod. Otago: University of Otago Press, 1987.

Coward, Harold, and David Goa: *Mantra: Hearing the Divine in India* Chambersburg, Pa.: Anima Books, 1991.

Fauja Singh and Gurbachan Singh Talib: *Guru Tegh Bahadur: Martyr and Teacher*. Patiala: Punjabi University, 1975.

Gurdas, Bhai: *Kabbitt Savaiye*. Ed. Onkar Singh. Patiala: Punjabi University, 1993.

Gurdas, Bhai: *Varan*. Ed. Gursharan Kaur Jaggi. Patiala: Punjabi University, 1987.

Gurdit Singh, Giani: "Adi Bir da Rachna Kal, "*Prakash*, June 30, 1952,

Gurdit Singh, Giani: *Bham ate unahan di Rachna*. Ludhiana: Punjabi Sahitt Academy, 1961.

Harvey, Alper: *Understanding Mantras*. Albany: State University of New York Press, 1989.

Hawley, John Stratton, and Mark Juergensmeyer: *Songs of the Saints of India*. New York: Oxford University Press, 1988.

Hawley, John Stratton: "Author and Authority in the *Bhakti* Poetry of North India. "*Journal of Asian Studies*, 1988.

Hawley, John Stratton: "The Music in Faith and Morality. " *Journal of the American Academy of Religion,* 1984.

Piar Singh: *Gatha Shri Adi Granth*. Amritsar: Guru Nanak Dev University, 1992.

Shackle, Christopher; Mandair, Arvind-Pal Singh: *Teachings of the Sikh Gurus: Selections from the Sikh Scriptures*. United Kingdom: Routledge, 2005.

Shri Guru Granth Sahib by Dr Gopal Singh M.A Ph.D.: Published by World Book Centre in 1960

5

Main Figures

The evolution of Sikhs began with the emergence of Guru Nanak as a religious leader and a social reformer during the fifteenth century in Punjab. Their identity was formalised and wielded into uniform practice by Guru Gobind Singh on March 30, 1699. The latter baptised five persons from different social backgrounds to form the social brotherhood of the Khalsa. The first five, Pure Ones, then baptised Gobind Singh into the Khalsa fold. The Sikhs founded a nation, under Ranjit Singh, in the nineteenth century in which they were preeminent. They were known for their military prowess, administrative capabilities, economic productivity and their adaptability to modern western technology and administration.

The Sikhs revere Guru Granth Sahib as their supreme teacher, as it is a literal transcript of the teachings of the Sikh Gurus. The tenth Guru appointed Guru Granth Sahib as his successor. Compiled by the Sikh Gurus, and maintained in its original form, Sikhs revere Guru Granth Sahib as their supreme guide. Non-Sikhs can partake fully in Sikh prayer meetings and social functions. Their daily prayers include the well being of whole mankind. The concept of saint-soldier is a unique feature of Sikhism. Every Sikh is required to aspire to sainthood by his devotion to God and service to mankind, but also, according to the situation, to adopt the role of the soldier.

A Sikh is also commanded, if necessary and circumstances allow, to lay his or her life down to protect the poor and weak, regardless of race, religion, sex or creed. The Sikhs look at the martyrdom of the 9th Guru for trying to protect Hindus from religious persecution, in Delhi, on 11 November 1675 AD, as an example to be followed. Sikhs are required not to renounce the world, and aspire to live a humble life. Seva (service) is an integral part of Sikh worship, very easily observed in the Gurdwara.

Visitors of any religious or socio-economic background are welcomed, where Langar (food for all) is always served. The Sikhs also revere Bhaktas or Saints belonging to different social backgrounds. The work of these Bhagats is collected in Guru Granth Sahib, and is known as Bhagat-Bani (holy word of bhagat) as against work of Sikh Gurus being known as Gur-Bani (holy word of Guru).

MAIN FIGURES IN EARLY PERIOD

Guru Nanak

Guru Nanak Dev (1469- 1539), was the founder of Sikhism, and the first of the ten Sikh Gurus. Shri Guru Nanak Dev Ji was born 20 October 1469 into a Hindu Khatri family, in the village of Rai Bhoi Ki Talwandi, now called Nankana Sahib (after the Guru), near Lahore, Pakistan. Today, his birthplace is marked by Gurdwara Janam Asthan. His father, Kalidas Chandarana, later known as Kalyan Das Bedi, also known as Mehta Kalu was the patwari (accountant) of crop revenue for the village of Talwandi under the Muslim landlord of the village, Rai Bular, who was responsible for collecting taxes. Guru Nanak's mother was Tripta Devi and he had one older sister, Nanaki.

At the age of five years Nanak is said to have voiced interest in divine subjects. At age seven, his father Mehta Kalu enrolled him at the village school as per the norm. Notable lore reccounts that as a child Nanak astonished his teacher by describing the implicit symbolism of the first letter of the alphabet, which is almost straight stroke in Persian or Arabic, resembling the mathematical version of one, as denoting unity or oneness of God. Other childhood accounts refer to strange and miraculous events about Nanak such as a poisonous cobra being seen to shield the sleeping childs head from the harsh sunlight.

Guru Nanak was married to one Sulakhni. His marriage took place with her in the town of Batala. The marriage party had come from the town of Sultanpur Lodhi. He had two sons from this marriage; Shri Chand and Lakhmi Chand. The former was a deeply spiritual person and founded a renunciate/ascetic subsect known today as Udasis. The younger son grew up to become immersed in worldly life.

Nanak's teachings come down today foremostly in the Guru Granth, a vast collection of revelatory verses recorded in sloaks. From these some common principles seem discernible. Firstly a supreme Godhead who although incomprehensible manifests in a variety of religious forms, the Singular 'Doer' and formless source of all forms. It is described as the indestructible or timeless form and in both impersonal and personal forms. Salvation or liberation depends on the grace ('nadir'- glance) of God alone and although outside the power of the individual, manifests through the individual whom is seen to be unceasing in their efforts. Religious awakening is compared to undergoing a living death.

Nanak describes the dangers of the self and calls upon devotees to engage in worship through God's name and singing of God's qualities, discarding doubt in the process. However such worship must be selfless (seva) which could be said to be similar in principle to the nishkaam worship elabourated in the Bhagavad Gita. God's name cleanses the individual to make such worship possible. This is related to the revelation that God is the Doer and without God there is no other. He warns that hypocrisy and falsehood are pervasive in humanity and that religious actions can also be in vain. However the practice of satsang is considered exalted. It may also be said that ascetic practices are disfavoured by Nanak who suggests remaining inwardly detached whilst living as a householder.

Nanak put the greatest emphasis on the worship of True Name (naam japna). One should follow the direction of Awakened individuals rather then the mind (state of manmukh- being led by the mind)- the latter being perilous and leading only to frustration.

In the context of his times, reforms that occurred in the wake of Nanak's teachings and the bhakti movement at large included bhakti devotion being open to all castes, women not to be marginalised from its institutions, and both Godhead and Devotion transcending any religious consideration or divide, as God is immanent and not separate from any individual.

Guru Angad

Guru Angad was born in 1504. Guru Angad invented and introduced the Gurmukhi script and made it known to all Sikhs. The scripture of Guru Granth Sahib is written in Gurmukhi. This scripture is also the basis of the Punjabi language. It became the script of the masses very soon.

Guru Angad was a model of self-less service to his Sikhs and showed them the way to devotional prayers. He took great interest in the education of the children by opening many schools for their instruction and thus greatly increased literacy. For the youth he started the culture of Mall

Akhara, where physical as well as spiritual exercises were held. He collected the facts about Guru Nanak Sahib's life from Bhai Bala Ji and wrote the first biography of Guru Nanak Sahib. He popularized and expanded the institution of 'Guru Ka Langar' started by Guru Nanak Sahib earlier.

Guru Amar Das

He was born in 1479. He took up the courage of spirituality to fight against caste restrictions, caste prejudices and the curse of untouchability. He strengthened the culture of the free kitchen, Guru Ka Langar and made his disciples, whether rich or poor, whether high born or low born have their meals together sitting in one place. He thus founded social equality amongst the people.

Guru Amar Das introduced the Anand Karaj marriage ceremony for the Sikhs, replacing the Hindu form. He also completely abolished amongst the Sikhs, the custom of Sati, in which a married woman was forced to burn herself to death in the funeral pyre of her husband. The custom of Paradah (Purda), in which a woman covered her face with a veil, was also done away with.

Guru Ram Das

He was born in 1534. Guru Ji founded the city of Amritsar and started the construction of the famous Golden Temple at Amritsar, the holy city of the Sikhs. He requested the, Muslim Sufi, Mian Mir to lay the cornerstone of the Harmandir. The temple remains open on all sides and at all times to every one. This indicates that the Sikhs believe in One God who has no partiality for any particular place, direction or time. The standard Sikh marriage ceremony known as the Anand Karaj is centered on the Lawan, a four stanza hymn composed by Guru Ram Das Ji.

The marriage couples circumscribe the Guru Granth Sahib as each stanza is read. The first round is the Divine consent for commencing the householder's life through marriage. The second round states that the union of the couple has been brought about by God. In the third round the couple is described as the most fortunate as they have sung the praises of the Lord in the company of saints. In the fourth round the feeling of the couple that they have obtained their hearts desire and are being congratulated is described.

Guru Arjan Dev

He was born in 1563. He was the third son of Guru Ram Das Ji. Guru Arjan was a saint and scholar of the highest quality and repute. He compiled the Adi Granth, the scriptures of the Sikhs, and wrote the Sukhmani Sahib. To make it a universal teaching, Guru Ji included in it hymns of Muslim saints as well those of low-caste pariah saints who were never permitted to enter several temples.

Guru Arjan Dev completed construction of Shri Darbar Sahib also known as Golden Temple in Amritsar. Shri Darbar Sahib welcomes all without discrimination, which is symbolised by the four doors that are open in four directions. Guru Ji became the first great martyr in Sikh history when Emperor Jahangir ordered his execution.

Guru Har Gobind

He was born in 1595. He was the son of Guru Arjan Dev and was known as a "soldier saint," Guru Hargobind organized a small army, explaining that extreme non-violence and pacifism would only encourage evil and so the principles of Miri-Piri were founded. Guru Ji taught that it was necessary to take up the sword in order to protect the weak and the oppressed.

Guru Ji was first Gurus to take up arms to defend the faith. At that time it was only emperors who were allowed to sit on a raised platform, called a takhat or throne. At the age of 13, Guru Hargobind erected Shri Akal Takhat Sahib, ten feet above the ground and adorned two swords, Miri and Piri, representing temporal and spiritual power.

Guru Har Rai

He was born in 1630, spent most of his life in devotional meditation and preaching the teachings of Guru Nanak. Although, Guru Har Rai was a man of peace, he never disbanded the armed Sikh Warriors, who earlier were maintained by his grandfather, Guru Hargobind.

He always boosted the military spirit of the Sikhs, but he never himself indulged in any direct political and armed controversy with the Mughal Empire. Guru Ji cautiously avoided conflict with Emperor Aurangzeb and devoted his efforts to missionary work.

Guru Har Kishan

He was born in 1656. Guru Har Kishan was the youngest of the Gurus. Installed as Guru at the age of five, Guru Ji astonished the Brahmin Pundits with his knowledge and spiritual powers. To the Sikhs he proved to be the very symbol of service, purity and truth. The Guru gave his life while serving and healing the epidemic-stricken people in Delhi.

The young Guru began to attend the sufferers irrespective of cast and creed. Particularly, the local Muslim population was much impressed with the purely humanitarian deeds of the Guru Sahib and nicknamed him Bala Pir (child prophet). Even Aurangzeb did not try to disturb Guru Harkrishan Sahib sensing the sensitivity of the situation but on the other hand never dismissed the claim of Ram Rai also.

Guru Tegh Bahadur

He was born in 1621 in Amritsar and founded the town of Anandpur. The Guru laid down his life for the protection of the Hindu religion. He was a firm believer in the right of people to the freedom of worship. It was for this cause that he faced martyrdom for the defence of the downtrodden Hindus. So pathetic was the torture of Guru Tegh Bahadur that his body had to be cremated clandestinely at Delhi while his severed head was secretly taken four hundred kilometres away to Anandpur Sahib for cremation.

Guru Gobind Singh: He was born in 1666 and became Guru after the martyrdom of his father Guru Tegh Bahadur. He created the Khalsa in 1699, changing the Sikhs into a saint-soldier order with special symbols and sacraments for protecting themselves. After the Guru had administered Amrit to his Five Beloved Ones, he stood up in supplication and with folded hands, begged them to baptize him in the same way as he had baptized them. He himself became their disciple. The Five Beloved Ones were astonished at such a proposal, and represented their own unworthiness, and the greatness of the Guru, whom they deemed God's representative upon earth.

He gave the Sikhs the name Singh (lion) or Kaur (princess). He fought many battles against the armies of Aurangzeb and his allies. He had lost his father, his mother, four sons, finally, after his famous letter (the zafarnama) to Aurangzeb, in which he indicted the Grand mughal with his treachery and Godliness, the attacks against the Guru and his Sikhs were called off. Aurangzeb died soon after reading the letter. Soon, the rightful heir to the Mughal throne sought the Gurus' assistance in winning his kingdom. It was the envie and fear of the growing friendship between the new Emperor and the Guru which lead to the sneak attack of the Pathan assasins of Wasir Khan who inflicted the wound which later caused the Guru's death. Thus the tree, whose seed was planted by Guru Nanak, came to fruition when Guru Gobind Singh created the Khalsa, and on 3 October 1708, appointed Guru Granth Sahib as the Guru.

Bhai Mardana

Bhai Mardana (1459-1534) was a devotee and attendant of the Sikh founder Guru Nanak and Bhai Bala. He was with Guru Nanak in all of his journeys across India and Asia. Mardana was born a muslim to a Mirasi couple, Badra and Lakkho, of Talvandi Rai Bhoe, now called Nankana Sahib, in Sheikhupura district of Pakistan. It is said that Mardana first contacted Guru Nanak to seek help as many people in his family were dying at a young age. Guru Nanak gave him the assurance that henceforth people in his clan will not die early. It is said that the name Mardana came from this assurance- Mar- Da- Na meaning des not die. Guru Nanak and Mardana were brought up in the same village. The Miharbdn Janam Sakhi says that Mardana was ten years elder to Guru Nanak and was his companion since his childhood days. It further states that Mardana sang hymns written by Kabir, Trilochan, Ravidas, Dhanna and Bern. According to Ratan Singh Bhangu, Prachin Panth Prakash, Guru Nanak as a small boy gave Mardana a string instrument improvised from reeds to play on while he sang the hymns.

WhenGuru Nanak took charge of the granaries and stores of the Nawab of Sultanpur Lodhi, he became known for his genorosity. Mardana, was by then married and had two sons and a daughter,Mardana went to meet Nanak as Nanak's father wanted news of his son, Mardana never went back from his trip and was with Gurun Nanak from then on. He used to play the rabab or rebeck as Guru Nanak spoke his words about God.

When Nanak planned to travel the world to spread his message, he wanted Mardana to accompany him, Mardana wanted to marry off his daughter before doing so, Bhai Baghirath a disciple of Guru Nanak helped Mardana materially to enable the daughter's marriage and allow Mardana to accompany Guru Nanak.

The chronicles of their travels uses Mardana to show worldly doubts and bring forth Guru Nanak's message, in many situations Mardana is portrayed as doubtful and wanting clarifications in every situation. The Puratan Janam Sakhi tells of these situations.

In 1534, Mardana, fell ill at Kartarpur The sickness was intense and it was clear that he would not survive. As he was born a Muslim, Guru Nanak is said to have asked him how to dispose of his body, and Mardana is said to have left the choice to his Guru. It is said that The Guru had his body consigned to the river Ravi, and had hymns sung and karha prashad, the sacrament, distributed among the mourners. He consoled Mardana's family including his son Shahzada, asking them not to weep as Mardana had returned to his heavenly home. Mardana also wrote poetry. One of his compositions appears in Guru Granth Sahib in Bihdgare ki Var along with two others of Guru Nanak's addressed to Mardana. As per the composition Mardana is convinced that an evil body may be cleansed of sin in sangat.

Bhai Bala

Bhai Bala, (1466 - 1544 AD) Born in Talvandi Rai Bhoi, now called Nankana Sahib in Pakistan. He was a childhood friend and all his life a constant companion of Bhai Mardana and Guru Nanak. He travelled with Guru Nanak and Bhai Mardana on all their great journeys around the world including China, Mecca and around India. He died in Khadur Sahib, in his late 70s in 1544 AD. His mortal remain were cremated at the site of Gurdwara Tapiana Sahib.

Mai Bhago

Mai Bhago is one of the most famous women in Sikh history. She is always pictured on horseback wearing a turban with her headscarf gracefully flowing in the wind, courageously leading an army into battle. A staunch Sikh by birth and upbringing, she was distressed to hear in 1705 that some of the Sikhs of her village who had gone to Anandpur to fight for Guru Gobind Singh had deserted him under adverse conditions. She rallied the deserters, persuading them to meet the Guru and apologize to him. She led them back to Guru Gobind Singh Ji in the battlefield at Muktsar (Khidrana) Punjab. She thereafter stayed on with Guru Gobind Singh as one of his bodyguards, in male attire. After the death of Guru Gobind Singh at Nanded in 1708, she retired further south. She settled down at Jinvara, where, immersed in meditation, she lived to a ripe old age.

Banda Singh Bahadur

Baba Banda Singh Bahadur (1670-1716) was a Sikh warrior known for his struggle against the Mughal Empire in the early seventeenth century. The title Baba (Elder) in Sikhism denotes respect.

Famous for the sack of the Mughal provincial capital, Sirhind, he is revered as one of greatest Sikh warriors as well as one of the most hallowed martyrs of the Khalsa. His confrontation with the Mughal administration in Northern India, though brief, was strong enough to shake its foundations. The agrarian uprising that he led in the Punjab was the foundation on which the Dal Khalsa, the Sikh Misls and Maharaja

Ranjit Singh built the edifice which finally culminated with Ranjit Singh capturing Lahore in 1799 and establishing the Sikh Kingdom of the Punjab. One of the most revolutionary acts of Banda Bahadur, after establishing his authority in Punjab, was the abolition of the zamindari system, and granting proprietory rights to the actual tillers of the land.

Mata Sundri

Mata Sundari Ji was the second wife of Guru Gobind Singh (1666-1708), was the daughter of Bhai Ram Saran, a Kumarav Khatri of Bijvara, in present-day Hoshiarpur district of the Punjab. She was married to Guru Gobind Singh at Anandpur on 4 April 1684. On 26 January 1687, at Paonta, she gave birth to Sahibzada Ajit Singh, the eldest son of Guru Gobind Singh. Consequent upon the evacuation of Anandpur on the night of i6 December 1705, Mata Sundari, along with Mata Sahib Devan, was escorted by Bhai Mani Singh to Delhi.

She rejoined Guru Gobind Singh in 1706 at Talvandi Sabo, where she heard the news of the martyrdom of her son and the other Sahibzadas as also of the death of her aged mother-in-law, Mata Gujari. She went back to stay at Delhi while Guru Gobind Singh left Talvandi Sabo for the South.

At Delhi, Mata Sundari adopted a young boy whom she named Ajit Singh because of his resemblance to her own late son. After the passing away of Guru Gobind Singh at Nanded in October 1708, the Sikhs looked up to her for guidance. She appointed Bhai Mani Singh to manage the holy shrines at Amritsar and also commissioned him to collect the writings of Guru Gobind Singh. She also issued under her own seal and authority hukamnamas to sangats. The hukamnamas since discovered and published bear dates between 12 October 1717 and 10 August 1730.

Mata Sundari was disappointed in her adopted son, Ajit Singh. Emperor Bahadur Shah treated him as the successor of Guru Gobind Singh, called him to his court and gave him a robe of honour in September 1710. This went to his head and he started living in style as a courtier. He grew arrogant and haughty even towards Mata Sundari who disowned him, and migrated to Mathura.

Ajit Singh was later convicted for murder and was put to death on 18 January 1725. Mata Sundan returned to live in Delhi where she died in 1747. A memorial in her honour stands in the compound of Gurdwara Bala Sahib, New Delhi.

MAIN FIGURES IN MEDIEVAL PERIOD

Maharaja Ranjit Singh

Maharaja Ranjit Singh called The Lion of the Punjab (1780-1839) was a Sikh ruler of the Punjab. Maharaja Ranjit Singh was a Sikh born in 1780. At the time much of Punjab was ruled by the Sikhs, who had divided the territory between factions. Ranjit Singh's father Maha Singh was the commander of the Sukerchakia misl (faction) and controlled a territory in west Punjab based around his headquarters at Gujranwala. Ranjit Singh succeeded his father at just the tender age of 12.

The Sikh Maharaja Ranjit Singh after several campaigns he united the Sikh factions into one state and he took the title of Maharaja on April 12, 1801 (to coincide with Baisakhi day), with Lahore having served as his capital from 1799. In 1802 he took the holy city of Amritsar.

He then spent the following years fighting the Afghans, driving them out of western Punjab. He also captured Pasthun territory including Peshawar. This was the first time ever that Pastuns were ruled by non-muslims. This event has a very important historical perspective. For more than a thousand years invaders had come down from the Khyber pass and ruled eastern lands. Ranjit Singh reversed this trend. When the Sikh empire finally fell to the English, they were able to retain this state. He captured the state of Multan which encompassed the southern parts of Punjab, Peshawar (1818), Jammu and Kashmir (1819) and the hill states north of Anandpur, largest of which was Kangra.

He also modernised his army, hiring European mercenaries to create the first modern Indian Army, the effect was to create a powerful and heavily armed state and at this point Punjab was the only state not controlled by the British. He brought law and order, yet was reluctant to use the death penalty. He stopped Indian secular style practices by treating Hindus and Muslims equally. He banned the secular "jizya" tax on Hindus and Sikhs. In his multi-ethnic empire he was famous for its tolerance with Muslims and Hindus holding high states of office. The Empire was effectively non-secular as it did not discriminate against Hindus and Sikhs, relatively modern and had great respect for all religions of the Empire. This was in sharp contrast with the ethnic & religious cleansing of past Moghul rulers. Ranjit Singh had created a state based upon Sikh and hindu noble cultures, where everyone worked together, regardless of background. Where citizens where made to look at the things that they shared in common, e.g. being Punjabi, rather than any religious differences.

The British at this time, on the subcontinent, where expanding and consolidating their grip on power. Whereas, in Punjab they had met a comprehensive road block for complete supremacy, on the subcontinent. Ranjit Singh had stopped the ever expansion of the British Empire, during this time- around Punjab, and this could have been permanently entrenched by competent political heirs. Ranjit Singh died in 1839 and the state went to his eldest son Kharak Singh.

The Kingdom, that he had worked so hard to build, began to crumble due to poor governance and political mismanagement by his heirs. His successors died through accidents and murder, while the nobility and army struggled for power till the end of the Second Anglo Sikh War, when it was annexed by the British from his youngest son Duleep Singh. However, after the First Anglo Sikh War, Punjab effectively ceased to be an independent state and all major decisions where made by the British Empire. The Punjabi Army had been reduced under the peace treaty, with the British Empire, to a tiny skeleton force. Moreover, massive punishing war compensation had destroyed any meaningful, independent fiscal policy. Most historian believe competent political heirs would have forged a highly durable, independent and powerful state (Ranjit Singh had done during his rule).

Ranjit is remembered for uniting the Punjab as a strong state and his possesion of the Koh-i-noor diamond. His most lasting legacy was the beautification of the Harmandir Sahib, holiest site of the Sikhs, with marble and gold from which the popular name of the "Golden Temple" is derived.

He was also known as Sher-e-Punjab, the Lion of Punjab and is considered one of the 3 Lions of India, the most famous and revered heros in North Indian history - the other 2 Lions are Rana Pratap Singh of Mewar and Shivaji the Maratha. The title of Sher-e-Punjab is still widely used as a term of respect for a powerful man.

Sant Attar Singh

Sant Atar Singh of Mastuana, the most charismatic figure in latter-day Sikh piety, was born on 13 March 1866 in the village of Chima, in Sangrur district of the Punjab. His father, Karam Singh, was a farmer of humble means and could not afford to send him to a school in town. So Atar Singh was apprenticed to Bhai Buta Singh, head of the Nirmala dera or monastery of Bhai Ram Singh, in his own village. He acquired proficiency in the Sikh religious religious texts and also read philosophical treatises such as the Vichar Sagar. Side by side with his progress in Sikh learning, he developed a deeply religious cast of mind. While tending his cattle, he would become absorbed in reciting hymns from the Guru Granth Sahib.

At the age of seventeen, Atar Singh enlisted as a gunner in the Artillery, later getting himself transferred to the 54th Sikh Battalion stationed at Kohat. There he received Sikh initiation in the cantonment Gurdwara and continued his study of the Scripture under the guidance of its granthi Bhai Jodh Singh. He was still in the army when he took a vow not to marry.

This was a stimulating period of time in the Punjab. English education and Christian missionary activity had created a new ferment. The Arya Samaj was the Hindu response to the situation and the Singh Sabha represented the Sikh reaction. Atar Singh became involved in the Singh Sabha's dual concerns of restoring the purity of Sikh belief and custom and rejuvenating Sikh society and of promoting Western education among the Sikhs.

In the first instance, he went on a pilgrimage to Shri Hazur Sahib at Nanded, holy to Guru Gobind Singh. In 1888, Atar Singh was placed in the reserve list and, in 1891, he got his name finally struck off the rolls of the army to devote himself solely to preaching the holy message of the Gurus. He toured extensively in Jammu and Kashmir, Sindh and the North-West Frontier Province. In the Pothohar region, many Sikhs and Hindus received pahul at his hands.

Master Tara Singh, who later became famous as a political leader, and Bhai Jodh Singh, eminent theologian and educationist, were administered the rites of Khalsa baptism by him at Dera Khalsa. In Jammu and Kashmir, he visited Srinagar, Mirpur and other towns which had Sikh populations.

In Jammu and Kashmir, he visited Srinagar, Mirpur and other towns which had Sikh populations. At Peshawar, in the North-West Frontier Province, he was received with honour not only by the Hindus and the Sikhs, but also by the Pathans. Sant Kalyan Singh of Peshawar became a devotee. In Sindh, he visited Sakkhar, Hyderabad and Karachi.

In 1902, he founded his main centre in the Malva region, at Gursagar Mastuana, near Sangrur. By his extensive tours and his melodious and resonant recitations of the Gurus' bani before vast audiences, he created a new religious fervour in the Sikh community. Many were impressed by his gentle and spiritual manner and were drawn into the fold of Sikhism.

To receive baptism at his hands was considered especially meritorious. New Gurdwaras sprang at in several places in the wake of Sant Atar Singh's visit.

After 1920, Sant Atar Singh focused his attention on the area around Damdama Sahib where Guru Gobind Singh had sojourned in 1706 before proceeding to the South. At Damdama Sahib, he raised a magnificent bunga and turned it into a major centre for the propagation of Sikhism. He sent abroad four Sikh young men - Teja Singh, Amar Singh, Dharmanant Singh and Hari Singh Basra - for the twin-purposes of receiving higher education and spreading the Gurus' message.

Teja Singh set up in London the Khalsa jatha of the British Isles, and later went to the United States of America. He took his Master's degree at Harvard University and lectured on Sikhism widely in America and Canada, besides espousing the cause of Punjabi immigrants. Dharmanant Singh received his Ph.D. degree from London University specializing in Platonic studies.

The Khalsa College Committee, Amritsar, requested Sant Atar Singh, to represent it at the Delhi Darbar in 1911. However, he went to Delhi as a guest of the Maharaja of Jind. He was a distinguished participant in the ceremonial procession taken out from Patiala House in Delhi in which, apart from the people in general, the chiefs of Patiala and Jind participated. As he rode on an elegantly caparisoned elephant, he looked the very picture of holiness. He was naturally the centre of attention, overshadowing the princes.

Equally with preaching the Word of the Gurus, Sant Atar Singh concerned himself with the promotion of modern education among Sikhs. He associated himself actively with the Sikh Educational Conference and participated in its annual sessions, presiding over that of 1915 at Firozpur. He helped found several institutions such as Khalsa High School, Lyallpur, Khalsa High School, Chakval, Missionary College, Gujranwala, Guru Nanak Khalsa College, Gujranwala, Malva Khalsa High School, Ludhiana, and Akal College, Mastuana.

In 1914, he went to Banaras at the invitation of Pandit Madan Mohan Malaviya to participate in the ceremonies for laying the foundation of the Sanskrit College. Maharaja Ripudaman Singh of Nabha, who was an admirer of Sant Atar Singh took him to Varanasi in his own saloon. Under the tent near the site of the college, Sant Atar Singh performed a series of five akhand paths, or continuous, uninterrupted readings of the Guru Granth Sahib, Maharaja Ripudaman Singh saying the Rahrasi every evening. As these recitations of the Guru Granth Sahib were concluded, Maharaja Gangs Singh of Bikaner offered concrete in a silver plate and Santji laid the foundation of the building by applying it to the eleven bricks of gold supplied by the Raja of Kashi. After the ceremonies were over, Sant Atar Singh remained in Varanasi for a week as the guest of the Raja who treated him with deep reverence.

Sant Atar Singh shared the Sikh community's wider social and religious concerns. He supported the Gurdwara reform movement, and took part in the divan held at Nankana Sahib by the Shiromani Gurdwara Parbandhak Committee in honour of the Nankana Sahib martyrs in 1921. He was invited to attend the Bhog ceremonies at the conclusion of the Akali morcha at Jaito.

Fateh Singh Ahluvalia

Son of Bhag Singh, and a grand-nephew of Jassa Singh Ahluvalia, leader of the Ahluvalia misl and of the Dal Khalsa, who in 1758 proclaimed the sovereignty of the Sikhs in the Punjab. Fateh Singh succeeded to the Ahluvalia chiefship in 1801. He was the chosen companion of Maharaja Ranjit Singh, with whom he in 1802 exchanged turbans in a permanent bond of brotherhood. Fateh Singh took part in almost all the early campaigns of Ranjit Singh - Kasur (1802-03), Malva (1806-08), Kangra (1809), Multan (1818), Kashmir (1819) and Mankera (1821). He fought in the battle of Haidru (1813) and held command in the Bhimbar, Rajauri and Bahawalpur expeditions. In 1806, Fateh Singh acted as the plenipotentiary of Ranjit Singh and signed the first Anglo-Sikh treaty with Lord Lake at the time when the Maratha chief, Jasvant Rao Holkar, had sought shelter in the Punjab.

Close association with the ruler of Lahore brought Fateh Singh ample rewards. The Maharaja had bestowed upon him the districts of Dakha, Kot, Jagraoh, Talvandi, Naraingarh and Raipur after his Malva campaigns. He possessed extensive territories on both sides of the Sutlej yielding an annual revenue of 1,76,000 rupees in 1808; in 1836, his territories were estimated to be worth 1,600,000 rupees annually.

The cordiality between the two chiefs was strained by Fateh Singh's direct communications with the British over the question of Bhirog and Kotla chiefships, the construction by him of a strong citadel at Isru and his constant pleas for British protection. Feeling unsafe at Lahore, Fateh Singh fled across the river in 1825 to his Sutlej territory and sought British protection. Ranjit Singh promptly seized his trans-Sutlej possessions, but showed willingness to forgive him if he returned to Lahore.

The rift between the Allluvalia chief and Maharaja of Lahore was, however, soon repaired. Fateh Singh returned to Lahore in 1827, and the Maharaja received him with honour restoring to him all his possessions. Later in his life, Fateh Singh lived at Kapurthala where he died in October 1836.

Maharaja Kharak Singh

Son of Maharaja Ranjit Singh, he was born on 9 February 1801. He was married to Chand Kaur, daughter of Jaimal Singh Kanhaiya, in 1812. The Maharaja brought him up in the family's martial culture and assigned him to a variety of' military expeditions. While barely six years old, he was given the nominal command of the Sheikhpura expedition (1807); was placed in charge of the Kanhaiya estates in 1811; and deputed in 1812 to punish the recalcitrant chiefs of Bhisnbar and Rajauri. He was invested with the command of Multan expedition (1818) as well as of Kashmir (1819). He was also sent on similar campaigns undertaken by Ranjit Singh for the conquest of Peshawar and against the Mazaris of Shikarpur.

Frail in constitution, Kharak Singh ascended the throne in June 1839 on the death of his father. From the very first day he had to encounter the envy of his powerful and ambitious minister, Dhian Singh Dogra. Dhian Singh resented especially the ascendancy of the royal favourite Chet Singh Bajva, a trusted courtier who had also been Kharak Singh's tutor. The Dogas started a whispering campaign against the Maharaja as well as against Chet Singh. It was given out that both the Maharaja and his favourite were surreptitiously planning to make over the Punjab to the British and surrender to them six hands in every rupee of the State revenue and that the Sikh army would be disbanded. To lend credence to these rumours, some fake letters were prepared and discreetly intercepted. Gulab Singh Dogra, Dhian Singh's elder brother, was charged to work upon Kharak Singh's son, Kanvar Nau Nihal Singh, then travelling in his company from Peshawar to Lahore. Misled by these fictitious tales, the young prince became estranged from his father.

Matters came to a climax when, in October 1839, Dhian Singh made a plot to assassinate Chet Singh. Early on the morning of 9 October the conspirators entered the Maharaja's residence in the Fort and assassinated Chet Singh in the presence of their royal master, who vainly implored them to spare the life of his favourite.

Kharak Singh was removed from the Fort and he remained virtually a prisoner in the hands of Dhian Singh. Kanvar Nau Nihal Singh took the reins of the government into his own hands, but he was helpless against the machinations of his minister, who continued to keep father and son separated from each other. Dhian Singh subjected Kharak Singh to strict restraint upon the pretext that he might not escape to the British territory. Doses of slow poison were administered to the Maharaja, who was at last delivered by death on 5 November 1840 from a lonely and disgraceful existence.

MAIN FIGURES IN MODERN PERIOD

Sant Dalip Singh

Son of Ishar Singh and Har Kaur, was born in 1883 at the village of Lahri, in Hoshiarpur district. He was hardly five years old, when his father died. He was brought up by his maternal grandfather, Nihal Singh, at his village Dumeli. He received his early education from a local Sikh priest, who also trained him in the singing of gurbani.

Dalip Singh was a child with peculiar traits. He was fond of solitude. One day he wentout and did not return home. He built for himself a cell (the site, now called Baba Rana) for meditation. He was then a youth of about twenty. He remained wrapped up in deep meditation for forty-eight days in his cell. As he refused to return home, the residents of the village built for him a cottage. He ground the grain into flour and did his own cooking, refusing to accept food even from his own mother. In his cottage, he started a small langar (free kitchen) for the poor and needy.

He was convinced that selfless service to fellow men was the essence of true religion and the highest worship of the Almighty. Whenever he came across a disabled, blind, dumb, lame, sick or orphaned child, he brought him to his cottage and looked after him. He brought up many such children and trained them for earning their livelihood. Sant Sarvan Singh Ghandhari, born blind, and Giani Harbans Singh born a cripple, who are now running the dera of Sant Baba Dalip Singh, grew up under his care. The former was enabled to earn his Master's degree in Music (Classical and Instrumental) and the latter to qualify for practice in the indigenous system of medicine.

Baba Dalip Singh combined with his saintly disposition a revolutionary urge gave shelter to the Babar Akalis engaged in anti-government activities and provided them with food and money. He himself took part in the Akali movement and led a jatha during the Jaito morcha.

During the Hindu-Muslim riots in 1947, he saved the lives of many Muslims at great personal risk. Sant Dalip Singh died in 1948.

Giani Zail Singh

Giani Zail Singh was first punjabi to become president of India. Born on 5 May 1916, son of Mata Ind Kaur and Bhai Kishan Singh in a small village named Sandhwan, near Kot Kapura, formerly prince state of Faridkot. Kishen Singh was village carpenter. He also had some land to till. He was devout Sikh and was known in the countryside for his simple and upright manner. Zail Singh was youngest of Five brothers and sisters. Zail Singh lost his mother at his early age. He was brought up by the sister of his mother named Daya Kaur. He had little formal education. He inherited the family's broad interest in religious learning and gained easy fluency in reading the Guru Granth Sahib. He acquired a fairly wide knowledge of Sikh doctrine and history. He was accepted for admission to the Shahid Sikh Missionary college at Amritsar, without fullfilling the miminum entry condition of marticulation. What immpressed authorities was his flair for public speaking.

His native Faridkot was small unit politically and geographically., peaceful and quiet. It ruler, Raja Harinder Singh was a colourful personality. He was full of energy and ambition. One of his aims was to open the doors of modern progress for his state and have it counted among the more progressive territories of the region. Because of Raja's friendly nature he knew almost two three families of all the villages of his territories. Raja was an easy mixer with common folks. In the year of Indian Independence, 1947 Nehru came to Faridkot asking Raja to align himself with India. Nehru encouraged the local extremsits. When Raja was away in Malerkotla they formed a parallel government. Raja was in a rage. He immediately put an end to revolt and send out a very angry cable to Nehru and Patel, two indian leaders who were negotiating with the Indian Princes. Since Zail Singh was aligned with the people who were protesting against the Raja, he had to bear the Raja's brunt.

Giani Zail singh had emerged from one of the smaller units. He was dedicated and single minded with limitless powers of concentration. In 1949, a non party government was founded in PEPSU with Gian Singh Rarewala of Patiala as Chief Minister and Giani Zail Singh as Revenue minister. Then after the elections in 1951, in the congress government formed on 23 May 1951, he became Agriculture minister. From 1956 to 1962 he served as a Member of Indian parliament (Rajya Sabha). In general elections in 1972, he became chief minister of Punjab. In the 1980 General elections Giani Zail singh was elected as Member of Parliament of Lok Sabha, Indira Gandhi the president of the Congress party made him minister of home affairs. In 1982 Giani Zail Singh was unaanimously elected by the congress party as a choice for President. Giani Zail Singh won almost by a unianomous vote of the nation. Even the dissident parties such as Akalis and Communists supported him.

Eventhough Giani Zail Singh achieved much in his life but he did not aligned himself with the Akalis in Punjab, the leading group of Sikh political aspirations. Giani Zail Singh owing to his humble background was always trying to immpress his bosses (especially Indira Gandhi, Prime Minister of India), he even once said "I will sweep the door of her house if Madam tells me to do so". Such comments from a person of such stature made him unpopular in Sikhs and Akalis. Earlier when he was Chief Minister of Punjab he dangerously brought religion into politics. He would often visit Gurdwaras and give them huge grants.

He named many roads on the name of Sikh Gurus. Obviously this type of politics was to undermine Akalis who were openly working for Sikhs and Sikhism causes. His dirty politics with religion brought in front Jarnail Singh Bhindrenwale who was simple minded and zealously working for Sikh causes and hated both Congress and Akalis. Zail Singh supported Bhindrenwale and brought back the rule of Congress in Punjab under Darbara Singh as chief minister. When he was president of India, Indira Gandhi ordered Army attach on Golden Temple called Operation Blue Star without disclosing these orders to the President of India, Zail Singh., eventhough Army is under the direct command of President of India. This incident alone shows that President is merely a puppet at the hands of Prime Minister. Giani Zail Singh visited Golden Temple four days after the army attack.

After this attack many Sikh resigned from their posts, many Sikhs revolted in army, but Giani Zail Singh remained firmly attached to his ceremonously post, this showed his true colours and respect for Sikhs and Sikhism. Then when Indira Gandhi was murdered by two Singhs named Beant Singh and Satwant Singh, Giani Zail Singh made Rajiv Gandhi, the Prime Minister of India. Rajiv Gandhi's party and henchmen killed more then 7000+ Sikhs (Government of India estimates), but Sikh president of India could do nothing. SO! this biography of Zail Singh is being presented as a dark chapter in Sikh history, the darkest hour of this century in Sikh history that was 1980's. In 1994 when he was on a pilgrimage to Takht Shri Keshgarh Sahib his car met with a serious accident. He died on 25 December 1994.

Master Tara Singh

Master Tara Singh was born in a Punjabi Hindu Malhotra family of Rawalpindi. It is indeed remarkable that from humble origins he arose to the top of Sikh leadership, culminating with the creation of Punjabi State in Independent India. He initiated into Khalsa when he was ten or twelve years old. A fierce sewadar and helpful to all Sikhs he was among those cream of crop who strive to become a perfect Soldiers of their community. Tara Singh Malhotra is remembered for two things, one steering Sikhs towards opting for India in 1947 and other to campaingn for the state of Punjab in Independet India.

His first duty to serve Khalsa on the political arena came when he was invited to Round Table conference at Shimla after the end of the Second World War by the Governor-General, Lord Wavell, to ease the political situation in the country, the Sikhs were given representation along with other communities. Pleading on their behalf, Master Tara Singh who was among the twenty-one Indian leaders invited, argued that the creation of Pakistan would be more injurious to his community than to any other community. He told governor general that Sikhs are scattered all over the Punjab and are not in majority in any district. He vigorously campaigned against the demand of Pakistan by Muslim League and made many enemies.

He along with other Sikh leaders met with the leader of Muslim League Mohammad Ali Jinnah at the house of Hardit Singh Malik. Here is a quote from the book "Heritage of the Sikhs by Harbans Singh" "Mr Jinnah, who outwardly maintained an attitude of sullen and studious disregard towards the Sikhs, tried to cajole them privately. He knew in his heart of hearts that Sikh opposition to Pakistan was one real obstacle in his way and made several secret overtures to the leaders of the community. He chided them for being too subservient to Congress influence and held out all kinds of allurements, including the formation of an autonomous Sikh area within Pakistan. Some British of ficers also conveyed similar offers to Sikh leaders "to enable them to have political feet of their own on which they may walk into the current of world history." Plans were made to have Master Tara Singh and Jinnah talk together.

A meeting took place in Delhi on April 2, 1946, at the house of Sir Teja Singh Malik, a retired chief engineer who had also been minister in the princely states of Jaipur and Patiala. Besides Master Tara Singh and Jinnah, Maharaja Yadavinder Singh of Patiala, his prime minister, Sardar Hardit Singh Malik who was the host's brother, and Giani Kartar Singh joined the meeting. Malik Hardit Singh was assigned to presenting the Sikh viewpoint as the principal spokesman. Jinnah's one overriding concern was to have the Sikhs rescind theiropposition to Pakistan and lend his demand their support instead. He was prodigal of assurances, and told the Sikh leaders that the Sikhs would have a position of honour in the new State. But he refrained from elabourating. Malik Hardit Singh tried to extract from him a more specific enunciation and raised some concrete issues.

He said that in Pakistan there would presumably be a parliament, a cabinet, armed services, and so on. He wished Jinnah to say what exactly would be the Sikhs' position in these and other instruments of State. Jinnah dodged by inviting the Sikhs to set forth their demands in writing and by citing the instance of Zaghlul Pasha of Egypt. Zaghlul Pasha, he said, asked the Copts, the Christian minority, to give him their charter of demands. Without having a look at what was written in document, Zaghlul Pasha signed, "I agree." " That is how I shall treat the Sikhs," said Jinnah. Hardit Singh continued his thrusts and said, "You are being very generous, Mr Jinnah, but how about your succcessors? What is the guarantee that they would implement the assurance given by you?" "My friend, in Pakistan my word will be like the word of God. No one dare go back on it," replied Jinnah. "

Since these meetings were private and there was never promised anything on paper, Sikh leaders did not trusted the Promised given to them by Jinnah and were vindicated of their foresight when Pakistan's army launched an attacked against Bengali Muslims in Bangladesh with mass destruction and gross human rights violations. Considering the current pathetic state of minorities like Hindus and Christians, Sikh leaders like Tara Singh did indeed had a great foresight by not believing in the private concessions of Jinnah.

After repeated attempts of rioting, Indian leaders agreed to the partition of country. Tara Singh and many Akali leaders were furious as they were going to loose their houses and lands. On March 3 1947, Tara Singh at Lahore along with about 500 Sikhs declared from a dias "Death to Pakistan" when about 50,000+ strong muslim crowd went berserk outsie. Tara Singh and his Akali men narrowly escaped their death, the next day fourth March 1947, wide scale rioting in Lahore and adjoining areas started. As Jinnah had declared "Muslims are no believers of non-violence", each muslim tried to prooved his point by plundering, pillaging, raping and other un describeable acts.

Rioting at other places in Punjab stated as a retaliation to the killings by Muslims in Lahore and Rawalpindi. In this greatest holocaust ever, More then one million humans were murdered by Muslims, Hindus and

Sikhs in Punjab. Tara Singh migrated to East Punjab and was active in Akali politics until his death in 1967 on the eve when Akali Party was going to form their first government in new state of Punjab.

Sobha Singh

A painter famous especially for his portraits of the Gurus, was born on 29 November 1901 in a Ramgarhia family of Shri Hargobindpur, in Gurdaspur district of the Punjab. His father, Deva Singh, had been in the Indian cavalry. At the age of 15, Sobha Singh entered the Industrial School at Amritsar for a one-year course in art and craft. As a draughtsman in the Indian army he served in Baghdad, in Mesopotamia (now Iraq). He left the army to pursue an independent career in drawing and painting. In 1949, he settled down in Andretta, a remote and then little-known place in the Kangra valley, beginning the most productive period of his life.

Sobha Singh was skilled in the western classical technique of oil painting. His themes came from, the romantic lore of the Punjab, Indian epics and from the Sikh religious culture. His paintings of Punjabi lovers Sohni and Mahinval and Hir and Ranjha became very famous. Sohni-Mahinval was rated to be a real masterpiece ; its impact upon the Punjabi consciousness was of a lasting nature. What gave Sobha Singh the utmost satisfaction was his paintings of the Gurus of the Sikh faith. As he put it., "Painting the Gurus is nearest to the ultimate in the evolution of my real self." His earliest painting in the series was of the birth of Guru Nanak done in 1934. The child Nanak was depicted in Mata Tripta's lap, surrounded by his sister Nanaki and other women of the family, while Siva, Rama, Sita and the Goddess Sarasvati appeared from out of the skies to shower flowers on the holy child. The motif clearly bore the influence of Christian art of the middle ages.

The earliest portrait. of Guru Nanak by Sobha Singh captioned nam khumari nanaka charhi rahe din rat (Let the rapture of the Lord's Name, saith Nanak, keep me in inebriation day and night) was painted in 1937. The Guru is shown here with eyes lowered in a mystic trance. Several later versions of Guru Nanak's portrait by him are preserved in the Chandigarh Museum. The portrait he made in honour of the 500th birth anniversary of Guru Nanak in 1969 won the widest vogue. Likewise, he made a portrait of Guru Gobind Singh for his 300th birth anniversary in 1967 which also became very popular. Sobha Singh painted pictures of other Gurus as well- Guru Amar Das, Guru Tegh Bahadur meditating in his basement chamber at Baba Bakala and Guru Har Krishan healing the sick in Delhi. Earlier in his career, he had attempted a painting depicting

Queen Nur Jahan in the presence of Guru Hargobind, but. its prints were sealed following a protest frorn the Muslims in 1935.

Among Sobha Singh's portraits of contemporary personalities that. of' Norah Richards, the matriarch of Punjabi theatre, was done with a rare delicacy and feeling. Murals by him embellish the art gallery of Parliament House in New Delhi. The panel depicting the evolution of Sikh history features Guru Nanak with Bala and Mardana on one side, and Guru Gobind Singh in meditation on the other. Much acclaimed and honoured in his lifetime, Sobha Singh died in Chandigarh on 21 August 1986.

REFERENCES

Banga, Indu: ed. *Five Punjabi Centuries*. New Delhi: Manohar, 1997.

Bhagat Singh: *Maharaja Ranjit Singh and His Times*. New Delhi: Sehgal Publishers Service, 1990.

Bhatkhande, V. N. A.: *Comparative Study of Some of the Leading Musical Systems of the 15th, 16th, 17th, and 18th Centuries*. Baroda: Indian Musicological Society, 1972.

Bosch, Gulnar K., John Carswell, and Guy Petherbridge: *Islamic Bindings and Book Making*. Chicago: Oriental Institute, University of Chicago, 1981.

Brown, Kerry: *Sikh Art and Literature*. Routledge, 1999.

Brown, Kerry: ed. *Sikh Art and Literature*. New York: Routledge, 1999.

Callewaert, Winand M., and Pater G. Friedlander: *The Life and Works of Raidas*. New Delhi: Manohar, 1992.

Deol, Harnik: *Religion and Nationalism in India*. Routledge, 2000.

Duggal, Kartar Singh: *Philosophy and Faith of Sikhism*. Himalayan Institute Press, 1998.

Foley- Garces, Kathleen: *Death and Religion in a changing World*. M.E Sharpe, 2005.

Fowler, Jeaneane: *World Religions: An Introduction for Students*. Sussex Academic, 1997.

Ganeri, Anita: *Guru Granth Sahib and Sikhism*. Black Rabbit Books, 2003.

Gupta, Hari Ram: *History of the Sikhs Vol.1; The Sikh Gurus, 1469-1708.* Munshiram Manoharlal Publishers, 2000.

Gurmat Granth Pracharak Sabha: Encyclopedia of The Sikhs, Punjabi University Patiala.

Hoiberg, Dale; Indu Ramchandani: *Students' Britannica India.* Popular Prakashan, 2000.

Jarnail Singh: *Shri Gourou Granth Sahib.* 4 vols. Providenciales, West Indies: Intellectual Services International, 1998.

Kashmir, Singh: "Shri Guru Granth Sahib - A juristic Person"., Global Sikh Studies.

Keene, Michael: *New Steps in Religious Education.* Nelson thomes, 2002.

Khalsa, S. S. Shanti Kaur: ed. *The History of Sikh Dharma of the Western Hemisphere.* Espanola, NM: Sikh Dharma Publications, 1995.

Khushwant Singh: *A History of the Sikhs.* 2 vols. Princeton: Princeton University Press, 1984.

Kohli, Surinder Singh: *A Critical Study of Adi Granth.* Delhi: Motilal Banarsidass, 1976.

Manmohan Singh: *Shri Guru Granth Sahib.* 8 vols. Amritsar: Shiromani Gurdwara Prabandhak Committee, 1962.

Mann, Gurinder Singh: *The making of Sikh Scripture.* Oxford University Press, 2001.

Nayar, Kamala Elizabeth; Jaswinder Singh Sandhu: *The Socially Involved Renunciate: Guru Nanak's Discourse to the Nath,* 2007.

Nizami, Khaliq Ahmad: "Some Aspects of Khanqah Life in Medieval India. " *Studia Islamica,* 1957.

Nizami, Khaliq Ahmad: *Some Aspects of Religion and Politics in India during the Thirteenth Century.* Delhi: Idarah-i Adabiyat-i Delli, 1974.

Nripinder Singh: *The Sikh Moral Tradition.* Columbia, Mo.: South Asia Publications, 1990.

O'Connell, Joseph T.: et al., eds. *Sikh History and Religion in the Twentieth Century.* Toronto: University of Toronto, 1988.

Pashaura Singh: "Sikh Self-Defintion and the Bhagat Bai". M. A. diss., University of Calgary, 1987.

Penney, Sue: *Sikhism*. Heinemann, 14.

Shackle, Christopher: *A Guru Nanak Glossary*. London: School of Oriental and African Studies, 1981.

Shackle, Christopher: *An Introduction to the Sacred Language of the Sikhs*. London: School of Oriental and African Studies, 1983.

Singh, Ganda; Gurdev Singh: *Perspectives on the Sikh Tradition*. Singh Brothers, Amritsar (India), 1996.

Singh, Gurbachan; Sondeep Shankar: *The Sikhs: Faith, Philosophy and Folks*. Roli & Janssen, 1998.

Singh, Kushwant: *A history of the Sikhs*. Oxford University Press, 2005.

Singh, Sangat: *The Sikhs in History*. Singh Brothers, 1995.

Singh, Sangat: *The Sikhs in History*. Singh Brothers, 1995.

Smith, Wilfred Cantwell: *What Is Scripture: A Comparative Approach*. Minneapolis: Fortress Press, 1993.

Talib, Gurbachan Singh: *Shri Guru Granth Sahib*. 4 vols. Patiala: Punjabi University, 1985.

The Sikh Religion', M.A. Macauliffe, Preface xxii, 1909.

Trumpp, Ernest: *The Adi Granth or the Holy Scripture of the Sikhs*. Delhi: Munshiram Manoharlal, 1978.

6

Scriptures

Guru Granth Sahib was accumulated in the year 1603 by the fifth Guru, Arjan Dev, (Also known as the the Adi Granth). It is the teaching collection of Sikh scriptures. Arjan included in this both his own writings and the ideas of the four former Gurus, along with other material he conceived important. Despite the diversity of authors, there is a coherent message that a person should work to attain religious dismission through belief and reflection in the divine Name. Altogether, the Adi Granth comprises of 5,894 hymns, all formatted according to the musical evaluate in which they are sung. Curiously, 937 of the songs and poems were compiled by well-known bhakti saints who were not part of the Sikh culture, admitting the North Indian saint Kabir and five Muslim lovers.

In the Guru Granth Sahib, all the Hindu names as well as "Allah" is used when concerning to God. Thus it can be seen that from the identical commencing, Sikhism was interpreted as an inclusive faith which tried to comprehend and enrich other Indian religious cultures. Although the material in the Adi Granth is treated as divinely inspired, it is not conceived to be the actual words of God. The Adi Granth is unusual in that it not only contains religious texts written by the Sikh Gurus, but it also comprises material from two other religious faiths: Hinduism and Islam. The Adi Granth is considered so highly that extremum measures are taken to assure that it stays holy.

It is not allowed to be translated because any rendering would necessarily compromise some of its meaning. This can cause troubles because the Adi Granth is written in Punjabi, a language which is not easy to understand and which many young Sikhs in the West have little contact with. Some would like to see the Adi Granth understood into English in order to assure that young Sikh do not drift away from the faith of their antecedents, an controversy which will likely grow in strength as time passes. The Adi Granth is the direction of worship services, held at Gurdwaras ("gates to the Gurus").

A granthi contributes the service reads from the Adi Granth and Sikhs who sit in its comportment must remove their shoes and cover their heads out of respect. The granthi who understands from the Adi Granth is not considered a leader so much as simply someone in the community who has a greater agreement of the text. Sikhs may have a copy of the Adi Granth in their dwellings, but the book must have its own room. Like at a Gurdwara, the book must be retained a pedestal of pillows and it is not unusual for a Sikh to read from the religious text every day.

There are a few other important Sikh texts, none of which are regarded consecrated literature and none of which experience anything close to the level of cultism accorded to the Adi Granth. One is the Dasam Granth (the book of the Tenth Guru), considered by most Sikhs as an introduction of Guru Gobind Singh.

The third significant religious text among Sikhs is the Janam Sakhis (life stories), a accumulation of writings which lionize the life of Guru Nanak. They were mostly penned around the mid-seventeenth century and they portray Nanak as the grooviest of all teachers and spiritual leaders.

The principal Sikh scripture is the Adi Granth (First Scripture); more ordinarily called the Guru Granth Sahib. The Sikhs do not consider this as their "holy book" but as their eternal and current "Guru", Guide or Master. It was called Adi Granth until Guru Gobind Singh, the tenth and final Guru in human form conferred on it the title of the Guru in 1708, after which it was called Shri Guru Granth Sahib or Guru Granth Sahib, for short. The Granth has 1430 pages and is divided into 39 chapters. All imitates are exactly alike. The Sikhs are forbidden from making any alters to the text within this Scripture.

DIVINE WORDS

Sikhism understand the sheer and sovereignty of God, creator of all that is: everything is depending on his will. He does not become present within the world, a belief which is in counterpoint with the Hindu conceptions of avatars, but makes known his will and way. In distinguishing this, meditation (nam simaran) on sabda, "sound," is of predominant importance, especially through repeating of the Name, or on the hymns of the Guru Granth Sahib. Karma and samsara are accepted: the way to release or dismission is to move one's life against one's headstrong and disordered inclination (haumai) into alinement with the will (hukam) of God. This is only possible because of the help of God, the equivalent of grace, described by several words such as kirpa, nadar, prasad. Karma decides the nature of our birth, but the door of salvation is found only through grace. A Sikh moves from being a wayward wrong doer(manmukh) to being one who is devoted to and engaged in the Guru (gurmukh), The manmukh gives way to the five evil cacoetheses and is lost in mara (understood by the Sikhs as the error which attributes higher value to the material world than to the spiritual). Those who move from manmukh to gurmukh pass through stages (khand)" dharm khand, living appropriately, or according to the dharma; gian khand, deep knowledge; saram khand, effort or joy; karam khand, effort or joy; sach khand, bliss outside words and beyond rebirth, merging with the divine as a drop in the ocean or a spark in the flame. The attainment of sach khand does not hinge upon ascetic renunciation of this world, but on finding and following the will of God in everyday life. Therefore, Sikhs can stay grihash, householders, in demarcation to the four asramas of the Hindus, for whom grhastra is just one stage, to be followed by liberal forswearing.

RELIGIOUS SCRIPTURES

Adi Granth

Adi Granth literally signifies "the first book." This is the early compilation of the Sikh Scriptures by Guru Arjan, the fifth Sikh Guru, in 1604. This Granth (Book) is the Holy Scripture of the Sikhs. The tenth Sikh Guru, Guru Gobind Singh contributed further holy Shabads to this Granth during the period 1704 to 1706. Then in 1708, before taking leave for his celestial abode, Guru Gobind Singh asserted the Adi Granth as the perpetual Guru of the Sikhs and the Granth then turned known as the Shri Guru Granth Sahib.

The original copy of the scripture, called Adi Granth, collected and documented by Guru Arjan Dev still exists today and is kept at Kartarpur which is a town about 15 km. north west of the city of Jalandhar, Panjab, India. This is the only Holy Scripture in the world which was written by the collapses of the religion during their lifetime. All other holy scriptures were finished after their founders had left for their heavenly abodes. Further, this is the only holy scripture that can be considered a "universal Granth" because it contains the verses of both Hindu and Muslim saints.

Compilation: One of the classic reductions of Sikh history pertains to the conceptualization of the holy scripture, the Guru Granth Sahib.

The event is broadly described in the briefest terms. The Holy Volume was collected by Guru Arjun (AD 1563-1606) and the first copy was wrote by Bhai Gurdas at his dictation — this is all we learn from most of the generators. What amount of planning, minute attending to detail and went into this work is glossed over.

An old text which gives some elaborate information is the "Gurbilas Chhevin Patshahi". Written in AD.. 1718, this, in fact, is the oldest source. Although it does not go into the proficient and literary minutiae, it narrates the entire opertion from the beginning of the arrangement of the Holy Volume to its induction in the newly built Harimandir Sahib at Amritsar.

Why Guru Arjun attempted the task is variously explained. One commonly assumed assumption is that the codification of the Gurus' composings into authorized volume was begun by him with a view to maintaining them from falsifying by schismatical groups and others.

Bani: The "Bani", Gurus inspired vocalization, had always been the object of highest veneration for the Sikhs as well as for the Gurus themselves. It was corresponded with the Guru himself. "The bani is the Guru and the Guru bani" sang Guru Ram Das in measure Nat Narain. By collecting the canon, Guru Arjun cared to affix the seal on the sanctified word. It was also to be the repeated fountain of inspiration and the means of self-prolongation for the community.

Guru Arjun called Bhai Gurdas to his comportment and conveyed to him the wish that the authorships of the Gurus as well as those of some of the saints and sufis be collected. Massages were charged to the disciples to gather and carry to him the hymns of his predecessors. Baba Mohan, son of Guru Amar Das, Nanak III, had two manuscript assemblages of the Gurus' hymns hereditary from his father.

Bhai Gurdas travelled to Goindwal to bring these pothead but the proprietor refused to see him. Bhai Buddha, one of the most former Sikhs from Guru Nanak's days, was likewise averted from his door. Then Guru Arjun went himself. He sat ha the street below Mohan's attic executing him on his tambura. Mohan was demilitarized to hear the hymn. He came below with the pothis and presented these to the Guru. As says the Gurbilas, the pothis constituted placed on a palanquin bedighted with precious stones. The Sikhs carried it on their berms and Guru Arjun walked behind shoeless. He resisted to ride his horse, saying that the pothis were the very emotional state of the four Gurus — his predecessors.

The building of the Granth was not an easy task. It demanded sustained labour and a stringent intellectual discipline. Extracts had to be made from a vast amount of material. Besides the composings of the four preceding Gurus and the Guru Arjun who himself was a poet with a rare religious insight, there were songs and hymns by saints, both Hindu and Muslim. What constituted genuine had to be sifted from what was counterfeit. Then the selected material had to be attributed to conquer musical measures and transliterated in a minutely laid out order.

Guru Arjun carried out the work with sinful exactness. He formatted the hymns in thirty different ragas, or musical patterns. A accurate method was followed in setting down the composings. First came shabads by the Gurus in the order of their sequence. Then came hands, vars, and other poetic forms in a set order. The themes of the Gurus in each raga equaled followed by those of the Bhaktas in the same format. Gurmukhi was the script used for the arrangement.

A genius, unique in religious insight and not careless with methodology design, had created a scripture with an glorified mystical tone and a high degree of establishment. It was large in size—nearly 7,000 hymns, constituting authorships of the first five Sikhs Gurus and fifteen Bhaktas and sufis from different parts of India, admitting Shaikh Farid, Kabir and Ravidas.

The Holy Book consisted of 974 leaves, or 1948 pages, with several dummy ones at the end of a raga when there were not shabads enough to fill the division assigned to it. The site of these tremendous labours is now distinguished by a shrine called Gurdwara Ramsar.

The completion of the Granth Sahib was, says the "Gurbilas", celebrated with much exultation. In thanksgiving, karah prasad was developed in huge quantities. Sikhs came in packs to see the Holy Book. They exulted in their hearts by a sight of it and bowed before it in veneration. Among the visitors was Bhai Banno, who had led a radical of Sikhs from Mangat, in western Punjab.

Binding: Guru Arjun, who knew him as a committed Sikh, instructed him to go to Lahore and have the Book bound. Banno sought the Guru's permit to be appropriated to take the Granth Sahib first to Mangat for the Sikhs there to see it. The Guru appropriated this, but ordered him not to carry at Mangat, or at any former place, more than a night.

As Bhai Banno left Amritsar with his consecrated charge, it happened to him to have a second copy transliterated. The first copy, he argued, would remain with the Guru. There must be an extra one for the sangat. The Guru's focus was that he should not stay longer than one night at a place, but he had said nothing about the time to be exhausted on the journey. So he proceeded with his plans and sent a Sikh to purchase paper.

He proposed to his comrades that they should travel by easy butts of five miles a day. The time thus saved was applied in transcribing the holy text. Sikhs wrote with love and devotedness and nobody shirked his duty whether it was day or night. By the time they accomplished Lahore, the second copy was ready. But Banno had increased it some questionable texts. He had both volumes bound and brought back to Amritsar as fast as he could.

It was settled to spend the night at Ramsar and return to Amritsar the next morning. The Granth Sahib leant on a seat under the canopy, whereas the Guru and the Sikhs slept on the ground. A adherent had to be chosen to take charge of the Granth Sahib. As says the Gurbilas, Guru Arjun lay awake through the night reflecting on the question. His choice officially fell on old Bhai Buddha whose devotion was universally clapped.

As they awoke, the Guru and his Sikhs made washings in Ramsar. The former there upon practiced his wonted speculation. At dawn, the entire sangat marched towards Harimandir. Bhai Buddha carried the Holy Book on his head and Guru Arjun took the air behind swinging the whisk over it. Musicians sang shabads. Thus they reached the Harimandir. The Granth Sahib was ritualistically installed in the centre of the inner sanctuary on September 1, 1604. Bhai Buddha opened it with revere to obtain from it the divine command, as Guru Arjun stood in attendance behind.

Installation: Guru Arjun addressed that during daytime the Holy Book should remain in the Harimandir and by night, after, Sohila was read, it should constitute taken to the room he had built for himself. As evening encouraged by two watches, Bhai Buddha recounted Sohila and made the final ardas or supplication. The Granth Sahib was closed and wrapped in silks. Bhai Buddha held it on his head and abutted towards the chamber indicated by Guru Arjun. The Guru led the sangat singing hymns.

The Granth Sahib was committed on the appointed seat, and the Guru slept on the basis by its side. Daily, in the small hours of the morning as the stars twinkle in the pool beneath, the Holy Book is taken out in state to the Harimandir and brought by night to rest in the room marked for it by Guru Arjun. The practice continues to this day. But the volume is not the same. That master copy was taken to Kartarpur when Guru Arjun's successor, Guru Hargobind, left Amritsar in 1634. There it authorized into the possession of his grandson, Dhir Mall. It has since stayed in that family.

Guru Granth Sahib

Guru Granth Sahib is more than just a Holy Scripture of the Sikhs. The Sikhs treat this Granth (holy book) as a living Guru. The holy text spans 1430 pages and comprises the actual words spoken by the founders of the Sikh religion (the Ten Gurus of Sikhism) and the words of several other Saints from other religions including Hinduism and Islam.

Guru Granth Sahib was given the Guruship by the last of the living Sikh Masters, Guru Gobind Singh in 1708. Guru Gobind Singh said before his death that the Sikhs were to treat the Granth Sahib as their next Guru.

When one chatters a Gurdwara (a Sikh temple), the Guru Granth Sahib classes the primary part of the Darbar Sahib or Main Hall. The holy book is directed on a dominant platform and covered in a very beautiful and beautifully coloured fine cloth. The platform is always addressed by a canopy, which is also decorated in expensive and very attractive colored materials. The text in which the Granth is wrote is a script called Gurmukhi (literally "From the Guru's mouth"), which is believed a modern growth of the ancient language called Sanskrit.

History: Guru Nanak bestowed the "Word of God" to grounds upon Earth. Through his Hymns and Prayers, he inspired and elated kindness to live a life of truth, morality and mysticism. These enlightening words were sung by his companions, Bala and Mardana, and by the Sangats which grew up in the region of Guru Nanak. In his later years at Kartarpur, it became anticipated for the members of the Sikh population to sing certain hymns on a daily root: Japji in the morning; So Dar and So Purakh, the early period of Rehiras, in the evenings.

Guru Angad, Guru Amar Das and Guru Ram Das all perched Shabads (hymns), and the Sikhs began to collect these in books called Pothis. chant these Shabads, the Sikhs became vehicles for the atmosphere of the "Word of God", and they accomplish a state of higher realization, a inspirational meditative union with God and Guru.

Even early in Sikh history, however, there were individuals, and dissimulators to the Throne of Spirituality. The elder brother of Guru Arjun, Prithia, compiled his own hymns and authorized them off as writings of Guru Nanak. There were many different accumulations of Shabads, and many disagreeing versions of the same Shabads. Guru Arjun realized that a homogeneous, documented collection of the Guru's Bani was needed to safeguard the truthfulness of the Shabad.

The most accomplished collected works of Shabads of Guru Nanak, Guru Angad and Guru Amar Das was in the will power of Mohan, a son of Guru Amar Das. Guru Arjun sent Bhai Gurdas to Mohan's home in Goindwal, to request this assemblage of Shabads. Mohan felt cold-shouldered at having been passed over for Guruship — his father, Guru Amar Das, had seen the Divine Light in Guru Ram Das, and had contributed the Guruship upon him. Mohan rejected to answer the door when Bhai Gurdas knocked, and Bhai Gurdas gave to Guru Arjun unrewarded.

Guru Arjun then sent Baba Buddha to Mohan's house. Baba Buddha was by then a very former and esteemed man in the Sikh community, having been an adherent of all the Gurus, from Guru Nanak through Guru Arjun. When Mohan did not respond Baba Buddha's knock, he entered the house anyway. Inside, he found Mohan in a deep pondering trance. Mohan's younger brother converted Baba Buddha not to disturb him, and Baba Buddha also return to Guru Arjun empty-handed.

Gazing upon Guru Arjun's illuminated face, feeling the love and glowing emanating from him, hearing the sweet words of love and humility, Mohan's heart was muffled, and opened at last. He admitted Guru Arjun's true place on the throne of Guru Nanak, and gave all of the Shabads in his self-control to Guru Arjun.

Guru Arjun then set to accumulate the Shabads into a single volume, the Adi Granth. He sieved through the Shabads which had been passed down from the first four Gurus, and strained those which had been added by imposters. Bhai Gur Das established the scribe who recorded the Words of Guru Arjun. When he asked Guru Arjun how he could discern between the true and the false Shabads, Guru Arjun replied, "Even in a great herd of cows and calves, the mother cow will distinguish the cry of her calf, above all others. Just so, the True Shabad reverberates truly, and is easily recognized from the false."

Guru Arjun added a great numerous of his own Shabads to those of Guru Nanak, Guru Angad, Guru Amar Das and Guru Ram Das. He also contributed Shabads of thirty-six Hindu and Muslim Saints, amongst them Kabir, Ravi Das, Naam Dev, Trilochan and Sheikh Farid. This was the beginning time any religion comprised the works of sincere devotees of other religions into its own scripture; it reflects the universality of thought which underlies the Sikh belief in One God, and the one family of humankind as children of God.

Guru Arjun left some white pages in the Granth. When Bhai Gur Das asked the purpose of this, he replied that one of the Gurus to follow him would add the Shabads in their apropriate place at the proper time. In time the shabads of Guru Teg Bahadur, the ninth Expression of the Guru's Light, were added by Guru Gobind Singh and thus the Siri Guru Granth Sahib was accomplished.

The Adi Granth was finished in 1604, and established in the Golden Temple; Baba Buddha was nominated Guru Granthi. Guru Arjun told his Sikhs that the Adi Granth was the incarnation of the Guru, and should be treated with all the respect concorded to himself. When Guru Arjun first accomplished the Adi Granth, he placed it on his own bed and slept on the floor. Its words were composed without any spaces or breaks, which nowadays is difficult for most people to follow.

Guru Gobind Singh, the tenth and last of the Sikh Gurus to take individual form, prescribed the entire Granth Sahib at Talwandi Sabo now called Damdama Sahib. Dhir Mal, the son of Baba Gurditta and grandson of Guru Hargobind, had taken ownership of the Adi Granth; he denied to give it to Guru Gobind Singh when the Guru asked for it. Dhir Mal razzed the Guru, "If you are a Guru, then develop your own." Guru Gobind Singh proceeded to dictate it to Bhai Mani Singh, who commemorated it on paper. While some have questioned the authenticity of this story, it is well for us to remember that, of course, Guru Gobind Singh was no average person at all. And, in the old days of bards and story-tellers, it was not strange for them to recite from memory entire epic poems. Hajis, for example can recount the entire Qur'an and many Hindus priests could enumerate the Mahabarata. In a time when many people could not read or write oral customs were very important. The SGGS is like the Qur'an and the Gita is set in the form of Music and rythm building them much easier to remember.

Guru Gobind Singh incorporated the Shabads of his father, Guru Teg Bahadur, but he did not admit his own Shabads; instead, he placed them in a classify Granth, the Dasam Granth. The Dasam Granth is not reverenced as Guru, however. The great task of re-writing the entire Guru was finally finished in 1705. The "Damdama Sahib Bir" as it is now known was then taken to Nanded where it was based.

Guru Gobind Singh based this elaborated version of the Adi Granth as Guru on October 20, 1708. This day is celebrated today as Guru Gadi Day. At the time of his death, he announced that the Word of God substantiated in the Siri Guru Granth Sahib was to be Guru for all time. He said, "O Beloved Khalsa, let any who desire to behold me, behold the Guru Granth. Obey the Granth Sahib, for it is the visible body of the

Guru. Let any who desire to meet me, diligently search its Bani." Thus the Word of God, which has manifested as Guru in Nanak, and had passed through the ten incarnations of Guru, was now returned to its form as the Word, the Bani, the Shabad.

Structure: Within it's 1430 pages, the shabads (hymns) of the Shri Guru Granth Sahib are arranged in thirty-one Ragas, the cultural Indian musical measures and scales. Within the Ragas, they are arranged by order of the Sikh Gurus, with the shabads of the Hindu and Muslim Saints following. The shabads are written in several metres and rhythms, and are organized accordingly. For instance, Ashtapadi-eight steps, or Panch-padi-five steps. The Shri Guru Granth Sahib is written in Gurmukhi script, but the shabads were written in many different languages including Punjabi, Sanskrit and Persian.

The original bir of Guru Granth Sahib did not contain an index. However, this is provided in some modern print of the bir to make it easy to find the location of some of the common banis. For example, from the index, it can be seen that the Japji Sahib starts at page 1 and ends at page 8; Sukhmani Sahib is located from pages 262 to 296; the Bara Maha bani can is found at pages 133 to 136; The bani called Anand Sahib (Bliss) can be found at pages 917 to 922, etc.

The Guru Granth Sahib begins with the word "Ek Onkar" – The All Pervading Being. From this Word to the tenth Word "Gur-parshad" is called the Mool Mantra. After this is the rest of the composition called the Japji composed by Guru Nanak Dev. This comprises 38 Pauris or stanzas, a Prologue and an Epilogue. This is one of the morning prayer of the Sikhs.

The next composition has two parts-(1) "So Dar" and (2) "So Purkh". The Bani, "So Dar" contains 5 Shabads and "So Purkh" contains 4 Shabads. This form most of the evening prayer of the Sikhs and is called the Rehras. After this is the Bani called Sohila (full name, Kirtan Sohila), which contains 5 Shabads and is the bed-time prayer.

Ragas: The Adi Granth starts with the non-raga section which begins with Japji as the first entry followed by Rehras and ending with Kirtan Sohila. Then begins the main section consisting of 31 Ragas or chapters. A raga is a musical structure or set of rules of how to build a melody. It specifies a scale, as well as rules for movements up and down the scale; which notes should figure more and which notes should be used more sparingly; etc. The result is a framework that can be used to compose or improvise melodies in, so that melodies in a certain raga will always be recognizable yet allowing endless variation.

Just as a raga has emotional overtone, so each chapter has spiritual implication. The thirty-one ragas appear in the following serial order: Shri raga, Manjh, Gauri, Asa, Gujri, Devagandhari, Bihagara, Wadahans, Sorath, Dhanashri, Jaitshri, Todi, Bairari, Tilang, Suhi, Bilaval, Gond (Gaund), Ramkali, Nut-Narayan, Mali-Gaura, Maru, Tukhar, Kedara, Bhairav (Bhairo), Basant, Sarang, Malar, Kanra, Kalyan, Prabhati and Jaijawanti. Within the 1430 pages are found Saloks of Bhagat Kabir, Sheikh Farid, Guru Tegh Bahadur, etc.

Historical Volumes of the Siri Guru Granth Sahib: There are three historical volumes of Shri Guru Granth Sahib. These are:

- Kartarpur Vaali Bir: As described above, Guru Arjun dictated the Adi Granth to Bhai Gur Das. This first volume, or Bir, was made in Amritsar and later transferred to Kartarpur, where it remains today. The opening lines are in the hand of Guru Arjun, and it bears the signature of Guru Hargobind at the end. There are several blank pages, left by Guru Arjun to hold the writings of Guru Teg Bahadur.Apart frommany handwritten copies of Shri Guru Granth Sahib possessed by several persons and found in some Gurdwaras the most important is the Bir recension at Kartarpur,near Jullundur in the custody of Sodhi Amarjit Singh, a descendant of Dhirmal

- Bhai Banno Vaali Bir: After completing the Adi Granth, Guru Arjun asked one of his Sikhs, Bhai Banno, to take the manuscript to Lahore to have it bound. During this journey, Bhai Banno had a copy made for his own use. He inserted a few Shabads of his own choosing, however. This version remains with his descendents.Hand written Manuscript of Bhai Banno wali Bir is said to be available at Gurdwara Banno Sahib in Kanpur city in India.

- Damdama Vaali Bir: This is the volume dictated by Guru Gobind Singh at Damdama Sahib to Mani Singh. In it, Guru Gobind Singh included the Shabads of Guru Teg Bahadur. The volumes of the Siri Guru Granth Sahib which preside over our Gurdwaras now are copies of this edition.

The Message: The Guru Granth Sahib provides unique and unequalled guidance and advice to the whole of the human race. It is the torch that will lead humanity out of Kaljug, (the dark era) to a life in peace, tranquility and spiritual enlightenment for all the nations of the World. The main message can be summarized as:

- All Peoples of the World are Equal
- Women as Equals
- One God for All
- Speak and Live Truthfully
- Control the Five Vices
- Live in God's Hukam
- Practice Humility, Kindness, Compassion, Love, etc

NON-RELIGIOUS SCRIPTURES

Dasam Granth

The Dasam Granth historically known as Dasven Padshah Ka Granth is a scripture of Sikhism, containing texts composed by the 10th Sikh Guru, Guru Gobind Singh. The compositions of the Granth set out the ideas, thoughts and guidlines for the future of the Nanak panth as enshrined in the Khalsa. The Jaap Sahib, Tvye Prasad Sawaiye (Amrit Savaiye) and Benti Chaupai, all compositions from the Dasam Granth, are part of the daily prayers Nitnem of the Sikhs, which serve, as well, as a part of the Sikh initiation Khande di Pahul.

Structure: The Dasam Granth contains 1428 pages and is the collection of the writings of the 10th Patshah, Shri Guru Gobind Singh Ji. It contains his Jaap Sahib, the Akal Ustat or praise of the Creator, the Vachitar Natak or Wonderful Drama, in which the Guru gives an account of his parentage, his divine mission, and the battles in which he had been engaged. Then come three abridged translations of the Devi Mahatamya, an episode in the Markandeya Puran, in praise of Durga the Goddess of war (Chandi Chritras: Chandi Chritra I, Chandi Chritra II, Chandi Ki Var).

Then follows the Gyan Parbodh, or awakening of knowledge; Chobis Avatar-accounts of twenty-four incarnations of the Vishnu, according to the Hindus, and Brahmavatar and Rudravtdr, selected because of their warlike character; the Shabad Hazare; quatrains called Sawaiyas, which are religious hymns in praise of God and reprobation of idolatry and hypocrisy; the Khalsa Mahima, or words in praise of the Khalsa; the Shastar Nam Mala, a list of offensive and defensive weapons used in the

Guru's time, with special reference to the attributes of the Creator; the Tria Charitar, or tales illustrating the qualities, but principally the deceit of women; the Kabiovach Bainti Chaupai will "absolve the suffering, pain or fear of the person, who will even once recite this Bani"; the Zafarnama, containing the tenth Guru's epistle to the Emperor Aurangzeb; and Hikayats, several metrical tales in the Persian language.

The Dasam Granth is said to have been compiled by Bhai Mani Singh Ji, a companion and disciple of the Guru, after the tenth Guru's death. It is understood that Bhai Mani Singh spent nine years at this task, by getting copies from other disciples and filling in some of the gaps by memory.

There are many compilations in existence and many are still being discovered. The current version in wide circulation closely follows the edition ascribed to Bhai Mani Singh.

There are three main editions:

- One edition said to have been written by Bhai Mani Singh in his own hand.
- A volume at the Gurdwara at Patna.
- A volume at the Gurdwara at Sangrur.

Contents: They consist of eighteen works written in four languages: Braj (frequently highly Sanskritised), Hindi, Persian and Punjabi. The Dasam Granth can be conveniently divided into three sections:

- Mythological
- Philosophical
- Autobiographical

The largest portion is mythological and is devoted to retelling well known tales of Hindu mythology and adding in a reworking from a Gurmat perspective. The Chandi Charitra I and II and Var Bhaguti Ki (Chandi di var) recount the battles of the deity Durga and the Chaubis Avtar are tales of the incarnations of Vishnu.

It is a common false impression by some uninformed people that Guru Gobind Singh workshipped the Hindu deities he wrote about. They are misled by the compositions on Shri Ram Chandra Ji, Baghwan Krishan Ji, Vishnu in the Chaubis Avtar and the vars of Chandi. They assume that since Guru Ji praised them in verse, he must have admired and worshipped them also. These often 'learned' persons fail to recognize the fact that nowhere in his writings does Guru Ji accept them as anything other than the creations of the Formless Akal.

In reality Guru Sahib wrote about them in the language of the people drawing from the mythological lore current at that time. He wrote about their exploits in colouful martial language to raise courage in the hearts of all who read them. It is meaningless to make one's own deductions while ignoring the words of the Guru which are very clear.

The Contents of the Dasam Granth are:

- Jaap (meditation)
- Akal Ustat (praises of God)
- Bachitar Natak (autobiography of the Guru)
- Chandi Charitar I & II (the character of Goddess Chandi)
- Chandi di Var (a ballad to describe Goddess Durga)
- Gian Prabodh (the awakening of knowledge)
- Chaubis Avtar (24 incarnations of Vishnu)
- Brahm Avtar (incarnation of Brahma)
- Rudar Avtar (incarnation of Shiv)
- Shabad Hazare (ten shabads)
- Swayyae (33 stanzas)
- Khalsa Mehma (the praises of the Khalsa)
- Shastar Nam Mala (a list of weapons)
- Triya Charitar (the character of women)
- Zafarnama (epistle of victory, a letter written to Emperor Aurangzeb)
- Hikayats. (stories)

Language: The Dasam Granth is all rhymed poetry. It was designed to be heard, so there is considerable repition, and a variety of metrees to hold the attention. The language of most of the Dasam Granth is largely Braj veering towards Sanskrit at one extreme and simple colloquial Hindi at the other. The Braj dialect is a variety of medieval Hindi with a mixture of Sanskrit, Persiona, and Arabic words. The Zafarnama and the Hikayats are in Persian using Gurmukhi characters and several passages in other works are in Punjabi. The 'author' not only used this melange of languages but also coined words half Arabic half Sanskrit (and sometimes words without any meaning just to create a musical effect). Some of this kind of writing has great power and beauty.

Most of the poetry of the Dasam Granth is hardly intelligible to the modern Punjabi reader without the aid of a commentary. Experts tell us that the Guru's poetry is of the highest order:

The descriptions of scenes of battle are couched in extremely vigorous staccato rhyme often reduced to lines of one word each. The battles waged by Chandi and the Guru's encounters with the hill chiefs at Bhangani and Nadaun are among the most stirring that exist.

Janamsakhis

Janamsakhis, literally Birth Stories, are writings which profess to be biographies of the first Guru, Guru Nanak Dev Ji. These compositions have been written at several stages after the demise of the first Guru. They all record miraculous acts and supernatural conversations. Many of them contradict each other on material points and some have obviously been touched up to advance the claims of one or the other branches of the Guru's family, or to exaggerate the roles of certain disciples.

It may be incidentally mentioned that it was the Gospel according to Barnabas which Muhammad used in the composition of the Quran." The falsification of old or the composition of new Janamsakhis was the result of three great schisms of the Sikh religion: The Udasis, the Minas and the Handalis.

Though from the point of view of a historian the janamsakhis may be inadequate, they cannot be wholly discarded because they were based on legend and culture which had grown up around the Guru in the years following his demise, and furnish useful material to augment the bare but proved facts of his life. The main janamsakhis which scholars over the years have referred to are as follows:

Bhai Bala Janamsakhi: This is probably the most popular and well known Janamsakhi, in that most Sikhs and their Janamsakhi knowledge come from this document. This work claims to be a contemporarry account written by one Bala Sandhu in the Sambat year 1592 at the instance of the second Guru, Guru Angad. According to the author, he was a close companion of Guru Nanak and accompanied him on many of his travels. There are good reasons to doubt this contention:

Guru Angad, who is said to have commissioned the work and was also a close companion of the Guru in his later years, was, according to Bala's own admission, ignorant of the existence of Bala. Bhai Gurdas, who has listed all Guru Nanak's prominent disciples whose names were handed down, does not mention the name of Bala Sandhu.

Bhai Mani Singh's Bhagat Ratanwali, which contains essentialy the same list as that by Bhai Gurdas, but with more detail, also does not mention Bala Sandhu. It is only in the heretic janamsakhis of the Minas that we find first mention of Bhai Bala. The language used in this janamsakhi was not spoken at the time of Guru Nanak or Guru Angad, but was developed at least a hundred years later. Some of the hymns ascribed to Nanak are not his but those of the second and fifth Gurus.

At several places expressions which gained currency only during the lifetime of the last Guru, Guru Gobind Singh (1666-1708), are used e.g WaheGuru Ji ki Fateh. Bala's janamsakhi is certainly not a contemporary account; at best it was written in the early part of the 18tyh Century.

This janamsakhi has had an immense influence over determining what is generally accepted as the authoritative account of Guru Nanak Dev Ji's life. Throughout the nineteenth century the authority of the Bala version was unchallenged. An important work based on the Bahi Bala janam-sakhi is Santokh Singh's Gur Nanak Purkash commonly known as Nanak Parkash. Its lengthy sequel, Suraj Parkash carries the acount up to the tenth Guru and contains a higher proportion of historical fact, this was completed in 1844.

In the first journey or udasi Guru Nanak Dev left Sultanpur towards eastern India and included, in the following sequence: Panipat (Sheikh Sharaf) Delhi (Sultan Ibrahim Lodi) Hardwar Allahbad Banaras Nanakmata Kauru, Kamrup in Assam (Nur Shah) Talvandi (twelve years after leaving Sultanpur) Pak Pattan (Sheikh Ibrahim) Goindval Lahore Kartarpur.

The Second udasi was to the south of India with companion Bhai Mardana. Delhi Ayodhya Jagannath Puri Rameswaram Shri Lanka Vindhya Mountains Narabad River Ujjain Saurashtra Mathura. The third udasi was to the north: Kashmir Mount Sumeru Achal. The fourth udasi was to the west. Afghanistan Persia Mecca Madina Baghdad

Vilayat Vali Janamsakhi: In the year 1883 a copy of a janamasakhi was dispatched by the India Office Library in London for the use of Dr.Trumpp and the Sikh scholars assisting him. (it came to be known as the Vilayat Vali or the foreign janamsakhi.) This janamsakhi was the basis of the accounts written by Trumpp, Macauliffe, and most Sikh scholars. It is said to have been written in 1588 AD. by Sewa Das.

Hafizabad Vali Janamsakhi: A renowned Sikh scholar, Gurmukh Singh of the Oriental College, Lahore, found another janamsakhi at

Hafizabad which was very similar to that found by Colebrook. Gurmukh Singh who was collabourating with Mr.Macauliffe in his research on Sikh religion, made it available to the Englishman, who had it published in November 1885. This biography agrees entirely with the India Office janamsakhi.

Bhai Mani Singh's Janamsakhi: The fourth and eveidently the latest is the Gyan-ratanavali attributed to Bhai Mani Singh who wrote it with the express intention of correcting heretical accounts of Guru Nanak Dev Ji. Bhai Mani Singh was a Sikh of Guru Gobind Singh Ji. He was approached by some Sikhs with a request that he should prepare an authentic account of Guru Nanak Dev Ji's life. This they assured him was essential as the Minas were circulating objectionable things in their version.

Other Janamsakhis: Many other janamsakhis have since been discovered. They follow the above in all material points. The term Puratan janamsakhis means ancient janam-sakhis and is generally used with reference to the composite work which was compiled by Bhai Vir Singh and first published in 1926. Of the still existing copies of the Puratan Janam-sakhis the two most important were the Colebrooke and Hafizabad versions. The first of these was discovered in 1872, the manuscript had been donated to the library of the east India company by H.T. Colebrooke and is accordingly known as the Colebrooke or Vailaitwali Janamsakhi. Although there is no date on it the manuscript points to around 1635.

According to the Puratan Janamsakhi Guru Nanak Dev was born in the month of Vaisakh, 1469. The date is given as the third day of the light half of the month and the birth is said it have taken place during the last watch before dawn. His father Kalu, was a khatri of the Bedi sub-cast and lived in a village Rai Bhoi di talwandi, his mothers name is not given. When Guru turned seven he was taken to a pundit to learn how to read. After only one day he gave up reading and when the pundit asked him why Guru lapsed into silence and instructed him at length in the vanity of worldly learning and the contrasting value of the Divine Name of God.

The child began to show disturbing signs of withdrawal from the world. He was sent to learn Persian at the age of nine but returned home and continued to sit in silence. Locals advised his father that Nanak should be married. This advice was taken and at the age of twelve a betrothal was arranged at the house of Mula of the Chona sub-caste. Sometime later Nanak moved to Sultanpur where his sister Nanaki was married. Here he took up employment with Daulat Khan. One day Nanak went to the river and while bathing messengers of God came and he was transported to the divine court. There he was given a cup of nectar (amrit) and with it came the command "Nanak, this is the cup of My Name (Naam). Drink it." This he did and was charged to go into the world and preach the divine Name.

The first three sakhis recount the greatness of Raja Janak and describes an interview with God wherein Raja Janak is instructed that he is to return to the world once again to propagate His Name. Details of Guru Nanak's birth are given in the fourth sakhi and his father was Kalu, a Bedi and his mother Mata Tripta. The account of Guru Ji learning to read from the pundit is also recounted here. After the interlude at Sultanpur Guru Nanak Dev set out to Mount Sumeru. Climbing the mountain Guru Ji found all nine Siddhus seated there – Gorakhnath, Mechhendranath, Isarnath, Charapatnath, Barangnath, Ghoracholi, Balgundai, Bharathari and Gopichand. Gorakhnath asked the identity of the visitor.

Non-Religious Compositions of Guru Har Rai And Guru Tegh Bahadur

The printed version of the Adi Granth, the Sikh scripture, contains no compositions by the seventh Guru, Har Rai, and one hundred sixteen by the ninth Guru, Tegh Bahadur. This study introduces to textual scholarship a couplet attributed to Guru Har Rai in two seventeenth-century manuscripts and seven couplets and two padas attributed to Guru Tegh Bahadur in a number of early manuscripts. It also discusses a notice found in seventeenth-century manuscripts recording a verse of the fifth Guru, Arjan, supposed to have been written in a manuscript copy of the Adi Granth by Guru Har Rai. The study also introduces six seventeenth-century manuscripts of the Adi Granth.

Textual Studies: Textual studies on the Adi Granth, the Sikh scripture, have tended to concentrate on a limited number of issues, usually the presence or absence in manuscripts of certain compositions characteristic of the Banno and Kartarpur versions. Beyond this, most writing has focused on trying to prove either the Kartarpur or Banno versions the "original" text or on textual issues such as the position of invocations in the printed text and the authenticity of the Ragamala listing of ragas that concludes the volume. As a result, many other interesting textual issues have been ignored, particularly those raised by later manuscripts and other versional cultures of the Granth.

We will discuss three such neglected textual issues: a couplet attributed to the seventh Sikh Guru, Har Rai; a notation in some manuscripts referring to Guru Har Rai's having inscribed a verse of the fifth Guru, Arjan, in a copy of the Adi Granth; and two sets of non-canonical compositions attributed to the ninth Guru, Tegh Bahadur. The study also introduces to Adi Granth scholarship six seventeenth-century manuscripts of the Adi Granth.

Four Versions of the Adi Granth: Culture and twentieth-century scholarship recognize four texts or versions of the Adi Granth: the Kartarpur version, said to have been compiled by Guru Arjan in 1604; the Banno version, said to be descended from a direct copy of Guru Arjan's manuscript, to which a number of extra compositions were added; the Lahore version, which lacks the extra material of the Banno version and has a different order at the end of the text; and the Damdami version, said to have been compiled by the tenth Guru, Gobind Singh, in 1706, which lacks the extra compositions of the Banno version and is said to have been the first text to contain the works of Guru Tegh Bahadur.

The Damdami text forms the basis of the printed Adi Granth. In the Adi Granth, the pada and dohara of Hindi cultures are referred to as shabad and shloka and the corpus of compositions of a particular author or the text as a whole as bani. The manuscript contains all the extra compositions characteristic of the Banno version, except that only the first line of the Surdas composition "Chhadi mona Hari bimukhana ko Sanga" is given in Saranga raga, where later Banno texts usually contain the entire pada. The chalitru joti joti samavana ka listing of the death dates of the Gurus at the end of the index goes up to the eighth Guru, Harikrishan, who died in 1664.

The manuscript appears to be the earliest extant dated text to contain the works of Tegh Bahadur as an integral part of the appropriate raga sections of the Granth itself. Unlike the published Damdami version, though, raga Jaijavanti has been placed before rather than after raga Prabhati, and the text contains fifty-six rather than fifty-seven salokas of the ninth Guru, including three of the extra-canonical salokas presented in this paper.

The second seventeenth-century manuscript is in British Museum. Although the catalogue of the Museum's manuscripts dates the text to the nineteenth century, the manuscript actually consists of two distinct sections, an older portion on Kashmiri paper and a newer completion on Sialkoti paper, most probably necessitated by damage to the original volume. The index has been produced by the hand that completed the text. The manuscript is of the Lahore version and has had the Ragamala added in a third hand at the end of the text.

The older section of the manuscript would appear to have been completed before the final quarter of the seventeenth century and does not contain the compositions of the ninth Guru, which have been added on new folios by the second scribe. The orthography of the older section is particularly archaic, and in common with a number of other late seventeenth century Lahore-version manuscripts, the rubrication of the text has been done in red ink.

As in a number of other old texts, each folio is numbered on the reverse rather than on the obverse. The first folio of the text proper is illuminated in the style of the Dehra Dun and Kartarpur manuscripts. Unlike later manuscripts, some sections of the earlier portion of the text end with the invocations vahuGuru, vahuGuru gariba nivaja Ji, Guru gariba nivaja Ji, and Guru sati. The invocation of Siri raga contains the uncharacteristic phrase shri satigura gariba nivaju rather than the full or abbreviated forms of the mulamantara found in most manuscripts. The completion of the text in the hand of the second scribe contains the shloka attributed to Guru Hari Rai.

Four other seventeenth-century manuscripts are in the collection of Takht Shri Harimandar Sahib, Patna. The first is a Lahore-version manuscript that contains a nisana of Guru Gobind Singh on the folio facing the beginning of the text proper. Both folios are illuminated. The manuscript has a chalitru joti joti samavana ka that contains the death dates of the Gurus to the eighth Guru Harikrishan. This is followed by a notice of the shloka said to have been inscribed on a copy of the Granth by Guru Har Rai. The manuscript is said to have formerly been the text used for worship in the shrine. The second manuscript is a Lahore text to which the compositions of the ninth Guru and the material characteristic of the Banno version have been added in another hand.

The manuscript has had the nisana of an unknown figure. The shloka vara te vadhika section contains the shloka attributed to the seventh Guru. The third manuscript is a Lahore manuscript dated 3 January 1699 to which the compositions characteristic of the Banno version have been added in another hand. The text has a chalitru containing the death dates of the Gurus to the eighth Guru, Harikrishan, which is followed by a notice of the shloka written on a copy of the Granth by Guru Har Rai. The fourth Patna volume is one of which some brief notice has been taken in scholarship on Adi Granth manuscripts. The manuscript is a Lahore version text written by Ram Rai, son of Uttam Chand the goldsmith to which the compositions characteristic of the Banno version have been added in another hand.

The index and text proper have been completed by the original scribe up to the Mahala chaupada section of Maru raga, after which two new hands have completed the text. The compositions of the ninth Guru are in the same hands as the rest of the text throughout. The chalitru in the hand of one of the scribes who completed the text lists the death dates of the Gurus to Tegh Bahadur, although the entry for his death date is in a darker ink than the other entries. The leaf indicating that he did indeed stop writing the text and index midway through Maru raga, has been bound at the end of the text. The reverse of the leaf contains a notice regarding the shloka, written on a copy of the Granth by Guru Han Rai.

This granth is a copy of Fatehchand's granth, which is a copy of the Pushkar granth. The Pushkar granth has been corrected against the big granth that the fifth Guru got written by Gurdas. Jagna Brahman's granth is more correct than others, and the Pushkar granth has been corrected against Jagnas text. This brief notice is the earliest extant reference to the textual authority of the copy of the Adi Granth written by Bhai Gurdas for Guru Arjan. The two other manuscripts mentioned, Jagna's granth and the Pushkar granth, are not known either to culture or to scholarship. Adi Granth scholarship has failed to notice a shloka (couplet) attributed to Guru Hari Rai found in the shloka vara te vadhika section of two of the above seventeenth-century Lahore-version manuscripts. The printed edition of the Granth does not contain any compositions by the seventh Guru.

Although the shloka is clearly marked in both texts as a composition of Guru Har Rai, the seventh Mina Guru, Miharban, also used the marker Mahala and the chhapa Nanak, leaving open the possibility of a mistaken attribution. The shloka does not, however, appear in any of the extant texts containing the works of Miharban. At the same time, though, none of the available texts on the lives of the Sikh Gurus has any reference to Guru Har Rai's having composed any bani, and the shloka is not attested elsewhere in the Sikh culture. It cannot therefore be securely attributed to Guru Har Rai.

A number of seventeenth-century Lahore-version manuscripts also contain a notice reproducing a shloka supposed to have been written in a manuscript copy of the Granth by Guru Har Rai. The notice appears after the index of the manuscript and before the beginning of the text proper, the same location in which some seventeenth-century manuscripts have a nisana. It seems likely, therefore, that it represents a transcription of a nisana added to an earlier manuscript.

The shloka quoted in both the above notices is a slight variation on the shloka to the thirty-fifth pauri of Guru Arjan's Bavana akhari in Gauri raga, an acrostic composition based on the fifty-two letters of the Nagari script. The choice of this verse is an unusual one, since most extant nisanas (including the three published exemplars attributed to Guru Har Rai) consist of the mulamantara. Like this putative nisana, a nisana in the hand of Guru Gobind Singh in a Banno manuscript dated 1744 also consists of a verse from Bavana akhari in this case the first two tines of the nineteenth pauri. It is unclear whether the existence of two nisanas containing extracts from Bavana akhari implies anything about the popularity of this composition in the seventeenth century.

The notice accompanying the shloka in the Patiala and Patna manuscripts raises the question of whether the phrase "at the time of sitting on the throne" refers to Har Rai's installation as Guru. Two pieces of information in the text allow us to come to some conclusions, but in both cases we are hampered by the fact that there seem to be no extant contemporary documents about the life of Guru Har Rai. The first piece of information is the date given in the text, the second half of the month of Poh (December-January) in an unspecified year. This date does not match those given by most later Sikh documents for Guru Har Rai's accession.

The second important piece of information is the text's mention of the camp of Thappal in Sirmor. Early Sikh sources do not refer to Guru Har Rai's having gone to Sirmor state, and Sarup Das Bhalla's Mahima prakasha implies that Har Rai's installation as Guru took place at Kiratpur. An interesting piece of testimony about the Guru's presence in Sirmor is, however, provided by the Dabistan-i mazahib, an account of Indian religious groups written in Persian. According to the Dabistan, Guru Har Rai went to Thapal in Sirmor in 1645-46, a year after his accession to the Guruship. His departure is said to have been occasioned by an attack on the state of Bilaspur (in which Kiratpur was situated) by Mughal forces under the command of the faujdar of Kangra, Nijabat Khan.

The importance of the Dabistan's testimony would seem to be bolstered by its author's claim to have spent a number of years in Punjab and Kashmir and to have visited Guru Hargobind in Kirstpur in 1643-44. Some of the supporting information given by the Dabistan is, however, somewhat problematic. In identifying the location of Thapal, the text states that it is in the domain of Raja Karam Parkas. Karam Prakash had indeed ruled Sirmor during the years 1616-30, but at the time this section of the Dabistan was written in 645-46, his brother Mandhata Prakash was ruling the state.

Further, according to Mughal chronicles, the only major Mughal campaign led by Nijabat Khan in the Punjab hills was against Shrinagar in Garhwal in the opening months of 1635. The Mughal forces lost the campaign, and Nijabat Khan lost his post as Faujdar of Kangra. Although he was subsequently appointed to other posts, he seems never to have regained the faujdari of the hill region. The other hill campaigns mentioned in Mughal chronicles do not match either the date or the location mentioned in the Dabistan: a skirmish between the Mughal faujdar Shah Quli Khan and Raja Bhupat Dev of Jammu campaign against Jagat Singh of Nurpur, and a campaign against Shrinagar in Garhwal led by Khalilullah Khan. Some other pieces of information given in the Dabistan's account of the Sikh Gurus also raise doubt about the text's accuracy. There seems, for example, to be a major problem in the text's chronology: the Dabistan gives the death date of Guru Hargobind as Sunday, twenty February 1655, whereas the chalitru joti joti samavana ka in early Adi Granth manuscripts unanimously give the date Sunday, three March 1644.

We cannot, however, conclude on the available evidence that Har Rai was installed as Guru at Sirmor or that he wrote the quoted shloka in an Adi Granth manuscript on the occasion of his accession to the Guruship. The notice may instead refer to Guru Har Rai's having inscribed an Adi Granth manuscript after a more quotidian act of sitting on the throne of Guruship to give darshan to devotees. The memory of this occasion was presumably preserved in writing in the manuscript in which the shloka was recorded and subsequently copied by later scribes.

Available chronicle accounts of the life of Guru Har Rai do not mention either his having inscribed a copy of the Adi Granth or his having composed any poetry during his Guruship. Both early and later chronicles agree, however, that the singing and recitation of the bani of his predecessors was a prominent feature of Guru Har Rai's court. Kesar Singh Chhibbar's Bansavalinama comments on the frequency with which the bani was recited and expounded, a point also emphasized by Saurp Das Bhalla's Mahima prakasha and Santokh Singh's Shri Gurapratapa suraja. Mahima prakasha also narrates three stories that illustrate Guru Har Rai's deep regard for the bani.

In the first, the Guru uses a shard from an old ghee-pot that had been given lustre by the sunlight to explain how the bani brings out a person's hidden qualities. In the second story, repeated in all major Sikh chronicles, Guru Har Rai banishes his eldest son Ram Rai for altering a word in a shloka of Guru Nanak when questioned about its meaning b y the emperor Aurangzeb.

In the third, Guru Har Rai injures his knee while rushing to get off a bed in order to show respect by sitting on the ground when two Sikhs begin to sing the bani. Culture states that a manuscript volume of the bani preserved at Gurdwara Manji Sahib in Kiratpur was given by the Guru to his daughter Rup Kaur on the occasion of her marriage. Thus, while Sikh culture emphasizes the deep respect given to the bani by Guru Har Rai, it does not actually endorse the suggestion that he composed any of his own. It is likely that the act of inscribing a quotation of the works of his predecessors on a manuscript copy of the Granth would not have been recorded in the major chronicles anyway, since there are no chronicle references to substantiate the extant nisanas attributed to the ninth and tenth Gurus. The culture's stress on the Guru's reverence for the bani of his predecessors does, however, increase the likelihood that the notice regarding the inscribed shloka may derive from an actual incident.

The case of the non-canonical compositions attributed to the ninth Guru is somewhat more complex than either that of the shloka attributed to Guru Har Rai or the notice regarding the shloka written by him on an Adi Granth manuscript. The published Adi Granth contains fifty-nine shabads and fifty-seven salokas attributed to Guru Tegh Bahadur. The earliest extant text to contain the ninth Guru's compositions as part of the body of the manuscript is the Dehra Dun volume, which also had Guru Tegh Bahadur's bani as a part of the main text. Most seventeenth-century manuscripts that were written before the addition of Guru Tegh Bahadur's compositions to the Adi Granth have had them added in a later hand, usually in a group at the end of the text but occasionally on new folios or in the margins of the appropriate raga sections.

As is to be expected from so complex a textual history, extant manuscript texts of Guru Tegh Bahadur's bani contain a fair number of variant readings, and raga Jaijavanti, which was used for the first time by the ninth Guru, has been placed in different positions in several manuscript of the Granth. In addition, some texts display differences in the order of salokas and shabads. Where the printed Adi Granth contains twelve compositions by Guru Tegh Bahadur in Sorathi raga. It is not, however clear whether the composition actually appears in any of the texts in which it is cited in the index. There is also some evidence of cross fertilization between the works of Guru Tegh Bahadur and the wider Braj devotional culture: the Guru Tegh Bahadur composition "Pritama jar lehu mana muhi" in Sorathi raga appears with some variant readings in Dhansari raga under the chhapa Surdas in the introductory vinaya section of the printed Surasagara. Without reference to manuscript traditions of the Surasagara, it is impossible to establish at what point this cross-fertilization occurred.

A number of compositions not present in the printed Adi Granth are attributed to Guru Tegh Bahadur in some Banno-version Adi Granth manuscripts. The compositions fall into two groups: two padas in Siri raga and a group of six salokas and a transcribed Persian bait in the shloka vara te vadhika section. Three of the salokas appear in the Dehra Dun manuscript, although all three have subsequently been deleted with hartal (correction paste). All seven verses appear in India Office, London, while six of them appear in an undated manuscript formerly at Gurdwara Dehra Sahib.

The Persian bait quoted and translated in the manuscripts is, in fact, one of the maxims on the conduct of war and battle that occur at the end of the first bab of the seventh-century Persian author Shaikh. Since the Bustan was in the curriculum of north Indian Persian schools, it would have been read and known by all who were literate in the language. As such, the presence of a translation of the verse in some Adi Granth manuscripts underlies the pervasive influence of the Persian culture at all levels of pre-modern north Indian tradition.

It is, however, impossible to attribute with any certainty the Braj translation of the verse. Further, unlike the salokas of Guru Tegh Bahadur in the published text of the Adi Granth, none of the Braj verses given above contains the chhapa Nanak. They cannot therefore be attributed with any certainty to Guru Tegh Bahadur. Although the salokas are therefore of uncertain provenance and occur in only a small number of extant manuscripts, their relatively early date must render them of interest to textual scholars. This is particularly the case with the three salokas found in the Dehra Dun manuscript.

Two Padas: In addition to the salokas given above, there are also two padas attributed to Guru Tegh Bahadur in Siri raga in some manuscripts. The published Adi Granth does not contain any compositions by the ninth Guru in this raga, the first in the text.

The two padas do not seem to be represented in early Adi Granth manuscript traditions and cannot therefore be understood to have borne early associations with Guru Tegh Bahadur. They do, however, have intrinsic interest as examples of compositions associated with the ninth

Guru by some within the eighteenth-century Sikh community: it may be that the compositions were recorded because some scribes or singers felt that the ninth Guru should be represented in the first raga in the Adi Granth.

Alternately, they may represent part of an oral or musical repertoire of non-canonical compositions attributed to the Guru by some within the community.

In sum, then, neither the single shloka attributed to Guru Har Rai nor the padas and salokas attributed to Guru Tegh Bahadur can be said with any certainty to have been composed by them. Nonetheless, all are of significant interest, since at least some sections of the seventeenth- and eighteenth-century Sikh community seem to have accepted them as the Gurus' compositions.

It may well be that the compositions represent part of independent oral or musical repertoires of non-canonical compositions attributed to the Gurus: they may, therefore, be analogous to the oral repertoires of non-canonical compositions attributed to Guru Nanak in janamasakhi accounts of his life. Their inclusion in manuscripts of the Adi Granth shows the concern of scribes to create what they felt were "complete" texts of the Granth and indicates the possibilities for variation present in manuscript traditions of the Granth even into the eighteenth century.

In particular, the shloka attributed to Guru Har Rai and the notice recording a verse written by him in an early manuscript underline the neglect by textual scholars of seventeenth-century Lahore version manuscripts of the Adi Granth, while the compositions attributed to the ninth Guru hint at the issues created by the complex and varied textual histories attendant upon adding his work to the Adi Granth.

In addition, the association of one of the salokas with Shaikh Bustan reflects the importance of Persian literature in pre-modern north India and the prevalence of borrowings from that culture at all levels of literary and popular tradition.

Neither the shloka attributed to Guru Har Rai nor the compositions associated with Guru Tegh Bahadur solve any textual problems; indeed, they raise new ones. Further work on Adi Granth textual traditions is likely to yield new data and to enrich the study of the relationship between the manuscript texts and traditions of the Adi Granth.

REFERENCES

Anant, L. B. Ram: *Kabir Granthavali*. Delhi: Regal Book Depot, 1968.

Bahura, Gopal Narayan: ed. *The Padas of Surdas*. Jaipur: Maharaja Savai Man Singh II Museum, 1982.

Callewaert, Winand M, and Bart Op de Beeck: eds. *Devotional Hindi Literature*. Vol. 1. New Delhi: Manohar, 1991.

Callewaert, Winand M.: and Mukund Lath, eds. *The Hindi Padavali of Namdev*. Delhi: Motilal Banarsidass, 1989.

Chahil, Pritam Singh: *Shri Guru Granth Sahib*. New Delhi: Crescent Printing, 1995.

Chaturvedi, Parashuram: *Kabir Sahitya ki Parakh*. Alahabad: Bharati Bhandar, 1964

Coward, Harold: *Sacred Word and Sacred Text: Scripture in World Religion*. New York: Orbis Books, 1988.

Ganda Singh: "Nanak Panthis from the Dabistan-i-Mazahib. " *Punjab Past and Present*, 1967.

Gandhi, Surjit Singh: *Perspectives on Sikh Gurdwara Legislation*. New Delhi: Atlantic Publishers, 1993.

Gangoly, O. C.: *Rags and Raginis*. Bombay: Nalanda Publications, 1935.

Gonda, J.: *Mantra Interpretation in the Satpatha-Brahmana*. Leiden: E. J. Brill, 1988.

Gopal Singh: *Shri Guru Granth Sahib*. 4 vols. Delhi: Gurdas Kapur and Sons, 1960–1962.

Grewal, J. S.: *Guru Nanak in History*. Chandigarh: Punjab University, 1979.

Grewal, J. S.: *The Sikhs of the Punjab*. New York: Cambridge University Press, 1990.

Gupta, Mataprasad: ed. *Kabir Granthavali*. Alahabad: Lokbharati, 1969.

McLeod, W. H.: "Guru Nanak and Kabir. " *Proceedings of the Punjab History Conference*. Patiala: Punjabi University, 1965.

McLeod, W. H.: "Hakikat Rah Mukam Raje Sivanabh ki. " *Proceedings of the Punjab History Conference.* Patiala: Punjabi University, 1969.

McLeod, W. H.: *Guru Nanak and the Sikh Religion.* Oxford: Clarendon Press, 1968.

McLeod, W. H.: *The Evolution of the Sikh Community: Five Essays.* Oxford: Clarendon Press, 1996.

Pashaura Singh: "An Early Sikh Scriptural Tradition: The Guru Nanak Dev University Manuscript 1245. " *International Journal of Punjab Studies*, 1994.

Pashaura Singh: "Scriptural Adaptation in the Adi Granth. " *Journal of American Academy of Religion*, 1996.

Pashaura Singh: "The Text and Meaning of the Adi Granth. " Ph. D. diss., University of Toronto, 1991.

Piar Singh: *Gatha Shri Adi Granth and the Controversy.* Grandledge, Mich.: Anant Education and Rural Development Foundation, 1996.

7

Teachings

Sikh beliefs conform to neither Western nor Eastern standards. Sikhs believe in Universal Love above all else, as the key to Truth. The law of karma and the cycle of birth and death including reincarnation is also a central teaching. Sikhs believe in a single Supreme God, who is within and outside of all, and refute idolatry. The basic teachings of Sikhism are to earn an honest living, to share ones earnings, and to contemplate on the essential truth, the Name.

The Sikh religion prohibits idolatry, the observance of a caste system, and the use of alcohol or tobacco. Sikhs also avoid meat that is not humanely slaughtered, and prefer a vegetarian diet. Kosher and Halal meats are forbidden because they are believed to be inhumanely slaughtered.

Sikhism "Deep within the self is the light of God. It radiates throughout the expanse of his creation and through the teachings of Guru all the darkness of spiritual ignorance is dispelled", these words elucidate the honest wisdom of Sikhism. A progressive religion well ahead of its time when it was founded over 500 years ago, The Sikh religion today has a following of over 20 million people worldwide and is ranked as the worlds fifth largest religion. The word 'Sikh' in the Punjabi language means 'disciple', Sikhs are the disciples of God who follow the writings and teachings of the Ten Sikh Gurus. The wisdom of these teachings in Shri Guru Granth Sahib is practical and universal in their appeal to all mankind. Sikhism preaches a message of devotion and remembrance of God at all times, truthful living, equality of mankind and denounces superstitions and blind rituals. Sikhism is open to all through the teachings of its 10 Gurus enshrined in the Sikh Holy Book and Living Guru, Shri Guru Granth Sahib. The Sikh religion believes in only one God who has no form and no relative as well.

Sikhism is wholly an Indian religion in the sense that its founders were all of Indian origin. Secondly its religious scripture and teachings are wholly Hindu. Sikhism fully subscribes to the fourfold principles of Karma-Samsara-Jnana-Mukti. Sikhism is marked out as a Guru-centered religion much more than any other Indian culture. Guru is given a place of great importance in Nyaya, Advaitism, Nathismand, Kabirpanth, but the Guru is held in the highest esteem in Sikhism. Unlike any other form of Hinduism, it enjoins upon the Sikhs to fight against social injustice and in defence of one's faith.

SPIRITUAL TEACHINGS

Sikhism is an organized religion predominant in the state of Punjab in India. It is an offshoot of radical Hinduism and mystic Sufi traditions pravelent during the fifteenth century onwards.

Sikhism is thought to have started from the teachings of an Indian mystic, Guru Nanak. Many saints in that period taught against the institutionalization of the Hindu religion and against the hegemony of the priestly classes which divided people based on caste, profession, etc. In orthodox Hinduism, the role and the place in the social ladder of a person is strictly determined by his profession and his caste (which in many cases is also based on race). Orthodox Hindus of that period also had an elabourate priestly class (membership to which was obviously restricted by race, caste or lineage) which wanted to maintain its power and control over people. Spiritual and mystic saints of that period, who had no agenda to divide people, rebelled against these aspects of society.

They saw the corruption that institutionalized religions lead to and propagated a message of equality, of personal effort and devotion, of the importance of individual experience, and of the authority of an experienced teacher rather than of books, idols, pilgrimages or rituals. Most saints of that period were born in orthodox Hindu and Muslim families. Many of them, after having mystical experiences, rejected the lies being perpeterated by the religious and political rulers of that time. They formed a close group of disciples which carried on their traditions. Due to their egalitarian outlook, many people from the working classes converted to their teachings.

One of these mystics, Guru Nanak Dev daringly rebelled against the prevailing rituals and exhorted his disciples to chant the God's name to have a mystical experience instead of following any rituals or priests. There were many contemporaries of Nanak who gave the same message but in his case, a lineage started. From his close disciples, Nanak appointed a successor to carry on his message.

The second teacher, Lehna (known after his appointment as Guru Angad Dev) carried on Nanak's message and stressed on divinity within a household existence (instead of the prevailing custom of leaving home and family for the life of a hermit).

Lehna appointed the paternal uncle of his son-in-law, Amar Das Bhalla as the third Guru. Amar Das was again born in a Hindu family and regularly went for pilgrimages to Haridwar and Jwalamukhi. He was however, radical in his outlook and gave a message of social and gender equality and the abolition of cruel customs like Sati.

Amar Das nominated his son-in-law, Ram Das Sodhi, as the fourth Guru. Ram Das, at the end of his life, nominated his youngest son, Arjun Sodhi (reverentially called Guru Arjun Dev) as the fifth Guru. Arjun Sodhi compiled the writings of many mystics including the first four Gurus and his own, into a combined text called the "Adi Granth". Apart from establishing a scriptural text, he put in place many other ritual and institutional measures amongst his disciples: Establishing a holy shrine in Amritsar (now known as the Golden Temple), authoring of prayers to be recited regularly at certain times of the day, founding of the towns of Tarn Taran, Kartarpur and Hargobindpur (the last named after his son), establishing an organizational structure of masands (authorized teachers), etc.

These measures, and some other political acts (such as helping the King's detractors) were justifiably seen as the formation of another political power center and the Guru was imprisoned, tortured and killed by the Mughal King Jehangir. Before he died, Arjun Dev, nominated his son Hargobind (aged only eleven) as the sixth Guru and exhorted him to start forming an army against the regime. Hargobind Sodhi founded the Sikh seat of power, the Akal Takht. He also started behaving like a regular king with a court, royal regalia, etc. Due to his miltiary overtures and some petty squabbles with the Mughal King, he was imprisoned many times and fought many battles.

Hargobind Sodhi formed the distinct identity of Sikhs as a warrior class. He had four sons. The eldest of them, Gurditta Sodhi, died when he was 24. As was common in patriarchy at that time, the eldest son used to be the successor of a King. If he is dead, then either the next eldest son or one of the grandsons from the eldest sons are the next candidates. Hargobind called the eldest son of Gurditta, Dhir Mal, to receive the succession but Dhir Mal did not come. The throne thus passed to the second son of Gurditta, Har Rai Sodhi.

Har Rai Sodhi continued to wield temporal power over the disciples and subjects. When time came to name his successor, his eldest son, Ram Rai Sodhi, disappointed him and he nominated his younger son (or the younger son was implicitly nominated after his fathers' death), Harkishan Sodhi (then only five years old) to be the next King. However, Harkishan died of smallpox when he was only eight years old.

Several stories abound as to how the ninth Guru was chosen but the fact that Teg Bahadur was a son of the sixth Guru, Hargobind had an obvious bearing on the matter. He was appointed the ninth Guru amidst much squabbling.

Aurangzeb, the last Mughal King, wanted the Kashmiri Pandits to convert to the Muslim faith. Teg Bahadur helped the Pandits keep their faith (he challenged Aurangzeb to convert him first) and infuriated Aurangzeb. He was tortured and killed by Aurangzeb. He had nominated his son Gobind Rai Sodhi to be the tenth Guru and King.

Gobind Rai was only nine years old when he became the Guru. He was a poet as well as a warrior and fought many guerrilla battles with Aurangzeb's army. He had four sons, all of whom died in his conflicts with Aurangzeb. Guru Gobind Rai instituted the baptising ceremony of Sikhs, gave them a distinct identity of being turbaned with long hair and beards, and instituted many other rules and rituals (giving every Sikh man and woman the last name of Singh and Kaur, respectively).

The drive for mystical salvation had become a social, political and military movement. The focus shifted completely from salvation to social justice.

Today Sikhism is an organized religion, with its own scriptures, rituals, temples, places of pilgrimage, code of conduct, division between Sikhs and non-Sikhs, a distinct identity, a corrupt priest class, huge donations at the altars for worldly gains, and so on. Sikhs used to be easily identifiable by their turbans and full flowing beards.

The basic tenets of Sikh spirituality are orthodox as well as modern as that of any other Indian religion: A timeless, formless, eternal God. Rebirth, reincarnation, sins and pieties, singing of hymns and asking for blessings and forgiveness, chanting and reading the holy book as the principle spiritual practices, protesting pedantry and pretensions, having a moral code of conduct, hagiography and miracle tails about the Gurus, the concepts of baptising, blasphemy, of being an apostate and a fallen Sikh, of holy water and holy baths.

What Gurus preached, practiced, and lived is Sikh religion. The purpose of the incarnation of the Gurus, their life samples and cause for which they died is glorious religion - Sikhism. The divinity which flowed like nectar from their holy lips is most luminous and eternal Sikh scripture called Shri Guru Granth Sahib. Sikhism is nothing else but the glowing purest of the pure lives lived by our Great Gurus in this darkest of the dark age of kalyug.

When the God almighty desires to establish a new dharma in the deteriorating scenario in humanity, descent of the almighty and all-compassionate Lord becomes inevitable. His most beloved ones thus incarnated in human garb then establish the kingdom of God in the midst of the perishable and sinking humanity. Those Incarnations set the highest examples of truth, purity and sacrifice, thereby opening new frontiers of reaching the Almighty and chart out hitherto unexplored tracks and paths reaching out to the ultimate reality. What was thus established by Great Gurus is Sikh religion and what was so gloriously followed in their Holy footsteps is Sikh way of life – Sikhism.

REDEMPTION

In order to attain redemption one must live honest life and meditate on God. Sikhism shows the way to attain redemption and become one with God. Sikhism instructs that you do not have to fast, abstain, go on renunciation, or enter a monastery in order to meet God. All you have to do is have faith, recites the name of God and remember him for each possible moment. Guru Ji themselves got married and lived a family life and showed everyone that you can meet God while living a family life. Furthermore, teachings says that your mind has to be detached from this world, you have to look this world as a temporary place, you will not be here forever, one day you will have to die. What you do while you are alive is critical, so make your decisions wisely. Furthermore, you do not have to detach yourself from this world physically, you can lead a normal family life and still be able to meet God. The life to lead in order to attain redemption is clearly explained by Ninth Guru Guru Teg Bahadur. He said:

Mortals are attached to this fake world and are not detached from it even for a moment. Your wealth, your spouse and everything you posses, which you think as of your own, Nanak says, the truth is that none of them shall go along with you at the time of your death. Mortal view this world as his own, but nothing here belongs to him. Mortal's consciousness dwindles all the time because of money and among millions is one, who actually remembers God. Mortal have not enchanted the praises of Lord and have wasted all of his life. Mortals do not remember the name of Lord, and are completely drenched in money. All naïve and foolish mortals are worried about money. Nanak says, without reciting the name of Lord, this life is useless. Without reciting the name of Lord, you shall be caught in the cycle of birth and death again. For the one who does not recite the name of Lord, the use of his body is no greater than that of any animal that walks on this earth. Nanak says, everything is useless without reciting the name of Lord.

The one who goes to pilgrimages, sustain fast, make donations and by doing so take pride in his mind. His actions are like of an elephant that takes bath in the river and rolls in mud. Mortals are made of flesh and blood and consider themselves intelligent and clever. Mortals are very proud of their body; it all perishes in an instant. Nanak says, the mortals who have recited upon the Name of Lord wins upon this world.

Be aware of three phases of life, childhood, youth and old age. Youth passes away in no time and you shall attain an old body. Mortal wished never to die but death came upon him. Mortal plotted to deceive it but death stood on his very own threshold. Nothing comes in mind when you are old and death stand at your threshold. Mortals did not do what they were suppose to, and remained entangled in greed. Says Nanak, all the time has passed away, mortal did not worship God, then and why is he crying now? Mortal have not loved the One who gave him the body and wealth. Mortal's head shakes, feet stagger, and eyes become dull and weak. Nanak says, this is the condition mortals face, and why still they do not recite the Name of Lord? Nanak Says, O my naïve friend, when death is near you, you shake and tremble helplessly. Have you recited the Name of Lord, you would not have feared death. Nanak says, human body is hard to attain, do not waste it. Mortals have numerous friends in good time and none in bad. Nanak says, tell your conscience to recite the Name of Lord, and He shall be your companion in the end (at the time of death).

God has given you body, wealth, peace, and house to live. Nanak says, why don't you recite the name of Lord? Lord is the only giver of peace and happiness, and there is none else. God is the savior of sinners. He is the destroyer of fear, eradicator of evil-mindedness and the protector of every orphan. Nanak says, He always resides near you, make an attempt to know Him. Immerse your mind in Him, just like the fish in the water and you shall not be caught in the cycle of birth and death again. Always recite the One, by reciting whom you attain redemption. And redemption is attained only by reciting the name of God. Your dignity lies in merging in the one whom you originated from. Nanak says, tell your conscience to recite the name of Lord, and you shall be able to meet Him.

The one who is not affected by happiness, pain, greed, emotional attachment and egotistical pride. The one who is beyond praise and slander, and treats iron and gold alike. The one who is not touched by pain or pleasure, and treats his friends and enemies alike. The one who does not terrorize anyone and neither is afraid of anybody. The one who leaves all the materialistic things, renounces wealth and have detached himself from this world. The one who recites the name of God day and night, Nanak says, that person is the one who knows what is redemption, that person becomes spiritually aware, that is the person whose future is bright and that person becomes the image of Lord. The truth is that by become the image of Lord it means that there remains no difference between God and that individual. Just like a drop of water merges in the ocean.

Mortals have wandered lost and confused through countless lifetimes and yet they have not overcome the fear of death. Nanak says, tell your conscience, reciting the name of Lord, and you shall merge in the fearless Lord.

All mortals in this whole world roam around like beggar; Lord is the giver of all. Nanak says, by reciting Him in the heart, all work comes to completeness. The ones who always long happiness should start reciting the name of Lord. Tell you tongue to recite the Name of Lord and tell your ears to hear the Name of Lord. Says Nanak, tell your conscience if you do so, you shall not be caught in the cycle of birth and death ever. Consider this world just like a dream. Nothing here is true besides God. Says Nanak, tell your conscience that all mortals are created in this world just like ripples on the water, who comes in existence and fade away all the time. Nanak says, nothing in this world is yours.

You should be worried if death was to wipe only you. But this is the condition everyone in this whole world has to face, no one is stable here. The one who has taken birth has to die; everyone has to perish. The world and its affairs are totally fake, be aware of this my friend. Just like a sand castle, this world will not last long. This world is like a dream, nothing lasts forever here. Nanak says, this is the time to sing praises of Lord and give up all entanglements. Nanak says, stable is the worshipper of God, enshrine this in your mind. Stable is the Name of Lord and stable is Lord. Says Nanak, rare are ones who have enchanted the praises of Lord.

Whenever a mortals who recites the name of Lord loses strength and is caught in worldly means and cannot do anything at all to save himself. He then asks God for help, God helps him with the strength which is greatest of all. Then he regains his strength and is able to do forsake this world. He knows that the almighty God is with him. Nanak says, everything is in the hand of God; He is the greatest saviour and protector. Nanak has enshrine the Name of Lord in his heart and he says there is nothing else equivalent to it. Its His Name by reciting all the troubles disappear and Lord Himself come in appearance.

DEVOTION TO GOD

Guru Nanak describes the attributes of God in the prayer, Japji, There is but one God. His name is True and Everlasting. He is the Creator, Fearless and without Enmity, the Timeless Form, Unborn and Self-existing. Sikhism rejects the theory of incarnation. God does not take birth. He is self-existent and not subject to time; He is eternal; He can be realized through the teachings of a spiritual guide or Guru, but such a guide must be perfect. Sikhism believes in a personal God. The devotee is compared to a bride yearning for union with her husband and waiting on his pleasure to do his bidding.

The Gurus have called God by different names-Ram, Rahim, Allah, Pritam, Yar, Mahakal. There is no such thing as a God of the Hindus or a God of the Muslims. There is the Only One God who is a presence, and is called WaheGuru by the Sikhs.

He is present in all things and yet they do not cover His limitless expanse. When God is seen through the universe, we think of him as Sargun(Quality); when we realize His transcendence, we think of Him as Nirgun(Abstract). God is both in and above the universe. God is the Whole and the world a part of that Whole. A complete knowledge of God is impossible. Guru Nanak says, "Only one who is as great as He, can know Him fully." We can only have some glimpses of Him from His works. The universe is His sport in which He takes delight. The world is a play of the Infinite in the field of the finite.

By His order, all forms and creatures came into existence. It is the duty of man to study the laws of the universe and to realize the greatness and glory of the Supreme Being. He has created an infinite number of worlds and constellations. The world in which we live is a small atom as compared to other worlds. Scientists like James Jeans, Hoyle and Narlikar have confirmed this theory.

There are atheists who deny the existence of God. They are in a way free from moral rules and the stings of conscience. However, the atheist finds no meaning and purpose of life. He misses the inspiration and consolation of religion. He misses the companionship of God and Guru, and has, no future to hope for.

Again, there are agnostics who are not certain about God, because they do not wish to get 'involved'. They fear that religion may entail austerity and sacrifice. Such people regard religion as a gamble and are not prepared to take the plunge. In Sikhism, the belief in the existence of God is a must. The disciple knows that God is knowable, but is not known to him. It is for him to study the scriptures and follow the instructiosn of the Guru to learn about God. A thorough knowledge, serious effort and steadfast devotion are necessary.

Moreover having a belief in God turns men's minds to His qualities: love, justice, charity, mercy, peace, wisdom, truth, goodness and beauty. When we meditate on His qualities, we imbibe often unknowingly some of these traits. Throughout the ages, prophets have given their concepts of the Creator. To the Christians, God is revealed as a Trinity: God, His son Jesus and the Holy Ghost. The Hindus accept the theory of incarnation and affirm that God appears in human form to save the world at the times of crisis. Islam believes in the one God who gave his message to Mohammed the Prophet. Ths Sikh Gurus emphasise the unity of God. He is the Creator, Sustainer and Destroyer. He manifests himself as Nam, "The Truth" and "the Word".

Undoubtedly, you can live without a belief in God. You can inflate your ego. But the spirit will remain stunted and starved. You can develop the spirit only through spiritualiy, which means pracitising a devotion to God. God does not insist that we worship him. Some people are under the impression that God, just like an army commander, demands respect and worship. God does not need man's flattery or praise. Guru Nanak says: "If all people start praising Him, it will not make the least difference to His greatness." Just as the sun does not need light of the lamps so in the same way, God does not need the praises of men.

People worship Him from a sense of duty, Dharma. They are convinced that God who made this universe can be known and loved. Those who know His nature and qualities are wonder-struck by His greatness. In their ecstasy, they exclaim "WahGuru", Wonderful Lord. They want to love Him as devotedly as a wife loves her husband.

Moreover, many people feel that human life is the supreme opportunity for spiritual attainment. A worldly man who makes no effort towards spirituality stands in great danger of joining the cycles of birth and death. A sense of spiritualiy is a sheet-anchor for the individual. It gives purpose and meaning to life. Guru Arjan writes in The Sukhmani Sahib, "The seed of the Lord's Divine knowledge is in every heart." Thus, a sense of emptiness may be replaced by a sense of richness. Only those who are egoistic and wallow in their material possessions, refuse to accept the comfort of divinity.

Man is not potentialy evil, but is weak and ignorant. When temptation faces him, he is likely to succumb to it. At that moment, he needs a support, an inspiration. If he remembers his divine essence and calls on his moral courage, he will get the necessary strength to overcome the temptation. A positive approach to God will yield results. Union with God is our goal. Truth, Goodness, Beauty, Love, Purity, Peace, Wisdom, Justice, Mercy etc. are the ladder to Him. By concentrating on these qualities, we through auto suggestion, imbibe such qualities. Man rises to God, while God stoops to lift man.

ETHICAL ACTIONS

Family life is central to Sikhism, and extended families will have a male or female head (one of the senior members). Sikhism emphasizes love and care for one another. The family is a broad network of support, advice, and practical help to all its members.

Marriage is the preferred state for Sikhs. Many marriages are arranged, and are seen to unite two families. The choice is made from a similar caste because the couple will then be matched in social grouping and expectations. Officially, the giving of dowries is forbidden in India and by Sikhs, but social custom is still sometimes strong. The practices of suttee (a widow throwing herself on her husband's funeral pyre), female infanticide, and purdah (separation and seclusion of women) are all strictly forbidden for Sikhs. Widows are allowed to remarry, and marriage with other faiths is allowed if it does not require conversion of the Sikh. In cultural cultures, Sikh women are expected to remain at home foliowing marriage. However, this is changing, and some Sikh women continue with their chosen careers after marriage. The cultural differences between countries, and the interaction between culture and modernity, continue to change the way Sikhism is practiced around the world.

Sexual expression is considered a natural part of marriage, and Sikhs are expected to avoid sex before marriage and adultery. Some aspects of society - for example, pornography and prostitution - are seen as wrong and likely to lead to unacceptable behaviour. Young men and women are often kept apart until they are married, to help them to avoid temptation. Traditionally, homosexuality is seen as unacceptable, particularly because it is not seen to fit into the Sikh concept of family life. Contraception is acceptable to Sikhs, who do not think of sex as simply for procreation. However, operations such as sterilization are considered to harm the body, and are only acceptable if necessary because of risks to health. Abortion is unacceptable within Sikh teaching. Divorce is permitted but not common. The extended family usually attempts to help couples reconcile their differences. After divorce, both the man and the woman are allowed to remarry.

Sikhism holds that all religions are different paths to the same destination. Many Hindu and Muslim verses are included in the Guru Granth Sahib. Sikhs should not offend other faiths, and should accept the equality of all. This is one of the reasons why only vegetarian food is served in the langar (communal kitchen of the Gurdwara), so that a person of any religion might visit and be able to eat without embarrassment.

Sikhs believe that the body is given by God, and should be looked after and maintained in its natural state as far as is possible. Drugs, tobacco, and alcohol are strictly forbidden (according to the teachings of the Adi Granth 554). Cutting or shaving of any body hair is forbidden, as is dyeing grey hair. Most men and some Khalsa women wear a turban, which marks that they are Sikh, and most Sikhs wear a steel bracelet (kara), a symbol of God's unity and eternity. Halal meat is forbidden, and some Sikhs are vegetarian.

Everything given, Sikhs believe, is given to God, and Sikhs are taught to give a tenth of their savings to charity, and not to discriminate between potential recipients. Giving of labour, resources, and general abilities is central to the practice of Sikhism. Learning to give begins in the Gurdwara, where everyone joins in all the tasks of sweeping, cleaning, and cooking, for the good of the whole community. Care of people in need is important; Guru Nanak set up a centre for the care of lepers, and Sikhs today are taught to provide for the needy in charitable service to others. Guru Nanak's teaching on sewa helped to change the attitudes of some of the

Hindus of his time, who believed that suffering was an unchangeable part of karma, and that helping people of a different caste would make them impure. Sikhs have been known to offer food and aid to people on both sides of battle lines, and to give aid to groups of people in need regardless of their ethnic or religious background.

Sikhism strongly opposes any form of oppression or tyranny, and Sikhs are obligated to defend the weak. However, if all attempts at reconciliation and peace between nations have failed, defence by fighting is considered appropriate, and is called a Dharam Yudh, a war in defence of righteousness. It must be undertaken as a last resort, and must not be fuelled by wishes of revenge. Civilians must be unharmed, no property taken, people must not be humiliated, nor their places of worship desecrated, and the least force necessary must be used.

Sikhism teaches that the soul does not die, and that its future course is governed by current actions. People who do not choose to improve their actions will be reborn endlessly, and will suffer from a sense of being distant from God.

MESSAGE OF HARMONY AND LOVE

The message of oneness of God and universal kinship of humankind of Guru Granth Sahib serves as a model for harmony and world peace. It promotes inter-faith dialogue and spiritual elevation of all humankind. Its message of love and peace continues to inspire the generations.

Sikhism is, in principle, a casteless society. But in fact it is religionless society, which condemns the barriers of all religions. Sikhism believes in equality of religions and respects them as different paths for salvation, and does not categorize any religion as superior or inferior. Simultaneously, it does not associate with any of them, as it condemns any barriers for mankind what so ever. There is a peculiarity in the peace-loving, spiritual and social teachings of Sikhism that goes hand in hand against the oppression of humanity by the upper castes, society and State.

REFERENCES

Badan Singh, Giani: ed. *Adi Shri Guru Granth Sahib Ji Samik (Faridkot valalika).* 4 vols. Patiala,

Dil, Balbir Singh: *Amar Kavi Guru Amardas.* Patiala: Punjab Language Department, 1975.

G. B. Singh: *Shri Guru Granth Sahib dian Prachin Bi[an.* Lahore: Modern Publications, 1944.

Ganda Singh: ed, ed. *Hukamname.* Patiala: Punjabi University, 1985.

Ganda Singh: ed. *Punjab, 1849–1960 Bhai Jodh Singh Abhinandan Granth,* Ludhiana: Punjabi Sahitt Academy, 1962.

Grewal, J. S.: *Sikh Ideology Polity and Social Order.* New Delhi: Manohar, 1996.

Hans, Surjit: *A Reconstruction of Sikh History from Sikh Literature.* Jalandhar: ABS Publications, 1988.

Harbans Singh: *The Heritage of the Sikhs.* New Delhi: Manohar, 1983.

Jodh Singh, Bhai: *Bhai Jodh Singh Gadd Saurabh.* Ed. Piar Singh. Patiala: Punjabi University, 1986.

Joginder Singh: *Japji de like.* Jalandhar: Hindi Press, 1981.

Kalal, Koer Singh: *Gurbilas Patishahi 10.* Ed. Shamsher Singh Ashok. Patiala: Punjabi University, 1986.

McLeod, W. H.: *Sikhism.* New York: Penguin, 1997.

Mishra, Bhagavatsvarup: ed. *Kabir Granthavali.* Agra: Vinod Pustak, 1969.

Mishra, Bhagirath, and Rajnarayan Maurya: eds. *Sant Namdev ki Hindi Padavali.* Pune: Pune University, 1964.

Nahar Singh: "Some Documents regarding Sacred Sikh Relics in England. " *Punjab Past and Present,* 1974.

Nikki-Guninder Kaur Singh: *The Name of My Beloved.* San Francisco: Harper SanFrancisco, 1995.

Nirankari, Surinder Singh: ed. *Nirankari Gurmati Prarambhata.* Amritsar: Young Men's Association, 1951.

Pritam Singh: ed. *Sikh Concept of the Divine.* Amritsar: Guru Nanak Dev University, 1985.

Qaiser, Iqbal: *Historical Sikh Shrines in Pakistan.* Lahore: Punjabi History Board, 1998.

Sahib Singh: *Bhagat BaGi Samik.* Amritsar: Singh Brothers, 1974.

Sainapati: *Shri Gur Sobha.* Ed. Ganda Singh. Patiala: Punjabi University, 1988.

Santokh Singh, Bhai: *Shri Gurpratap Suraj Granth*. Vol. 6. Ed. Bhai Vir Singh. Amritsar: Khalsa Samachar, 1963.

Seva Singh: *Shahid Bilas*. Ed. Giani Garja Singh. Ludhiana: Punjabi Sahitt Academy, 1961.

Sevadas: *Parchi Patishahi Dasvin ki*. Ed. Piara Singh Padam. Patiala: Kalam Mandir, 1988.

Shan, Harnam Singh: *Guru Granth Sahib di Koshkari*. Patiala: Punjab Language Department, 1994.

Sikh Itihas Research Board: Shiromani Gurdwara Prabandhak Committee, 1982.

Suri, Sohan Lal: *Umdat-ut-Tvarikh*, daftar III. Trans. V. S. Suri. Delhi: S. Chand and Company, 1961.

Suri, Sohan Lal: *Umda-ut-Tvarikh*, daftar IV. Trans. V. S. Suri. Chandigarh: Punjab Itihas Prakashan, 1972.

Teja Singh, and Ganda Singh: *A Short History of the Sikhs*. Patiala: Punjabi University, 1989.

Vaudeville, Charlotte: *A Weaver Named Kabir*. Delhi: Oxford University Press, 1993.

8

Moral Value System

People who are suffering can look into the teachings of Sikhism, which will give them hope and courage and allow them to once again become useful members of the society. Besides these ceremonies, Sikhs are also encouraged to organize prayer ceremonies such as Akhand Path, a non-stop cover to cover reading of the Guru Granth Sahib or Sukhmani da Path to commemorate joyous occasions such as births, marriages or when moving into a new house. This rise in divorces has caused a lot of social problems, especially among teenagers and young children. During the ceremony, all family members, relatives and friends of the deceased, are encouraged to pay their last respects. Within the holy scriptures of the Guru Granth Sahib, Guru Nanak Dev, the first Guru mentioned and emphasized an important statement regarding morality, "Greater than the Truth is Truthful living". Besides that, Sikhs are supposed to earn an honest living and willingly give help to the poor and the needy sincerely.

Discrimination against women has been a major problem in societies worldwide and is still strongly present in many Asian societies. Besides that, the children themselves will have an opportunity to ask their parents for advice and get help in certain aspects of their lives. Sikhs are encouraged to provide voluntary services such as physical services or donation services. This aspect not only plays an important role in the family but also in the society. Sikh parents are encouraged to teach their children about the disadvantages of consuming alcohol and drugs through Sikhism. These bonds between family members are essential, as it is the basis for building relationships and unity in the society.

Sikhism is a considered to be a practical religion and stresses on the importance of ethics and moral values. These teachings have laid a solid foundation in which Sikhs have looked into from time to time while bringing up their families.

MORAL VALUES

Morals are based on what we believe is right and wrong and they are not negotiable. Many people do not have the morals and values that keep them doing bad things. We do not think that morals have anything to do with sex or gender. When we put someone else's feelings or needs before our own, we feel that we are practicing good ethics. For example, when we have a project to complete and we know that it is important to do it on time, we will not make excuses to procrastinate. Class and race barriers that keep many people in bad situations compound lack of job opportunity and pay equity for some groups in the formal economy. Maybe if we had continued down the wrong path, the feeling would have subsided but, for me, the feeling has always been enough to push me back on the right path. In addition, we will not participate in behaviour that is harmful to someone else just because everyone else is doing it.

In our opinion, morals are mostly about being a good person and treating others well. For example, not everyone believes that it is not all right to steal, cheat, hurt people and commit crimes. If we know, in our heart, that something is wrong, we will not try to come up with reasons to make it right.

The Sikhs must believe in the following moral values:

1. Equality: All humans are equal before God – No discrimination is allowed on the basis of caste, race, sex, creed, origin, colour, education, status, wealth, etc. The principles of universal equality and brotherhood are important pillars of Sikhism.

2. God's spirit: Although all living beings including plants, minerals and animals have been created by God, only the human being contains God's Spirit which is capable of becoming a Gurmukh.

3. Personal right: Every person has a right to life but this right is restricted and has certain duties attached. Simple living is essential. A Sikh is expected to rise early, meditate, and pray, consume simple food and perform an honest day's work, carry out duties for your family, enjoy life and always be positive, be charitable and support the needy, etc.

4. Actions count: Salvation is obtained by one's actions – Good deeds, remembrance of God – Naam Simran, Kirtan, etc

5. Living a family life: Encouraged to live as a family unit to provide and nurture children.

6. Sharing: It is encouraged to share and give to charity 10 percent of one's net earnings.

7. Accept God's will: Develop your personality so that you recognize happy events and miserable events as one – the will of God causes them.

8. The four fruits of life: Truth, contentment, contemplation and Naam, (in the name of God).

MORALITY IN LIFE

Duties imply obligations, to oneself, to the family, to society, to one's country and humanity at large. Some duties are mentioned in the Scriptures and some are laid down by the State. Man has to obey both, because if he infringes them, he will reap the consequences thereof.

Man's duties as an individual includes looking after his body and his health. He must avoid that food and drink which will impair his physical or mental well-being. Moderation is the principle which should guide one's choice in this field. Secondly, man must develop his mind through education and training and be able to earn his living. He must support his family (and his near relatives). Married life is the normal state for an a individual, unless they are either physically or mentally retarded. One must earn his living by fair and honest means. The amassing of wealth by the exploitation of labour is forbidden in Sikhism, Thirdly, one must serve others as far as possible, share one's food and also support projects of public welfare. Voluntary service to the poor and sick are recommended by the Gurus. There are also certain dues required of an individual as the member of an organization. For example Khalsa Sikh has to maintain the Five K's and follow the Khalsa discipline.

The basic principle is that one must so conduct oneself that he sets an example which others can follow. In any event they should behave to others as they expect others to behave towards them. The duties to others may also depend upon the holding of a particular office. As a member of the human family others must be treated with consideration. Neither slander others nor cause mischief nor harm to them. He should be kind not only to his neighbours, but to one and all. He should be ready and willing to help those who are less fortunate than himself and participate in projects of social concern like orphanages, widow's homes and institutions for the care of the sick and the handicapped. There is also a duty to one's superiors like parents, teachers and the Head of the community or the State. One must respect national leaders, obey one's parents and teachers.

Seek the advice of the family elders in cases of need. Teachers should be respected for they give knowledge through teaching and example. Similarly, one must show courtesy and consideration to the aged and the handicapped.

The duties to equals or peers include politeness and cordiality in one's dealings with them. Frankness and fairness will play a large part in oiling-the smooth flow of social life. The duties to one's subordinate include trying to understand their problems~ and being able to sympathize with them in their times of crisis or distress. It is one's duty to help any who seek one's help, even those who on account of shyness may no ask for aid.

Certain religions exclude social morality and the betterment of the environment from the sphere of duty. Sikhism believes in moulding one's environment for moral goals. The Gurus paid a lot of attention to social reform, particularly in abolishing cruel practices like untouchability, infanticide and suttee.'Prudence lies in considering what is right or wrong for society or the social group as a whole. Man has the faculty of discrimination and he also has the capacity to distinguish between good and bad. There are choices or options open to man in many cases and then he must exercise his intellect to find out what is in favour of human sociability and the public good. Sometimes the choice may be difficult, as for example, cultural practice versus moral compliance. In such a case the choice should fàll on the ethical option or the one which promotes the quality of life. The Gurus protested against the tyranny of their Rulers and the corruption of bureaucracy, as well as caste prejudices and rivalries. They exposed the priestly class for their greed and hypocrisy.

It is man's duty to monitor his own environment and raise his voice against inequality and injustice. He must use his power of reason for the betterment of society and the improvement of his surroundings. Prudence would even seem to recommend force, for a good purpose or a moral issue. Similarly, the social practices which promote inequality among men, the segregation of sexes, superstition and pollution, were condemned by the Gurus, They took steps to remove these promoters of inequality and myth. The begging mendicants pretending to holiness were dubbed as social parasites. The Gurus emphasized the use of reason in demolishing social ills and abuses.

Professional duties pertain to the relationship which a professional person has with his client, for example the duty of a doctor to his patient, of a lawyer to his client, of a merchant to his customer, or a landlord to his tenant. Besides there are also the duties of elected representatives or of holders of honorary position like the President of a mutual-benefit Society or the Secretary Trustee, of a temple or a charitable organization.

The general duty of a professional is to discharge his functions efficiently, and with a sense of responsibility and sincerity. He must safeguard the interests of his client and give him the necessary truthful guidance and direction. A doctor's duty to his patient is very delicate, for he is dealing with a human being in trouble, therefore he must give him his undivided attention and greatest professional devotion. He cannot afford to be indifferent or negligent. Similarly it is the duty of a lawyer or attorney to offer sound advice, to his client. He must not prolong the case to make more money or do any thing to obstruct the course of justice. Many litigants get dissatisfied with their legal counsel, because the latter have adopted unfair means to gain advantage from them. Honesty and fair play are the tests of professional competence.

With regard to elected or fiduciary positions, the duties are even more onerous and sensitive. There is an element of morality in such appointments, The representative is duty bound to pay attention to the wishes of the electorate or the people he is supposed to serve. As a trustee, he must safe-guard the interest of the entire group which elected him. He must look after the assets and property of any Trust, as if these were his own. Though law regulates the nature and functions of office-bearers it is important that people in power perform their functions, impartially and with care and integrity. Office bearers must act consciously in the interest of their beneficiaries and man's duty to speak out against the malpractice

Justice as a virtue implies respect for the rights of others. It also stands for fairness and impartiality. The neglect or violation of the rights of others is a moral lapse. The Guru condemned the usurpation of another's right as ineligious like the eating of pork by a Muslim or beef by a Hindu. Delay and the denial of justice, is generally due to greed and selfishness. Justice must be done with a good heart, and not by shedding crocodile tears. Justice lies in apportioning correctly, what is the due of others, even if they have not the courage to ask for it.

In a wider sense, justice means the non-exploitation of others. Unfortunately in our modern competitive society, exploitation is sometimes condoned on - the grounds of the survival of the fittest. Trampling on the rights of others is justified as an ingredient of ambition and go-getting. It is generally agreed that many get rich as quickly as they can, even when this cannot be done without employing dishonest and underhand means. Making a quick buck is an art which involves cunning and trickery. Moreover, in our present-day society, the rich or the strong often get away with it. The Gurus censured the Rulers for looting the peasants and compared it to 'Devouring men at night.' Moreover, justice in its real sense connotes equity and not legalisticism. It forbids preferential treatment to any person, religious or social group. Justice in its essence manifests selflessness or the conquest of the ego, and is one of the means for self realisation.

MORAL VALUES FOR LEADER

Guru Nanak's purpose of truth did not divide the world into spiritual and secular. Political and social order is for him inseparable from the universal order, a divine harmony in which every part has its role to play, its dharma. Humans who forget God, abuse earthly power. The fundamental issue is spiritual, not political. All authority is ultimately God's. From analogy with the Sikhs' conduct of their religious affairs it might be imagined that they disapprove of monarchy or favour democracy. In fact the Gurus never criticised the political system of kingship, only its abuse. After the death of Guru Gobind Singh in 1708 AD., many of his followers flocked to his nominated deputy, Banda Bahadur, and treated him as king.

Throughout the eighteenth century Sikhs fought as members of misals (military groups), each with its chieftain who exercised more or less princely power. More successful than his contemporaries in his pursuit of power, Maharaja Ranjit Singh ruled a united Punjab from 1799 to 1839. Although regarded by some as the golden age of Sikh polity, by others Maharaja Ranjit Singh's period is perceived as one in which Sikhism lost its distinctive character and lapsed into Hinduism. The difference between his reign and that of the eighteenth-century Sikh rulers was one of degree and not of kind.

Authority is God's, and as the Guru uniquely mediates the divine to other human beings, the Guru is the ultimate human authority. During the lives of the ten Sikh Gurus, this spiritual authority was recognized by their followers and evident in a style of sovereignty increasingly parallel to the Mughal rulers' administration. The chauri (an emblem of authority) was waved above the Guru as he gave audience. From at least the time of Guru Arjan Dev, representatives called masands had responsibility for devotees in designated areas (manjis). This reflected Mughal imperial administration and continued until the system was abolished by Guru Gobind Singh. On assuming Guruship in 1606 AD., Hargobind also assumed military leadership - miri (temporal power) - as well as piri (spiritual authority), symbolised by two swords. The Guru was sache padshah, the true emperor.

In 1699 Guru Gobind Singh founded a new model of authority. Guruship was henceforth vested not only in his person but also in his khalsa. This consisted of those Sikhs who had taken amrit (that is, made a distinctive act of commitment) and accepted the responsibilities and identifying marks now required of them. From Guru Gobind Singh's death in 1708, the scriptural compilation of hymns, the Adi Granth, was to be Guru, the Guru Granth Sahib. The Guru Granth Sahib continues to be treated with the external signs of respect due to the highest authority. For example, most Sikh families do not have a complete volume of the scriptures at home, because as Guru it requires an upstairs room to be devoted exclusively to it. A random reading is accepted daily as the Guru's hukam (order, guidance) for the day.

The Guruship of the Khalsa or the Panth has been emphasised less. However, a gurmata, a decision taken by consensus of the congregation in the presence of the Guru Granth Sahib, is binding. This is particularly true of any gurmata taken in the Akal Takht, the building facing the Golden Temple in Amritsar, and issued as an edict (hukamnama) to all Sikhs. A recent instance was the hukamnama issued in 1978 AD. which ordered all Sikhs to boycott the Sant Nirankari sect. At times of crisis during the eighteenth century, the Dal Khalsa (Sikh army) would gather at Amritsar and act on the basis of whatever gurmata was reached. Akal Takht is the principal seat of authority but there are four other Takhts recognized by Sikhs.

For religious purposes, such as administering khande di pahul, the initiation ceremony inaugurated by Guru Gobind Singh in 1699, authority is represented by the panj pyare (five beloved ones), that is, five Sikhs of known orthodoxy and good character. In the Gurdwara all are equal, although only those proficient in reading the Gurmukhi script can publicly read the scriptures and act as granthi. Giani (learned) is the respectful title given to Sikhs proficient in interpreting the Guru Granth Sahib.

There is no priesthood in Sikhism. It is important to realise this, especially as the media and many Sikhs now use the words 'priest' and even 'high priest'. The latter usually refers to the senior jathedar (leader of the panj pyare) at the Akal Takht, Amritsar. A sant is a religious teacher who attracts followers. Some sants wield enormous influence on Sikh religion and politics. Sant Jarnail Singh Bhindranwale in India and Sant Puran Singh (Kerichowale Baba) in Britain are recent, very different examples. Although the election of office holders on Gurdwara management committees is ideally by consensus of the gathered congregation (sangat), individual Gurdwara constitutions differ on the best procedure. In Gurdwaras set up by the followers of a sant, his choice is final.

In accordance with Guru Nanak's insights, both ruler and ruled must be disciplined. The pursuit of power and pleasure leads both astray, and a conflict of interests results. The ruler has, above all others, the task of maintaining justice. He or she must be a person of integrity. Guru Gobind Singh re-emphasised this in his Zafarnama (Epistle of Victory) addressed to the emperor Aurangzeb, reproaching him for his faithlessness in breaking an oath.

When the tenth Guru died, Sikhs had political leaders, but the community (Guru Panth) were careful that they did not have religious powers since the Guru Granth Sahib was the spiritual leader. In the nineteenth century Maharaja Ranjit Singh ruled over an independent Punjab which was not a Sikh state but a place where people were free to practice any religion. He, like any ruler, Sikh or other, could be challenged if they abused their power. The ideal of the Kshatriya or ruler for the Sikh is expressed by Guru Amar Das when he said: 'He alone is a kshatriya who is brave in good deeds. He yokes himself to charity and alms giving. Within the field bounded by the protecting fence of justice he sows seed which benefits everyone'.

MORAL DUTIES OF SUBJECTS

Sikhs must always keep the law if it is in accordance with Sikh principles. However, when those in power are unjust, Sikhs are exhorted to resist the oppression. In the last resort this will possibly involve armed resistance. Unfortunately, acts which one Sikh regards as justified violence against an otherwise immovable oppressive regime can appear to others, Sikh and non-Sikh alike, as irresponsible terrorism. A positive example for Sikhs is Guru Tegh Bahadur who pleaded the cause of the Kashmiri Brahmins to the Mughal rulers and his execution is seen as a death for religious liberty.

A favoured method of drawing attention to injustice is the morcha (campaign), a mass protest, as when Sikhs protested peacefully against the abuse and corrupt managements of their Gurdwara. This led to the passing of the Sikh Gurdwaras Act in 1925. Similarly Sikhs courted arrest in the early 1960s, demanding a state where Punjabi was the officially recognized language.

MORAL VALUES IN SOCIETY

People belonging to different regions and faiths have different customs, habits, and manners. It is therefore necessary that the individual should not be upset by them. He must accept non-conformity and diversity as an inescapable fact of life. However, this does not imply that he should change his stand because of others. He must remain firm in his own convictions and make no compromise on principles; he must control any feeling of prejudice or violence when he sees people whose manners or customs are not to his liking. Racialism is a prevalent disease among the most civilized societies today; it is in fact a form of superiority writ large. Tolerance puts a human and charitable construction on the apparently peculiar conduct of others. The tolerant person does not feel angry or upset.

He keeps his cool in times of excitement or anger. Even if he feels mentally disturbed he will not show his impatience or annoyance. Just as a sensible person tolerates the foolish behaviour of a child, in the same way, the tolerant person will be able to stand ignorance or lack of politeness in others. Why should one expect that others will always behave to us as one wants them to behave? Tolerance accepts dissent and even opposition. This quality is particularly needed by Rulers and religious teachers, because without it, they are likely to allow or condone many follies and atrocities against those who differ from them.

Self-control is necessary in desires, words and actions. It is generally agreed that man's mind runs after lower things as a matter of course. The eyes, the ears, the tongue, the hands and feet are to be used for good purposes to act at the right moment. Temperance is like a fence which prevents one from straying into the wilderness. It is the golden mean between self-indulgence and rigid regimentation. Temperance is just the right way for the householder. He should enjoy the normal comforts and amenities of life, but at the same time, he must keep his passion and desire under control. This self regulation would result in a balanced and harmonious existence.

Chastity or continence, is emphasized in Sikhism, because in the human body lies the divine presence and as such, the body has to be kept clean and perfect. Those things which harm the body or cause sickness and disease have to be scrupulously avoided. Sex is to be limited to one's wife. Pre-marital or extra-marital sex is forbidden to a Sikh. He should consider females older to him as his mother, equal to him as a sister, and younger than him as a daughter. He should never entertain evil thoughts in the company of women. Marriage is a sacrament and the purpose thereof is companionship and help on the spiritual path, rather than sexual enjoyment. The marriage ideal is summed up in the maxim: 'one soul in two bodies.' Fidelity to one's married partner is the essence of continence.

Patience implies forbearance in the face of provocation. Some say that it is natural to be angry, but one should think twice before giving vent to anger. Patience gives moral courage to bear the unexpected, such as sudden hardships and sorrows. It may be noted that saints and great men are tested through the fire of suffering, though they have not done any thing to deserve that suffering. The challenge of life are intended to evaluate the mettle of man. Even the performance of duty may involve the facing of difficulties and personal injury, but that is no excuse for shirking one's duty. One must pray for God's help and grace to overcome the difficulties.

There are people, who are in a position to injure or even to crush their opponents with the power they possess, but they control resentment and anger, because they firmly believe that if another loses his head, they should not lose theirs. Moreover patience keeps their mental faculties in balance. Their minds are tranquil. They do not cry or rail bitterly against their enemies or at God for their misfortunes or deprivation.

Contentment is an attitude of mind which accepts victory or defeat in the same way. A contended man is active; he tries his best to go forward, but he does not despair if he cannot achieve what he wants. Contentment has no place for fear, fatalism, inertia or sloth. Contentment does not mean a compromise with poverty and privation. In the modern world, the common man has opportunities for self-advancement and affluence. He must develop his own potentialities and work hard to move forward; at the same time, he should not become proud through his achievement or feel frustrated in case of failure.

God is the ultimate arbiter of man's destiny, and He will not leave 'an iota of a man's effort uncompensated.' Unfortunately, in this modem competitive world, one seems to keep multiplying one's needs and commitments, in order to keep up with the Jones, thus only adding to one's tensions and difficulties. The contented man knows the limits of his own needs and so does not feel frustrated if he is unable to get what his neighbor or friend has, in spite of his best efforts. Truly conceited people realise the distinctions between means and ends. Wealth and position are the means and not the ends of life. If one has a large amount of wealth, then some must be devoted to the benefit of the community and for altruistic purposes. The hoarding of wealth and the prestige of office are not to be used as means for self-aggrandisement or inflation of the ego.

Detachment implies an ever increasing non-attachment to all things of a material nature. It does not imply renunciation or asceticism or indifference to the world in which we live. It implies devotion to duty and the performance of the chores of daily life. The Sikh serves the family and the community, but he does not get deeply involved in their problems. His attitude is that of a nurse attending a patient. She ministers to their care and comfort, but maintains her distance. Similarly, a Sikh has to live the life of a family man at the same time, he ought to adopt an attitude as that of a trustee in reference to his near and dear ones.

Guru Nanak has given the example of the lotus in the pond which is unaffected by the mud or the movement of the water. In the same way, the 'detached' individual keeps him self away from worldly things. They live in the world, but are not involved in worldliness. They keep their heads high and look to a more spiritual goal.

Here is a story which reveals how detachment is possible in normal life. A Ruler once asked a saint to tell him how he could practice detachment. The holy man told the king that he had just one week more to live, that his death would occur after that. period.

The king believed the holy man, and fearing death, led a good life, doing his duty, avoiding evil things and constantly thinking of his coming death. After the week when he did not die as forecast, the holy man returned to the King's palace and asked him how he has passed the seven days. The king replied that he had spent that period like a traveller in an inn. He had done his duties as usual, but his mind was not involved in the routine. He had avoided doing any thing wrong, fearing that God would call him to account after his end. He had also prayed as much as he could during this period. The holy man told the king that this was what was meant practising detachment in life.

The individual alone, must overcome his own ego and pride. This is most easily done on the path of humility, regarding oneself as the lowest of the low and considering all others as being superior. The humble man, will serve others without material motive or the expectation of reward. He does this through his love of God and man. God is present in every living soul, and therefore to injure the feelings of another person is to hurt the God in him. Those who are vain and the haughty have an inflated ego and as such do not mind exploiting their fellow men. Even some holy men are not free from pride and prejudice. Guru Tegh Bahadur warned pious people of that pride, which is subtle and unobtrusive.

Modesty is generally appreciated as a virtue. Humility is not depreciation of oneself, but rather recognition of one's own faults and of how much one falls short of the ideal. It was a practice among the Sikhs before Guru Gobind Singh, to greet each other by touching the other's feet. This was an expression of the Sikh's humility. In the Sikh religion, the opportunity to touch the feet of saintly beings or even the dust of the feet of the congregation, is regarded as a great blessing.

PRACTICAL ASPECTS

Sikhism recommends an active life in which family has a great role to play. Life of a householder is the best institution to fulfil the Sikh ideal of contributing to the development of the human society. Here the children learn to know the individual as well as the corporate Code of Sikh Conduct through this institution.

Family in Sikhism is a training school for social, cultural, political and spiritual makeup. It is a training school for Seva and charity. From the family of birth, the religious and ethical ideas are implanted in the child. It is worth to mention here that Bhai Mani Singh took all the traits of sacrifice from his forefathers. Guru Arjan Dev implanted the spirit of sacrifice in the wider family by offering his life to upkeep righteousness.

The Sikh families believe in monogamy. The marriages are normally arranged by the parents with consent of the children. Extra-marital and pre-marital relationship is not allowed in Sikh families. Marriage is considered to be a sacrament. According to the concept of Lavan (Marriage hymns), divorce is not encouraged in Sikhism. It is expected of the couple to help and support each other in the family to attain God.

Sikhs believe in Nam Simran while living a family life which has all the elements of love, optimism, laughter, pride, pity, joy, gratitude, respect, purity, service and sacrifice. The concept of family life teaches to love and respect the parents, grand parents and society at large. It cares for the vulnerable. It provides psychological foundation for the future and helps in improving the quality of life. It provides emotional care for its members and opportunity to practice democratic decision making. Sikh family preserves human values, cultural identity and historical continuity.

Those who live in the situations of God loving families, carry with them into society an urge to strive, the ability to work toward an ultimate goal to attain God, an acceptance for the opinions and defects of others, responsibility, good judgment, sense of kinship plus an unshakable belief in the benefits of sharing and co-operation with human beings. All of these family values are needed in to-day's world.

The Sikhs usually live in extended and joint families under one roof. The parents and grand parents take care of their children and grand children. The members of the family help each other economically, socially, psychologically and spiritually. The children are moulded in Godly crucible by the parents who take all the possible measures to develop their personality according to Sikh values of tradition and religion. The children learn from their families about the concept of universal brotherhood and desire to progress as a world unit by praying for universal welfare.

The Seniors or grand parents have a great role to play in make up of the good families. They are head of the families. They have got experience of life. They have gone through the ups and downs in life.

They are the people to pass on to the future generations the values of religion, history, tradition, society and their heritage. They are always seen energetic and doing some or the other thing in Indian society unlike sitting in the rocking chairs. Many a times they work as family counsellors or volunteer professional consultants in the society. They are successful mentors in many families.

The grandparents can be supportive of their married children. These are often the grandparents that tell the night stories which develop an increased sense of familial, social, cultural, historical, and religious heritage in the children. More often, these days, the young parents want their parents to approve of the way they raise their children. Such suggestions sometimes are considered as criticism which prove to be most devastating. Simultaneously it may be kept in view that grandparents do not have evil motives.

Many grandchildren confide more in their grandparents than in their own parents. Children learn the most important things about themselves from the grandparents. Grandparents have bigger lap than the great seas but sometimes the grandparents are accused of spoiling the grand children by raising them in the old fashion or by giving them gifts or being permissive or being too much generous. The Bible says that too much of even a good thing can be taken as bad.

Grandparents and grandchildren often enjoy a special bond. The grandparents many a times influence future of their grandchildren. An ancient proverb says, The crown of old men is the grand children. The grand parents have years of parenting experience under their belts. Having learned from their mistakes, they may be more competent in handling children than they were when they were younger in age. The grandparents bequeath a legacy of happiness, emotional health, increased sense of well-being and morale that benefits everyone in the family and society at large. There is always a payback reward for raising a good family and a nation of outstanding vision.

REFERENCES

Album Central Sikh Museum: Amritsar: Shri Darbar Sahib, 1996.

Archer, John Calrk: "The Bible of the Sikhs. " *Punjab Past and Present*, 1977.

Attar Singh: ed. *Socio-Cultural Impact of Islam on India*. Chandigarh: Punjab University, 1976.

Avtar Singh: *Ethics of the Sikhs*. Patiala: Punjabi University, 1983.

Bachittar Singh: Giani, ed. *Planned Attack on Aad Shri Guru Granth Sahib*. Chandigarh: International Centre of Sikh Studies, 1994.

Banga, Indu: ed. *Five Punjabi Centuries*. New Delhi: Manohar, 1997.

Barque, A. M.: *Eminent Sikhs of Today*. Lahore: Barque and Company, 1942.

Barrier, N. G.: and V. A. Dusenbery, eds. *The Sikh Diaspora: Migration and Experience beyond Punjab*. Columbia, Mo.: South Asia Books, 1989.

Bhagat Singh: *Maharaja Ranjit Singh and His Times*. New Delhi: Sehgal Publishers Service, 1990.

Bhatkhande, V. N. A.: *Comparative Study of Some of the Leading Musical Systems of the 15th, 16th, 17th, and 18th Centuries*. Baroda Indian Musicological Society, 1972.

Bosch, Gulnar K., John Carswell, and Guy Petherbridge: *Islamic Bindings and Book Making*. Chicago: Oriental Institute, University of Chicago, 1981

Grewal, J. S., and S. S. Bal. *Guru Gobind Singh*: Chandigarh: Punjab University, 1987.

Griffin, Lepel H., and Charles Francis Massy: *Chiefs and Families of Note in the Punjab*. Lahore: Punjab Government Press, 1939.

Matringe, Denis: "A study of Saix Farid's verses and Their Sikh Commentaries in the Adi Granth. " In Anna Libera Dallapiccola and Stephanie Zingel-Ave Lallemnat, eds. *Islam and Indian Regions*. Stuttgart: Franz Steiner Verlag, 1993.

McLeod, W. H.: "Guru Nanak and Kabir." *Proceedings of the Punjab History Conference*. Patiala: Punjabi University, 1965.

McLeod, W. H.: *Guru Nanak and the Sikh Religion*. Oxford: Clarendon Press, 1968.

McLeod, W. H.: "Hakikat Rah Mukam Raje Sivanabh ki. " *Proceedings of the Punjab History Conference*. Patiala: Punjabi University, 1969.

McLeod, W. H.: *The Evolution of the Sikh Community: Five Essays*. Oxford: Clarendon Press, 1996.

Nahar Singh: "Some Documents regarding Sacred Sikh Relics in England. " *Punjab Past and Present*, 1974.

Nikki-Guninder Kaur Singh: *The Name of My Beloved.* San Francisco: Harper SanFrancisco, 1995.

Nirankari, Surinder Singh: ed. *Nirankari Gurmati Prarambhata*. Amritsar: Young Men's Association, 1951.

Nirbhai Singh: *Bhagata Namadeva in the Guru Grantha*. Patiala: Punjabi University, 1981.

Nizami, Khaliq Ahmad: "Some Aspects of Khanqah Life in Medieval India. " *Studia Islamica*, 1957.

Smith, Wilfred Cantwell: *What Is Scripture: A Comparative Approach*. Minneapolis: Fortress Press, 1993.

Suri, Sohan Lal: *Umdat-ut-Tvarikh*, daftar III. Trans. V. S. Suri. Delhi: S. Chand and Company, 1961.

Suri, Sohan Lal: *Umda-ut-Tvarikh*, daftar IV. Trans. V. S. Suri. Chandigarh: Punjab Itihas Prakashan, 1972.

Talib, Gurbachan Singh: *Bani of Shri Guru Amar Das*. New Delhi: Sterling Publishers, 1979.

Prajnanananda, Swami: *A Historical Study of Indian Music*. Delhi: Munshiram Manoharlal, 1981.

Pritam Singh: "Keertana and the Sikhs. " *Journal of Sikh Studies*, 1976.

Pritam Singh: "The Translation of the Guru Granth Sahib into Devanagari Script. " *Journal of Sikh Studies*, 1977.

9

Movements

The Sikh religion, which was founded by Guru Nanak, gradually developed into a major religious movement in the sixteenth century. Because of the egalitarian message of the Gurus large number of peasants came into the fold of Sikh faith. Banda Singh Bahadur, a recluse who embraced Sikhism under the influence of Guru Gobind Singh at Nanded in the present Maharashtra, moved to Punjab. He organized the Sikh peasantry who rose in arms against the feudal lords in Punjab and liberated most of the Punjab from the Mughal rule and introduced the concept of peasant-proprietor in Punjab.

While the movement got a temporary setback after the arrest and subsequent torture to death of Banda Singh Bahadur and his followers, the Sikhs organized themselves into fighting brigades and re-emerged in the form of twelve confederacies in the eighteenth century. One of the leaders of these confederacies, Ranjit Singh of the Shukerchakia Misl, conquered Lahore and laid the foundation of a powerful Sikh kingdom in north India which extended from the Khybar Pass in the North-West, Sutlej in the East, China in the north and deserts of Sind in the South. As a result of Sikhs' rise to political power there was qualitative increase in the number of followers of the Sikh faith. Political patronage coupled with economic prosperity created a general sense of inertia and slackness towards religious and moral values among the Sikhs. The ruling class started following practices which were not in keeping with the Sikh culture and teachings of the Sikh Gurus.

To take the Sikh community out of these non-Sikh like practices movements of reform and purification emerged among the Sikhs. The Nirankari Movement, the Kuka or Namdhari Movement, the Singh Sabha Movement and the Akali Movement (1920-25) are some of the important manifestations of reform within Sikhism. A splinter group of the Nirankaris which owes its origin to Buta Singh and has developed as a major sect under the name of Sant Nirankari, is not considered a part or sect of Sikhism and the Sikhs are advised by their leadership not to have any association with this sect. Similarly, another powerful movement of reform known as the Radhaswamis with their headquarters at Beas near Amritsar, is not considered a sect of Sikhism though all the preceptors of this sect happen to be Sikhs as also the majority of their followers. Some of the Saints of late have made serious efforts to restore cultural moral and spiritual values of the Sikh faith but their followers and missions work under the broader theme of Sikhism and cannot be described as separate movements.

RELIGIOUS MOVEMENTS

Nirankari Movement

The Nirankari movement owes its origin to Baba Dayal Das (1783-1855) a bullion merchant of Peshawar (Pakistan). A contemporary of Maharaja Ranjit Singh, this simple God-fearing man assailed the non-Sikh like practices that had entered in the Sikh society, especially in the lifestyles of the elite under Maharaja Ranjit Singh. He vigorously preached against idol-worship and exhorted his followers to worship only the One Nirankar (Formless One). Hence those who followed his teachings came to be known as the Nirankaris. The main focus of the teachings of Baba Dayal was to worship the one formless God popularly called Nirankar and he described himself as Nirankari - the follower of Nirankar.

He preached against the worship of God-men and disapproved of going on pilgrimages or performing other Brahamanical rites and rituals. Baba Dayal got a wide response to his movement of reform within Sikhism from some of the members of the business community from Peshawar and nearby areas. However, when Baba Dayal moved to Rawalpindi he met opposition both from the priestly class as also the Bedi Khatris who claimed to be descendants of Guru Nanak. Baba Dayal and his followers were boycotted both by the Hindus and the Sikhs of Rawalpindi and the neighbourhood. Unmindful of the opposition Baba Dayal continued with his mission of popularising worship of Formless One and introduced several reforms in the Sikh society. Impact of Baba Dayal's teachings on the contemporary Sikh society can be gauged from the fact that Ludhiana Christian Mission which was watching the developments in Punjab after its annexation to the British empire in 1849 took a special note of Baba Dayal's activities as mentioned in its report for the year 1853: Sometime in the summer we heard of a movement... which from the representations we received seemed to indicate a state of mind favourable to the reception of Truth. It was deemed expedient to visit them, to ascertain the true nature of the movement and, if possible, to give it proper direction.

On investigation, however, it was found that the whole movement was the result of the efforts of an individual to establish a new panth (religious sect) of which he should be the instructor... They professedly reject idolatry, and all reverence and respect for whatever is held holy by Sikhs or Hindus, except Nanak and his Granth. They are called Nirankaris from their belief in God as a spirit without bodily form. The next great fundamental principle of their religion is that salvation is to be obtained by meditation on God. They regard Nanak as their saviour, in as much as he taught them the way of salvation. Of their peculiar practices only two things are learned. First, they assemble every morning for worship, which consists of bowing the head to the ground before the Granth, making offerings and in hearing the Granth read by one of their members, and explained also if their leader be present. Secondly, they do not burn their dead, because that would assimilate them to the Hindus; nor bury them, because that would make them too much like Christians and Musalmans, but throw them into the river. In 1851 Baba Dayal founded a Nirankari Durbar four miles outside the town of Rawalpindi which came to be later known as Dayalsar.

After his death Baba Dayal's mission was continued by his eldest son Baba Darbara Singh. The movement gained momentum during Baba Darbara Singh's time. He issued Hukamnamas to his followers as to how should they live their lives according to the teachings of the Sikh Gurus. He quoted extensively from the Guru Granth Sahib and exhorted his followers to lead simple life, keep away from alcohol and idolatrous worship. He also advocated simple marriage and introduced the practice of Anand Karaj. This marriage ceremony, requires four circumambulatory rounds around Guru Granth Sahib while the Ragis sing relevant hymns, called Lavan, from the Guru Granth Sahib. This practice is said to have been introduced by the Sikh Gurus but fell in disuse as a result of growing Brahmanical influence on the Sikh society. It did not gain currency among the Sikhs till the passage of Anand Marriage Act by the Central Legislative Assembly of India in 1909. Concerted efforts of Baba Darbara Singh and his supporters resulted in the Nirankari Movement getting momentum. By the time his brother Baba Ratta succeeded him the number of Nirankaris had risen from sixty one in 1853 to four thousand in 1909. To propagate the teachings of Baba Dayal Baba Ratta organized a network of missionaries called biradars who propagated the message in their respective areas as a labour of love.

The Nirankari Movement had both Keshadharis (those supporting uncut hair) and Sehajdharis (those who did not support uncut hair but had full faith in the teachings of the Sikh faith) among its followers. Their common passion was to live life according to the tenets of Sikh faith and to sing glory of Formless One. Baba Ratta was succeeded by his son Baba Gurdit Singh (1909-1947). During long tenure of Baba Gurdit Singh Nirankari Movement made rapid progress. Several allied organizations such as the Nirankari Balak Jatha, and the Nirankari Youngmen's Association on the pattern of Young Men Christian Association were founded and many pamphlets discussing important issues of Sikh theology giving supporting evidence from Gurbani as interpreted by the predecessors of Baba Gurdit Singh were published. It is interesting to note that during this period the three more powerful manifestations of Sikh reform movements - the Namdhari, the Singh Sabha and the Akali Movement had also played an important role in creating religious, social and political awareness among the Sikhs. Since the Nirankari leaders' main concern was religious renaissance they did not attract any hostility either from the leadership of their successive movements or from the government of the day.

However, the Nirankari Movement got a major setback with the partition of Punjab in 1947 and subsequent migration of the Nirankaris to Indian Punjab. It was only in 1958 that the Nirankaris were able to set up Nirankari Durbar in Chandigarh with Baba Gurbakash Singh as its head. While the original Nirankaris have scattered to such far off places as Bombay and Calcutta, the Sant Nirankari Mission with its head quarters at Delhi has emerged as a powerful movement with large number of followers hailing from different religious traditions although it has nothing in common with the Nirankari Movement started by Baba Dayal.

The Namdhari Movement

Another powerful movement of religious revival and reform that developed within Sikhism was the Namdhari Movement, literally meaning devotees of the Holy Name. They were also called the Kukas because of their practice of screaming while chanting which in Punjabi means kukan. The Namdhari Movement had its birth in the Attari District – the North-West frontier of Punjab. Baba Balak Singh (1797-1862) an inspired soul preached the message of Sikhism which was according to the teachings of the Sikh Gurus – shorn of empty rituals and worldly pomp and show.

Inspired by his simple teachings devout Sikhs from the nearby areas flocked to Baba Balak Singh. Ram Singh (1816- 65) who was then serving in the Sikh army heard of Baba Dayal's teachings and one day went to pay his personal respect to him at Hazro.

The first meeting seems to have electrified the young Ram Singh who decided to leave his job in the army and dedicate the rest of his life to the practice and preaching of the spirituality and simple way of life taught by the Sikh Gurus. Dr. Ganda Singh believes that Baba Ram Singh who became the founder of the Namdhari Movement, is one of the most misunderstood and misrepresented socio-religious leaders of the nineteenth century Punjab. According to him Baba Ram Singh was a religious man and the movement launched by him was a "purely religious movement aiming at the revival of the Sikh faith". Baba Ram Singh believed that the decline in spiritual and moral values among the Sikhs was due to the Sikh elite and custodians of the Sikh shrines going away from the teachings of the Sikh Gurus.

He believed that during the hey days of Maharaja Ranjit Singh's rule Brahmanical rites and rituals had slowly creeped in the Sikh society. Inspired by the example of Baba Balak Singh, Baba Ram Singh started preaching the teachings of the Sikh Gurus. Impressed by his devotion and dedication Baba Balak Singh named Baba Ram Singh as his successor. In keeping with the teachings of earning livelihood through manual work Baba Ram Singh took to cultivation in partnership with some fellow villagers. According to Dr. Fauja Singh, "Baba Ram Singh's life was both of an ideal farmer and an ideal man. He combined in his daily conduct whole-hearted devotion to God, strict observance of morality in everything done and unstinting industry in his chosen profession." Baba Ram Singh attached special importance to the vows of the Khalsa and advised his followers to take Khande-ka-Pahul (baptism of the double edged sword) as introduced by Guru Gobind Singh. Followers of Baba Ram Singh were distinguished by their all white dress made of home-spun khadi and a white turban tied in peculiar style and a woolen rosary.

They were advised to follow a strict moral code and believe in One Formless God and Guru Granth Sahib as their scripture. While the followers of Baba Ram Singh continue this practice, with the passage of time they also started calling Baba Ram Singh as the Guru and his successors as successive Gurus which is not in keeping with the Sikh doctrine. Like the teachings of Nirankari Babas, Baba Ram Singh also exhorted his followers not to worship tombs and graves and not to accord special status to the Bedis and Sodhis who claimed special privileges because of being descendants of the Gurus. Regard for personal hygiene required the Namdharis to have full hair bath early in the morning before starting their religious routine. While advocating abstinence from falsehood, slander, adultery, eating of flesh, use of liquor, hemp or opium, they attached special importance to the protection of cow which later brought them into conflict with the butchers and later with the British authorities. No caste distinctions were recognized and women were freely admitted to the ranks of the followers and encouraged to fully participate in all community functions.

Female infanticide, forced widowhood and dowry were strictly forbidden. Simple marriages without dowry and sometimes mass marriages of couples were encouraged. Baba Ram Singh encouraged his followers to breed horses, learn horse-riding and carry a staff or club and recite chandi-di-var, a composition of Guru Gobind Singh invoking martial spirit. To spread the movement Baba Ram Singh appointed Subas (governors), Naib Subas (deputy governors) and Jathedars (group commanders) who operated in the assigned areas and kept regular liaison with the Namdhari headquarters at Bhaini Arayian (Ludhiana district of Punjab) which later came to be reverentially known as Bhaini Sahib. Baba Ram Singh's special focus on instructions in the Sikhs' native language Punjabi in Gurmukhi script, his emphasis on use of swadeshi cloth and boycott of mill-made or imported cloth and use of own system of transportation and sending messages, as against the newly introduced railways and postal facilities and his followers attacking some Muslim butchers for killing of cows created suspicions among the British officials about Baba Ram Singh's mission.

Though Baba Ram Singh's mission was specially marked by teachings of righteousness, toleration and mercy yet some of his followers got out of control and in a fit of religious frenzy committed certain excesses which resulted in a clash with the Government. Some of his more fanatic followers, who became excited over the killing of cows, murdered the butchers at Amritsar, Raikot and Malerkotla and were as a punishment, blown off from the cannon's mouth. Though there is difference of opinion among the scholars regarding whether the movement was religious or political, there is no denying the fact that the official action against the Kukas created great hatred for British rule in the minds of the people in the Punjab. People's anger against the British might have prepared the ground for the subsequent religio-political struggle of the Akalis in the early twentieth century.

REFORM MOVEMENTS

Singh Sabha Movement

The year following the persecution of the Kukas and the suppression of their movement saw the birth of the Singh Sabha (1873 AD..). The Singh Sabha movement and its activities had a much wider appeal to the Sikh masses and, consequently, made a far greater impact. The promoters of the Singh Sabha movement, most of whom belonged to the educated class, were connected with other socio-religious movements in the Punjab and were aware of similar movements in the country. They ascribed the corruption in the Sikh religio- social life to the lack of education among the Sikhs.

They believed that religious reformation could be brought about only when the masses were made aware of their cultural heritage. The movement gained quick support from the Sikh elite and such prominent Sikh scholars of the time as Bhai Vir Singh, Bhai Kahan Singh, Bhai Ditt Singh and Professor Gurmukh Singh joined the ranks of the Singh Sabha. Though the Singh Sabha aimed mainly at religious reform through the spread of education and consciously refrained from discussing political questions or in any way incurring the displeasure of the British rulers, the religious propaganda of some of its preachers had marked political overtones. For instance, when it was argued that vicious social customs and the neglect of religion and education were the direct causes of the political downfall of the Sikhs, most of the preachers put it as an axiom that 'never had the Sikh nation fallen so low or was in so wretched a plight as during the British rule.' And again, 'never was the education', they argued, 'backward, temporal resources so straitened and disease and poverty so rampant.'

Following perhaps the advice of the Singh Sabha leadership who, either because of their own vested interests as landed magnets or because of their perception of the interests of the Sikhs, did not want to incur the displeasure of the British rulers. These Updeshaks did not hold the British Government directly responsible for the manifold social and religious ills; but it was difficult to totally dissociate 'the idea of responsibility of the Paramount Power from the deplorable state of affairs that was depicted by these preachers'. While referring to the golden days of Maharaja Ranjit Singh's rule in the Punjab, they compared the present degraded conditions of the Sikhs with the past hardships under the Mughals. It was suggested that this similarity in conditions under the Mughals and the British 'was due to the similarity in causes'. However, the major contribution of the Singh Sabha leadership lay in the creation of a network of Khalsa schools, colleges and other centres of learning. The Singh Sabha leaders felt that the spread of education among the Sikhs needed support and friendship of the British rulers. They, therefore, sought the patronage of the Viceroy and other British officials. Soon after the establishment of the Khalsa Diwan, at Lahore, an active campaign was started for the foundation of a central college for the Sikhs around which was to be organized a network of schools in the outlying districts. Educational activities of the Singh Sabha received ready support and patronage from the Government of India and the British officials in the Punjab.

It was with this assistance from the British officials and the rulers of the Sikh princely states that the Khalsa College was founded at Amritsar in 1892. Though the promoters of the Khalsa College and their British patrons founded the college for purely educational advancement, the students and some of the teachers there could not escape the influence of the prevailing political unrest in the state and the growing movement of nationalism in the country. The C.I.D. officials reported to the authorities that the Khalsa College had, by 1907, 'become an important centre for inculcating national feelings among the students'. It was reported that some of the teachers were addressing openly seditious lectures' to their students and instilled anti-British feelings in their minds'. In any case, the teachers of the college had failed to 'mould students into loyal subjects of the British crown'. When Gopal Krishna Gokhale visited Amritsar, the students of the college in their enthusiasm unyoked the horses of the Baghi carrying him and themselves drove it to the college. Much to the chagrin of the British Principal of the college Gokhale was made to address the students advising them to participate in the freedom struggle. It was perhaps due to the influence of these politically active teachers and the inspiration of Gokhale, Gandhi and other nationalist leaders that the students demonstrated twice against the European officers who visited the college with a view to suggesting certain measures to curb the growing anti-British feeling among the college students.

To check the growing political consciousness and feelings of nationalism in the college, the Government of the Punjab reconstituted the college managing committee so as to ensure better official control over its affairs. By the new arrangement, the Commissioner of the Lahore Division became the ex-officio President and the Deputy Commissioner of Amritsar, the Director of Public Instructions, the Political Agent, Phulkian States and the European Principal became ex-officio members of the new managing committee. With all the members being nominated and removable by the Government, the college virtually passed into the hands of the Government. As a result some of the earlier members of the committee and the teachers with advanced political views were made to resign who started a Sikh National College at Lahore with Niranjan Singh, younger brother of Master Tara Singh, as its Principal. This aroused the anger of the extremists among the Sikh leaders. Master Sunder Singh tried to arouse popular feelings by asserting that the college was no longer in the hands of the Sikhs.

In an anti-British pamphlet entitled Ki Khalsa Kalaj Sikhan da Hai?, published in 1911, he accused the British Government of 'having robbed the Sikhs of their college just as they had, by gross breach of faith, previously swallowed up the Punjab'. The pamphlet also denounced the pro-British Sikh leaders like Sardar Sunder Singh Majithia as 'traitors for their having brooked the official interference in the Khalsa College'. Paradoxically the college which was patronised by the ruling Sikh families and the British officials to produce educated loyal students was transformed into a nursery of Sikh nationalism. The movements of socio-religious reform and education among the Sikhs exposed the evils which had slowly crept into the Sikh social and religious life and indirectly inculcated in them a desire for reform. The growing political unrest in the Punjab in the early twentieth century, the influence of the nationalist press and above all the growing forces of nationalism in the country further added to the growing unrest among the masses and prepared the ground for the coming Akali struggle directed against the Mahants and other vested interests in Sikh shrines on the one hand and against the British imperialism in Punjab on the other.

Akali Movement

Cumulative effect of the internal forces of purification among the Sikhs, such as the Nirankari, Namdhari and the Singh Sabha movements and also external influences such as the rise of nationalism in the country, the propaganda of the native press, the impact of the Ghadrites' activities above all the tragedy of Jallianwala Bagh, set the stage for the Akali Movement for Gurdwara Reform (1920-25). Reform was initiated by the local Akali Jathas in their respective areas, but soon two representative bodies of the Sikhs - the Shiromani Gurdwara Parbandhak Committee (SGPC) and the Shiromani Akali Dal - came into existence. These two bodies were not only able to obtain control over all the important Sikh shrines through peaceful agitations, but also strengthened the forces of nationalism in the state by ejecting the Mahants, priests, government-appointed managers and other pro-British interests, and by providing a new nationalist leadership to the Sikh community.

After successfully gaining control over the Gurdwara Babe-di-Ber in Sialkot through peaceful methods, the Akali Jathas, next paid attention to the premier Sikh shrines at Amritsar. Corrupt and non-Sikh practices in the precincts of the Golden Temple and the Akal Takht and official control over its management had been a source of great discontentment among the Sikhs much before the beginning of the Gurdwara Reform Movement. While the reformers were anxious to free these premier shrines from evil influences and indirect official control as early as possible, British officials in the state carefully tried to forestall any effort at reform or change in the existing system of management.

The loyalty and support of government-appointed priests and other vested interests was treated by the British Government as symbolizing the 'proverbial loyalty' of the Sikh community as a whole. These priests of the Akal Takht were made to issue Hukamnamas (religious injunctions) against Ghadrite heroes which described them as thugs and which called upon the Sikh masses not to give them any shelter. After the tragedy of Jallianwala Bagh, Arur Singh, the government-appointed manager of the Golden Temple, invited General Dyer to the temple and, after honouring him with a Saropa (robe of honour), declared him a 'Sikh'.

While the reformers were agitating for the termination of official control over the Golden Temple and the authorities were trying to soft-pedal the issue by deferring the question till the implementation of the Reforms Scheme in the Council, the walk-out of the priests of the Akal Takht in protest against the entry of newly baptized 'low caste' members of the Khalsa Biradari into the premises of the Golden Temple virtually brought these important shrines under the control of the reformers, who appointed a representative committee for their management.

Thus far the Akalis had gained control over important Sikh shrines through peaceful means and without shedding much blood. But the tragedy of Nankana, in which over 130 peaceful Akali reformers were done to death by Mahant Narain Das and the mercenaries hired by him, proved a turning point both in the annals of the Akali struggle for Gurdwara reform as also the official policy towards the Movement. The involvement of British officials in the Nankana tragedy, particularly that of C.M.King, Commissioner of Lahore Division, and the support extended to Mahant Narain Das by the British officials, convinced the Akali leadership that the bureaucracy was supporting the vested interests in the Sikh shrines.

The Government of India's criticism of the Punjab Government's failure to deal with the Akali Movement, firmly and consistently from the beginning and of the local officials for not having taken the necessary precautions to avert the tragedy, provided British officials in the state with the excuse to come out in open support of the Mahants. In consultation with the Viceroy and other members of his Council, the Punjab Government now inaugurated a 'strong policy' towards the Movement with the two-fold objectives of (i) suppressing the reformers by force and (ii) weakening the growing Akali agitation with promises of 'suitable legislation'. The implementation of this new policy resulted in the subsequent agitation over Key's Affair and later opened new fronts, first at Guru-Ka-Bagh and then at Jaito in the erstwhile princely state of Nabha.

After taking over the management of the Golden Temple and the Akal Takht at Amritsar, the Akali reformers formed a Provisional Committee for their management. Sardar Sunder Singh Ramgarhia, who held the dual office of Secretary of the newly based committee of management under the S.G.P.C. and also the government-nominated Sabrah (custodian), still controlled the keys of the Toshakhana (treasury of the temple). To ensure its complete control over the shrines, the S.G.P.C. asked Sardar Sunder Singh Ramgarhia to hand over the keys of the Toshakhana to its President. But before the Sarbrah could do so, the Deputy Commissioner of Amritsar forestalled the Akali move by immediately sending Lal Amar Nath, an Extra-Assistant Commissioner, who took away the keys from Sardar Sunder Singh Ramgarhia.

This action created a stir within the Sikh community, which was already agitated over the tragedy of Nankana. A period of intense protest through the press and on the platform followed the official taking over of the keys. Noticing the flood of protest and indignation in the central districts of Punjab and the increasing sympathy of several sections of the Sikh population with the Akali Movement, the Government of India advised the Punjab authorities that the only way of severely rebuffing the increasing non-cooperation of the Sikhs was to successfully prosecute five or six leading men, especially Dan Singh and Jaswant Singh.

Accordingly, the Deputy Commissioner of Amritsar arrested these leaders when they were addressing a Sikh Diwan (congregation) at Ajnala, near Amritsar, on 26 November, 1921.

The Akali reaction to the arrests of these leaders was immediate. As soon as the news reached Amritsar, the S.G.P.C., reached Ajnala and continued the proceedings of the Diwan. The authorities declared the assembly illegal and arrested all its members. However, instead of checking the advance of the Movement, the arrests gave a fillip to the Akali agitation.

The S.G.P.C. by a resolution called upon the Sikhs 'to hold religious Diwans everywhere to explain the facts about the Keys Affair'.

REVIVALIST MOVEMENTS

Radhasoami Satsang

Radha Soami Satsang Beas (RSSB) was founded by Baba Jaimal Singh Ji Maharaj in 1891 at a site on the East bank of the River Beas, in Beas, Punjab Northern India. Today this site is called Dera Baba Jaimal Singh. Sant Seth Shiv Dayal Singh, was the first leader of Radhasoami Community, taught 'Surat Shabd Yoga,' often the teachings are referred to as Sant Mat, the Teachings of the Saints.

Today Radha Soami Satsang Beas is succeeded by Babaji Gurinder Singh, who was officially appointed by Maharaj Charan Singh (Guru). Radha Soami Beas satsang is a non-profit charitable society and is an autonomous body, which doesn't bear allegiance to any of the other Radhasoami/Sant Mat groups or satsangs.

'Radha' means Soul & 'Soami' means Lord. Hence Radhasoami can be translated into meaning Lord of the Soul. The Radha Soami teachings lay down a method for Self Realization leading to God Realization, through the means of Surat Shabd Yoga. Satsang describes a group that seeks truth, and Beas refers to the town near which the main centre is located in northern India. There are a number of other contemporary movements that use the name 'Radha Soami' but Radha Soami Satsang Beas is not associated with any of them.

The technique of the yoga/meditation is imparted under the instructions of a teacher (present day teacher: Baba Gurinder Singh), or his personally selected representitives. It is through this union of the soul with the Audible Life Stream that gives this meditation practice its name - The Surat Shabd Yoga. To assist in the practice of the Surat Shabd Yoga, one must be a lacto vegetarian (no eggs, fish, fowl or meat), abstain from recreational drugs and alcohol, and confine sexuality to a legal marriage. The vegetarian diet encourages respect and empathy for all life and acknowledges that there is a debt to be paid for taking any life. The required lifestyle aids concentration, calming and centering the mind.

Before one decides to adopt the Surat Shabd Yoga meditation, one is strongly advised by the present master Baba Gurinder Singh Dhillon, to research not only Radha Soami Satsang Beas philosophy and teachings, but any other mysticism teachings or yoga systems that may interest the seeker. This allows the seeker to be 100% intellectually satisfied that this is the right choice for them as individuals. Also that they are able to adhere to the vegetarian diet and the lifestyle change of no alcohol or recreational drugs and are able to take time out to practice the meditation.

People are able to practice the Surat Shabd Yoga meditation, while still remaining a part of their community and religious customs. It is a solitary practice that is done in the quiet of one's own home for 2 1/2 hours each day. Members commit themselves to a way of life that supports spiritual growth while carrying out their responsibilities to family, friends and society.

The teachings are also referred to as Sant Mat, meaning 'Teachings of the Saints' (past and present). The Radha Soami Satsang Beas community and members are from diverse ethnic, social and religious backgrounds. The teachings are available to anyone interested and no fees are charged for imparting the doctrine or Surat Shabd Yoga system. Today the Beas ashram, known as simply the 'Dera', maitains a Langar (free kitchen) and has lodgings for Sadhus, Sewadars, Satsangis and others.

Three Charitable hospitals were built and run by RSSB. Beas Hospital, Sikanderpur Hospital and the Bhota Hospital provide free medical care for the rural community surrounding it and aid the needy. They include free accommodation of relatives of their patients. Also has helped in relief efforts of victims of natural disasters. An annual eye clinic gives medical aid to people suffering eye-ailments, including the removal of cataracts. Volunteers are from diverse ethnic, cultural and social backgrounds.

Jaito Morcha Movement

The Jaito Morcha movement refers to the movement by those Sikhs who protested the forced abdication of the ruler, Maharaja Ripudaman Singh, of the princely state of Nabha from 1912-23, by the British. Because Ripudaman Singh was an Akali supporter who was sympathetic to the nationalist movements on behalf of Indians, the British forced his abdication in favour of his young son Pratap Singh. When a number of Sikhs came together to protest and attempt to reinstate Ripudaman Singh, the police interrupted and made arrests. 500 Akali Sikhs had begun a peaceful march to protest the abdication of the Maharaja on February 9, 1924 and the situation escalated to a point of violence. When the Akali Sikhs had marched more than 10k in order to reach the Gurdwara Tibbi Sahib, they were stopped by the British administrator Wilson Johnston.

As the Sikhs refused to stop in reaching their destination of the Sikh temple Tibbi Sahib, Johnston ordered his troops to open fire. This senseless act resulted in the death of 19 Akali Sikhs and the injury of 29.

Gurdwara Reform Movement

The Gurdwara Reform Movement came about because of the desire for Sikh values and traditions to once again be revived and adhered to. Brought on by the efforts of the Singh Sabha Movement as well, what the Gurdwara Reform Movement responded to more specifically, was the authority of the "Mahants," or professional priests who belonged to the Udasi sect, in all Sikh Gurdwaras. According to the movement, the Mahants were believed to have been stealing the offerings and income made to the Gurdwaras for their own personal uses, such priests therefore needed to be abolished from all Sikh temples.

Although at first, the British tended to support the Mahant priests, the pressures from the Sikh community forced them to change positions and instead they passed the "Sikh Gurdwaras and Shrines Act" in 1922. According to the Act, a committee was to be chosen by the British government, which would in turn handle all matters pertaining to the Gurdwaras in India. Because the control of the committee was chosen by the British, the Akali leaders opposed the original draft of the bill. Therefore, a second draft of the bill was made which granted the Akali council members more authority. In general, what the Act ensured was the betterment of all Sikh Gurdwaras through positive control and leadership.

REFERENCES

Attar Singh: *Socio-Cultural Impact of Islam on India*. Chandigarh: Punjab University, 1976.

Avtar Singh: *Ethics of the Sikhs*. Patiala: Punjabi University, 1983.

Balbir Singh: *Ragmala da Saval te Jodh Kavi ate Alam*. Amritsar: Khalsa Samachar, 1969.

Bal, Giani Rajinder Singh: *Bhai Banno DarpaG ate Khare vali Bi[*. Jalandhar: Central Town, 1989.

Bhandari, Sujan Rai: *Khulastut Tvarikh*. Trans. Ranjit Singh Gill, ed. Fauja Singh. Patiala: Punjabi University, 1972.

Bhalla, Sarupdas: *Mahima Prakash, Bhag Duja*. Ed. Gobind Singh Lamba and Khazan Singh. Patiala: Punjab Language Department, 1971.

Brown, Kerry: *Sikh Art and Literature*. New York: Routledge, 1999.

Cole, W. Owen, and Piara Singh Sambhi: *The Sikhs: Their Religious Beliefs and Practices*. Brighton: Sussex Academic Press, 1995.

Cole, W. Owen: *Sikhism and Its Indian Context 1469–1708*. New Delhi: D. K. Agencies, 1984.

Dass, Nirmal: *Songs of Kabir from the Adi Granth*. Albany: State University of New York Press, 1992.

Denny, Frederick M., and R. L. Taylor: *The Holy Book in Comparative Perspective*. Columbia: University of South Carolina Press, 1993.

Griffin, Lepel H., and Charles Francis Massy: *Chiefs and Families of Note in the Punjab*. Lahore: Punjab Government Press, 1939.

McLeod, W. H.: *The Sikhs: History, Religion and Society*. New York: Columbia University Press, 1989.

McLeod, W. H.: *Historical Dictionary of Sikhism*. Lanham, Md.: The Scarecrow Press, 1995.

McLeod, W. H.: *Sikhism*. New York: Penguin, 1997.

Pritam Singh: *Sikh Falsafe di Roop-Rekha*. Amritsar: Guru Nanak Dev University, 1975.

Randhawa, Harveen Kaur: *"Early Printing History of Guru Granth Sahib."* M. Phil. term paper, Guru Nanak Dev University, 1985.

Randhir Singh: ed., *Prem Sumarag Granth*.Jalandhar, 1965.

Robert O. Ballou: *The Portable World Bible*, Penguin Books, 1976.

Santokh Singh: *Philosophical Foundations of the Sikh Value System*. New Delhi: Munshi Ram Manohar Lal Publishers, 1983.

Sardool Singh Kavishar: *Sikh Dharam Darshan*. ed. Dr. Wazir Singh, Patiala: Punjabi University, 1969.

Sher Singh: *Philosophy of Sikhism*. Ludhiana: Chardi Kala Publications, 1966.

Taran Singh: *GurbaGi dian Viakhia PraGalian*. Patiala: Punjabi University, 1980.

Teja Singh: ed. *Shabadarth Shri Guru Granth Sahib Ji*. 4 vols. Amritsar: Shiromani Gurdwara Prabandhak Committee, 1969.

10

Reformers

REFORMERS IN EARLY PERIOD

Baba Buddha

Baba Buddha was one of closest companions of the Guru Nanak (the first Guru of Sikhism) and is one of the most revered and holy saints in Sikhism. He holds one of the most important and pivotal positions in Sikh history. The first head Granthi of Shri Harmandir Sahib. Baba Buddha Ji was alive during many of the Sikh Guru's lives. He was nicknamed "Buddha" by Guru Nanak Dev because although he was a young boy, he had the wisdom and knowledge of an old man. Baba Budha Ji ia also credited with starting the martial culture of the Sikhs. The Budha Dal Nihang Singsh attribute their beginnings to Baba Budha Ji himself.

Bhai Mani Singh

Bhai Mani Singh, a great Sikh personality of eighteenth century, occupies a very esteemed position in Sikh history. He assumed the control and steered the course of the Sikh destiny at a very critical stage in their history. A great scholar, a devoted Sikh, and a courageous leader, Bhai Mani Singh willingly laid down his life to uphold the dignity of the Sikh religion as well as nation. The nature of his martyrdom has become a part of the daily Sikh Ardas (prayer).

Bhai Mani Singh is said to have been brought in the early years of his childhood to the presence of Guru Tegh Bahadur at Anandpur. He was approximately of the same age as the Guru's own son, Gobind Rai. Both grew up together - Gobind Rai and Mania were the names they went by in those pre-Khalsa days. Mani Singh remained in his company even after he had ascended the religious seat as Guru. Mani Singh accompanied the Guru to the seclusion of Paonta where Guru Gobind Singh spent some three years exclusively given to literary work.

Bhai Mani Singh took Amrit at the hands of Guru Gobind Singh Ji on the day of the creation of Khalsa. When Guru Gobind Singh Ji left Anandpur on the night of December 20, 1704, his family got separated at river Sirsa in the confusion created by the Mughal attack. Bhai Mani Singh took Mata Sundri Ji and Mata Sahib Devan to Delhi via Ambala.

In 1706, Bhai Mani Singh escorted Guru Sahib's wife and Mata Sahib Devan to Talwandi Sabo where the Guru was staying. When Guru Sahib left Agra with Emperor Bahadur Shah for Nander in 1707, Mata Sahib Devan and Bhai Mani Singh accompanied him. Afterwards Bhai Mani Singh escorted Mata Sahib Devan Ji back to Delhi where she lived with Mata Sundri Ji for the rest of her life.

Mata Sundri Ji came to know of the trouble that was brewing between the Tat Khalsa and Bandai Khalsa military factions of the Sikhs. She appointed Bhai Mani Singh as the Granthi of Harimandir Sahib and sent him to Amritsar with Mama Kirpal Singh (Chand), the maternal uncle of Guru Gobind Singh Ji. On his arrival at Amritsar in 1721, Bhai Mani Singh restored peace among the Khalsa and put the affairs of Harimandir Sahib in order.

Bhai Mani Singh acted as scribe when Guru Gobind Singh Ji - the then Guru of the Sikhs - dictated Shri Guru Granth Sahib. He also transcribed many copies of the holy Sikh scriptures which were sent to different preaching centers in India. He also taught the reading of Gurbani and its doctrine to the Sikhs.

Bhai Sahib was responsible for collecting the Gurbani of Guru Gobind Singh Ji and compiling it in the form of Dasam Granth (Book of the Tenth Guru). Besides this, Bhai Sahib also authored Japji Sahib Da Garb Ganjni Teeka (teeka means translation and explanation of a work). He expanded the first of Bhai GurDas's Vaars into a life of Guru Nanak which is called Gyan Ratanawali. Mani Singh wrote another work, the Bhagat Ralanawali, an expansion of Bhai GurDas's eleventh Vaar, which contains a list of famous Sikhs up to the time of Guru Har Gobind.

In his capacity as a Granthi of Darbar Sahib at the Golden Temple, Bhai Singh is also stated to have composed the Ardaas (Supplication) in its current format; he also started the culture of mentioning deeds of several Gursikhs with the supplication.

Bhai Taru Singh

Born in Punjab during the reign of the Mughal Empire, Bhai Taru Singh was raised as a Sikh by his widowed mother. During this time,

Sikh revolutionaries were plotting the overthrow of the Khan and had taken refuge in the jungle. Bhai Taru Singh and his sister gave food and other aid to the rebels. An informant reported them to Zakaria Khan, the governor of Punjab, and the two were arrested for treason. Though his sister's freedom was bought by the villagers, Bhai Taru Singh refused to seek a pardon.

After a period of imprisonment and torture, Singh was brought before the Khan and given the choice of converting to Islam or being executed. As a symbol of his conversion, Singh would have to cut off his Kesh and present it as an offering to the Khan. Upon his refusal, and in a public display, Bhai Taru Singh's scalp was cut away with razors to prevent his hair from ever growing back.

The exact method of his execution is somewhat ambiguous. Sikhs believe that once Singh had been returned to prison to await a slow death, Zakaria Khan was stricken with unbearable pain and the inability to urinate. As a last resort, he sent an apology to the Khalsa Panth for his persecution of the Sikhs and begged for their forgiveness. It was suggested that if Zakaria Khan had his own scalp hit with Bhai Taru Singh's shoes, his condition might be lifted. Although the shoe cured the Khan's condition, he died 22 days later. Upon hearing that he had miraculously outlived the Khan, Bhai Taru Singh died as well.

Bhai Gurdas

Bhai Gurdas (1551-1636) was a Punjabi Sikh writer, historian, missionary, and religious figure. He was the original scribe of the Guru Granth Sahib and a companion of four of the Sikh Gurus. Bhai Gurdas was born in 1551 in Goindwal, a small village in the Punjab. His father was Bhai Ishardas who was a first cousin of Guru Amar Das. His mothers name was Jivaniand she died in 1554 when Gurdas was only three.

He was adopted by his uncle Guru Amar Das. He learned Sanskrit, Brijbhasha, Persian and Punjabi (Gurmukhi) and eventually began preaching Sikhism. He spent his early years at Goindval and Sultanpur Lodhi. At Goindval he listened to scholars and swamis who kept visiting the town while traversing the Delhi-Lahore road. He later moved to Varanasi where he studied Sanskrit and Hindu scriptures. There, he was subsequently initiated into Sikhism. After Guru Amar Das died, his successor Guru Ram Das, appointed Gurdas as the Sikh missionary to Agra.

In 1577, Bhai Gurdas contributed his labour to excavating the pool at the Harimandir Sahib. Twenty years later, he went on an expedition to

Kartarpur and recited many of the early hymns to Emperor Akbar. This was at a time when many of the Sikhs were becoming very anti-Muslim in tone and family feuds within the Gurus' family had put Sikhism in danger. Akbar received the verses positively and became convinced there were no anti-Muslim suggestions.

After Guru Ram Das died, Bhai Gurdas formed a close relationship with the fifth Guru, Guru Arjan Dev. Guru Arjan Dev had great respect for him, and regarded Bhai Gurdas as his maternal uncle. It is said that the Mughal emperor Jahangir was growing jealous of the popularity of Sikhism, and Bhai Gurdas was sent to Kabul, Kashmir, Rajasthan, and Varanasi again to preach Sikhism.He even went to Shri Lanka, preaching the name of the Guru among the masses and showing them the true way of life.

He completed the Adi Granth in 1604. It took him nearly 11 years to complete this task. Bhai Gurdas not only wrote the Adi Granth as dictated by Guru Arjan Dev but also supervised four other scribes, Bhai Haria, Bhai Sant Das, Bhai Sukha and Bhai Manasa Ram. He assisted these scribes in the writing of several scriptures. His other works in Punjabi are collectively called Varan Bhai Gurdas.

Mian Mir

Mian Mir was a renowned Sufi saint of Lahore. He belonged to Sistan in Central Asia. His original name was Shaikh Muhammad. He was born about 1550 AD. He had a religious bent of mind. As a child he attentively listened to religious sermons. He became a disciple of Shaikh Khizr of the Qadiri order of Sufis. Sufis believed in spreading Islam by peaceful means. As India was a great field for conversion, Mian Mir decided to come here. He was then about 25 years old. He settled at Lahore. He resided in the suburbs of the city called Begampura. The whole area is now called after him Mian Mir.

Mian Mir was such a holy man of God that the boons granted by him turned into reality. People thronged to him in large numbers from far and wide. Guru Arjan often visited Lahore to see the birth-place of his father and meet his relatives. On the occasion of one of such visits he called on the Pir. The two men of God met and became life-long friends. Mian Mir was thirteen years older than Guru Arjan.

Guru Arjan was responsible for the construction of many tanks and buildings. In 1589 he planned to build a temple in the centre of the holy tank called Amritsar or the tank of nectar. As the temple was to be thrown open to people of all castes, creeds and climes, he invited Mian Mir to lay the foundation stone of the Han Mandar. He came to Amritsar wearing a religious mendicant's long cloak made up of patches of coarse wool and a cone-cap made of a number of gores with a rose flower on top.

Mian Mir was given one of the warmest welcomes for which Guru Arjan was famous. The two holy men embraced each other in sincere love and regard. The purpose of the temple was disclosed to the Sufi saint. The Guru pointed out that the Hindu temples and Muslim mosques were built on a raised plinth. The Sikh temple would be erected on a lower plinth than the surrounding area. The idea was that God could be attained by bending low in submission and humi-lity. The Hindu temples and Muslim mosques were closed on three sides and had only one doorway facing east and west respectively. His temple would be open on all the four sides implying that it would welcome persons of all the four castes, Brahmans, Kshatriyas, Vaishas and Shudras; to all the four religions in the world, Hinduism, Buddhism, Islam and Christianity, and to all the people from any country or climate from north, south, east and west.

The Muslim saint was highly delighted at the fine objectives the Guru had in mind. He was deeply impressed with his pleasing. personality, charming manners and the divine light shining in his face,. words and deeds. The foundation-stone was laid. Hymns were sung in the praise of God and sweets were distributed among the audience. A mason with his tools stood by. As the holy man had placed the stone irregularly, the mason corrected its posture in order to place bricks on it properly. The saint expressed sorrow at the mason's mistake and remarked that the temple would have to be rebuilt in course of time The prophecy came out true about a century and a half later when Ahmad Shah Abdali blew it off with gunpowder.

In 1606 Guru Arjan was implicated in the affair of Khusrau, the rebel son of Jahangir. He was imprisoned in the Lahore fort and was barbarously tortured. When Mian Mir heard about it, he came to see the Guru. He found Guru Arjan calm and serene having completely resigned himself to the will of God. Mian Mir suggested to the Guru whether he should intercede with Emperor Jahangir on his behalf The Guru forbade him saying that God's will must have its course unchecked, as it was not proper to interfere with its working. He only asked for the Saint's blessings for his son Hargobind.

A couple of years after the death of Guru Arjan, his son and successor Guru Hargobind, a lad of thirteen, called on Mian Mir at Lahore. In the monastery (Khanqah) there were many disciples of Mian Mir including a young girl Kaulan. She was the daughter of Rustam Khan, the Qazi of the Capital. Being religious-minded from childhood, she became a disciple of Mian Mir. She had made up her mind to become a nun, but in Islam there was no room for a woman to lead the life of a nun. She therefore decided to become a disciple of Guru Hargobind: Her father grew furious at such a proposal. He tried his best to dissuade her from her intention. Having failed in this. attempt he began to persecute her. She fled to Mian Mir who sent her to Amritsar under proper escort. She was given a separate house to live, and she was immortalised by the construction of a tank named after her Kaulsar. He is called the founder of Mian Khail branch of the Qadiri order. He passed away on 11 August, 1635. He was buried at village Hashimpur.

Bibi Bhani

Bibi Bhani was daughter of Guru Amar Das, the third Sikh Guru and the wife of Guru Ram Das, the fourth Sikh Guru and the mother of Guru Arjan Dev, the fifth Sikh Guru. She was married to Bhai Jetha who was a most devoted Sikh of Guru Amar Das. He was a dedicated Sikh and enjoyed serving the Guru and his Sangat.

She had two brothers named Bhai Mohan Ji and Bhai Mohri Ji and an older sister named Bibi Dani Ji, who was married to a pious Sikh named Bhai Rama. She was born to Mata Mansa Devi on 19 January 1535 at Basarke Gillan, a village near Amritsar. She was married on 18 February 1554 to Bhai Jetha (whose name was later changed to Guru Ram Das), a Sodhi Khatri from Lahore. Bhai Jetha later moved to Goindval which was an upcoming Sikh town and carried out voluntary service (Sewa) in the construction of the Baoli Sahib.

Guru Amar Das was very impressed with the Sewa performed by Bhai Jetha and so a marriage was arranged between Bibi Bhani, his daughter and a dedicated devotee, Bhai Jehta. After marriage, the couple remained in Goindval serving the Guru and the congregation (Sangat). Later, on the near completion of contruction of the Gurdwara at Goindval, Bhai Jetha was deputed by the Guru to go and establish a habitation at present-day Amritsar. This place was also later caller Ramdasar. Here, on a piece of land gifted, according to one version, by Emperor Akbar to Bibi Bhani at the time of his visit to Guru Amar Das.

Three sons, Prith Chand (1558), Mahadev (1560) and (Guru) Arjan Dev (1563) were born to her. A popular story mentioned in old chronicles describes how devotedly Bibi Bhani served her father. One morning, it is said, as Guru Amar Das was absorbed in meditation, Bibi Bhani noticed that one of the legs of the low wooden seat on which the Guru sat was about to give way. she at once put forward her hand to support the stool. As the Guru ended his devotions, he discovered how her hand was bleeding from the injury she had sustained. He blessed her saying that her progeny would inherit the Guruship. Bibi Bhani died at Goindval on 9 April 1598.

Bibi Bhani was mother of Guru Arjan Dev, the Fifth Guru. Undoubtedly, Guru Arjan Dev was brought up as a model GurSikh. Guru Arjan Dev was the first Sikh Martyr. Guru Arjan Dev compiled Adi Granth by collecting all the writings of Gurus before him and installed it at Golden Temple. This granth now called the Shri Guru Granth Sahib is central of Sikhism and the current and perpetual Guru of the Sikhs. Guru Arjan Dev also completed the construction of Golden Temple or Harimandir Sahib.

She was a symbol of service. In the Sikh history, she is known as an embodiment of service. There is special status of Bibi Bhani in the life of Guru Amardas by the way she cared for her father proving that there was no difference between a son and a daughter. Both can equally serve their parents.

There is a superstition in Punjabi tradition that a father does not get any service done from the daughter, but Bibi Bhani used to serve her father before marriage and kept serving him even after her marriage. We can learn a lesson from her way of serving that one can continue doing worldly duties along with daily religious service or worship.

Domestic circumstances never became any obstacles and she kept serving her father humbly and with devotion, even after she became the mother of three sons. She very gladly and regularly kept giving bath to her father and used to keep a watch so that no body disturbed him during his meditation. So much so that when a leg of that bath-stool was broken, she kept her arm underneath it, so that his meditation was not disturbed. Only Bibi Bhani could do that. She was married in the beginning of 1553. She served Bhai Jetha not only as a husband but also as a saint.

She was so contented that she never complained about the poverty of her in-laws. She kept serving her father even after her marriage, as her in-laws were local. She continued doing her worldly duties along with the service of her father. Her husband continued serving in the common kitchen even after his marriage.

They had three sons, Prithi Chand, Maha Dev, and Arjan Dev. Prithi Chand was arrogant, lazy, and dishonest, but still wanted the Guruship after his father. He wanted that his Mother should recommend him for Guruship. She advised him that the decision made by his father would be on merit and she remained neutral. When Guru Arjan Dev was selected for Guruship, Prithi Chand misbehaved with his father.

Bibi Bhani snubbed Prithi Chand and admonished him. She said to him that the decision made by his father was impartial. This has been the culture from the time of Guru Nanak. She also said, "Your father was also selected on the basis of his service and humility." Bibi Bhani always stood for truth.

Her eldest son, Prithi Chand, was ignored due to his haughty nature and the youngest one, Guru Arjan Dev, was made the fifth Guru by his father. Prithi Chand claimed that he was the fifth Guru and through his agents collected the offerings of the devotees before they could see Guru Arjan Dev. He, thus, tried to fail the common kitchen run by Guru Arjan Dev. Bibi Bhani and Bhai Gurdas, a devotee of Guru Arjan Dev, foiled the conspiracy of Prithi Chand and the common kitchen continued as usual. After the death of Guru Ram Das, Bibi Bhani helped her son, Guru Arjan Dev, in every activity undertaken by him and advised him She persuaded Guru Arjan Dev to remarry after the death of his first wife.

REFORMERS IN MEDIEVAL PERIOD

Sant Sohan Singh

Sant Sohan Singh was a common man like any other Sikh hailing from a remote village in the Punjab. Over the years he so developed himself spiritually and so endeared himself to the Sikhs in Malaya and Singapore, that he became an institution by himself. He was head and shoulders above the average Sikh not only in matters spiritual but also in physical stature. Yet he moved about among them unassumingly, claiming no better place than the commonest of them and using no high sounding language to impress them with the spiritual stature he had attained.

Sant Sohan Singh exercised influence in the religious and social activities of the Sikh community of these regions. He performed the naming ceremonies of numerous children born in Sikh homes. He blessed innumerable newly wedded Sikh couples. He performed the last rites of many Sikhs. He addressed unaccounted congregations in different towns on Sikh festivals or other occasions. He visited Sikhs settled in remote areas whenever and wherever he was requested to do so.

He maintained these visits right into the eve of his life, notwithstanding poor health and difficulty in walking. Perhaps he was doing his best to follow: "Every day and night that passes lessens your remaining hours; so fulfil your mission in accordance with the will of the Guru."

Sant Sohan Singh was on one such tour when he was taken seriously ill and was admitted to the Ipoh General Hospital. After a brief period he passed on to Sachkhand whither everyone must proceed.

In the eyes of the Sikhs of this region Sant Sohan Singh was no comman man. The news of his death spread very fast and Sikhs came to Ipoh from distant towns as far north as Penang. Under normal circumstances his remains would have been cremated in Ipoh soon after he passed away. But the community decided that the cremation should take place in Malacca, which was more or less his headquaters for a period of 45 years.

The cortege started on the last journey of 255 miles to Malacca at 1.00 am on 25 May 1972. At every town on the way Sikhs of all ages and both sexes came out in large numbers to pay homage to the man who had been one with them, many of whom he knew by name. From every town cars joined the great procession, the likes of which has not been known to the Sikh community. The cortege reached Malacca at about midday. Meanwhile large numbers of Sikhs converged on to Malacca from all towns in the South including Singapore 150 miles away.

The cremation over, for the first time the Sikh community felt a sort of vaccum around them. Very soon they were convinced that no other person could fill that vaccum. They stopped looking for a man to take the place of Sant Sohan Singh.

Instead gradually they developed the attitude that they could show his living spirit in a practical manner. They appreciated that the body dies, not the soul. They started the Sant Sohan Singh Memorial Fund and registered one society in Malaya and another in Singapore.

At the rear of the Malacca Gurdwara, which he managed for 45 years, they erected a new building to house a religious school - Sant Sohan Singh Dharmak Vidyalia - for training young boys willing to adopt the religious path and work as granthis, parcharaks and ragis.

There is dire need for such an institution under the present circumstances. There are few properly trained granthis in this region. In the near future the community can look forward to granthis raised in the local environment able to appreciate the problems of the local people.

Sohan Lal Suri

Sohan Lal Suri is famous for his monumental work in Persian, ' Umdat ut-Twarikh, a chronicle of Sikh times comprising five daftars or volumes. Little is known about Sohan Lal's early life except that he was the son of Lala Ganpat Rai, a munshi or clerk successively under Sardar Charhat Singh and Sardar Mahan Singh of the Sukkarchakkia misl. Ganpat Rai had kept a record of important events of his own time which he passed on to his son around 1811 enjoining upon him to continue the work of writing a history of the Punjab.

Lala Sohan Lal who, according to his own statement, was well versed in Persian, Arabic, mathematics, astronomy and numerology, was inspired to take to historiography by, besides the example of his father, Sujan Rai Bhandari's Khulasat ut Twarikh which covers the period from Hindushahi rulers of the tenth and eleventh centuries to 1704 in the reign of Aurangzeb. While acknowledging his debt to Sujan Rai Bhandari, Sohan Lal Suri mentions another motive that prompted him to write his book. In the beginning of the first daftar of ' Umdat ut-Twarikh, he remarked referring to himself in the third person : "In fact the purpose and reason for which he undertook the novel and noteworthy compilation was that ever since the time of the Sultanate the writing of such works was looked upon as the proof of literary ability, which distinguished a scholar from an ordinary man. Learned men received due recognition and encouragement from the rulers of the time. " The sources for his voluminous Twarikh, 7,000 pages of manuscript in shikasta or running Persian script covering the period from the birth of Guru Nanak in 1469 to the annexation of the Punjab in 1849, are his own knowledge of contemporary events, the notes bequeathed to him by his father and the historical or legendary material bearing on the subject available to him.

Besides his magnum opus, the ' Umdat ut-Twarikh, Lala Sohan Lal Suri wrote 'Ibrat Namah, lit. an account that teaches a lesson. It is a small poetical composition on the tragic murders of Maharaja Sher Singh, Raja Dhian Singh and the Sandhanvalia Sardars and their associates in September 1843. The title of another work of his, Selections from Daftar II, is deceptive. The manuscript contains brief notes on courtiers, rajas, diwans, learned men, saints and ascetics living in the year 1831 ; a genealogical table of the author's family up to 1836 ; a funeral oration on the death of his father, an account of the Sutlej chiefs, a description of the institutions of the English; a brief description of the author's meeting with Captain Wade, later Colonel Sir Claude Martin Wade, British political agent at Ludhiana, and copies of certain letters and testimonials. He is also said to have written treatises on mathematics, astronomy and geometry.

Faqir 'Aziz ud-Din, Maharaja Ranjlt Singh's favoured minister, introduced Sohan Lal to Captain Wade as a historian of the Sikh court. At Captain Wade's request the Maharaja allowed Sohan Lal to visit Ludhiana, where he used to read out to his host from the ' Umdat ut-Twarikh twice a week. He also presented the latter with a copy of the work which is still preserved in the Royal Asiatic Society Library in London. After the annexation of the Punjab to British dominions in 1849, Lala Sohan Lal Suri was awarded a jagir worth Rs. 1,000 per annum in the village of Manga, in Amritsar district, to which he probably retired to pass his remaining years.

REFORMERS IN MODERN PERIOD

Bhai Lachhman Singh

One of the Nankana Sahib martyrs, was the leader of the jatha of more than one hundred Sikhs who were attacked in Gurdwara Janam Asthan (birthplace of Guru Nanak) by the custodian of the shrine, Mahant Narain Das, and his accomplices, and killed to a man.

Lachhman Singh was born to Mehar Singh and Har Kaur in 1885 at the village of Dharovali, in Gurdaspur district of the Punjab. Mehar Singh, who retired as a police inspector in 1888, had been awarded for his meritorious record six squares of land in Chakk No. 33 in canal colony in Sheikhupura district. Four years later, he shifted his family of four sons and a daughter to this village, which began to be called Dharovali after their original village. Lachhman Singh passed his boyhood herding cattle and learning to read Gurmukhi and recite gurbani. In 1901, he was married to Indar Kaur, daughter of Buddh Singh Bundala of Chakk No. 64. In 1910, he joined Khalsa Parcharak Vidyala, a missionary school at Tarn Taran, and returned after two years training to devote himself to the cause of education and to spreading Sikhism in the canal colonies.

He started a girls primary school and a Khalsa orphange in his village with donations collected from the farmers. Reports about the corruption and licentiousness of Mahant Narain Das, who was in control of the principal holy shrine, Gurdwara Janam Asthan, at Nankana Sahib, led Lachhman Singh to call a public convention in his village, Dharovali, on 1-3 October 1920. The Shiromani Gurdwara Parbandhak Committee, which was formed at Amritsar on 15 November 1920, also decided to convene a conference at Nankana Sahib on 4-6 March 1921 with a view to exerting pressure on the Mahant to reform himself and make over control of the Gurdwara to a democratically elected body. Lachhman Singh learnt about the conspiracies Mahant Narain Das was hatching against the reformers. He and Kartar Singh Jhabbar, another equally dashing leader of the Bar Khalsa Diwan, decided on 17 February 1921 that they would proceed to Gurdwara Janam Asthan and claim possession of the shrine on behalf of the Panth.

The date fixed was 20 February when the Mahant, according to their information, was scheduled to attend a Sanatan Sikh conference at Lahore. Lachhman Singh was to march with his jatha from Dharovali through the darkness of the night of 19 February and Kartar Singh Jhabbar from Sachcha Sauda was to join him with his comrades at dawn at Chandarkot canal waterfall bridge, about 8 km north of

Nankana Sahib. They sent a special messenger to Amritsar to secure the concurrence of the Shiromani Gurdwara Parbandhak Committee. The Committee did not agree and deputed Dalip Singh of Sahoval to go and dissuade Lachhman Singh and Kartar Singh Jhabbar from taking any precipitate action. Dalip Singh succeeded in contacting Kartar Singh Jhabbar and bringing him round to the viewpoint of the Shiromani Gurdwara Parbandhak Committee. Then they drafted a hukamnama, signed by six prominent leaders including Kartar Singh Jhabbar, to be delivered to Jathedar Lachhman Singh to stop him from proceeding to Nankana Sahib.

Lachhman Singh had meanwhile left Dharovali along with his comrades. They offered the ardas and prayed for the success of their mission. Volunteers from villages en route increased their number to more than 130. Taking a short cut, they went by the village of Mohlan and not by Chandarkot bridge, 3 km south, which was the rendezvous fixed for a meeting with Kartar Singh Jhabbar. Dalip Singh who was carrying the hukamnama combed the area round Chandarkot till the small hours of 20 February but failed to locate Lachhman Singh's jatha.

Exhausted by his fruitless wandering, he retired for rest to Uttam Sirrgh's factory, about a mile away from Gurdwara Janam Asthan leaving his companion, Waryam Singh, to continue the search. The latter did meet Lachhman Singh and delivered to him the message commanding him to halt and go back with the jatha. The jatha was bound by the ardas it had offered before setting out on its march. So Lachhman Singh refused to comply and entered, along with his companions, Gurdwara janam Asthan at 5.45 a.m. chanting hymns.

All of a sudden bullets began flying in from the southwest corner of the roof of the Mahimankhana or guest house of Mahant Narain Das. Those squatting in the compound below were killed in the shooting. The Mahant's men then descended and pounced upon their prey with swords, hatchets and other lethal weapons and made short work of the devotees. A bullet-hole was made in the silver-plated door of Chaukhandi, the sanctum-sanctorum, where Lachhman Singh sat in attendance behind the Guru Granth Sahib. His companions stood in front in a row to protect the Holy Book from desecration. All of them including Lachhman Singh fell to the bullets fired by the Mahant's men who had broken open the door. This happened on 20 February 1921.

Baba Puran Singh

Baba Puran Singh also affectionately called "Kericho wala Babaji" or simply because he lived most of his adult life in this rural Kenyan town (Kericho is a small town in Western Kenya, Africa), where now stands a very impressive Gurdwara. Baba Ji influenced and changed the lives of many in the U.K. from 1974 until Babaji passed away in 1983. Baba Ji was a great Gursikh who reached the lives of many people across several continents. He practiced the purest of love for the congregations. His first love was Gurbani - Everything that he taught was from the Shri Guru Granth Sahib and the lives of our Gurus.

The small town of Kericho is home to Africa's largest Gurdwara or Sikh place of worship. It is a living monument, dedicated to the memory of one of the greatest Sikh saints of the twentieth century outside India, a saint who lived in Kenya for 57 years of his total 84 years of life. The saint has immortalised the town of Kericho, changing for the better the lives of hundreds of thousands of Sikhs worldwide as well as uplifting the local community through many development initiatives within the town itself. Baba Puran Singh propagated faith with immense simplicity, across class, creed, denominations, gender and status, through utmost humility, compassion, selflessness and infinite love. He is the founder of the international charitable organization, Guru Nanak Nishkam Sewak Jatha, which promotes the spirit and practice of selfless service (nishkam sewa) in the name of Guru Nanak Dev, the founder of the Sikh faith.

Bhai Vir Singh

Bhai Vir Singh was a poet, scholar and exegete, a major figure in the Sikh renaissance and in the movement for the revival and renewal of Punjabi literary traditioin. His identification with all the important concerns of modern Sikhism was so complete that he came to be canonized as

Bhai, the Brother of the Sikh Order, very early in his career. For his pioneering work in its several different genres, he is acknowledged as the creator of modern Punjabi literature.

REFERENCES

Ashok, Shamsher Singh: *Shiromani Gurdwara Prabandhak Committee da Punjab Sala Itihas 1926 ton 1976*. Amritsar: Punjab Language Department, 1970.

Chhibbar, Kesar Singh: *Bansavlinama Dasan Patishahian ka*. Ed. Rattan Singh Jaggi. Chandigarh: Punjab University, 1972.

G. B. Singh: *Gurmukhi Lippi da Janam te Vikas*. Chandigarh: Punjab University, 1981.

Hawley, John Stratton, and Gurinder Singh Mann: eds. *Studying the Sikhs: Issues for North America*. Albany: State University of New York Press, 1993.

Hunter, Dard: *Paper Making: The History and Technique of an Ancient Craft*. New York: Dover Publications, 1974.

Juergensmeyer, Mark, and N. G. Barrier: eds. *Sikh Studies: Comparative Perspectives on a Changing Tradition*. Berkeley Religious Studies Series. Berkeley: University of California Press, 1979.

Kirpal Singh: ed. *Janam-Sakhi Prampra: Itihasak DrishtikoG ton*. Patiala: Punjabi University, 1969.

Kohli, Surinder Singh: ed. *Punjabi Sahitt da Itihas*. 3 vols. Chandigarh: Punjab University, 1973.

Lal Singh, Giani: ed. *Guru Arjan Dev: Jivan te Rachna*. Patiala: Punjab Language Department, 1988.

Macauliffe, Max Arthur: *The Sikh Religion: Its Gurus, Sacred Writings and Authors*. New Delhi: S. Chand and Company, 1985.

Mahan Singh, Giani: "Bahoval vali Pothi Sahib. " *Khe[a*. New Delhi: Bhai Vir Singh Sahitya Sadan, March 1980.

Mahan Singh, Giani: *Param Pavitar Adi Bi[da Sankalna Kal*. Amritsar: Khalsa Samachar, 1952.

McLeod, W. H.: *Early Sikh Tradition: A Study of the Janam-sakhis*. Oxford: Clarendon Press, 1980.

McLeod, W. H.: *Textual Sources for the Study of Sikhism*. Chicago: Chicago University Press, 1990.

Padam, Piara Singh: ed. *Sufi Kavidhara*. Patiala: Kalam Mandir, 1993.

Pritam Singh: ed. *Pahili Patishahi, Shri Guru Nanak Dev*. Ludhiana: Punjabi Sahitt Academy, 1969.

Talib, Gurbachan Singh: *Bani of Shri Guru Amar Das*. New Delhi: Sterling Publishers, 1979.

Tatla, Darshan Singh: *The Sikh Diaspora: The Search for Statehood*. London: University College London Press, 1999.

Udasi, Swami Harnamdas: *Adi Shri Guru Granth Sahib dian Puratani Bi[an te Vichar*. 2 vols. Kapurthala: Kantesh Pharmacy, 1969.

Vir Singh, Bhai: *Santhaya Shri Guru Granth Sahib*. 7 vols. Amritsar: Khalsa Samachar, 1972.

Vir Singh, Bhai: *Shri Ashm Guru Chamatkar, Bhag I te II*. Amritsar: Khalsa Samachar, 1990.

11

Major Sects

Like all the spiritual customs the world over that have different sects, so Sikhism also has many dictates that represent the faith concording to their special view and beliefs. These several orders have adopted the subject matter of Dharma that Guru Nanak Dev spoke of, and dispersed this wisdom to the bulks in their own unequaled way.

The Sikh religion is not a completely singular faith; there are diverse sects which are predictable by the Sikhs. For example, one is called as the Udasis, a group which was found by an elder son of Guru Nanak Dev, Baba Shri Chand. They have taken the oath of chastity and wearing a yellow robe, carry around a mendicancy bowl to receive food or donations. They are very similar to Hindu ascetics in their mannerisms and habits and they possess been active as missionaries of the Sikh faith. Another group is known as the Sahajdharis, which means slow adopters. This actually covers several smaller sects, all of which incline to be shaven like Hindus and obstinate to Sikh culture. They have largely refused the more militant instructions which were encouraged by Gobind Singh, the tenth and last human Guru.

Another group is called as the Keshadharis (hair wearers) and it, too, covers a number of littler sects. The Nihangs are the most militant of all Sikhs, they carry variety of arms and are more willing to take action to defend their religion. They regard themselves as covering in the culture of Guru Gobind Singh's Khalsa army and live a semi-nomadic life-style. The Nirmalas, on the other hand, are much less militant than average and members tend to lead meditative lives while secluded in monasteries. Another group categorized with the Keshadharis are the Nirankaris, established by Baba Dayal. They focus on the formless, eternal nature of God and accept the being of a continuing line of living Gurus. Another group is known as the Namdhari or Kukas. This is a reform radical which formulated in the ninteenth century and they follow a living Guru who is condescended from the master Gurus.

AKALIS

The Akalis (also known as Nihangs) thought in non-humoring and chastity. They believe in three Granths: The Adi Granth, the Dasam Granth and the Sarob Loh Granth. They conceive that all have equal status and supplement each other; in the Akali/Nihang perspective it is not potential to fully comprehend the Adi Granth without the other two Granths. The Nihangs believe in the oral custom of giving kathas (oral discourses on the scripture), and do not expense their history. Today not all Nihangs are continent, some marry and some till the land. Nihangs conceive that they are the real Khalsa who practice martial arts and live their lives as Guru Gobind Singh outlined. The Nihangs consequently powerfully conceive and rigidly adhere to the rahit (code of conduct).

The Akalis/Nihangs were at their peak in the eighteenth and early nineteenth centuries. At this time they were called Akalis and were known to be dauntless, skilled and brave warriors. They saw themselves as forming the elite corpus of the Khalsa. They believe themselves to have developed from the times of Guru Gobind Singh. The Akalis earned a reputation for being valiant soldiers during the reign of Maharaja Ranjit Singh. The Akalis, as armed groups on horseback, offered Sikhs fortification from Muslim ill-treatment in the 1750s to the late 1780s. These army groups had several divisions (called misls) which finally gained control over areas of varying sizes. Initially these groups of horsemen were agitating the Mughals, then the Afghans. The ultimate conqueror was Ranjit Singh who captivated and united all the misl groups and ruled an undivided Panjab in the 1800s. One of Ranjit Singh's most famous warriors was the continent Akali Phula Singh (1716-1823), who was the Nihangs grooviest leader.

The Nihangs dress is the most distinct and prominent of all the Sikhs, for they are rigorous supporters of the code set down in the rahit literature. They are all Keshdhari (uncut hair), they put on weapons most notably the sword and the steel quoits around their blue turbans. Their general dress colour is blue, with a long blue shirt (chola). The style of their turbans is also quite unique. It is very tall and likely three to four times the length of convention Khalsa Singh's turbans. The tall turban called a damala is overcame by a cloth or a flag (pharhara). Around this turban are directed one or two steel or iron rings (quoits). The vertical position of where this ring is worn signifies the people religious skill; the higher the ring the keener the religious growth.

The Nihangs are divided into four Dals (armies); Tarna Dal, Baba Bidhi Chand Dal, Baba Bhindran Dal, and Baba Budha Dal, (which are named after Akali Leaders known as Jathedars). The supreme commander will nominate a successor, usually a celibate like himself.

The Nihangs pass half their time traveling the Panjab on horseback and half decided domesticating the land. Whilst going they set up camps (deras) at several locations. The Five Takhts are: Akal Takht in Amritsar is paramount; Keshgarh Sahib in Anandpur, Harimandir Sahib in Patna, Huzur Sahib in Nander, and Damdama Sahib in southern Panjab. These four are all located at sites in history linked with Guru Gobind Singh. Decisions are arrived at (hukam-namas) by the Sarbat Khalsa (all the represented community) binding on all the Sikhs. These types of orders only issue from the Akal Takht in Amritsar. Nihangs meet on several festivals, most remarkably at Anandpur for the Holla Mahalla festival, where they establish their martial art and give preachings on their scriptures.

NIRANKARIS

The Nirankaris conceived that at their time contemporaneous Sikhs had become lax in their practice of nam-simaran (remembrance of the divine Name), and had fallen into the ritualism practices of Hinduism. They reanimated the focus on inner repeating of the name via the mantra; glory to the Formless One. They refused all Gods and Goddesses and all types of offerings made to them. Similarly they rejected all Brahmanical rites and rituals, and pilgrimages. They assumed that the death of a body is to be rejoiced and not mourned. They do not drink, smoke or eat any meat. The Nirankaris conceived that women are not impure at childbirth, that marriages and other crucial events should not be fixed according to paid astrologers, that dowries should not be publicly exhibited, and that no fee should be charged for performing ceremonies. They believed and emphasised the amorphous aspect of the divine; Nirankar, hence their name. However the key belief that questions their orthodoxy is the belief in the continuance of the line of human Gurus after Guru Gobind Singh. They hence do not judge in the orthodox view of the Adi Granth being the last and only Guru endless for àll Sikhs.

The Nirankaris originate the North West region of Punjab during the final years of the reign of Maharaja Ranjit Singh. The sect was founded by Baba Dayal Singh (1783-1855), a Sahajdhari Sikh whose primary mission was to bring Sikhs back to the Adi Granth and Nam-simaran. His successor Baba Darbara Singh founded many centres outside Rawalpindi and wrote about the indispensable teachings of Baba Dayal. The sect had grown substantially and the third successor, Sahib Rattaji (1870-1909) kept the Nirankaris in order via strict attachment to their rahit (Khalsa code of conduct). At this time they numbered in the thousands and some had taken interest in the Singh Sabha causes, under the fourth successor Baba Gurdit Singh. The Nirankaris helped to bring the Anand Marriage Bill in 1908-9 to the care of the Sikh populace. Their fifth Guru Sahib Hara Singh (1877-1971) started to regroup the sangat and was succeeded by his eldest son Baba Gurbakh Singh. However because their tension was largely upon Guru Nanak's message, and the times were prevailed by Singh Sabha Sikhs emphasizing Guru Gobind Singh's Khalsa, their voices went unheard. This was exasperated by the shift from Sahajdhari (shaven) to Keshdhari (unshaven) Sikhs. Finally with their powerlessness to keep in step with the troubled social changes of the British Raj they were soon marginalized.

NAMDHARIS

The Namdharis consider in the theology belief of recalling the divine Name (Nam-simaran) and the use of a prayer beads in this practice. They think in the irregular view of personal Guruship, which did not end with the tenth and cultural understood to be the last Guru, Gobind Singh. They are strict vegetarians who do not drink or smoke. They assert the Hindu belief that the cow is holy and should therefore not be killed for human uptake. They believe in certain ritualism practices like the fire ceremony (havan) which involve the practice of pheras (circummambulating the fire) during a wedding ceremony. They consider that food not cooked from their own hands should not be eaten. They also consider in the efficaciousness of mantras/holy words.

The Namdharis were founded by Guru Balak Singh (1797-1862) in north-west Punjab. He was a prude and emphasized the grandness of the divine Name for redemption and drew most of his followers from the poorer castes, namely the Jats. However, in Ludhiana their second Guru, Ram Singh had the keenest impact. He was the first reformist to emphasise the Khalsa Singh identity under colonial rule, but did not exclude the Sahajdharis in his addresses. The Namdhari's zeal for the auspices of the cow brought them into direct engagement with the British government. However before the end of the ninteenth century the Namdharis disposed their militancy to return to simple piety. They conceive themselves the instigators of India's fight for freedom since they ostracized British education, law courts, railways and post office services.

All Namdharis put on only white home-spun clothing. Their turbans have a particular style, being tied horizontally across the brow, called Sidha Pag (straight turban). Because the British, fearing revolution, blackballed the right to carry arms, Namdharis carried sticks to represent the sword of the Khalsa warrior. Many wore a knotted woollen cord about their necks which assisted as a rosary.

KHALSA

Khalsa refers to the corporate body of all christened Sikhs. The Khalsa was in the first place demonstrated as a military order of "saint-soldiers" on 30 March 1699, by Guru Gobind Singh, the tenth Sikh Guru. It was the call given by the Guru to all his disciples baptized in the Amrit Sanchar ceremony. The symbolic having in mind of Khalsa translates as "belonging exclusively to Guru Gobind Singh". Guru Gobind Singh depicts in his book, the Dasam Granth the characters of Khalsa. A Sikh who has been started in Khalsa is called as a Khalsa Sikh or Amritdhari, as fought to Sahajdhari.

The word "Khalsa" means "pure", Khalsa's are Sikhs which have changed the holy Amrit Ceremony started by the 10th Sikh Guru, Guru Gobind Singh. The Khalsa order was initially produced on Baisakhi Day March 30 1699, with Guru Gobind Singh christening 5 Sikhs and then in turn asking the five Khalsa's to baptize him. Following this the Guru in person baptized thousands of men and women into the Khalsa order. The Khalsa baptism ceremony is contracted as part of ones own personal spiritual development when the start is ready to fully live up to the high prospects of Guru Gobind Singh. All Sikhs are awaited to be Khalsa or be functioning towards that objective.

The Khalsa sacrament ceremony involves drinking of Amrit (sugar water stirred with a dagger) in the comportment of 5 Khalsa Sikhs as well as the Guru Granth Sahib. The beginner is taught in the following; (a) You shall never remove any hair from any part of thy body, (b) You shall not use tobacco, alcohol or any other inebriants, (c) You shall not eat the meat of an animal licked the Muslim way, (d) You shall not commit adultery. The initiate is expected to wear the physical symbols of a Khalsa at all times as well as adopt the Khalsa Code of Conduct.

In order to become a fellow member of the Khalsa, one has to assume the 'Nash doctrine', or the doctrine of destruction. A individual has to give up his or her previous religion (Dharam Nash), give up the practice of ritualistic or superstitious behaviours (Karam Nash), and also give up any caste preeminences (Kul Nash). Instead, the new member assumes Sikhism as his or her religion, the Khalsa Rehat as his or her code of behavior, and Singh or Kaur as his or her blood line.

Guru Gobind Singh was the first to turn a fellow member of the Khalsa on the day he preceded the introduction ceremony, complied by the 'Five Beloved Ones', Bhai Daya Ram of Lahore (Khatri), Bhai Dharam Chand of Delhi (Jat), Bhai Himmat Das of Dwarka, Gujarat (a washerman), Bhai Mohkam Chand of Puri, Orissa (a calico-printer), and Bhai Sahib Chand of Bidar, Karnataka (a barber). They were all applied the surname 'Singh', and they were told that from that day advancing they were no longer determined as Jats, Khatris, high castes, or low castes. Rather, they were equal brothers and sisters.

This was adopted by a mass generalization of disciples into the Khalsa Panth. Everyone who understood in the principles prophesied since Guru Nanak Dev Ji, was receive to take Amrit and become a member of this new community. Different writers have given unlike figures concerning the number of Sikhs who took Amrit that day. According to secret reports sent to the emperor and subsequent writings of Sikh authors, it is said that more than 40,000 people became Sikhs on this instance. Taking Amrit was conceived a great honour.

The educations of the Khalsa were indistinguishable to, and the climax of, the teachings of the religious and social rotation begun by Guru Nanak. Communities who once detested each other were brought together into a single brotherhood under the following teachings:

1. To have respect for each other with mutual love and affection.

2. To pray together, treating God by the names assigned to Him in any and every language, with equal affection and regard.

3. To break bread with each other, side by side, disregarding of status, caste, belief, or even non-belief.

The mandate announced by Guru Gobind Singh for the founding of the Khalsa may briefly be described with the following three points:

1. To spread righteousness and to jointly and systematically oppose repression or injustice.

2. To end the hate for individuals of different faiths.

3. To inculcate self-confidence and promote the common masses to stand up for their rights, live a humiliate but not weak life, have self-respect but not self-importance, and to serve society as respectable saint-citizens.

Decisions pertaining the Sikh Rehat Maryada, or Sikh Code of Conduct, are the obligation of the Guru Khalsa Panth itself, the collective body of the Khalsa. They are to be esteemed and obeyed as edicts of the Guru would be.

Five K's

In those days Hindus of honorable families wore five decorates: gold ear rings, a necklace, gold or silver bangles, finger ring and a waist belt of gold or silver. The user felt proud of exhibiting his superior social position. At the same time he ran the risk of missing these articles as well his life intonation.

Guru Gobind Singh allowed for to his followers five jewels which were amongst reach of everyone down to the poorest peasent and the lowest labourer. Instead of producing fear in the mind of the user of losing these jewels, Guru Ji's five jewels made his Singh bold, brave and amazing. These jewels were kesh or long hair, Kangha or comb, Kirpan or dagger, Kara or steel bracelet and Kachcha a pair of knickerbockers. These symbols gave Khalsa a sembelence of unity, close brotherhood and equality. They formulated group awareness. Guru Gobind singh gave the Khalsa a new uniform. This was the religious uniform which at once annulled one to be able to hide their individuality and face danger boldly, and to remain united in close affinity.

Kanga: Comb. A symbol of hygiene and discipline as opposed to the matted unkept hair of ascetics. A Khalsa is expected to regularly wash and comb their hair as a matter of self discipline.

Kirpan: Ceremonial Sword. A symbol of lordliness and the Sikh battle against injustice. It is worn purely as a spiritual symbol and not as an arm. When all other means of self auspices fail, the Kirpan can be used to defend yourself or others against the enemy.

Kara: Steel bracelet. A symbol to prompt the wearer of constraint in their actions and commemoration of God at all times.

Kacha: Drawers. A symbol signifying self control and chastity.

Kesh: Long hair. A symbol of spiritualism. The Kesh reminds a Khalsa to behave like the Guru's. It is a mark of commitment and group awareness, showing a Khalsa's adoption of God's will. Long hair have long been a common element of many religious prophets of several religions such as Jesus, Moses and Buddha.

UDASIS

Udasis had taken a spiritual vow of chastity and disinherited worldly ways, but still regard themselves as Sikhs. The largely Vedantic, idealistic beliefs led them away from Bhakti to a knowledge and meditation of the divine, such that there was a shift from an own God to an impersonal reality. Although they believe in the Adi Granth and pay it great respect, they do not consider in the householder (grihasti), nor in the accumulation of wealth and property. Additionally Guru Nanak's definition of udas was to make use of all things in this world and not believe them one's own, but only God's property, and ever to acquire a desire to meet Him in udas.

The Udasis were founded by Baba Shri Chand (1494-1629), the eldest son of Guru Nanak. Udasi, from the root 'udas' means disengagement, withdrawal from worldly life, solitary, sadness and grief, and so refers to one who renounces. He lived a continent life of apostasy and asceticism. During the seventeenth century the Udasis grew in number and were esteemed by the early Sikh Panth. Early Sikh records demonstrate that there were ten major Udasi orders.

During eighteenth century, the Udasis got away the ill-treatment of the Mughal rulers. Since they conceived themselves as Sikhs, this naturally led them to look after the Sikh shrines in the nonexistence of Khalsa Singhs and the Akalis/Nihangs. Here they executed a key role in keeping Sikh teaching alive. Anand Ghan, an Udasi scholar of the late eighteenth and early ninteenth centuries, wrote comments on the Adi Granth from a mostly Hindu-Vedantic view.

The Mahants (in charge of the Gurdwaras) of the nineteenth and early twentieth century, often arrogated an Udasi descent, though their life style had substantially changed. The crucial occasion in Udasi history came in 1921 when a Mahant of Nanakana Sahib Gurdwara, taking to be an Udasi, engineered the massacre of a large group of Akalis who were looking for non-violently to reclaim the temple. Today they are seen as Sahajdhari or Sanatan Sikhs as fought to Khalsa Singhs.

Udasi wear their hair long and matted. The matted hair represents their renouncement of worldly life. Many go around bare and smear ash on their bodies, again symbolizing their death to the world of family relatives business and caste.

NIRMALAS

Nirmala educations integrated Sikh teachings and doctrines within a mostly Vedantic framework. Like the Udasis they were celibates, and did not believe in agreeing private funds. The Nirmalas, with the Udasis, form part of the Sanatan Sikh world-view and share many of its beliefs; along with impression in meditative and biblical recitation and study, they reflected, in addition to the Adi Granth, on the Vedas, Shastras, Puranas and Epic literature.

Nirmalas as digressing ascetic preachers, promulgated Sikh teachings in and outside the Punjab. They were thus the first gypsy movement to teach the ideas of the Gurus. The most famous Nirmala was Pandit Tara Singh Narotam (1822-91), who devoted his entire life to the explanation of Sikh theology. He wrote over ten books and reference materials. The deeply authoritative Giani Gain Singh (1822-1921) was taught by him. Sant Attar Singh (1867-1927) one of the most powerful Sikh Sants, also had his formal training at a Nirmala establishment. Today they form a well respected and highly conditioned organization with many institutions. As a decriminalize part of Sikh History they are assumed as a part of the Sikh Panth.

SANATAN SINGH SABHA

Sanatan Singh Sabha is the master Singh Sabha formed in 1873 by Sikhs in Amritsar. The Sanatan Sikhs consider Classical Sikhism as Sikhs to be a wider appellative of Sanatan Dharma by one who practices karma and bhakti (of God) in any way for the accomplishment of Moksha, or spiritual liberation.

As a strictly political response to the formation of the Sanatan Singh Sabha, a second Singh Sabha was formed and named the Tat Khalsa (True Khalsa) by The Governing British Administration based at Lahore in 1879. The British Raj applied the Tat Khalsa Singh Sabhia Sikhs to apply their 'divide and rule' policy which sought to negate Sanatan Sikhism in the name of 'reform' whereas Sanatan Sikhism is preponderantly inclusive, the Tat Khalsa is not.

The Sanatan world-horizon is essentially oral, personal, democratic, diverse, and reliant on past traditions and a historical in nature. The Tat

Khalsa world-view is textual, impersonal, elite, homogenous, historical, liberal and modern in nature. In the early there is an acceptance of the Indian culture and its value over Western culture and exploitation. In the latter there is a conflation and fundamental interaction between Western colonialism and Indian inherited traditions. The basic belief of Sanatan Sikhism is inclusively, i.e., religious diversity is natural and Sikhism can be wrote of a variety of unlike forms and practices, since boundaries are inherent fluid. The point of contention (with Tat Khalsa Sikhism) is that these practices are often inseparable from the practices evident in the Hindu and Muslim customs. Another springboard is when Sanatan Sikhs see Sikhism as an emergence of Hinduism. This is nauseous and mistaken in the Tat Khalsa's viewpoint.

Thus Sanatan philosophies are deeply embedded in the Hindu Holy Scripture such as the Vedas, Puranas, Shastras, admired poetic epics, myths and legends, aswell as in the practices of idol worship, worship of tombs, temples and other holy sites. There are also some Sufi, yogic and frugal practices too. A key point of contention is the Hindu canon of the avataras (divine incarnations) where God is conceived to incarnate in unlike forms at times when morality is about to be overcome by the forces of shadow. Sanatan Sikhs would include the Udasis and Nirmalas and conceive that the Amritdhari, Keshdhari and Sahajdhari are all Sikhs. Sanatan Sikhs also grip the Adi Granth and the Dasam Granth in adequate admiration.

The first Singh Sabha was founded at Amritsar in 1873. It was fundamentally bourgeois and Sanatan (eternal). It arose because of a comprehended dissolution of the Sikh faith, i.e., Sikhs were conceived to be falling into the folds of Hindu believed and practice. This was exasperated and combined by the rebirths of some Sikhs to Christianity - due to the extension of English-speaking education and Christian missionary camps in the 1880s. This induced a public tumult.

The Hindus, Muslims and Sikhs all represented these compound times as a menace to their customs and started reformist movements. The Sikhs thus introduced the Singh Sabha to recover a classifiable Sikhism. With the advent of the print media the task of detecting, defining (and to some extent creating) real Sikhism was worked out in print, journals and tracts, religious assemblies, preaching and public discussion. This cause rapidly elaborated and Sabhas were being formed all over the Panjab. However the primary other Singh Sabha was founded in Lahore, and was more reformist and radical, and which finally formed the crucial traits of the Tat Khalsa orientation. The Sanatan Sikhs (Udasis, Nirmalas and the Namdharis) were first challenged and finally marginalized.

AKHAND KIRTANI JATHA

They consider in the efficacy of kirtan (devotional singing) and on a regular basis hold nightlong sessions. This group also binds particular grandness to the meditation and repetition of the Sikh mantra 'Vahe-Guru' (wonderful Guru). The group discovers strict vegetarianism and will only cook with, and eat out of, iron utensils. All references to caste eminences are strictly forbidden. They reject the list of musical modes at the end of the Adi Granth, because of its qualities and do not repeat it when there is a complete reading of the scripture. However, conceiving that the words of the Guru Granth are literally the words of the Guru, they can be called fundamentalistic. Furthermore there is no interpretive explanation (katha) given of scriptural passages, since the meaning is assumed to be clear and crystal clear. The radical substitutes the archetype uncut hair (kesh) with a little under-turban (keshki), which both women and men bear.

Randhir Singh (1878-1961), a Jat from Ludhiana, started the apparent movement from his hanker periods in incarcerate, since he vehemently opposed British rule. He induced significant consternation with his vehement necessitates that he abide by his Khalsa's rahit (code of conduct) whilst in prison. His rigorous rendering did not allow him to eat out of anything not made in an all-iron vessel. He was linked with Teja Singh of Bhasaur and his Panch Khalsa Divan. His clique are known as the Bhai Randhir Singh da Jatha. The women are anticipated to wear the turban (Keski) as well as the common kesh (uncut hair). The grandness of the keski is warranted by the information that all the other five K's are extraneous and extra to the natural human form, exclude for the rough hair (kesh). Therefore it commands particular extraneous treatment.

PARSADI SIKHS

The Prasadi Sikhs are a arm of the Sikh religion. Most of them develop from Haryana, India. The virtually peculiarity of the Prasadis from thought Sikhs is that they do not consider in taking drugs. They conceive that this intervenes with the energy of one's atman, or soul, and obscures the innocence of the amritdhari, the Khalsa warrior.

Prasadis honor the Golden Temple of Amritsar and attend services in any Gurdwara beside other more orthodox Sikhs. Many Prasadis go forward to marry in the universal Sikh population. Like the Akalis, the Prasadis favour blue turbans on ceremonies, but in their case the blue is often a darker navy than their Akali counterparts. The Prasadis believe in the ability of women warriors and consider themselves true saint soldiers. Prasidis favour prayer, intonation and speculation as the true vehicle of wellness and curing and decontamination.

REFERENCES

Banga, Indu: ed. *Five Punjabi Centuries*. New Delhi: Manohar, 1997.

Brown, Kerry: *Sikh Art and Literature*. Routledge, 1999.

Callewaert, Winand M., and Pater G. Friedlander: *The Life and Works of Raidas*. New Delhi: Manohar, 1992.

Deol, Harnik: *Religion and Nationalism in India*. Routledge, 2000.

Duggal, Kartar Singh: *Philosophy and Faith of Sikhism*. Himalayan Institute Press, 1998.

Fowler, Jeaneane: *World Religions: An Introduction for Students*. Sussex Academic, 1997.

Ganeri, Anita: *Guru Granth Sahib and Sikhism*. Black Rabbit Books, 2003.

Hoiberg, Dale; Indu Ramchandani: *Students' Britannica India*. Popular Prakashan, 2000.

Kashmir, Singh: "Shri Guru Granth Sahib - A juristic Person"., Global Sikh Studies.

Keene, Michael: *New Steps in Religious Education*. Nelson thomes, 2002.

Khalsa, S. S. Shanti Kaur: *The History of Sikh Dharma of the Western Hemisphere*. Espanola, NM: Sikh Dharma Publications, 1995.

Kohli, Surinder Singh: *A Critical Study of Adi Granth*. Delhi: Motilal Banarsidass, 1976.

Mann, Gurinder Singh: *The making of Sikh Scripture*. Oxford University Press, 2001.

Nayar, Kamala Elizabeth; Jaswinder Singh Sandhu: *The Socially Involved Renunciate: Guru Nanak's Discourse to the Nath*, 2007.

Nizami, Khaliq Ahmad: *Some Aspects of Religion and Politics in India during the Thirteenth Century*. Delhi: Idarah-i Adabiyat-i Delli, 1974.

Nripinder Singh: *The Sikh Moral Tradition*. Columbia, Mo.: South Asia Publications, 1990.

Partridge, Christopher Hugh: *Introduction to World Religions*, 2005.

Pashaura Singh: "Sikh Self-Defintion and the Bhagat Bai". M. A. diss., University of Calgary, 1987.

Shackle, Christopher: *A Guru Nanak Glossary*. London: School of Oriental and African Studies, 1981.

Shackle, Christopher: *An Introduction to the Sacred Language of the Sikhs*. London: School of Oriental and African Studies, 1983.

Singh, Ganda; Gurdev Singh: *Perspectives on the Sikh Tradition*. Singh Brothers, Amritsar (India), 1996.

Singh, Kushwant: *A history of the Sikhs*. Oxford University Press, 2005.

Singh, Sangat: *The Sikhs in History*. Singh Brothers, 1995.

Smith, Wilfred Cantwell: *What Is Scripture: A Comparative Approach*. Minneapolis: Fortress Press, 1993.

Talib, Gurbachan Singh: *Shri Guru Granth Sahib*. 4 vols. Patiala: Punjabi University, 1985.

The Sikh Religion', M.A. Macauliffe, 1909.

12

Demographic Propagation

Numbering about 24 million global, the Sikhs are supporters of the fifth greatest religion in the world, Sikhism. The Sikhs make up 0.39% of the global population of which more or less 83% live in India. Of the Indian Sikh community 14.6 million, i.e. 76% of all Indian Sikhs, live in the northern Indian State of Punjab (India), where they form a bulk 59.9% of the population. Significant communities of Sikhs live in the Indian States of Haryana, Rajasthan, Uttar Pradesh, Delhi, Himachal Pradesh,Maharashtra, Uttarakhand and Jammu and Kashmir. The Sikhs as a political unit, distinct from other Indian traditions, can be said to have begun with the calvary of the fifth Sikh Guru, Guru Arjan Dev Ji in 1606, Sikh distinction was further enhanced by the establishment of the Sikh union or Khalsa, by Guru Gobind Singh Ji in 1699. This gives the Sikhs, as an organized political grouping, a comparatively recent history of around 400 years. Migrations of Sikhs during the era of the Gurus were limited to the limits of modern day India and Pakistan, and in particular restricted to the Sikh tribal heartland of the Punjab Region. The growth of the Sikh Confederacy and the development of the Sikh Empire (1716-1849), led to Sikhs transmigrating to conquered parts of their empire such as Ladakh and Peshawar. However these movements were limited, transitory and unsustained, depending on the Empire's wavering boundaries. During the time of the Sikh Empire, there was a net cultural immigration, with Napoleonic and British determines vying for the 'ear' of the then Sikh Maharajah Ranjit Singh. With honor to the Sikh distribution, the most significant political expression of this period was the diachronic constitution of a Sikh fatherland; the idea of a herculean Sikh state was a realism.

The Sikhs made enormous donations to Punjab from 1857 to 1947. Sikhs founded the city of Rawalpindi. Sikh agricultural and enterprising skills brought successfulness to Sheikhupura, Sialkot, Jhelum, Multan, Sargodha, Gujrat, Amritsar, Jullundar. Lahore, the capital of exclusive Punjab, had thriving Sikh neighborhoods.

The epoch of peace and successfulness turned into a incubus in 1947. The division of Punjab between India and Pakistan was a germinal disaster for Sikhs, unlike for the more legion Hindus and Muslims of the sub-continent. Islamic fiends made attacks on Sikh communities in villages and cities across West Punjab. Initially Sikhs thought the attacks were impermanent but their intensity increased after Pakistan's independence on August 14, 1947 when the Pakistani police and military broke down to protect the Sikh community. The Sikh communities were practically wiped out from Lahore, Rawalpindi, Multan, Sialkot, Lyallpur, Jhelum, Gujrat, Sargodha, Sheikhupura and other districts of West Punjab. The place of birth of Sikhism, Nankana Sahib, was burst away in West Punjab. Millions of Sikhs took flight to freedom and guard in East Punjab in India.

In 1960s and outside many Sikhs transmigrated to the UK and North America in explore of economic chances. Some of the Sikhs who had settled in eastern Africa were ejected by Ugandan dictator Idi Amin in 1972. Sikhs are primarily an agrarian community and with the forces of having only a limited amount of land, high birth rates and the want to make a better living, the male offspring of Sikh farmers were encouraged to migrate to foreign countries. Afterward the main 'push' factor for Sikh migration has been economical with significant Sikh communities now being found in Canada, the United Kingdom, the United States, Malaysia, East Africa, Australasia and Thailand.

ORIGIN

Historians conceive that Sikhism developed throughout the Bhakti movement amongst Hinduism and the Sufi branch of Islam, to which numerous independent beliefs and practices were added. At Sultanpur (Uttar Pradesh), Guru Nanak the beginner of Sikhism, experienced a vision to preach the way to nirvana and God. He is responsible the saying "There is no Hindu, there is no Muslim" which has since become one of the pillars of Sikhism. He instructed a strict theism, the brotherhood of humanity. He refused idol worship, and the Hindu conception of caste. Guru Nanak and Panth (his followers) later built the first Sikh temple at Katarpur. A succession of nine Gurus (regarded as rebirths of Guru Nanak) led the movement during the period from Guru Nanak's death until 1708. Sikhism advocated by Guru Nanak was largely a religious and spiritual movement, but even Guru Nanak proposed his followers to resist evil even to the point of sacrifice and martyrdom`. Later on Guru Hargobind Singh fortified on two swords `miri" (to defend and pursue political end) and `piri` (for safe guarding spiritual pursuit). But it was the last Guru Gobind Singh who instilled martial spirit into his Sikh followers called `Khalsa` and -who were to be called `Singh` (lion). The new order of Khalsa had to battle in defence of their religion, family and heart and their honor.

Sikhism of Guru Nanak was basically a religious reformist cause in the focus of Saint Poets of India. Guru Granth Sahib the hallowed book of the Sikhs comprises four poems of Trilochan, 62 of Namadeva and 240 Sakhis and 227 padas of Kabir. Most of the feature teachings of Sikhism like monotheism; crusade against idolatry and caste, externalism (bhaiachara), practice could be easily retraced to these saint poets, particularly Kabir. Kabir appears to be a present-day of Guru Nanak. Again, primitively, terms like Sikh, Saint, Sadhu, Bhakta and Sevak were employed in the same sense.

However, now, the term 'Guru' is to be employed for the first ten Gurus and for Adi Granth Sahib. All poets whose lines have been admitted in Adi Granth Sahib are called 'Saint. But 'Guru' is not to be called 'Saint'. However, one can memo that Guru Nanak: was significantly influenced by Saint Kabir. Sikh is really derived from the word 'Sisya'. Hence, Sikhism is the religion often Gurus and their followers Sisyas. A Sikh is one who is bequeathing to lay down his life for the sake of his Guru.

EARLY RISE

The growth of the Sikh community has been powerfully determined by the class of historical events. Guru Nanak, who was a Hindu by birth, turned at the time of religious reform movements in northern India. While his conceived shared many of the features of his contemporaries, his religious doctrine nevertheless marked a radical departure and soon attracted many followers. Guru Nanak was came through by nine other Gurus. Guru Angad (Guru between 1539 and 1552) established the Gurmukhi (from the mouth of the Guru) script in which Punjabi is written. Guru Amar Das (Guru between 1552 and 1574) founded Goindwall, a place of pilgrimage where Sikhs were promoted to gather twice a year. Guru Ram Das (Guru between 1574 and 1581) is remembered for founding the current site in Amritsar of the Darbar Sahib (Golden Temple) on land allowed by the emperor Akbar. When Guru Arjan Dev presumed the leadership of the community (1581-1606), Sikhism had developed a significant following in Punjab's central districts. During his Guruship the Darbar Sahib (1604) was finished and the Guru Granth Sahib (also known as the Adi Granth) was collected. Sikhism's altering influence, however, led the Mughal emperor Jahangir to check the development of the new faith. This move ensued in the calvary of Leader Arjan Dev in 1606.

Guru Hargobind (Guru between 1606 and 1644) responded to these growths by demonstrating a fortification at Amritsar and the Akal Takhat (seat of temporal authority) opposite the Harimandar Sahib (Temple of God) within the Darbar Sahib complex. The associating of these two forms of authority was further represented in his conclusion to wear two swords that signified the temporal and the religious. The leadership of the seventh and eighth Gurus (Guru Har Rai, Guru between 1644 and 1661; Guru Har Krishan, Guru between 1661 and 1664) was largely uneventfully as they sought to avoid a direct confrontation with the Mughal rulers, but their successor, Guru Tegh Bahadur (Guru between 1664 and 1675), was martyrized after making representations to the emperor Aurangzeb against the religious ill-treatment of Kashmiri "pundits" (from Sanskrit pandit, "teachers"). Guru Gobind Singh's Guruship (1675 to 1708) was marked by a developing conflict between the Sikh community and the Mughal and Hindu princely rulers in Punjab. In 1699, at Baisakhi, Guru Gobind Singh determined to further consolidate the development of the community by baptizing the Khalsa. Upon his death Guru Gobind Singh invested the Guruship in the Guru Granth Sahib. Thereafter the religious and the secular were was in the Guru Panth (the temporal Sikh community) and the Guru Granth Sahib (which would spiritually guide it).

With the break down of the Mughal Empire and the slump of Afghan charm in Punjab, the eighteenth century assured the rise of Sikhs to political power in the state. During what is known as the "heroic century," against significant odds, the Sikhs, who were the minority religious community in the state, accomplished political dominance in Punjab. This rise culminated in 1801 with the establishment by Ranjit Singh of the kingdom of Lahore, which admitted Afghan territories to the west and Kashmir to the east, and extended to the borders of Tibet. Although Ranjit Singh's state was the incarnation of Punjabi identity, its fortunes were largely led by a powerful military political orientation that was prevailed by the Khalsa.

Ranjit Singh's realm survived until 1849, when it was took over by the British. During the next century Sikh lucks waxed and waned as they were first covered with hunch by the ruling colonial rulers and then enrolled in large numbers into the Indian Army. In response to the competitive religious evangelicalism that took place in Punjab in the late ninteenth century among the three main traditions (Hinduism, Islam, and Sikhism) following the proselytizing activities of Christian missionaries, the Singh Sabha movement attempted to reassert Sikh identity by seeking the removal of Hindu influence and ritual that had accumulated the Sikh custom during the disruption of the Panth (Sikh community) in the seventeenth and eighteentheighteenth centuries. The employment of the Singh Sabha was finished by the Akali Movement (1920-1925), which successful removed Hindu mehants (hereditary custodians) of leading Gurdwaras, admitting the Darbar Sahib. This campaign launched the two premier institutions that have restricted Sikh affairs ever since: the Shiromani Gurdwara Prabandak Committee, which handles the occasions of the leading Gurdwaras, and the Akali Dal, its political wing.

Rise of Khalsa

The difference of Guru Gobind Singh Ji in 1708, after installing Guru Granth Sahib the last Guru, left the Sikh people with a legacy that was both inspiring and necessitating. Over the next century, they would face almost complete end followed by a golden age of sovereignty won in the scramble for freedom for the bursting Mughal Empire. The immediate successor to Guru Gobind Singh in his capability as generals of the Sikh army was a former ascetic who had been christened into the Khalsa and was popularly known as Banda Singh Bahadur (1670-1716). Banda Singh traversed into the Punjab from central India, where Guru Gobind Singh had departured.

Raising an stimulated army from the discontent peasants, town after town fell to Banda and his followers. They attained first at those who had caused the Guru so much trouble during his lifetime. Wazir Khan, the Mughal governor who supervised the execution of the two youngest sons of Guru Gobind Singh, was killed in a skirmish during the catch of Sirhind. The affect of the Sikh army on the social order was revolutionary.

The convulsion in the Punjab ruffled fledges in the capital, Delhi, and the once-compromising Mughal Emperor, Bahadur Shah, took draconian measurements. By ordering all non-Muslims to shave their beards, he efficaciously outlawed the Sikhs. The redoubtable Mughal army butted north and drove Banda Singh and his men back into their fastness in the Punjab Hills.

The end of Bahadur Shah in 1712 and the sequence to the throne of Farrukh Siyar the following year presented no respite. The new emperor coordinated regular expeditions against the Sikhs. Banda Singh, his peasant army and the fiercely freelancer Akali warriors, who had been the spearhead of the Khalsa victories, lived in the saddle, circumventing the imperial forces for three years. In December 1715, after three years of battling and a nine-month siege, Banda and his men were eventually starved into surrender. The capital was primed for a triumphant parade of the captured Sikhs to establish Mughal transcendence over this band of insurgents. Hundreds of Sikhs were decollated and their heads publically exposed.

The dreadful scene of murders contacted a climax as Banda Singh, denying to accept Islam as an alternate to death, watched his four year-old son, Ajai Singh, being hacked to pieces before his eyes. He himself was subjected to a tortuous end on June 9, 1716 by being pulled limb from limb. For the next two decades, the Sikhs stayed in persecuted remoteness, However, the Akali Sikhs brought a vital role in perfecting their guerrilla tactics, maintaining their faith and holding their place of respect in the eyes of the class.

As the once great Mughal court came down into scenes of murder and in-fighting, the predaceous rulers of Afghanistan and Persia infested India through Punjab; first in 1738, the Persians under Nadir Shah, and then the Afghans under Ahmad Shah Durani, who demonstrated his pillaging columns into India no less than nine times between 1748 and 1767. It was during these dispatches that they came face to face with the toughened Khalsa guerrilla warriors. Excellent horseman and sharpshooters in the Parthian mould, the Sikhs drew respect from friend and foe alike.

The pitiless guerrilla methods of the Khalsa were effective and reverenced. They carried out adeptly placed ambushes on horseback without allowing themselves to be maneuver into pitched battles. Depicting a small contingent of the main army into encounters, they would step by step break their antagonists' establishment and corporate strength.

Using this tactic constantly, the Khalsa could reduce an coordinated well-fitted out army into a harassed, incompetent and downhearted body of men. It was a way of fighting well suited to the individualistic bands of peasants and it turned the Sikhs into a practically indestructible army. In times of reversal, they would disband into the wastes of the Punjab plains. In better times, they would resurface in small groups that became the core of the strong and bendable organization which continued as a dissident movement whenever the Mughal rulers try to reassert their influence among invasion from foreign forces.

The Akalis were qualified and spiritual core of the Khalsa army. Despite early European account recitation Akalis as 'fanatics' or 'warlike', in the eyes of the eighteenth century Punjabi peasantry they had previously earned the reputation of being the truest Sikhs. This was largely due to the very useful role that they played in resisting successive invading forces during the most chaotic and disordered decades n the history of Punjab. present-day Sikh and Afghan writers pour praise on the nature and the behavior of the Akali Sikhs.

The Khalsa supplied the kindred spirit of the disparate Sikh communities, who had otherwise little or no communication. Like no other martial force in India, they obsessed a value system that forged them into the beau ideal of the Guru's warrior-saints. This spot as saintly defenders of the Punjab and its population, irrespective of faith, endeared them to the common people. A combination of their demoralizing revolutionary tactics and the groundswell of support from the peasantry led to a culture of extensive success. Ultimately, these evolved into twelve misls or confederacies. Twice a year, the complete army of the Khalsa, the Dal Khalsa, would meet at Amritsar to make decision on matters impressing the Sikh community; otherwise, the misls acted largely on the first step of their own leaders.

Capturing India's land held no magnetism for the Afghans and the Persians; they enter India simply to loot the dissolution Mughal state. On their return, they were met, while still battle-weary, by Sikh guerrilla forces and relieved of their booty. By the 1760s, the Khalsa army was powerful enough to have taken Lahore several times after defeating large Afghan forces. Lahore was captured again from the Afghans in 1767 and Sikh rule extended over the greater part of the Punjab. Soon afterwards, it spread to the hill country of Jammu and Kashmir. As the invading Persians and Afghans faded back to their homes in the west and Mughal power continued to wane, the Khalsa's power base and confidence grew.

By 1783, the Sikh forces were making successful sorties into the Mughal capital of Delhi. occupying it for eight months, together with the Red Fort. However, recognizing no political authority, the self-governing Akali warriors, the vanguard of the Sikh success, became marginalized as the Sikh chieftains started to organize themselves on territorial grounds. Success corrupted the idealism of the Sikh chiefs.

Numerous petty territorial disputes broke out between the misls, and Sikh fought against Sikh. Continued dissension led to the weakening of the misl organizations. In the ensuing disorder, the most powerful group, the Sukerchakia misl rose to supremacy under the leadership of a 17 year old warrior-chief, Ranjit Singh, who was later to be known and feared as the Sher-e-Punjab, the Lion of the Punjab. With innate intelligence, bravery and cunning, Ranjit Singh (1780-1839) consolidated the warring misls and again formed a united Khalsa brotherhood. By 1799, he had entered Lahore, the capital of Punjab.

FACTORS RESPONSIBLE FOR RISE

Eighteenth century is of historical importance because it witnessed the end of the rule of Mughals and Afghans, and the rise of Sikh power.The Sikhs, being engaged in a life and death struggle during this period.. The martyrdom of Guru Gobind Singh was not just an empirical fact, it symbolized a unique reality that Sikhism was a fresh ideology, and an urge to establish a new society with its own social and political codes, and fight out even violently as a last resort, forces which hampered their march to these goals. This being so, the stage was set for the Sikhs to resist with physical force what the Mughal state at that time stood for. Banda Singh Bahadur was the symbol of that response. He shook the mightiest empire in the world of his time to its very foundations. Within a short time, he became the master of the territories between the Jamuna and the Satluj, yielding an annual revenue of thirty-six lakhs of rupees. He founded a rule far different from that of the Mughals. It was committed to the welfare of all, irrespective of class, caste or creed. No communal group was special to him. Banda Singh proclaimed that his rule was to usher in a new era of harmony and mutual respect. He assumed royalty but did not flaunt it by sitting on a throne or by covering himself with a canopy. He issued coins, not in his name but in the name of the Khalsa. He introduced official seal, but that too was to declare that everything he had achieved was due to the grace of the SatGuru.

His rule, however, was short-lived, because the forces inimical to him, namely, the Mughal government, assisted by the Muslim religious elites, and Hindu political, religious, and social vested interests, combined together and defeated and executed Banda Singh in 1716. Even during this short period, the Sikhs' awareness sharpened and they were awakened to certain new realities. They demonstrated that the invincibility of the Mughals was a myth and that they could wrest independence if they had a will. Sikhs, under Banda Singh, by launching an offensive against the

Mughal rule and winning, set an example for others to follow. Though Khalsa sovereignty was short-lived, it went down into the memory of the people as a very good model of government and of governance. This fact alone was sufficient to sustain and boost the morale of Sikhs as it was a vindication of their belief that the Sikh ideology was a sure way to raise the status of the people. No wonder they soon regrouped to wage struggle not only for their survival, but also for asserting what they stood for.

For quite a long period after the execution of Banda Singh, they had to face persecution at the hands of the Mughal Subedars of the Punjab who were hell-bent to annihilate them. They cultivated a sense of Charhdi Kala. They developed a vibrant awareness of the role assigned to them by the Guru as members of the Panth. They organized themselves into Misls, voluntary organizations comprising equals, all soaked in Sikh ideology, and determined to reorganize society as per the Khalsa ideal. To successfully confront the Mughal and Afghan rulers, they evolved an organization, Dal Khalsa, a combination of all the Misls which not only fought militarily against the enemy, but also took care that the Sikh institutions and Sikh values were safeguarded properly. Ultimately, this organization emerged as the vanguard both in the military and social fields. So that its decisions might not be taken impulsively in contravention of Khalsa moral parameters, the Sikhs organized Sarbat Khalsa, an organization in which all the Sikhs, including the members of Misls, could participate.

It took unanimous decisions in the presence of Guru Granth Sahib often in the space between Shri Akal Takht Sahib and Shri Harmandar Sahib. These were called Gurmattas and were regarded by the Sikhs as holy and, hence, to be faithfully followed. With all these institutions and with the grit and the high spirit accompanied by the lofty targets, the Sikhs at long last succeeded in overthrowing the Mughals as well as Afghans even though the latter were led by Ahmed Shah Abdali, the ablest military commander of the contemporaneous world. Ahmed Shah Abdali's attempts at establishing Afghan rule in the Punjab and his hegemony over the rest of India were frustrated and the Sikhs established their principalities both in cis-Satluj and trans-Satluj Punjab, which accounted for over half of the Punjab. Not only this, they carried their forays into Indo-Gangetic Doab and considerably weakened the Mansabdars and other officials of the Mughals from which they found it hard to recover.

In this context, they raided Delhi fourteen times, proclaiming thereby, that the Khalsa power was the supreme and that its writ must be complied with without demur. At all-India level, they did destroy the prestige of the Mughal empire which was considered unchallengeable till then. However, they failed to evolve any suitable pan-Punjab model of governance which could appropriately replace the Mughal administrative apparatus. Like Marathas, they were more interested and involved in the affairs of their homeland.

All the same, they stopped forever the entry of invaders from across the Hindukush into the Indian subcontinent. Apart from the successful struggle against the Mughal oppressive state, hand in glove with the parochial Muslim and Hindu political and religious elites, the eighteenth century is significant in the life of the Sikhs from religio-social point of view as well.

At the spiritual level, Panth and Granth acquired unquestionable supremacy over the mind of the Sikhs. Sikh heroism was crested with spiritual glory. Martyrdom became a culture. The Sikh orders, Udasis and Nirmalas, deviated from the pristine objectives of projecting Sikhism in its unalloyed form. In the economic sphere, when the Sikhs came to settling down, they established themselves as peasant proprietors or as feudal chieftains, the development which clashed with egalitarian spirit of Sikhism.

SIKHISM IN OTHER PARTS OF WORLD

The existance of Sikh communities throughout the world presents a fascinating story of an immigrant community which originated in the Punjab, India, more than five hundred years ago. As everyone knows, male Sikhs are easily recognized by their turbans and beards.(But all men wearing turbans are not Sikhs.)Over the centuries, they have acquired a reputation for being sturdy, hard working and adventrous; they are a people who have earned the reputation for being extremely brave and loyal soldiers. They have also become known for being a militant people.

The Sikh homeland is the Punjab, in India, where today Sikhs make up approximately 61% of the population. This is the only place where Sikhs are in the majority. Sikhs have emigrated to countries all over the world - especially to English-speaking and East Asian nations. In doing so they have retained, to an unusually high degree, their distinctive cultural and religious identity.

Sikhs are not ubiquitous worldwide in the way that Disciples of larger world religions are, and they remain primarily an ethnic religion.

But they can be found in many international cities and have become an especially strong religious presence in the United Kingdom and Canada.

DEMOGRAPHICS

Numbering approximately 24 million worldwide, Sikhs make up 0.39% of the world population of which approximately 83% live in India. Of the Indian Sikh community 14.6 million, i.e. 76% of all Indian Sikhs, live in the northern Indian State of Punjab (India), where they form a majority 59.9% of the population. Substantial communities of Sikhs, i.e. greater than 200,000, live in the Indian States/Union territories of Haryana, Rajasthan, Uttar Pradesh, Delhi, Maharashtra, Uttaranchal and Jammu and Kashmir.

Sikh migration from the then British India began in earnest from the second half of the nineteenthninteenth century when the British had completed their annexation of the Punjab. The British Raj preferentially recruited Sikhs in the Indian Civil Service and, in particular, the British Indian Army, which led to migration of Sikhs to different parts of British India and the British Empire.

During the era of the British Raj, semiskilled Sikh artisans were also transported from the Punjab to British East Africa to help in the building of railways. After World War II, Sikhs emigrated from both India and Pakistan, most going to the United Kingdom but many also headed for North America. Some of the Sikhs who had settled in eastern Africa were expelled by Ugandan dictator Idi Amin in 1972. Subsequently the main 'push' factor for Sikh migration has been economic with significant Sikh communities now being found in Canada, the United Kingdom, the United States, Malaysia, East Africa, Australasia and Thailand.

Whilst the rate of Sikh migration from the Punjab has remained high, cultural patterns of Sikh migration, that favoured English speaking countries, particularly the United Kingdom has changed in the past decade due to factors such as stricter immigration procedures. Moliner states that as a consequence of the 'fact' that Sikh migration to the UK had "become virtually impossible since the late 1970s", Sikh migration patterns altered to continental Europe.

Italy has now emerged as a fast growing area for Sikh migration, with Reggio Emilia and the Vicenza state being areas of significant Sikh population clusters. The Italian Sikhs are generally involved in areas of agriculture, agro-processing, machine tools and horticulture.

Largest National Sikh Communities

Nation	Number
India	19,000,000
United Kingdom	500,000
Canada	225,000
USA	100,000
Malaysia	50,000
Singapore	20,000

REFERENCES

Avtar Singh: _Philosophical Perspectives of Sikhism_. ed. Gurnam Kaur. Patiala: Punjabi University, 1998.

Bhagat Singh Heera, Giani: _Gurmat Vichardhara_. New Delhi: National Book Shop, 1969.

Daljeet Singh: Sikhism: _A Comparative Study of its Theology and Mysticism_. New Delhi: Sterling Publishers, 1979.

Dhillon, Jaswinder Kaur: _Guru Nanak Keemat-Mimansa_. Amritsar: Guru Nanak Dev University.

Guninder Kaur: _The Guru Granth Sahib: Its Physics and Metaphysics_. New Delhi: Sterling Publishers, 1981.

Gurnam Kaur: _Sikh Value System and Social Change_. Patiala: Punjabi University.

Hawley, John Stratton, and Gurinder Singh Mann: eds. _Studying the Sikhs: Issues for North America_. Albany: State University of New York Press, 1993.

Hunter, Dard: _Paper Making: The History and Technique of an Ancient Craft_. New York: Dover Publications, 1974.

Juergensmeyer, Mark, and N. G. Barrier: eds. _Sikh Studies: Comparative Perspectives on a Changing Tradition_. Berkeley Religious Studies Series. Berkeley: University of California Press, 1979.

Kirpal Singh: ed. _Janam-Sakhi Prampra: Itihasak DrishtikoG ton_. Patiala: Punjabi University, 1969.

13

Socio-Political Influence

The Sikhs are one of the most enterprising people. Owing to their cosmopolitan temperament they have settled in all the nooks and corners of the world and have been contributing to enrich the country of their adoption by rendering very useful services. Because of their multifarious qualities and open mindedness they have earned good recognition and reputation at their work places. In U.S.A., Canada and U.K. they have been living since last decade of ninteenth century. Despite their very long and significant habitat in these countries, the Sikhs could not acquiant their fellow countrymen about their identity that they are the Sikhs belonging to the religion founded by Guru Nanak and nurtured by nine subsequent Sikh Gurus for a period of 239 years. Sikhs are the unique people who love humanity, serve humanity and seek 'welfare Unto All' when they pray before God, otherwise their prayer is considered incomplete. They have been instructed to help others, stand by the needies, support the weaks and remain egoless profused with a sense of humility dominating all the times. At the same time they are the people who can sacrifice their everything when their self respect is hit unnecessarily. They are the custodians of the righteousness and do not allow anyone to do injustice to them.

SOCIO-POLITICAL IDENTITY

A Sikh can be easily identified from amongst the crowds of hundreds and thousands. A man with beard and turban can well be easily recognized. Still some Sikhs wearing cultural dress give impression of a respectable monarch. Throughout the world one can observe Sikh men, women and children, dressed in fine clothes and colourful turbans, going towards Gurdwaras. A congregation in a Gurdwara makes one think of an assembly of heavenly people. The scared kitchen of a Gurdwara looks like the scene of a family feast where everyone seems to be trying to surpass each other to perform voluntary, selfless service.

Sikhism is a way of life, it is a tradition and it's a religion. Religion is an important part of every tradition. Faith in one God, honest earning, sharing with others, meditation, bowing before the Will of the almighty, Charhdi Kala, praying for the welfare of the whole of humanity, holy community kitchen (Langar), selfless voluntary service (Sewa), complete equality (Sangat, Pangat), equality for women, defending the poor, weak and downtrodden, tithe (Dasvandh) are the fundamental principles of Sikh religion. Most of these are unique only to the Sikh religion and Tradition. This, too, makes Sikh tradition distinct not only from the rest of east but also from the rest of the world.

The Sikhs have a distinct dress code, The Sikhs have their own different food. The Sikhs have their own sports. The Sikhs have their own rituals and customs regarding birth of child, marriage and death and also the Sikhs have their own Literature, their folk songs, dances and their own history. The history is a saga of chivalry and sacrifices.

These are a few basic points of the Sikh tradition that are specific to Sikhism only. Hence, Sikh tradition is a unique and is a lot different from that of others.

SIKHISM AND POLITICS

At the time of Partition, Punjab was so split up, that more than half of it got out of bounds for the Sikhs. They were debarred from primary, secondary and tertiary presence in areas wherein are situated so many Gurdwaras to remind them always of their heritage and history. Consequent upon rehabilitation, a large number of Sikhs did settle in Delhi, Western U.P., Rajasthan and places beyond several nooks and corners of the country. Irrespective of their overwhelming presence of so many ethnic and religious majorities, they are not invisible at those places.. At the same time to term those far-flung places integral to their geographic-linguistic zone partly imperiled by theirs and largely impeached by other's politics, will however be a misnomer.

All these factors are liable to call, the Sikhs to identity-politics that is raging in large parts of India and the countries around. The slogan of "Panth in danger" that the leadership in moments of crisis has loudly raised, goes to show that though covert it does hold appeal to the minds of the Sikhs. Luckily enough at other moments, they see through the politics involved and do not let this covert appeal turn into overt obsession. In the relative sense then, the Sikhs shun identity-politics. This is for several reasons, which, drawing upon their heritage and history, have molded their commonsense and directed their experience.

First, identity-politics is a call to alterity that visualizes survival of one entity through obliteration of the other. This goes against the grain of the historical heritage of the Sikhs which does compel its advocates to democrat borders from others but, by impelling them at the same time to cultivate bonds with them. Secondly identity-politics underlines one out of several identities which human beings have the potential and proclivity to and cultivate at the same time. For the historical heritage of the Sikhs, regional and linguistic identities are conterminous with the religious one. If desperation, opportunism and lack of vision drove the leaders to hold otherwise, the Sikhs in general did not become their playthings all the time. If not anathema, they have displayed aversion for such tactics of their leaders. Third, identity-politics tends to fetishes one denominational aspect so much that human beings have to petrify to one context in case they choose this obsession to over-ride their urge to grow, develop and progress, in life.

The historical heritage of the Sikhs has engendered in them this urge for growth, development and progress. Since it moulds their commonsense and directs their experience in the first instance, so emigration, without recall to goodsense in the second instance, has more and more become a way of life for them. This has resulted in their immigration to England, America, Canada, countries of south Asia and central Africa and molecularly to some of Latin America. There are so many places lying scattered over the globe which look like distant components of their geographic-linguistic zone in India. Of course, intervening distances pose spatial, social and cultural problems. Great ingenuity is called for to keep them under control. As such these problems cause lot of stress and strain to the real-life identity of the Sikhs. If they are neither alienated from their heritage nor obliterate by their verisimilitude, it is because nostalgia and alterity remain well within their control. Resilience is what marks their commonsense and underlines their experience.

It is problematic if in the twenty-first Century this will be enough of an asset to sustain them in the future. Involving choice, scope and opportunity to do and what not to do, sustenance is different from subsistence. Where the former is open ended the latter is in fact close-ending. To know if the strength to sustain themselves will be theirs in the next century, it is first imperative to grasp lineaments of social reality in the next century. To formulate it per the terms lately come in vogue, it will be the social reality of a new world order. Highly technologised and globalized, it will be a free for all so far go consumerism and the obsolescence of all objects meant for the purpose. Such will be social reality in the western countries in particular. To live it will be the destiny of the Sikhs because the level at which they are emigrating will betoken their presence more in those countries of adoption than here in the geographic-linguistic zone of birth. Then the pace at which the land is getting urbanized, this zone will tend to replicate change taking place in the western countries.

FUNDAMENTALISM

Is there such a thing as Sikh fundamentalism? Sikh theologians deny that such a concept can be applied to their faith and would presumably explain the recent situation in the following terms. Most Sikhs do not ever hear or read the term (or its translation) and few of those who do encounter it ever understand it. Of the tiny minority who do both hear and understand it practically all dismiss it as a term which could be applied to Sikh belief. It is a Western term, foisted on the Sikhs by the loose usage of journalists. The term is certainly used in recent publications with marked frequency.

It is, however, one which has been transferred from its Western context to the Islamic movements associated in particular with Iran, and from there was conveniently appropriated to describe the Sikh movement for Khalistan. The Khalistan movement was regarded as extreme and therefore it was fundamentalist. Is this a fair assessment. It is true that many of the participants in the campaign for an independent Sikh state (Khalistan) were correctly described as activists or militants, and many of them adopted a cultural view of their inherited faith. It is cultural in the sense that they revere their Gurus and the holy scripture.

It is also cultural in that those who upheld it adhered to a view of history which sanctifies the use of the sword when the need is compelling and when all other means have failed. Many of them could be described as fanatical in maintaining this particular faith. But this is not fundamentalism.

The term "fundamentalist" does not mean "cultural," on the one hand, nor "fanatical," on the other. It came to be increasingly used because journalists and other people in search of meaningful equivalents adopted this particular word as a loose equivalent of "fanatical."

Jarnail Singh Bhindranwale was a fanatical exponent of Sikh separatism. Therefore Jarnail Singh Bhindranwale was a Sikh fundamentalist. This view of fundamentalism as an equivalent of "cultural" or "fanatical" seems, on the face of it, to be a wrong use of the term. Fundamentalism, surely, concerns a belief in the inerrancy of holy scripture. Before accepting that this view is mistaken, however, there are at many questions which deserve to be considered. Is our understanding of the term "fundamentalism" in the Sikh context astray? Are there really any groups within the Khalsa which can legitimately be described as fundamentalist? What should we make of the views of some Sikh writers, mainly in English-language journals (particularly those which circulate amongst overseas Sikhs), who sound suspiciously like true fundamentalists? Are there some Sikhs who, under the influence of Western models, do adopt fundamentalism after all? What are we to make of the usage by journalists and other commentators who appropriated the term to refer to militant Sikhs? Their introduction of the term may not correspond to its original meaning, but introduce it they assuredly have. The strong defence of the term "fundamentalism" as applied to Khalistani Sikhs also needs to be considered.

Consideration of these six objections may perhaps lead us to modify the claim that fundamentalism is absent from the Sikh faith. Definition of fundamentalism is as follows. Fundamentalism, in its original and Christian sense, holds a central doctrine, together with a number of subordinate doctrines which flow from it. The central doctrine is the inerrancy of the Bible, and all the other issues which we associate with the fundamentalist faith are consequences of this one affirmation - such things as belief in the virgin birth or, at a vastly greater distance, hostility to abortion. This definition has subsequently been applied to Islam, where it seems to fit satisfactorily. Many Muslims also attribute verbal inerrancy to the Quran, just as fundamentalist Christians do to the Bible.

The transference to the Sikh community (the Panth) raises some doubts, but at least the Sikhs have a holy scripture and it is possible to argue that some of them attach a fundamentalist meaning to it. In theory at least it is possible to envisage fundamentalism within the Sikh Panth. With this definition in mind we can now proceed to consider each of the six objections which can be made to the original statement that there is no such thing as fundamentalism in the Sikh Panth. Is "Sikh fundamentalism" correctly understood? This question can be briefly considered and then set aside. Some Sikhs may be fundamentalists, but we must be careful not to align them with the more extreme forms of Western fundamentalism. Sikh fundamentalists (if the term is permissible) do not seek to build walls around themselves and to live lives separated from the remainder of their community or other communities.

There is no thought of a border which should be sealed, nor of modernist ideas which must be shut out. Whatever else may be said of this category of Sikhs, they are definitely prepared to face the world. If we are to declare some Sikhs fundamentalist, their fundamentalism must be understood in a modified form. At the same time the beliefs of certain groups within the Sikh Panth are indeed close enough to the definition offered above to warrant a closer examination.

Origins of Sikh Fundamentalism

How then do we explain the origins of these two distinctive meanings? What gives rise to the belief and behaviour which, in these varying senses, we describe as fundamentalist? The first usage is both very easy and very embarrassing to answer. It is embarrassing to answer because it means implicitly holding up these groups or sects to ridicule. Why are they fundamentalist. Why do they adhere so rigorously to a particular doctrine of the inspiration of holy scripture. The answer is that they have a singularly narrow view of life, one which enables them to shut out a vast range of belief and experience which inevitably presents a considerable degree of uncertainty. Or (to put the situation in rather different terms) they do not listen to other people with other experiences.

There are, in their midst, very few individuals who could be described as genuine thinkers or as authentic scholars. Indeed, one is constrained to say that they do not have a single person who could be so named.

This makes the explanation acutely embarrassing to offer, yet there seems to be no alternative. After all, it is the explanation which is characteristically offered for Western fundamentalism, with or without apology. The same explanation applies exactly to the Sikh case. The belief and behaviour of strict Sikh fundamentalists certainly differs from that of their Western counterparts because the scripture and the culture which they embrace are different. They are, however, truly fundamentalists, believing in the verbal inerrancy of their scripture. All castes are affected by it and many different classes, ranging from the simple faith of many of the Kukas through to the high-tech professional activities of many followers of Bhai Randhir Singh. There is actually a very general classification available at this point.

The Kukas and the Nihangs generally belong to the simpler orders of society, and one usually expects the poorer Jats or the Ramgarhias to be their members. The Nirankaris and the followers of Bhai Randhir Singh (at least the leaders) are, by contrast, generally drawn from the Bhapa castes (the Khatris and the Aroras, with a few Ahluwalias also drawn in). Most such fundamentalists usually live very quiet lives and only occasionally (as for example the Baisakhi Day march on the Amritsar meeting of the Sant Nirankaris in 1978) participate in the agitations which have been such a regular feature of the Panth's politics. Political activity, with all the agitations and disturbances associated with it, is particularly the state of the Jats (and especially the wealthier variety).

Needless to say, the wealthier ones require a large army of volunteers to conduct agitations and hold large processions, but for these they depend largely on their following in the villages. The Jats of the villages, whatever their level of prosperity, are the most likely to respond vigorously to the call of the Panth in danger, particularly if they are not engaged in harvesting at the time. This is not to deny the participation of other castes in politics. Master Tara Singh was, after all, a Khatri. Their involvement is, however, much less than that of the Jats. Even in the case of the Khatris it is less than their prominence in other areas of the Panth's activities would suggest.

The vast majority of those who participate in political activity are either Sikhs who adhere to Tat Khalsa views or are people without any great concern for doctrine. One does not expect to find many strict fundamentalists amongst them. The fundamentalists may well have a considerable sympathy for their co-religionists and likewise a rooted dislike of the Indian Government, but as actual activists they will not be very prominent. The case was, however, very different for the militant supporters of the Khalistan cause. Here we are dealing with the second meaning of the word "fundamentalist," the meaning which has been attached to it by journalists and adopted by some scholars. What persuaded these people to conduct campaigns and to wage guerrilla war against the Government of India? They were certainly Sikhs and their objective was an independent Sikh state of Khalistan.

The cause is now lost, but we should presumably expect that some new issue will eventually arise. The twentieth century has, after all, produced two earlier campaigns, in the Gurdwara Reform Movement and Punjabi Suba. In the strict sense of the word the proponents of Khalistan are not normally fundamentalists. It is only the transposition of the term on political grounds which justifies its application to them.

They may be called fundamentalists and we may have to become used to hearing the term applied to them, but strict fundamentalists they certainly are not. It appears, however, that those of us who stubbornly insist on the correct usage of the term have been fighting a losing battle. We may maintain that there are indeed fundamentalists among the Sikhs, but they do not include most Khalistanis or other political radicals. Rather, they are inconspicuous members of the Panth and are very rarely brought before the public gaze.

The reason for their fundamentalism is normally the influence of nurture or marriage, with relatively few joining such groups by direct conversion. But the term has been widely applied to the Khalistan militants and it will doubtless be applied to those of radical persuasion who may take their place. In vain will we protest that the word "fundamentalism" is not properly used when it is applied to the supporters of Khalistan, or to other radicals, and that the older, and more authentic meaning of the term has been compromised by such usage.

A second meaning has been conferred on the term and it seems safe to conclude that this dual usage will probably continue. For my part, though, the words "fundamentalist" and "fundamentalism" will retain a sole and exclusive meaning. The Khalistanis or other political radicals will seldom be true fundamentalists and should never be understood as authentic examples of Sikh fundamentalism.

CONTEMPORARY POLITICS

Sikhs are represented in Indian politics, with the current Indian Prime Minister Manmohan Singh, and the Deputy Chairman of the Indian Planning Commission Montek Singh Ahluwalia, all hailing from the community. The current Chief-minister of Punjab, Parkash Singh Badal, is a Sikh. Past Sikh politicians in India have included Dr. Gurdial Singh Dhillon, Speaker of the Parliament of India. Pratap Singh Kairon, Union minister, famous Sikh Indian independence movement leader and former Chief-minister of Punjab (India).

Prominent politicians of the Sikh Diaspora include the first Asian American to be elected as a full voting Member of United States Congress Dalip Singh Saund, the former mayoress of Dunedin Sukhi Turner, the current UK Parliamentary Under Secretary of State Parmjit Dhanda MP and the Canadian Shadow Social Development Minister Ruby Dhalla MP. Vic Dhillon, is a famous Sikh Canadian politician and current member of the Legislative Assembly of Ontario.

REFERENCES

Banga, Indu: ed. *Five Punjabi Centuries*. New Delhi: Manohar, 1997.

Bhagat Singh: *Maharaja Ranjit Singh and His Times*. New Delhi: Sehgal Publishers Service, 1990.

Bhatkhande, V. N. A.: *Comparative Study of Some of the Leading Musical Systems of the 15th, 16th, 17th, and 18th Centuries*. Baroda: Indian Musicological Society, 1972.

Bosch, Gulnar K., John Carswell, and Guy Petherbridge: *Islamic Bindings and Book Making*. Chicago: Oriental Institute, University of Chicago, 1981.

Brown, Kerry: ed. *Sikh Art and Literature*. New York: Routledge, 1999.

Callewaert, Winand M., and Pater G. Friedlander: *The Life and Works of Raidas*. New Delhi: Manohar, 1992.

Deol, Harnik: *Religion and Nationalism in India*. Routledge, 2000.

Duggal, Kartar Singh: *Philosophy and Faith of Sikhism*. Himalayan Institute Press, 1998.

Foley- Garces, Kathleen: *Death and Religion in a changing World*. M.E Sharpe, 2005.

Fowler, Jeaneane: *World Religions: An Introduction for Students*. Sussex Academic, 1997.

Gurmat Granth Pracharak Sabha: Encyclopedia of The Sikhs, Punjabi University Patiala.

Hoiberg, Dale; Indu Ramchandani: *Students' Britannica India*. Popular Prakashan, 2000.

Jarnail Singh: *Shri Gourou Granth Sahib*. 4 vols. Providenciales, West Indies: Intellectual Services International, 1998.

Kashmir, Singh: "Shri Guru Granth Sahib - A juristic Person"., Global Sikh Studies.

Keene, Michael: *New Steps in Religious Education*. Nelson thomes, 2002.

Khalsa, S. S. Shanti Kaur: ed. *The History of Sikh Dharma of the Western Hemisphere*. Espanola, NM: Sikh Dharma Publications, 1995.

Khushwant Singh: *A History of the Sikhs*. 2 vols. Princeton: Princeton University Press, 1984.

Kohli, Surinder Singh: *A Critical Study of Adi Granth*. Delhi: Motilal Banarsidass, 1976.

Manmohan Singh: *Shri Guru Granth Sahib*. 8 vols. Amritsar: Shiromani Gurdwara Prabandhak Committee, 1962.

Mann, Gurinder Singh: *The making of Sikh Scripture*. Oxford University Press, 2001.

Nizami, Khaliq Ahmad: *Some Aspects of Religion and Politics in India during the Thirteenth Century*. Delhi: Idarah-i Adabiyat-i Delli, 1974.

Nripinder Singh: *The Sikh Moral Tradition*. Columbia, Mo.: South Asia Publications, 1990.

O'Connell, Joseph T.: et al., eds. *Sikh History and Religion in the Twentieth Century*. Toronto: University of Toronto, 1988.

Partridge, Christopher Hugh: *Introduction to World Religions*, 2005.

Pashaura Singh: "Sikh Self-Defintion and the Bhagat Bai". M. A. diss., University of Calgary, 1987.

Singh, Gurbachan; Sondeep Shankar: *The Sikhs: Faith, Philosophy and Folks*. Roli & Janssen, 1998.

Singh, Kushwant: *A history of the Sikhs*. Oxford University Press, 2005.

Singh, Sangat: *The Sikhs in History*. Singh Brothers, 1995.

Singh, Sangat: *The Sikhs in History*. Singh Brothers, 1995.

Smith, Wilfred Cantwell: *What Is Scripture: A Comparative Approach*. Minneapolis: Fortress Press, 1993.

Talib, Gurbachan Singh: *Shri Guru Granth Sahib*. 4 vols. Patiala: Punjabi University, 1985.

The Sikh Religion', M.A. Macauliffe, Preface xxii, 1909.

Trumpp, Ernest: *The Adi Granth or the Holy Scripture of the Sikhs*. Delhi: Munshiram Manoharlal, 1978.

14

Religious Rituals and Traditions

Sikh ceremonies are simple, precise and practical guidelines laid out by the Gurus for the practice of the Sikh way of life. The Gurus emphasize that a Sikh should lead a disciplined life engaged in Naam Simran, meditation on God's name, Kirat Karni, living a honest life of a house-holder, and Wand kay Shako, sharing what one has with the community. This translates into hard work, honest living, love of fellow humans and through them service of the God, the primal power. This way of life is said to have been stripped of complications, myths, jargon, rituals and exploitation of man by man in the name of religion. No benefits are gained by where and to which family the person is born to – All have to undertake the rigours of Simran (meditation) and Sewa (selfless service) to progress spiritually.

All the Sikh ceremonies like birth, baptism, marriage and death, are simple, inexpensive and have a religious tone. They are held in the presence of Guru Granth Sahib and include Kirtan, the singing of appropriate hymns for the occasion, saying of Ardas - formal prayer, and the distribution of Karah Parshad, holy food, to the congregation. The baptism ceremony called Amrit, is the most important of all Sikh ceremonies.

RELIGIOUS RITUALS

Ardas

The phrase Ardas is derived from Persian word 'Arazdashat', meaning a request, a supplication, a prayer, a petition or an address to a superior authority. It is a Sikh prayer that is a done before performing or after undertaking any significant task; after reciting the daily Banis (prayers); or completion of a service like the Paath, kirtan (hymn-singing) program or any other religious program. In Sikhism, these prayers are also said before and after eating. The prayer is a plea to God to support and help the devotee with whatever he or she is about to undertake or has done. The Ardas is usually always done standing up with folded hands. The beginning of the Ardas is strictly set by the tenth Sikh Guru, Guru Gobind Singh.

Ardas is a unique prayer based on the fact that it is one of the few, well-known prayers in the Sikh religion that was not written in its entirety by the Gurus. The Ardas cannot be found within the pages of the Guru Granth Sahib due to the fact that it is a continually changing devotional text that has evolved over time in order for it to encompass the feats, accomplishments, and feelings of all generations of Sikhs within its lines. Taking the several derivation of the word, Ardas into account, the basic purpose of this prayer is an appeal to WaheGuru for his protection and care, a plea for the welfare and prosperity of all mankind, and a means for the Sikhs to thank WaheGuru for all that he has done.

The power that this single prayer possesses is astonishing. Starting with "pritham bhagautee simar kai, Gur Nanak laee dhiaa-e phir Angad gur tay Amardaas, Raamdaasai hoee sahaee and ending with Naanak naam charhdee kalaa, tayray bhaanay Sarbaht dah Phahla. The ardas encompasses so many Sikh and Humanistic values. It is more than just a prayer; it is a new concept of therapy for the elevation of the human spirit, mind and body.

In a congregational setting, the ardas is recited by one member of the assemblage with everyone standing reverentially, hands in prayer pose, facing the Guru Granth Sahib. Periodically throughout the recitation, the assembly as a whole repeats the word WaheGuru in order to support the idea that God, the Wondrous Guru, is the Supreme Being capable of anything. At the completion of ardas, the congregation bows down as one and places their foreheads on the floor to symbolize the fact that they will go as low as necessary to support WaheGuru and all that He stands for; in essence, they are placing themselves as the servants of God. Upon rising, the Sangat (congregation) proclaims WaheGuru Ji ka Khalsa, WaheGuru Ji ki Fateh. Immediately after uttering these words, one member of the assembly states the phrase, Bole So Nihal. In response to this statement, the entire Sangat heartily shouts, Sat Shri Akal or "True is the Timeless Lord". As one can see, the combination of the way that ardas is performed as well as the content of the prayer lends itself to the power of the supplication.

Importance: Ardas is read when the Guru Granth Sahib is moved and before the Guru Granth Sahib is opened. Ardas is read at a very specific time during the full reading of the Guru Granth Sahib as is done at an Akhand Path. During the Akhand Path, ardas is recited after Anand Sahib, a prayer in which the entire congregation stands and recites as one, and the distribution of Kara Parshad, a blessed offering made of wheat flour, butter, and sugar; but prior to the sangat taking Hukam (listening to a randomly chosen passage from the Guru Granth Sahib).

Ardas is read at the end of naming ceremonies, engagements, and the beginning of the Anand Karaj marriage ceremony. During the funeral ceremonies, ardas is said as the body is being taken away, while consigning the body to fire, when the pyre is fully aflame, upon returning to the Gurdwara, and after Anand Sahib is recited. Aside from all of the above occasions, Ardas is also recited during special circumstances in order to pray to WaheGuru for good luck and help in ones future endeavors such as at the beginning of school or before setting off on a journey.

One of the most momentous occasions when ardas is recited occurs during the ceremony where Sikhs take amrit in order to become amritdhari Sikhs or members of the Khalsa Panth. During this ceremony, the "five beloved ones" or Panj Pyare perform ardas, the prayer is repeated after the Amritdhari Sikhs take amrit, and then once more after all the expectations for an Amritdhari Sikh is revealed. Based on the fact that ardas is said so often within the course of such a significant ceremony, amrit, as well as with such frequency within such a large variety of ceremonies, one is able to understand how significant ardas is within the Sikh tradition.

Ardas incorporates a variety of images and ideas within its folds. It acts as a bridge that transgresses time to report the cruelties that have been inflicted upon the Sikh people while at the same time serving as a way for the Sikh people to seek guidance from WaheGuru' and thank him for the blessings that he has bestowed upon them. These events as they are portrayed in ardas provide the Sikh people with a sense of pride for their heritage and tradition. They are able to take strength from the martyrs and continue to support their faith secure in the knowledge that nothing could befall them that would be any worse than those crimes, which befell the martyrs. The dignity and courage that each of the persecuted people possessed through all of their suffering serves as an example for the Sikh people as a community. The rich and pure history that envelops ardas also serves as a means of educating the Sikh people. It is this quiet fervor that helped to shape the Sikhs as a people and mould them into what they are today.

The legendary stories and images from the past that it refers to within its context are perturbing yet at the same time evoke a sense of pride and courage within the Sikh community at large. Ardas not only accomplishes all of the above goals, but does so with a beauty and grace that is astonishing.

Amrit Sanskar

Amrit Sanskar or Amrit Sanchar or the Amrit ceremony is the Sikh ceremony of initiation or baptism. This practice has been in existence since the times of Guru Nanak Dev. During that time-period, this ceremony was known as Charan Amrit or Charan Phul or the Pag Pahul, the words Charan and Pag both signifying the foot of the teacher. During that time-period, the Guru would touch a container in which there was water and initiates would drink this water to be taken into the fold. When the Guru was not present, the masands or the local sangat leaders officiated. The water bowl was touched by the Guru's foot and then the devotees would drink it and seek blessings of the Guru. The Guru would guide the Sikhs about the Sikh teachings and instruct them to adopt them as a way of life

Khande di Pahul (Amrit Ceremony) was initiated in the times of Guru Gobind Singh when Khalsa was inaugurated at Shri Anandpur Sahib on the day of Baisakhi in 1699. Guru Gobind Singh asked a gathering of Sikhs, who was prepared to die for God? At first, the people hesitated, and then one man stepped forward, and he was taken to a tent. After some time, Guru Gobind Singh came out of the tent, with blood dripping from his sword. He asked the same question again.

After the next four volunteers were in the tent, he reappeared with the five, who were now all dressed like him. These five men came to be known as Panj Pyares or the Beloved Five. These five were initiated into the Khalsa by receiving Amrit. These five were Bhai Daya Singh, Bhai Mukham Singh, Bhai Sahib Singh, Bhai Dharam Singh and Bhai Himmat Singh. Sikh men were then given the name "Singh" meaning "lion" and the women received the last name "Kaur" meaning "princess"

Khande Di Pahul not only embodies the primary objects of Sikh faith and the promises connected therewith, but also is itself a promise to lead a pure and pious life to unite with Almighty Lord. It is about inward cleansing of the conscience and seeking unity with Supreme Lord through His Grace. The word Pahul is a derivative from the substantive, Pahu- which is an agent which brightens, accelerates or sharpens the potentialities of a given object.

It denotes the drinking of the Amrit or the Nectar. The Amrit is administered in the presence of the holy text of the Sikhs, the Guru Granth Sahib. The candidates take full bath, wear the five 5 Ks and present themselves before the Guru Granth Sahib for initiation of Amrit. The five Sikhs, who represent the five beloved, who had led a virtuous life and have strictly observed the Sikh discipline are chosen to prepare and administer the Amrit. The candidates for baptism are apprised of the Amrit conditions for acceptance before the ceremony is started. They are apprised about the pure and virtuous life they must lead. When the candidates agree to live by the discipline and code of Sikh conduct, the Panj Pyares start preparing the Amrit.

A Sarb Loh (Iron-steel) cauldron (Bata or bowl) is filled with clean water. Some Patashas (sugar crystals/plums) are poured into the water. The Five Beloveds then sit in Vir Asan (sit on ground with left knee down and the right knee up) around the cauldron. The mixture is stirred with a Khanda while the Panj Pyares recite path of five Banis (Japji Sahib, Jaap Sahib, Sawayae, Chaupai Sahib and Anand Sahib) from Shri Guru Granth Sahib and Dasam Granth with attention and full concentration on the Amrit preparation in the cauldron. The solution thus prepared is called Amrit (nectar of immortality).

The several ingredients and the aids to the preparation of this Holy Nectar are symbolic of a few things that are held in the highest regards by the Khalsa. The "Sarb Loh Bata" (Iron cauldron) signifies the strength of heart and mind. The chanting of hymns signify strong faith and cohesion in the devotees. The Khanda (the two-edged sword) signifies a spirit of valor and bravery.

Five handfuls of Amrit are given for drinking, five handfuls are sprinkled over the hair and another five are sprinkled into the eyes of each of the devotee who offer to be initiated. In this religion, it is believed that it should not be taken into mind that Amrit Chhakhna is the end purpose. It is the start of journey on a right path to attain pure and pious life which is essential to attain God (according to the Guru Granth Sahib. It is not something external.

Every Sikh is under an obligation and is required to submit himself to the order of the Khalsa. This can happen at any age and anytime they feel ready to fulfill their religious duties without fail. This is a pledge to remain under control, governess of the Ultimate reality. Amritdhari is the honour of being a member of the Panth (a disciplined force of the God).

A Sikh must live life according to terms of Sikhism. There is general understanding that novice must have lent period during which he must prepare to go the way of Guru and a voluntary firm decision to change life style and must be desirous and willing to live by the values and virtues of Gurmat. Then and then only, the novice will become worthy to get the gift of Almighty Lord's grace and attain eternal unity. Some people are of the view that initiation may be administered to a boy or girl when he or she reaches an intelligent age.

One who performs this external gesture without inner commitment to the ideas being expressed under doctrine of Amrit, is performing ritual. Without practice of the teachings in life and without cleaning inside and outside, such like initiation will be termed as ritualism. The Amrit Sanskar ritual is not external. The cleansing of the soul can only be done internally by the subject himself.

Amrit Sanskar is not ritualism, when novice promises and submits to the will of Gurmat, leads clean, pure and pious life according to concepts and doctrine of the Guru and emerges from the ordeal endowed with a totally different being from that which he possessed before his initiation

SOCIAL RITUALS

Religious rites in Sikhism which take place at several stages of life are called sanskar. For a man to attain several worldly stages he must go through several ceremonies at certain times in his or her life. The ceremony that takes place at these events is called a sanskar. The Sikhs have three main Sanskars or ceremonies in life. They are:

Naam Karan is a Sikh ceremony of naming a child and it usually takes place in a Gurdwara after the baby and mother are medically and physically fit to attended the Gurdwara. There is no limit or threshold to this timing and the family should not feel undue pressure of any kind as to the timing. The only matters that need to be taken into account are the well-being of the mother and child. It normally just involves the main family members attending at the local Gurdwara.

Anand Karaj is the name of the Sikh Marriage ceremony, meaning "Blissful Union" or "Joyful Union," which was introduced by Guru Amar Das. The four Lavan (marriage hymns which take place during the marriage ceremony) were composed by his successor, Guru Ram Das. It was originally legalised in India through the passage of the Anand Marriage Act 1909 but is now governed by the Sikh Reht Maryada (Sikh code of conduct and conventions) which was issued by the Shiromani Gurdwara

Prabandhak Committee. It dictates that only those who follow the Sikh religion may marry under the ceremony, therefore, Sikhs cannot marry persons professing to other religions under it. It also states that child marriage is invalid and that no account should be taken of the prospective spouse's caste. However, in practice, many Sikhs take preference in people from their caste.

In Sikhism death is considered a natural process and God's will or Hukam. To a Sikh, birth and death are closely associated, because they are both part of the cycle of human life of "Birth and Death of the body", which is seen as transient stage towards Liberation, complete unity with God. The soul being a unique form of energy from the source of all creation i.e. God, itself is not subject to death. Death is only the progression of the soul on its journey to God. In life, a Sikh tries always to constantly remember God (naam japna) so that he or she may be sufficiently prayerful, detached and righteous, and at death becomes one with God. "Lakh Akasha Akash" meaning countless galaxies or 'skies' also pervade or exit within the same One Almighty God along with all creation, including one and all of us.

Naam Karan

The Sikh ceremony of naming the child after its birth is known as the naam karan. When the baby and mother are medically and physically fit to attended the Gurdwara, naam karan ceremony takes place. There is no limit or threshold to this timing and the family should not feel undue pressure of any kind as to the timing. The only matters that need to be taken into account is the well being of the mother and child. It normally just involves the main family members attending at the local Gurdwara.

As soon as the family is ready to undertake this ceremony, the father or other senior member of the family should make contact with their local Gurdwara and make arrangements for this brief ceremony. On the day of this happy occasion, the family, all invited guests, the mother, and baby go to attend the normal weekly kirtan gathering of the Saadh Sangat, the holy congregation. The family should make arrangements to have Karah Prasad made for the occasion. Several Shabads of thanks, joy and support should be sung in the congregation followed by the short Anand Sahib. Then if a Sahaj Paath has been arranged, the Bhog of this reading should take place.

Then comes the main part of the ceremony which is the naming the baby. The Ardas is done in the normal way with a request to Guru Ji to grant the child good health; make him or her a dedicated Sewadar of the country & Panth; to enlighten the name of his family and Dharma; and to ask for a name for the child. The Ardas is followed by the Hukamnama. When the Hukamnama is taken, the first letter of the first word of the Hukam is the letter to be used to give the name to the child.

Once you have chosen the name for the baby, the word "Kaur" is added to the names of girls and the name "singh" is added to the names of boys. The Gianni will pronounce the name of the child in the Sangat and hail the Jaikara – Jo bole so nay-hal – Sat Siri Akal. That completes the ceremony. The parents should then begin calling the child with the name pronounced in the Sangat and this should be then registered with the legal authorities.

Anand Karaj

Anand Karaj is the Sikh marriage ceremony, meaning "Blissful Union" or "Joyful Union" that was introduced by Guru Amar Das. The four Lavan (marriage hymns which take place during the marriage ceremony) were composed by his successor, Guru Ram Das. It was originally legalised in India through the passage of the Anand Marriage Act 1909 but is now governed by the Sikh Reht Maryada (Sikh code of conduct and conventions) that was issued by the Shiromani Gurdwara Prabandhak Committee. It dictates that only those who follow the Sikh religion may marry under the ceremony; therefore, Sikhs cannot marry persons professing to other religions under it. It also states that child marriage is invalid and that no account should be taken of the prospective spouse's caste. However, in practice, many Sikhs take preference in people from their caste.

The Anand Karaj usually takes place at a Gurdwara (Sikh temple), although not necessarily so; the marriage may also be conducted at the bride's residence or any other place where the Guru Granth Sahib (Sikh holy book) has been installed. If the marriage takes place somewhere other than the Gurdwara, the place must be suitable and the Guru Granth Sahib must be installed properly. Any Amritdhari (man or woman who is a strict adherent of Sikhism) may perform the marriage ceremony.

The following are other important points that must be adhered to by the Sikh couple and their families: Both partners must be Sikhs. No consideration is to be given to Caste, Social Status, Race or lineage. No Dowry is allowed. No day is considered holier than any other; No astrological considerations are to be made; No superstitions are to be observed in fixing the date of the wedding. The religious ceremony to take place in a Gurdwara or home of the Bride in the presence of Guru

Granth Sahib. The religious ceremony must not take place in a hotel, wedding palace or Banqueting Hall. Burden of the cost of the wedding to be shared as equally as possible.

These days, the selection of the partners is left predominantly to the couple, with the families acting as supportive introduction service. However, in the past, the selection of the partners was left completely to the parents and other senior family members. This trend has slowly changed and communities will have varying attitudes to the selection process. Although, the ultimate choice of partners is always left to the would-be bride and groom, most couples will seek their parents consent and blessing.

The arrangements for the wedding are almost always undertaken by the parents of the couple, with the bride's side footing a larger slice of the total bill. The history of Anand marriage ceremony is traced back to the time of Guru Amar Das who composed the long 40 stanza hymn Anandu, in the Ramkali measure, suitable to be sung or recited on all occasions of religious import. His successor, Guru Ram Das, composed a four stanza hymn, Lavan, which is recited and sung to solemnize nuptials. During the time of Maharaja Ranjit Singh and his successors, however, this ceremony fell into partial disuse under renewed Brahmanical influence at court as well as in society.

The Nirankari reform movement of the mid nineteenth century made the practice of Anand ceremony a vital plank in its programme as did the later, more widely influential Singh Sabha. But there was opposition from the Arya Samajis and Brahman priestly classes, the former anxious to prove that the Sikhs were but a sect of the Hindus and hence subject to Hindu Law, and the latter apprehensive of a reduction in their clientele and income. The Sikh form of wedding ceremonial eventually received legal sanction through the Anand Marriage Act which was adopted in 1909.

The ceremony is now universally observed by the Sikhs. According to Sikh Rahit Maryada, a formal engagement or betrothal prior to marriage is not absolutely necessary, but if the parties so desire, the betrothal ceremony takes place usually at the boy's residence where a few near relations of the girl go with some gifts, sweets and fruit. The gifts may include a ring or kara and kirpan for the prospective groom. They are handed over to him in the presence of relations, collaterals and friends assembled usually in Sangat in the presence of Guru Granth Sahib.

Engagement: Formal engagements are not deemed necessary, however, if the parties so wish, the engagement will take place at the groom's residence. The relations of the bride will go to the groom's residence, taking with them a Kirpan (Sikh sword which is part of the five Ks) and some currency, both of which will be handed to the groom in the presence of the Guru Granth Sahib. The parents of the groom will present the bride with a dress and a gold ornament. In the West, it is now customary to present the bride with a wedding ring. It is argued by some that it is more in step with Sikhism if the ceremony takes place at a Gurdwara. Either way, the effects will a binding engagement of the couple.

Akhand Paath: This ceremony is optional, but is strongly suggested for a strong married life. It is a three-day prayer before all the other functions are to start. Here the Guru Granth Sahib is present and read non-stop, and divas and incense are also lit. Guests can come whenever they wish, in the first two days of the prayer, but should be present on the last day of the prayer in the morning hours. It is done in the morning hours because Sikhs believe that the morning is the most peaceful time of the day. At this prayer, breakfast, lunch, and dinner are provided depending on when you are present at the prayer.

Mendhi: A few nights or weeks before the main wedding, the Anand Karaj, ladies from one or both sides come together for a night of mendhi, dancing, food and singing. Here the bride's hands and feets are covered in a mendhi design. This is also where all the other ladies who are friends and family can get their hands stained in mendhi for the wedding. There is a saying in India that when you get married, and have mendhi applied to your hands, that the darker it is, the more love your future mother-in-law has for you. The groom, by tradition is also to have a little bit of mendhi on his palm or on the front of his hands. This function can be in a banquet hall, if large, or at home.

Sangeet: The sangeet is where ladies from both sides come together for a night of great food, dancing and singing. The sangeet is the Indian version of the Western bridal shower. At the sangeet, ladies sing cultural Indian songs, using the dholki (a two sided drum). This function is commonly in a hall, but can also be at home.

Chunni: After the "shagun" (engagement), the groom's family (usually close female relatives) comes to the girl's residence with the wedding "chunni" (veil) and is given gifts, gold ring and other jewellery. The boy's mother or close female relatives such as sisters and aunts puts a bit of mehendi (henna) on the girl's palms, a red chunni on her head, gold jewellery on her neck and ears, makeup, bindi on her forehead, sindoor on her forehead, and red bangles on her arms to symbolize her marriage.

Mayian: The mayian is a day before the main wedding. It consists of many ceremonies in one night.

Choora: On the day before the wedding, a ritual of chura (involving a set of ivory bangles) is performed at the bride's residence. Her maternal uncle makes a gift of clothes, jewellery and some cash called nankey-shak. He puts the bangles on his niece while the women sing cultural songs depicting the role of maternal uncles. Before the wedding ceremony, the bride-to-be takes a ritual bath and wears clothes provided by her maternal uncles, and she gets wed in those clothes. Similarly, the bridegroom-to-be also receives a set of clothes called jora-jama from his maternal uncles which he, too, wears at the wedding ceremony. It signifies the importance of the role of the mother's natal family at the wedding rituals, which also reinforcs the alliance established at her (mother's) own wedding.

Vatna: Vatna is the ceremony where the couple's families rub yellow tumeric paste (made out of chick pea flour and mustard oil) on their legs, face, and arms while they sit on a patri (a special red board with embroidery) and are under a red cloth held by four women. This ceremony is done to cleanse and balance the body for his/her marriage life. The culture of Vatna originally arrived from early ages when facilities weren't available to pamper the bride and groom prior to the marriage. Vatna in these days can be considered as a facial treatement which wasn't available in the olden days. There is always rangoli in front of where the groom/bride is sitting. A red thread is tied to the wrists of the bride and groom. After this the mother will clean the rangoli, and mix it with water, and put it on the front walls of the house. Indians say the longer it lasts, the more love a mother has for her son or daughter.

Jaggo: The Jaggo ceremony is where the family dances and sings on the road in front and around the beauitfully decorated wedding home. Jaggo is in the last hours of the night. They decorate copper vessels called "gaffers" with divas (clay lamps) and fill them with mustard oil and light them. The bride/bridegrooms maternal aunt (mammi) carries it on her head, and another lady will have a long stick with bells, and she will be shaking it. The ladies will then go into other friends and families homes and be welcomed by sweets and drinks, they will then dance there and move on. It is a loud ceremony, filled with joy, dancing, fireworks, and food. And if the family wishes the ladies' sangeet (ladies night of singing) and mendhi will follow the mayian and dinner.

Dinner: After all the ceremonies and family has started dancing into the early hours of the morning, dinner is served after the jaggo or last ceremony. Sweets are distributed to all guests families at all the ceremonies. All ceremonies nefore and after the Lavans are purely social, and do not have any religious significance. Hence, a Sikh can married with just the Lavans.

Wedding Day: The actual wedding day is really just one day, but Sikh weddings can last for many days, they are mainly 3-5 days. These include one day being the mendhi, another day being the Sangeet, and another being the Mayian ceremony. The wedding usually begins in the morning with the two sides meeting in a ceremony called "Milni". The word "Milni" literally means 'meeting', and typically involves an exchange of gifts by the father and maternal uncle of the bride and the groom. During the Milni, the family and friends of the bride and groom will assemble in the presence of the Guru Granth Sahib. An "Ardas" (prayer) called Asa di Var is read. When the Milni is complete, the parties retire for tea and other refreshments.

The marriage ceremony will then begin with the congregation gathering in front of the Guru Granth Sahib. The male takes his seat in front of the Holy Book and shortly afterwards, the bride will take her place on his left. The person presiding over the proceedings will first ascertain that both parties are Sikhs and that they both unequivocally agree to the marriage.

He will then ask the bride, groom and their parents/guardians to stand whilst the rest of the congregation remain seated and will then initiate an Ardas seeking the blessings of WaheGuru (the great giver of knowledge) and begging WaheGuru's grace on the couple.

The prayer publicly indicates the consent of the couple and their parents to the marriage. When this prayer has been said, the parties return to their seats as another short hymn is read. The officiant will then give a speech mainly directed at the couple explaining how the Sikh Gurus held marriage in high regard and how they taught that marriage is the highest and most ideal purpose to fuse two souls into a single spiritually inseparable one. High importance is also placed to the equality of the couple as this allows them to achieve the basic aims of life together and attain a deeper spiritual bond.

During the Anand Karaj, the four lavan (hymns composed by Guru Ram Das in the Suhi Raag section of the Guru Granth Sahib) are sung. They condition the love between husband and wife as the love between the human soul and the Almighty. Under these, the bridegroom and the bride vow to be faithful to each other in the presence of the Guru Granth

Sahib and the congregation. They accept the obligations of marriage by bowing before the Guru Granth Sahib.

During the main ceremony, the end of the cloth which is worn by the bridegroom is placed into the hands of the bride by her father/guardian. The four lavan are read by the person who is performing the marriage ceremony. After the first lavan has been read, the bridegroom will lead the bride around the Guru Granth Sahib whilst ragis (religious musicians) sing the same hymns. They will both sit down after having taken one trip around the Guru Granth Sahib. This step will be repeated until all four lavans have been read.

When the four lavans are complete, the hymn of Anand Sahib is read by the ragis. There is also an ardas, which marks the completion of the ceremony. A Holy "Vaak", which is a random reading of the of a hymn in the Guru Granth Sahib is read out whilst Krah Parsad (Holy food) is distributed to the whole congregation.

Lavans: The main part of the Anand Karaj is the reading and then the singing of each laav in turn. When the Laav is sung, the couple as a pair joint by a piece of cloth circle the Guru Granth Sahib. This has relevance to the occasion and should not be considered a ritual without meaning. When the couple circle the Guru Granth Sahib each time they making a commitment to God with the Guru as spiritual witness and support. And as one circles the Shri Guru Granth Sahib you are reminded that the Guru should be the center of your life, from which springs your spiritual guidance and understanding that you require for your souls long journey across this world ocean. The Shri Guru Granth Sahib is the center and the Sadh Sangat is your worldly witness and support.

The four nuptial rounds were written by Guru Ram Das for his own wedding. They explain the journey of the souls toward the Almighty. In them he tells us of the duties that a person undertaking a life of marriage should perform. In the first round, the Guru asks the partners to:

- Commit to righteousness
- Renounce sinful actions
- Remember, mediate and embrace Naam
- Only by good fortune, is real peace obtained
- Worship the one WaheGuru and all your sins will vanish

In the second round, the Guru asks the partners to advance further towards meeting the True Guru:

- Have fear of God and your ego will disappear
- Sing God's praises and feel His presence
- God is everywhere, outside and within, sing in Joy

In the third round, the Guru says that the partners mind is filled with Divine Love:

- Meeting the Sadh Sangat (Holy Congregation)
- Which is only obtained by good fortune
- Recite Gurbani and sing the Glorious Praises of the Lord
- The Naam will vibrates and resounds within your heart
- And you will know your future destiny.

In the final round, the Guru says that the partners mind become peaceful and they will have found the Lord:

- God's Will seems sweet to these Gurmukhs.
- You will lovingly focus your consciousness on the Lord, day and night
- All your desires will be fulfilled
- The Souls will blend with WaheGuru and only Naam will occupy your heart.

Doli: Before the groom departs with the bride, first the groom's party and then the bride's take lunch; the bride eats food provided by her parents-in-law and this is known as sauharian di rod. As the bride is about to leave her home, her mother, female relatives and close friends come out to see her off.

The band breaks into farewell songs. The bride and the groom leave together for the home of the latter's parents. The bride is usually accompanied by a younger brother, or traditionally, by the village barber's wife. This ceremony of the departure of the bride from her parent's home is known as doli, a word denoting the litter which was formerly used as transport for the couple; nowadays a decorated car is usually provided for this purpose.

As the car or carriage starts off, the father of the groom showers small coins over it, thus expressing his happiness over the successful conclusion of the ceremony. A basket of sweets (bhaji), to be distributed to the groom's kin and friends, is sent along with the bride. The couple is ceremonially received at the entrance of the groom's family house.

Then follows the ritual of uncovering the bride's face (munh vikhai) in the presence of the female kin, friends and neighbours of the groom. The bride is fed with cooked dal and rice (Khichadi) signifying that she has become a member of her husband's household. She removes her veil and offers obeisance to the senior women kin who give her gifts of money after sirvarna (revolving money around the head).

The custom of giving a reception by the groom's parents is becoming popular in urban society although some Sikh institutes do not allow this. The reception is held after the marriage ceremony. Close kin and friends of both families are invited. A day or two later the bride usually returns to her parental home. Only after the groom fetches her from there for the second time, may the marriage be consummated.

This second trip is called muklava. On this occasion and on her subsequent visits to her parents home, her parents give her gifts of clothes and ornaments. The word denotes the gifts given at the time of the marriage to their daughter and to the groom's parents by the bride's parents. The gifts given to the bride by the groom's parents are called van.

Besides, giving the dowry (again this is strictly against Sikh principles), consisting of all the things that the bride will need to set up a household clothes, ornaments, utensils, furniture and beddings the bride's parents undertake expenses on the marriage ceremony, feasting, illuminations, etc. All this is not to be taken as constituting the Sikh marriage, but is the general practice in Punjabi society. Sikh reformers since the emergence of the Singh Sabha have been urging simple and inexpensive marriages strictly in accord with the spirit of the anand ceremony.

Antam Sanskar

Antam sanskar in Sikhism refers to the death of an individual. To a Sikh, birth and death are closely associated, because they are both part of the cycle of human life of "coming and going" which is seen as transient stage towards Liberation, complete unity with God. Sikhs thus believe in reincarnation. The soul itself is not subject to death. Death is only the progression of the soul on its journey from God, through the created universe and back to God again. In life, a Sikh tries always to constantly remember death so that he or she may be sufficiently prayerful, detached and righteous to break the cycle of birth and death and return to God.

The public display of grief at the funeral such as wailing or crying out loud is discouraged and should be kept to a minimum. Cremation is the preferred method of disposal, although if it is not possible any other methods such as burial or submergence at sea are acceptable. As there is no grave a memorial to the dead or gravestone, etc. is discouraged, because the body is considered to be only the shell, the person's soul was their real essence.

At a Sikh's death-bed, relatives and friends should read Sukhmani Sahib, the Psalm of Peace, composed by the fifth Guru Arjan Dev, or simply recite "WaheGuru" to console themselves and the dying person. When a death occurs, they should exclaim 'WaheGuru' (the Wonderful Lord). Wailing or lamentation is discouraged.

If the death occurs in a hospital, the body is taken to the Funeral Directors or home for viewing before the funeral. In preparation for cremation (usually the day before or on the cremation), the body is first washed using yoghurt and water only while those present recite the Gurmantar WaheGuru or Mool Mantar. Then the body is lovingly dressed with clean clothes complete with the Five Ks (in case of baptized Sikhs). The body once fully clothed is transferred to a coffin.

The day of the cremation: On the day of the cremation, the body is taken to the Gurdwara or home where Shabads (hymns) from the Guru Granth Sahib, the Sikh Scriptures are recited by the congregation, which induce feeling of consolation and courage. Kirtan may also be performed by Ragis while the relatives of the deceased recite "WaheGuru" sitting near the coffin. This service normally takes from 30 to 60 minutes. At the conclusion of the service, an Ardas is said before the coffin is taken to the cremation site.

At the point of cremation, a few Shabads are sung and final speeches are made about the deceased person. Then the Kirtan Sohila, night time prayer is recited and finally Ardas called the "Antim Ardas" (Final Prayer") is offered. The eldest son or a close relative generally starts the cremation process – light the fire or press the button for the burning to begin. This service usually lasts about 30 to 60 minutes.

The ashes are later collected and disposed by immersing them in the nearest river. Sikhs do not erect monuments over the remains of the dead. After the cremation ceremony, there may be another service at the Gurdwara, the Sikh place of worship, call the Sahaj Paath Bhog Ceremony but this is optional.

Sahaj Paath Bhog Ceremony: After the death of a Sikh, the family of the deceased may undertake a non-continuous reading of the entire

Shri Guru Granth Sahib (Sahaj Paath). This reading (Paath) is timed to conclude within ten days of the death of the person. The reading may be undertaken at home or in the Gurdwara and usually takes place on the day of the cremation. The conclusion of this ceremony called the Bhog Ceremony marks the end of the mourning period.

Generally, all the relatives and friends of the family gather together for the Bhog ceremony on the completion of the reading of Guru Granth Sahib. Musicians sing appropriate Shabads hymns, Saloks of the ninth Guru Tegh Bahadur are read, and Ramkali Saad, the Call of God, is recited. After the final prayer, a random reading or Hukam is taken, and Karah Parshad is distributed to the congregation. Normally food from the Guru's kitchen, Langar, is also served.

OTHER RITUALS

Chardi Kala

Chardi Kala is an important expression used in Sikhism for a mind frame that a Sikh has to accept and practice. It loosely means a "positive, buoyant and optimistic" attitude to life and the future. Always be in high spirits, ever progressive, always cheerful, etc are some other terms used to describe this phrase. It reflects an eternally evergreen & blissful mental state of a Sikh.

Sikhism dictates that Sikhs believes in the Will of God (Bhana) and that God is without enemies (Nirvaar) and is always merciful. Hence acceptance of his Will is in the interest of and for the benefit of His Creation, even if at times one suffers severe hardship. This attitude of "Chardi Kala" is to allow one to sail through the ups and downs of life with as little harm as possible to the individual. To join and help others in their hour of need is part of this "Chardi Kala" spirit.

The Sikhs are a unique spirit-born people believing in Guru Nanak's basic concepts of Work, Worship and Charity and Gurmukh, Naam, Daan, Ishnan. Naam refers to the Power, the Energy, the Universal Cosmic Life Force and the vibrant manifestation of God in creation.

Chardi Kala signifies a perennially blossoming, unwilting spirit, a perpetual state of certitude resting on the unwavering belief in Divine justice. The Kala of Sanskrit origin gives a dominant meaning which is 'Energy'. Chardi, in Punjabi means rising, ascending, soaring. So, Chardi Kala would mean an intensely energized, ever–ascending state of the spirit of an individual or of a group. It is characterized by faith, confidence, cheerfulness, courage, fortitude, discipline and resolute willingness to uphold the cherished ideals and readiness to perform the assigned tasks even in the face of the most daunting challenge.

Courage is that state or quality of mind and spirit which enables one to face dangers with self-possession and resolution. Discipline resulting from training that leads to controlled behaviour, mentally and morally, is also an essential constituent of Chardi Kala. Perpetual readiness to act is another - he pursues the ideals he cherishes, makes no noise over a good deed, and proceeds to another. Kala also means "fine art", so actions in Chardi Kala become characterized by elegance and gracefulness. It also means playing a winning "Game" according to the accepted rules of the game.

Chardi Kala indicates the elation or high spirits of Sikhism. Chardi Kala, meaning "the positive attitude" is an equivalence of a mind that never despairs, never admits defeat and refuses to be crushed by adversities. It is the cherished ideal mood which the Gurus have preached and for which a Sikh daily prays in his Ardas (Prayer). "Nanak Naam Chardi Kala, tere bhane' Sarbat dah Phala"

Naam is the Power, the Energy that is always unlimited and never diminishes, no matter how much one partakes of it. In Gurbani Naam is also referred to as the Holy Life Force, as the Entity which is immanent and yet transcendent. As the Guru Granth Sahib tells us, "Says Nanak: Eternal is the foundation that the Guru has laid for my house and it becomes firmer with the passage of each day."

Chardi Kala is the superior and glorious state of mind in which there is no fear, jealousy or enmity and there is a constant celestial bliss of self-dignity, self-abundance and grandeur of soul. Chardi Kala is the indicator of a Sikh's absolute faith in One Akal-Purakh. The five K's of Khalsa, a gift from the Guru; are indicative of dignity and power. They are outer indications of the inner spirit that knows of no reverse or disappointment; of tht personality that is unconquerable in its hopes, of its spiritual radiance that is always a fountain of inspiration to others.

The life of the Spirit-born people imbibed in Naam makes the Khalsa noble, bold and free, self-less, flower-like and sun-like. They represent moral influence, radiating peace, good-will, friendship, fellowship, life, and vigour. They live in perpetual blossom like a flower with joy ever-lasting, and remain in a state of eternal bliss, not after death in some unknown region, but even now, here in this very life.

This is the central truth embodied in Shri Guru Granth Sahib, the universal scripture of mankind capable of dispelling the mist of ignorance and prejudice and propagating the light of Truth. This Truth is the metaphysical Reality, Beauty and Goodness that contributes to happiness. Man must not run away from the worldly life. The worlds of science and art co-exist and one can enjoy them by identifying himself with the Will of God, and by complete and unconditional acceptance of the direction of the Divine Will, he attains to the highest summit of spiritual bliss.

Dasvand

Dasvand literally means a tenth part and refers the act of donating ten percent of ones harvest, both financial and in the form of time and service such as seva to the Gurdwara and anywhere else. It falls into Guru Nanak Dev's concept of kirat karo. This was done during the time of Guru Arjan Dev and many Sikhs still do it up to this day..

In the time of Guru Amar Das, a formal structure for channelizing Sikh religious giving was evolved. He set up 22 manjis or districts in different parts of the country. Each of these "manji's" was placed under the charge of a pious Sikh (both male and female) who, besides preaching Guru Nanak's word, looked after the sangats within his/her jurisdiction and transmitted the disciple's offerings to the Guru. As the digging of the holy pool at Amritsar, and the erection in the middle of it of the shrine, Harimander, began under Guru Ram Das resulting in a large amount of expenditure, the Sikhs were encouraged to set aside a minimum of ten per cent (dasvandh) of their income for the common cause and the concept of Guru Ki Golak "Guru's treasury" was coined. Masands, i.e. ministers and the tithe-collectors, were appointed to collect "kar bhet" (sewa offerings) and dasvandh from the Sikhs in the area they were assigned to, and pass these on to the Guru.

The custom of dasvandh is found in documents called rahitnamas, manuals of Sikh conduct, written during the lifetime of Guru Gobind Singh or soon after. The culture has been kept alive by chosen Sikhs who to this day scrupulously fulfill this injunction. The institution itself serves as a means for the individual to practice personal piety as well as to participate in the ongoing history of the community, the Guru Panth.

Kirtan

Kirtan comes from Sanskrit kirtana. It became one of the pillars of Sikhism and in that context refers to the singing of the holy hymns from the Guru Granth Sahib to set music normally in Indian classical Raags format. The Sikhs place huge value on this type of singing and a Sikh is duty bound to listen and/or sing Guru-Kirtan as frequently as possible.

The Music traditionally has been Indian Classical Music, which is based on Ragas and taal (rhythmic beat patterns). Traditionally the Indian musical instruments the Harmonium and Tabla were used for this type of music. The Sikh Scripture contain 31 Ragas and 17 talas which form the basis for Kirtan music format.

While most Hindus and Sikhs devoutly sing Kirtan in its more cultural form, there are smaller groups that experiment with incorporation of non-Indian instruments like the guitar and synthesisers and interspersing Western themes like jazz into the fold.

The Sikh culture of Kirtan-Gurmat Sangeet-started by Guru Nanak at Kartarpur in 1521 was strengthened by his successors and particularly by Guru Arjan at Amritsar. In spite of several interruptions, kirtan continued to be performed at the Golden Temple and other historical Gurdwaras with due attention to raga, taal and dhuni.

The tradition of kirtan is as follows:

- Hymns from the following compositions only are permitted in kirtan: Adi Granth, Dasam Granth, vaars and kabits of Bhai Gurdas, Bhai Nandlal's poems.

- The kirtan-group is generally seated on the right side of the palki of Guru Granth Sahib. No special seats or cushions are provided for the singers. However, in big diwans (Assemblies), the use of platform or dais is allowed, provided it is lower than the palki (seat) of Guru Granth Sahib. This is done to enable the ragis and the congregation to have full view of one another.

- In the morning, kirtan of entire Asa-di-var (24 chhants, salokas and pauris) is completed. The singing of Asa-di-var is not to be interrupted by katha (exposition of a random hymn read from the Scripture) or lecture.

- Appropriate compositions of Gurbani are sung at certain functions. For example at the time of Anand Karaj (Sikh Wedding) Lavan, Anand and suitable shabads ar sung. At the funeral of a Sikh, appropriate shabads relating to death are sung. Kirtan Sohila is recited before cremating the dead body.

- Every hymn should be sung in the indicated raga and tala. The singer should use the appropriate laya, tan and palta. However, he must not forget the rasa and the appropriate ethos, mood and spirit of the hymn.

- Vars should be sung as indicated in the Scripture. For example Gauri var should be sung in Gauri raga, Ramkali var in Ramkali raga, with appropriate dhuni if indicated.

- Display of musical skill and excess of alaap and tan are not permitted, as they tend to make the minds of singers and listeners mercurial and unstable.

- Correct pronunciation and intonation of Gurbani is essential so that the audience may understand the wording and the meaning of the hymn. The singer is not supposed to introduce any words of his own or make interpolations in Gurbani. The use of extra words like ha, Ji, wahwah, piyara, etc., is against the spirit of Gurmat.

- The raga-technique and the sounds of instruments are subordinated to the singing of the hymn. What is brought out prominently by the musician is the Gurbani and its rasa, and not the musical expertise. Parallel quotations (parmans) to illustrate the theme are permitted during the kirtan.

- Any hymn that has been commenced should be completed. Lack of time is no reason for stopping the singing of a hymn in between.

- No kirtan is permitted during Akhand Path.

- The listeners should not make offerings (donations) to the musicians while the kirtan is in progress. Offerings can be made at the end of the kirtan. The best way is one followed by Sufi Congregations, where the listeners make the offerings to the president of the function or the organizer who respectfully hands over the collections to the leader of the music-group at the conclusion of the function. No ragi should interrupt his kirtan to acknowledge a donation or offering, nor should he mention the name of the donor. He should make a collective acknowledgement of the offerings at the end of the kirtan. This procedure is in accordance with Resolution No. 5 dated second January 1976 of the Kirtan Sub-Committee of the Shiromani Gurdwara Prabandhak Committee, Amritsar. In any case, interruption of kirtan to praise a donor or office-bearer of the Gurdwara or a distinguished visitor by name is absolutely forbidden, as it is against Gurmat (Guru's instructions).

Langar

The Langar or free kitchen was started by the first Sikh Guru, Guru Nanak Dev Ji. It is designed to uphold the principle of equality between all people of the world regardless of religion, caste, colour, creed, age, gender or social status. In addition to the ideals of equality, the culture of Langar expresses the ethics of sharing, community, inclusiveness and oneness of all humankind.

For the first time in history, Guruji designed an institution in which all people would sit on the floor together, as equals, to eat the same simple food. It is here that all people high or low, rich or poor, male or female, all sit in the same pangat.

The institution of Guru Ka Langar has served the community in many ways. It has ensured the participation of women and children in a task of service for mankind. Women play an important role in the preparation of meals, and the children help in serving food to the pangat. Langar also teaches the etiquette of sitting and eating in a community situation, which has played a great part in upholding the virtue of sameness of all human beings; providing a welcome, secure and protected sanctuary.

Everyone is welcome to share the Langar; no one is turned away. The food is normally served twice a day, every day of the year. Each week a family or several families volunteer to provide and prepare the Langar. This is very generous, as there may be several hundred people to feed, and caterers are not allowed. All the preparation, the cooking and the washing-up is done by volunteers and or by voluntary helpers (Sewadars).

Besides the Langars attached to Gurdwaras, there are improvised open-air Langars at the time of festivals and gurpurbs. Specially arranged Langars on such occasions are probably the most largely attended community meals anywhere in the world. There might be a hundred thousand people partaking of food at a single meal in one such langar. Wherever Sikhs are, they have established their Langars.

Guru ka Langar (literally, langar or refectory of the Guru) is a community kitchen run in the name of the Guru. It is usually attached to a Gurdwara. Langar, a Persian word, means 'an almshouse', 'an asylum for the poor and the destitute', 'a public kitchen kept by a great man for his followers and dependants, holy persons and the needy.' Some scholars trace the word langar to Sanskrit analgrh (cooking place). In Persian, the specific term langar has been in use in an identical sense. In addition to the word itself, the institution of langar is also traceable in the Persian culture. Langars were a common feature of the Sufi centres in the twelfth and thirteenth centuries. Even today some dargahs, or shrines commemorating Sufi saints, run langars, like Khwaja Mu'in ud-Din Chishti's at Ajmer.

The Langar is run by sevadars 'voluntary selfless' Sikhs and others who wish to help. It is a community kitchen and anybody can help in its running. These functions of Sewa brings a community feeling in the persons mind and destroy their ego and the feeling of "I" or "me" by the performing of this valuable service to humanity.

The langar continued to perform its distinctive role in days of the direst persecution. Bands of Sikhs wandering in deserts and jungles would cook whatever they could get, and sit in a pangat to share it equally. Later, when the Sikhs came into power, the institution of langar was further consolidated because of increased number of Gurdwaras running the langar, and assignment of jagirs to Gurdwaras for this purpose.

Simran

Simran in Sikhism signifies meditation. The prime purpose of meditation is to improve the quality of living. This is possible if we regularly become one with our inner spirit/self (Atma) which leads to union with the 'Creator', the 'Source of Being', the 'Source of Existence', more commonly known as WaheGuru Parmatma (God). Our Atma (soul) is the seed of Parmatma. Our Atma is like the wave which originates from the ocean, our God. It is the flame which originates from creator, momentarily takes shape and then recedes back into its source.

To most of us quality of life is primarily what we desire most in this human form. Basically these desires culminate into the following tangible/ objective categories: health, wealth and success. The first three are the sum total of all our materialistic desires. Human life, the Sikh way, as a grahasti (householder/worldly person) requires such aspirations - they are essential ingredients of human life. Sikhism does no advocate renunciation or becoming an ascetic. Sikhs must study/work hard, earn an honest living, be successful, share our earnings with those in need and, at the same time, seek spiritual enlightenment. Sikhs contribute positively to society, and do not become a burden on it.

Therefore, though the basic necessities of living, health, wealth and success are very important, we must place meeting WaheGuru as our prime motive in human life. Our efforts in getting closer to the ultimate aim of meeting WaheGuru bring us health, wealth, success and, most importantly, happiness. Happiness can only come with Naam Simran. I know a great number of successful people who are extremely unhappy because they lack spiritual nourishment, and suddenly find an emptiness which just cannot be filled. This emptiness is spiritual thirst. We must do something about this spiritual thirst from the earliest possible moment like right now, if we are already doing something about it.

REFERENCES

Bahura, Gopal Narayan: ed. *The Padas of Surdas*. Jaipur: Maharaja Savai Man Singh II Museum, 1982.

Callewaert, Winand M, and Bart Op de Beeck: eds. *Devotional Hindi Literature*. Vol. 1. New Delhi: Manohar, 1991.

Callewaert, Winand M.: and Mukund Lath, eds. *The Hindi Padavali of Namdev*. Delhi: Motilal Banarsidass, 1989.

Chahil, Pritam Singh: *Shri Guru Granth Sahib*. New Delhi: Crescent Printing, 1995.

Chaturvedi, Parashuram: *Kabir Sahitya ki Parakh*. Alahabad: Bharati Bhandar, 1964

Coward, Harold: *Sacred Word and Sacred Text: Scripture in World Religion*. New York: Orbis Books, 1988.

Ganda Singh: "Nanak Panthis from the Dabistan-i-Mazahib. " *Punjab Past and Present*, 1967.

Gandhi, Surjit Singh: *Perspectives on Sikh Gurdwara Legislation*. New Delhi: Atlantic Publishers, 1993.

Nripinder Singh: *The Sikh Moral Tradition*. Columbia, Mo.: South Asia Publications, 1990.

Pashaura Singh: "The Text and Meaning of the Adi Granth. " Ph. D. diss., University of Toronto, 1991.

Pashaura Singh: "An Early Sikh Scriptural Tradition: The Guru Nanak Dev University Manuscript 1245. " *International Journal of Punjab Studies*, 1994.

15

Society

Sikh is a person having belief in one God, the ten Gurus, the Guru Granth Sahib and other scriptures of the Sikh religion. Additionally he must believe in the importance of amrit. The word Sikh means a learner and, more specifically, a disciple of the spiritual teacher or Guru. For Sikhs the word Guru means God, as well as each of the ten human masters from Guru Nanak to Guru Gobind Singh, and the Guru Granth Sahib. Since Sikhs respect all religious paths theirs is not a proselytising faith.

Majority of Sikhs share a common traditional heritage. They originate from Punjab in North-East India, speak Punjabi, and every aspect of their lives is affected if not moulded by Punjabi traditional norms. Since 1947, when Punjab was divided between Pakistan and India, it has been the Indian state of Punjab with which Sikhs have identified. This traditional factor has to be borne in mind when looking at Sikhs' moral decisions, especially those concerning family life. Sikhs share many values (such as hospitality) with members of other faiths in the Indian subcontinent. For example, the maintenance and enhancement of one's family's izzat (honour) is a dominant concern. Misconduct, especially a woman's real or imagined sexual misconduct, brings shame on the whole family. During the twentieth century many Indians have emigrated. Although Sikhs constitute only 1.9 per cent of the population of India, they make up a much higher proportion of emigrants to the West. In Britain they probably outnumber Hindus and are a large community in Canada. Largely as a result of family dislocation, the younger generation of Sikhs are facing different issues from their parents at the same age.

It is traditionally on the older family members that the responsibility for decision-making rests. They are acutely aware of social pressures to conform within the Sikh community and these are likely to determine their conduct and advice. Certain major decisions are regarded as less a matter for the individual than in many families of non-Asian origin. Choice of career and, in particular, selection of a spouse are concerns for older relatives. Cultural behaviour, in terms of age, gender and status roles, is often at variance with contemporary non-Asian presuppositions and values. For young Sikhs in the West, faced with ethical choices in an environment far removed from Punjab, and for those in contact with them, it is helpful to be able to distinguish between time-honoured regional custom on the one hand, and Sikh religious principles on the other.

For example, family custom may dictate that sons and daughters marry members of the same cast. In rejecting this, as many Sikhs wish to, they are in fact not abandoning Sikh teaching, but acting in accordance with it. Those whose daily life is a constant remembrance (simran) of God will express God's will (hukam) in their actions. This is the shining message of the Gurus as set down in the Guru Granth Sahib, the holy scripture otherwise referred to as Adi Granth. Sikhs must recall God constantly, work honestly and share what they earn. Self-centredness (haumai) must give way to the Godward orientation of a gurmukh.

The gurmukh is a person who shuns lust, anger, greed, attachment to things temporal and pride (kaam, krodh, lobh, moh and ahankar). Sikhs must resist the temptation to renounce secular responsibilities, and must seek to live like a lotus, which is rooted in the mire, but unsullied by it. Because certain values were and are a basic part of Indian society, the Gurus did not emphasise them. Thus, a Sikh knows it is necessary to show hospitality to strangers and respect to the elderly. But because caste discrimination and religiosity were common problems, Guru Nanak and his successors proclaimed tirelessly the irrelevance of caste distinction and of superficial ritualism to the soul's reunion with God.

This emphasis on certain aspects of behaviour should not be taken to mean that other values are less important. A Sikh's conduct may find inspiration in certain compositions and traditions not included in the Guru Granth Sahib. Among these are the Vars of Bhai Gurdas and the numerous stories of Guru Nanak's life known as the janamsakhis. Equally inspirational are the compositions of Guru Gobind Singh, comprising the Dasam. Granth, and also the accounts of later Sikhs' heroism and martyrdom. Ever since the time of Guru Gobind Singh, codes of conduct (rahitnamas), for example Rahitnama Bhai Chaupa Singh and Prem Sumarg, have been in circulation. These lay down the behaviour required of Sikhs. Sikhs can decide questions of individual and corporate, moral and ritual conduct in the light of the most recent of these codes of practice, the Rahit Maryada, a guide to the Sikh way of life.

This was approved for issue by the Shiromani Gurdwara Parbandhak Committee, the central advisory body of the Sikhs, in 1945. It is available in both Punjabi and English. The few comprehensive studies of Sikh ethics so far undertaken do not tackle many major, highly complex and controversial contemporary issues such as nuclear war. These await serious scholarly attention and indeed recognition by most preachers.

Many Sikhs, young and old alike, act on the guidance of revered spiritual masters known as sants. They may have complete faith in their pronouncements, regardless of how little first-hand experience a sant has of some of his followers' perplexities. Some ethical issues, such as abortion, euthanasia and homosexuality, have not been publicly debated or discussed by scholars. Others, of central concern to Sikh identity, such as the cutting of one's hair or smoking, have received a great deal of attention. In the latter case, contemporary medical research is used to support the religious prohibition. Currently most Sikh concern is focused on the uneasy situation of Sikhs in India. This means that other controversial ethical issues are unlikely to receive so much attention. However, Piara Singh Sambhi and Gobind Singh Mansukhani have provided a Sikh response to important contemporary questions.

SOCIAL ORDER

The Sikh Gurus had a very high regard for the state of marriage, and they themselves entered into matrimony. They insisted that marriage is not merely a civil or social contract, but that its highest and most ideal purpose is to fuse two souls into one so that they may become spiritually inseparable.

In Guru Amar Das' words: They are not husband and wife who only dwell together. Only they who have one spirit in two bodies can be called husband and wife.

Verses such as the one above are used in the Anand Karaj (literally 'Ceremony of Bliss'), the Sikh marriage service, to impress upon the bridal couple the significance of marriage. The volume of the scriptures is the Guru in their midst, witnessing the marriage. Without the Guru Granth Sahib's presence no valid Sikh marriage can take place, and conversely, wherever it is appropriately installed is a fit place for the Anand Karaj, whether in a Western Gurdwara or in India under an awning near the bride's home. These affirm the life of the grihasth (the married householder as opposed to the celibate) and suggest the progression of conjugal devotion, while on the spiritual plane evoking the soul's gradual advance towards union with God.

Anand Karaj has been recognized as legal marriage in India since the passing of the Anand Marriage Act in 1909. In Britain, some Gurdwaras have registering officers who conduct a brief civil marriage on the day of the religious ceremony. Most Sikhs who marry in the West have a civil marriage in the Registry Office near the time of their engagement, but do not live together until after the Anand Karaj has been solemnised.

Indian culture, rather than specific Sikh religious teaching, demands that the couple have children, in particular a son to carry on the family name and to care for his parents in their declining years. In practice, women's sexual morality is more strictly enforced, but the Gurus condemned the adultery of men - even in thought.

Do not cast your eyes on the beauty of another's wife. The Sikh's underwear (kachha), worn by both sexes should remind them of the need for their marital fidelity. Monogamy has always been the Sikh norm. However both Guru Hargobind and Guru Gobind Singh had three wives, probably resulting from the fact that some devout Sikhs dedicated their daughters at birth exclusively to the Guru and his relatives.

Marriage is lifelong but there is no religious reason why Sikh widows and widowers should not remarry. In practice, perhaps influenced by the attitudes of Hindus, a woman is less likely to remarry than a man, although marriage to a close relative of her late husband is socially sanctioned.

Unlike Muslims, Sikhs of most castes may not marry cousins. In fact, they observe the general, unwritten Punjabi Hindu rules restricting marriage to members of the same subcaste (Jat, Ramgarhia, etc.) but of different gotra (clan). This precludes marrying anyone with the same family name as either of one's parents or any of one's grandparents. In villages men always marry women from a different village, in order to avoid moral laxity in village society where the men regard each other as brothers and the women as their sisters. This is a social convention and is not strictly observed among Sikhs living in the cities, whether in India or overseas.

Similarly, in the majority of Sikh marriages, parents and senior family members play a leading part in selecting the spouse. This is simply the way things are done in South Asian society; it is not a religious requirement. From a religious point of view what is required is that the future bride or groom be a Sikh. In practice, inter-marriage with Hindus has often occurred, but only according to the caste and got rules already outlined. For a Sikh girl to marry a non-Sikh would be considered more reprehensible than for a Sikh boy to marry out, for it is assumed that wife and children follow the father's faith.

Also, since marriage is a union of two families, it is felt that care must be taken to avoid needless future friction. This means ensuring that one's son's or daughter's life partner is from a background similar in its religious orientation and general outlook, as well as in its levels of education and income.

In practice, but not by any religious requirement, family relationships are based on the same expectations and presuppositions as in Punjabi Hindu society. Parents tend to indulge small children, especially boys, and to discipline older ones more strictly. A girl is brought up knowing she will one day be lost to another family whose love and respect she must earn, but looks to her brother for lifelong moral support. Boys know that they will be responsible for caring for their parents in their old age.

Folk songs, particularly those sung at the time of weddings, draw out the usual relationships of love (between mother and daughter, brother and sister) and potential friction (notably mother-in-law and daughter-in-law). In the West, many families conform outwardly - in terms of the number of relatives living under a single roof - to the norms of the nuclear family, but frequent reunions, especially at marriages, make children keenly aware of kinship ties, obligations and relative status.

For example, a man will feel bound to please his daughter's or his sister's in-laws. Since they have, as it were, taken a wife from his family, they enjoy higher prestige than those who gave the wife. Similarly, with her husband's younger brothers, a woman has an altogether more relaxed, joking relationship than with his elder brothers who have the greater status. This is very different from Western family life in which individual preference, rather than the nature of the relationship, determines relations (or the lack of them) with relatives and in-laws.

As in Hindu families cousins are regarded as brothers and sisters. Indeed in Punjabi villages there is a sense of blood relationship between all members of a zat.

In Punjab, as in Indian society generally, a child would not say 'thank you' to his or her parents. That would suggest that parental love is conditional and uncertain, rather than the prerogative of every child. To thank a relative in so many words would be to impose a distance and formality. Love is reciprocated in non-verbal ways. Parents know that they can rely on their sons to care for them in old age, and that their children will in turn lavish care on the next generation.

Among Sikhs resident in Western society, fewer relatives live together, both wives and husbands are at work and family ties are put to the test. More subtle influences are also at work. For example, the younger generation may think in terms of 'my friends' and 'my mother's friends'. In the past a parent's friend would automatically be a child's 'aunt' or 'uncle', and would be treated with the respect given to other older members of the family. Friendship was not seen in such an individualistic way as it often is nowadays in Western society.

Although marriage is regarded as the union of two souls and a lifelong bond, divorce increasingly occurs. Although it is permitted by Indian law, divorce is rarer among Sikhs in India than among Sikhs in the West. One reason is that in India women of all religions are less likely than those in the West to be financially independent of their spouses.

Wherever possible, Sikhs will endeavour to achieve a reconciliation between husband and wife. Consideration for the children may prevent divorce. 'If the wife and husband break off, their concern for their children reunites them'. When it does occur, divorce is regarded as extremely unfortunate. By many it is seen as a punishment for past wrong. Whatever the reason for the breakup, for divorced women the stigma persists. Parents will usually arrange a second marriage for their son or daughter if the first union has ended in divorce. A divorcee can be remarried in the Gurdwara.

SOCIAL CONDUCT

According to Sikhism, the mission of human life is the attainment of God and the realization is possible by observing the principles of truth in their true spirit. It is desired of a Sikh to live upto the discipline of Bani (Nam Simran) and Bana (Wearing of Five Kakars and keeping piety of outlook) to attain the ultimate goal.

Sikh code of conduct provides social, cultural, religious and spiritual teachings for governance of Khalsa corporate life. Sikh faith is established on observance of the principles and rules formulated by the Sikh Gurus in the true sense.

Sikhism is a way of life and the game of love needs truth and commitment on that way. In micro sense, Sikhism is concerned with individual life style (Gurmat and Reht Maryada style of life) of a Sikh but in macro sense, it is concerned with his corporate style of life (Sangat, Pangat, supermacy of Akal Takht and Wand Chhakna etc)conducted and governed truely at all the times and at all the places and in every behaviour according to the Word of God.

Sikhism is a way of life which believes in pure and pious living. It is a dynamic and practical religion. It has got certain principles and discipline to follow. More important than belief in the principles of the Sikh faith is the actual practice of the teachings of the Gurus. There are set rules and ways for the ideal life in Sikhism which determine Sikh beliefs and practices.

Sikh Code of Conduct is called Sikh Rehat Maryada. It is a manual and code of discipline for the followers of Sikh faith for social, moral, religious, spiritual and general living. According to the Sikh code of conduct published in 1945 by Shiromani Gurdwara Parbandhak Committee Amritsar, a Sikh must practice the concept of Bani (Spiritual life) and Bana (Uniform with Five Kakars). He must live upto the Internal and External code of conduct.

Internal Rehat Maryada means living a pure, pious and spiritual inner life. External Rehat Maryada means the outer code of conduct and visible living of virtuous life (Norm and Form). Rehat Maryada literally means "the code of conduct or way of life". Reht means mode of living or conduct and Maryada means culture, practice of the faith or code or discipline of life. It extends its meaning to life discipline. It meets the principles for ethical, moral and spiritual life. It is a code which tells the Sikh followers how to live and how not to live. It is a manual for the Sikh which tells him to live like a Lotus which has its roots in muddy water but its flower blooms floating pure and spotless over the muddy base.

Sikhism is essentially a practical religion. It gives great significance to voluntary discipline and self restraint in the physical, mental, moral and spiritual fields. Sikhism gives reverence to its holy traditions (Maryada), heritage, tradition and religious living. It does not call for blind and arrogant compliance of its way of life. Sikh Rehat is touch stone which reveals the purity and perfection of the Khalsa.

Sikhism believes in willing discipline of body and mind. It aims at serving the mankind and attaining the Ultimate Reality through Naam Simran, Sachi Kirt and Wand Chhakna. There is no use of coercion in observance of the discipline. It is not punitive. The code of Sikh conduct is positive, correctional and requires the devotee to attune with the Will of God. Sikhism believes in gradual progress of Sehaj Dharis to become the Khalsa. The deviants and slow movers are to be treated with sympathy and loving care so that they learn their roots and join the main stream.

Sikh Rehat Maryada has been evolved on the basic principles of God's universe, discipline of planetary system and the law of nature. Human body, mind and consciousness are gifts of the Lord leased to mankind for a pre-determined life time. Sikhism wants these gifts to be used for attainment of God through service of mankind.

Shri Guru Granth Sahib is the primary source of Sikh Code of Conduct. It is supported by Dasam Granth, Vars of Bhai Gurdas and writings of Bhai Nand Lal. The Rehat is further strengthened through the Rehat Namas of Bhai Nand Lal, Bhai Daya Singh, Bhai Desa Singh, Bhai Champa Singh and others. Gurbani says that blessed with infinite joy, without a trace of sorrow, is the house that Guru Nanak has inherited. Sikhism wants to keep peace and tranquillity in that house.

The doctrine of five Kakars gifted by Guru Gobind Singh helps the Sikhs to live life in full measure and with universal resources. The Guru ordained not only the Khalsa how to live but also how not to live. He gave certain do's and don'ts to the Khalsa Panth.

It is very essential to point out that no individual or individual organization has the authority to change or alter the Sikh Rehat Maryada as per personal needs and whims. Every Sikh is required to bow head before the Sikh Rehat Maryada published by Shiromani Gurdwara Parbandhak Committee. There is only one Rahit Maryada for the Khalsa Panth, it does not belong to any particular Jatha or entity, yet as Sikhs we are all obliged to follow it.

It is explicit in Gurbani that the principles of Gurmat are unchangeable and of permanent standing: The Instruction of the Guru is Unshakable. None can change it. Every Sikh must strengthen its rallying point i.e. Shri Akal Takht Sahib Amritsar failing which the Sikhs will lose their Vatican axle resulting in confusion everywhere.

TRADITIONAL VALUES IN SOCIETY

Family is the basic structure and unit in Sikhism. It is a strong and noble Sikh institution. Family was most important to all the Gurus who preached life of a householder rather than of renunciation. The Gurus believed that the family must procreate and continue the existence of the society. The family has economic and educational functions to perform so that family life becomes smooth and happy.

Sikhism teaches the followers to build a social structure on the basis of universal brotherhood, love for each other, equality, fraternity and Sarbat-Da-Bhala. It believes in individual as well as collective prosperity. It preaches that the human beings are sons and daughters of the same universal father (God). All of them have the same aim of realizing the ultimate Reality. Human race is one.

Sikhism recommends an active life in which family has a great role to play. Life of a householder is the best institution to fulfill the Sikh ideal of contributing to the development of the human society. Here the children learn to know the individual as well as the corporate Code of Sikh Conduct through this institution.

Family in Sikhism is a training school for social, cultural, political and spiritual makeup. It is a training school for Seva and charity. From the family of birth, the religious and ethical ideas are implanted in the child. It is worth to mention here that Bhai Mani Singh took all the traits of sacrifice from his forefathers. Guru Arjan Dev Ji implanted the spirit of sacrifice in the wider family by offering his life to upkeep righteousness.

The Sikh families believe in monogamy. The marriages are normally arranged by the parents with consent of the children. Extra-marital and pre-marital relationship is not allowed in Sikh families. Marriage is considered to be a sacrament. According to the concept of Lavan (Marriage hymns), divorce is not encouraged in Sikhism. It is expected of the couple to help and support each other in the family to attain God.

Sikhs believe in Nam Simran while living a family life which has all the elements of love, optimism, laughter, pride, pity, joy, gratitude, respect, purity, service and sacrifice.

The concept of family life teaches to love and respect the parents, grand parents and society at large. It cares for the vulnerable. It provides psychological foundation for the future and helps in improving the quality of life. It provides emotional care for its members and opportunity to practice democratic decision making. Sikh family preserves human values, cultural identity and historical continuity.

Those who live in the situations of God loving families, carry with them into society an urge to strive, the ability to work toward an ultimate goal to attain God, an acceptance for the opinions and defects of others, responsibility, good judgment, sense of kinship plus an unshakable belief in the benefits of sharing and co-operation with human beings. All of these family values are needed in to-day's world.

Sikhs generally encourage their children to study conscientiously at school and college, so preparing for the best career available to them. The professions of medicine and engineering are most attractive to parents and grandparents whose attitudes were moulded in rural Punjab. Teaching is also a respected occupation for both men and women.

As the word 'Sikh' means literally 'learner', and the concept of Guru or teacher is central to the faith, one might expect education to be a key concern. So it is, but in the sense of spiritual enlightenment rather than courses in the arts, sciences or practical skills. Before the provision of state education in Punjabi villages, children could learn in the Gurdwara to read and write in Gurmukhî. This is the script used for the Sikh scriptures, and it is also used by Sikhs to write Punjabi. In Britain, Punjabi classes are held in many Gurdwaras in order to make children literate in their mother tongue and enable them to read the Guru Granth Sahib.

Guru Nanak's compositions reveal his understanding of Sanskrit, Persian and Arabic in addition to the local vernacular, and as a young adult he used his skills as an accountant. Guru Gobind Singh was a proficient poet in Hindi, Punjabi, Sanskrit and Persian and set great store by training in martial as well as literary skills. In the late nineteenth century the Singh Sabha, a Sikh reform movement, set out to eliminate the social evils of illiteracy and ignorance by establishing schools and colleges. Since 1905 the Educational Committee of the chief Khalsa Diwan, Amritsar, has promoted education, providing scholarships and setting up educational institutions, for example for women and in backward areas. Despite this positive regard for secular education the Rahit Maryada makes no reference to education except to advocate that 'Every Sikh should learn Gurmukhi and read the Guru Granth'. From a religious point of view this is the most vital source of knowledge.

When the lamp is lit darkness is dispelled; similarly by reading religious books evil mindedness is destroyed. What matters ultimately is not book-learning but spiritual enlightenment and truth. An educated person is one who puts the garland of God remembrance round his neck. The scholars study more and more to gain knowledge. But they use it for vain discussion. True learning springs from reflection and is manifest in goodness of character.

In the janamsdkhis, the young Nanak tells his teacher how useless all his book knowledge is, by comparison with perpetual mindfulness of God's name. Western-style education encourages the student to assume increasing independence. For Sikhs a central truth is our dependence upon God and upon each other, and particularly the priority of family interests over individual concerns. The clearest statement on education by a Sikh writer is probably Piara Singh Sambhi's in Sutcliffe Dictionary of Religious Education.

Sikhs are proud of their reputation for hard work and initiative. Since they are expected to marry and live as householders, they are also expected to work hard to earn and to keep their families. After Partition in 1947 the hundreds of thousands of refugees from the Pakistan side of the new border built their lives anew without resorting to begging. In the rural, un-mechanized economy of Punjab's still-recent past there was some work for everyone. All but the handicapped had to work, and if performed in the right way, every work was noble.

According to Sikh teaching caste considerations should not affect one's attitude to accepting the work available. In practice hereditary caste preference has played its part, so that, for instance, only Sikhs of the leatherworking caste would be shoemakers. From a religious standpoint, however, only occupations incompatible with the Sikh code of conduct should be avoided, such as running nightclubs, selling alcohol and, in particular, selling cigarettes and tobacco.

Leisure is a necessary element of life. Festivals, marriages and the agricultural cycle in Punjab ensure periods of recreation. Bhangra dancing (for men) and gidha (for women) are enjoyed to the full. Rhythmic drumming, vivid costume and often humorous verses add to the fun. Reading and singing the hymns of the Guru Granth Sahib brings peace of mind and spiritual refreshment. These are the cultural pastimes.

In urban and Western society, leisure pursuits are to be enjoyed provided they do not conflict with morality and health. The company one keeps is vital to one's well-being. Smoking was forbidden by the Gurus. Together with drinking and gambling, it is prohibited for all Sikhs. In practice, the ban on smoking is almost universally observed, whereas many men see no inconsistency between their Sikh faith and the consumption of alcohol.

Sikhs have not yet thought out the implications of a world in which a growing number of individuals are destined to be technically unemployed for long periods of their lives. In the West, the Gurdwara is a place where the elderly, with time on their hands, find fulfilment in acts of services such as preparing tea or cleaning. But what of school leavers? Families may start a business, thereby avoiding the compulsory leisure of unemployment particularly for the young. Whether paid or unpaid Sikhs believe that work is essential for everyone's character to develop. Noblest is the work offered to God and the congregation as seva (service). Kar seva is voluntary manual work, sometimes on a vast scale, as when a Gurdwaraa is under onstruction. By extension, voluntary service to the wider community accords well with Sikh teaching and is to be undertaken by those who might otherwise be idle. So it would be appropriate for young Sikhs to be involved in local community projects of several kinds. Those in paid employment must be willing to share with those whose equally hard work is unpaid.

Sikh teaching is realistic in its approach to wealth: 'Those who have money have the anxiety of greed: those without money have the anxiety of poverty'. Poverty is not essential for holiness. All Sikhs are to earn honestly and share generously. They should give at least a tenth (dasvandh) of their earnings to others. Often they give in kind rather than cash: food for the langar (corporate meal) or building materials for a Gurdwara. There is no place for dishonesty or avarice. Nor should money be spent on pursuits such as gambling or drinking.

Riches must be honestly earned, not the result of exploiting the poor. This point is made most graphically in the janamsakhi story of Malak Bhago, the rich man who insisted that Guru Nanak should dine with him rather than with the carpenter, Lalo. Guru Nanak squeezed Bhago's fried 'puri', and blood dripped from it. When he squeezed Lalo's simple, hard-earned bread, milk flowed out. A popular janamsakhi story recounts how the youthful Guru Nanak struck a 'true bargain'. Instead of making financial profit with the money his father gave him for business, he spent it on feeding some religious mendicants.

According to the Adi Granth, wealth must not distract its owners from life's spiritual purpose: If the world were to be encrusted with diamonds and rubies, my bed studded with rubies; And if there were to be an alluring damsel, her face glistening with jewels, tempting me with seductive gesture, Forbid it, O Lord, that beholding such temptation I should forget Thee and fail to call to mind thy name. Wealth must be seen in perspective. In comparison with Nam (God's name, or essential reality) wealth is nothing. Material wealth is impermanent: 'Wealth, youth and flowers are short-lived as guests for four brief days'.

Value of Life

Respect for one's elders is a key principle of Asian society. Only through prolonged contact with Western values does care for the elderly become an issue to be discussed. Sikhs, in common with Indians of all other faiths, have always accepted the duty of sons to care for their parents (so the need for mothers to give birth to male children) in a society with minimal state welfare provision. Given the prevailing Punjabi attitudes there was little need for the Gurus to urge what was common practice. However, on the subject of respecting one's parents, Guru Ram Das said: 'Son why do you quarrel with your father due to whom you have grown to this age? It is a sin to argue with him'.

An initial reaction of Asians settling in the West was horror at a society in which the younger generation consigned their parents to institutions for the elderly. Fearful of the shame their family would suffer if fellow members of their community suspected neglect, Asians were reluctant to utilise such services as the local authority provided. Sikhs need to realise the increasing isolation felt by aged parents as they grow old and frail in surroundings where their earlier expectations of support and respect can't be realised and where they are cut off from neighbours and officials by lack of English.

The Gurdwara plays an important role in the West as a welcoming, familiar centre for the exchange of gossip; it also promotes an enhanced sense of selfworth through acts of seva such as hoovering or preparing tea for others. But the Gurdwara's potential as a day centre for the elderly, both Sikh and non Sikh, has yet to be developed. In Tarn Taran, Punjab, the Bhai Vir Singh Birdh Ghar, established in 1958, provides a free home for the elderly, funded by Sikhs' donations.

This is a pointer to the future, when in India, as in the West, families may be more fragmented. Along with other Asians, Sikhs have much to teach Westerners about family support for those needing care, and in turn their commitment to seva must extend beyond immediate kin and community. In the life of Guru Amar Das, whose twenty-two-year Guruship commenced at the age of 73, Sikhs have a reminder that age need not bring diminished responsibility or service.

Sikhs are to share their earnings with the needy. In the West, gifts to charities are one means of carrying out this obligation. In India, the Chief Khalsa Diwan set up an orphanage in 1906 in Amritsar. The Pingalwara, also in Amritsar, is a centre supported by voluntary donations, caring for the sick who are desperately in need of shelter. There is a Guru Nanak hospital for the handicapped in Ranchi.

CASTE SYSTEM

A total opposition of the caste system is a typical characteristic of the Sikh culture. Sikhism in fact originated as a voice of protest against the many prevalent ills of contemporary Indian society. The caste system was the most damaging and debilitating of them. It completely negated the humanitarian and egalitarian principles, fundamental to the Sikh creed. Guru Nanak, founder of Sikhism, and his nine spiritual successors strongly attacked the system. The advent of Sikhism in the midst of caste rigidities and superstitions was truly a radical beginning.

Caste defined as a hereditary social group comprising persons of the same ethnic stock, social rank, occupation and more or less distinctive mores" is a characteristic common to all societies the world over, and hardly shows anything more than social differentiations that have developed in varying degrees of discrimination or exclusiveness. In the Punjab, for instance, caste (jat) signifies only an ethnic group gotra (family, line or class). It is only when it develops into a system with its rigid stratification and permanent division of social status based on birth alone, as it did in India, that caste becomes a curse.

A system is qualitatively different from a casual or unintentional assortment of factors or forces. It is what distinguishes philosophy, religion or science from an unintegrated mass of doctrines and tenets. It is what distinguishes an army from a rabble, as it involves organization, arrangement, method and considered principles of procedure. Above all, a system presumes a direction, a plan, a purpose, an objective towards the fulfillment of which the functioning of the different parts of the system is oriented, coordinated and harmonized. Moreover, a system has its own cumulative power, thrust, momentum not easy to stem, and grip, hold and shackle almost impossible to unfetter. The caste system that developed in India over the millennia possessed all these ingredients and characteristics. And more, it was given the garb of religion, the Varnasrma Dharma, signifying divine origin or sanction for it.

Those social distinctions existed, as in other primitive societies, in pre-Aryan India is evidenced by the ruins of the Indus Valley civilization, but whether these were characterized by permanent divisions based on birth we do not know. The caste system in the Hindu society as generally understood definitely developed after the advent of the Aryans. Whether a four-fold division into occupational groups was historical necessity for the invaders is irrelevant here. The fact is that among the sacerdotal groups, the Brahmans, came to possess real power in matters social as well as religious and became, besides being the sole interpreters of religious texts, exclusive authors and arbiters of the social code. They divided society into castes and sub-castes meticulously arranged in a hierarchical social pyramid in which the social grade of each group and individual was fixed permanently by birth.

Each layer in the pyramid was superior in caste status (virtually in social status) to all the layers below it, and lower in caste status to all the others above it, irrespective of their political power and economic position. Even the Brahmans at the top of the pyramid and the untouchables at its bottom were graded among their own ranks. The privileges, disabilities, obligations, and duties, i.e. practically all aspects of social behaviour, of each sub-caste by fixed rules and codes were formulated by Brahmans particularly by Manu who claimed direct descent from Brahma, the creator of universe.

These sub-castes were, by and large, endogamous groups, and they worked sedulously to isolate themselves from each other in other social matters too. Mutual exclusiveness was caused predominantly not by social, but by ritualistic factors. Such factors as personal endowments, wealth, political power, colour and racial prejudices, and even taboos, which determined the hierarchical set-ups in other societies, were not the final determinants in the Indian caste system, though these did contribute to its development. Although individuals, groups and sub-castes were in the grip of a continuously downward process, there was practically no upward social mobility.

Caste system of the Varnasrama had its own intricacies. Its constituents were interdependent and interlocked, both horizontally and vertically, in a self-perpetuating social fabric. Within the sub-caste, each constituent of the system (hereditary functionalism, social and ritualistic taboos, pollution, religion, etc.) tied its own caste-knot around the individual.

The fundamental assumption of the caste ideology is that men are not equal, but are forever unequal. Permanent human inequality is the officially declared Brahmanical ideology, and this forms the basis of the Hindu social order. God Himself is the author of this inequality. The Veda was declared by Manu to be the direct revelation of God, and it is a Rig Vedic hymn, Purusa Sukta, which forms the source for the caste ideology. It says that God created Brahmans from His head, Ksatriyas from His arms, Vaisyas from His legs and Sudras from His feet. Even the Dharma Sastra of Manu is said to be the inspired word of the Vedas, almost of equal authority with them. Manu did not rest content with establishing the divine authority of the Vedas. His object thereby was to sanctify the caste system and the position of the Brahmans.

The process of the creation of a sovereign, autonomous society, the Sikh Panth, had started in the day of Guru Nanak himself. He had begun his career as a teacher of men with the significant utterance, "There is no Hindu, no Mussalman," and took clear-cut practical steps towards moulding a society of Sikhs (literally disciples) on independent ideological lines. He specifically condemned caste and caste ideology as perverse, and rejected the authority of the Vedas and supremacy of the Brahmans.

By contradicting Hinduism, Sikhism also delinked itself from that aspect of Hindu dharma which was, in day-to-day action, the main vehicle for providing religious sanction to the varnasrama dharma. The Gurus issued their own new version of dharma, which was, at least as far as caste was concerned, completely at variance with the Hindu mores. They made the Dharma perfect and universal by blending the four castes into one. Underlying the taboos on food and drink and the ostracization of the Sudra castes was the notion of pollution which was supposed to be incurred not only by partaking of food or drinks under certain conditions, but by the mere bodily contact with persons of certain low castes whose cultural occupation, whether actually followed or not, rendered them untouchable.

Besides denying the authority of the Vedas and Sastras, the Guru took some practical steps to impart an egalitarian thrust to the nascent Sikh community. The twin institutions of sangat (company of the holy) and pangat (commensality), where no discrimination on the basis of caste, birth or social status was observed, went a long way in inculcating in the Sikhs the spirit of equality, brotherhood and humanitarianism. The creation of the Khalsa by Guru Gobind Singh was the acme of the Sikh movement. The Khalsa made a clear break with the caste society. Of the five original initiates, the first batch of entrants to the Khalsa Brotherhood, there were three from the so-called Sudra castes, and one Jat, a caste then on the borderline of Vaisyas and Sudras.

For initiation into the Khalsa ranks, ritual (amrit or khande di pahul) was made obligatory, and during the ceremony the neophytes had to take five vows, viz. dharm nash, i.e. to sever connection with one's previous religious belief, karam nash, i.e. to free oneself from former rites, rituals, customs, etc.; kul nash, i.e. severance of all ties with lineage and birth, the fundamental basis of caste society; shram nash, i.e. obliteration of stigmas attached to trade or occupation, which gave the convert a sense of self-respect and dignity of labour; and bharm nash, i.e. discarding superstition, taboos and notion of pollution. The later Sikh literature of the eighteenth century (the Rahitnamas, specifically of varied authorship and composed at different times carrying the different emphases) is agreed on the point that the Khalsa broke away categorically from the caste ideology and caste society.

Testimony from contemporary non-Sikh sources substantiates this fact and historical evidence supports it. Guru Gobind Singh assigned the overall military command to a former Bairagi assisted by a council of five, selected irrespective of their former castes. Later, of the five divisions of Sikh guerrillas, one was captained by a convert from the so-called untouchable scavenger caste while another was headed by a former Ksatriya. Still later, when with further expansion of the Sikh army, the Dal Khalsa, it was divided into eleven misls; one was commanded by a low-caste warrior. Likewise, the overall command vested with one not born to the caste.

Sikhism mounted a frontal attack on citadel of caste and the individual pillars on which it was based. It must, however, be admitted that caste could not be totally uprooted, so strongly was it entrenched in the Indian soil, although it must be emphasized at the same time that the Sikhs never accepted either the religious validity of the caste system or that of its constituent pillars, its authors, interpreters and upholders, the Brahmans. The Sikhs have never owed allegiance to any scripture but Guru Granth Sahib, and it completely and categorically repudiates caste distinctions, ritualism and the Brahmanical ideology of pollution. Nor, since the time of the creation of the Khalsa, Brahmans have ever become a point of reference in the Sikh society in regard to social status or hierarchy, or for that matter for any purpose whatsoever. There has been no sacerdotal class or caste among the Sikhs, and stress on work ethics has amalgamated the other three castes into a single working class.

The only case where some vestiges of the caste system still remain is that of social discrimination against Mazhabi Sikhs (converts from scavenging caste) and Ramdasia Sikhs (formerly people engaged in leather work and weavers). They too have never been treated as untouchable and there has been no commensal or social discrimination against those among them who have taken the pahul (the rites) of the Khalsa. Also, there has been no discrimination against anyone while attending religious gatherings or dining in Guru ka Langar, i.e. community kitchen. The existence of remaining prejudices may be explained by several factors. First, it is a part of the dynamics of ideological mass upsurges that their initial momentum has always tended to taper off as time goes by.

After reaching ideological peaks, they have invariably reached a plateau and then slided somewhat back towards the levels they started from. It is due to the limitation of human nature and environmental hurdles that the transformation of human society in terms of its idealistic goals has been extremely slow, despite all religious and other progressive movements that have taken place. Revolutionary movements do leave behind more or less degrees of progress, but the critics usually tend to compare them with absolute standard instead of measuring the achievements in relative terms. It is always easier to point out shortcomings than to appreciate gains. The initial success of the revolutionary Sikh movement, it must be appreciated, attracted to its fold a large number of converts, mostly from the Hindu caste society.

During the tribulations and turmoils of the eighteenth century, the core elements of the Khalsa were deeply involved in a life-and death struggle against the tyranny of the oppressive Indian State and depredations of rapacious invaders, leaving the religious leadership in the hands of Udasis and Nirmala priestly classes whose religious and educational background was more akin to cultural Brahmanism than to orthodox Sikhism. The influence of these classes resulted in diluting the essentially anti-caste teaching of Sikh Gurus so much so that the nineteenth-century Nirankari and Namdhari movements professing to re-establish the purity of Sikh mores ended in Gurudom and sectarian exclusiveness.

Intra-caste endogamy is practiced only by some Khatri and Arora caste groups. In most cases, and invariably in the case of Jatt Sikhs, marriage is exogamous in relation to sub-caste, though endogamous in relation to class. In India, marriages are not based on pre-marital love, as in the West, and divorce is most difficult to obtain, if not practically impossible, because it carries with it social stigma. Joint family system has been and is still, commonly, the universal mode of life. A girl after marriage has to undergo a tremendous change in family relationships as well as in social environment, and has to make far reaching adjustments in her own behaviour and way of life. Such adjustments become easy if the change from parental home to the in-laws' is minimal, that is if the life-style of the two families is identical or similar. This is easily achieved if the marriage is arranged within the same occupational class which is what caste means among the Sikhs.

STATUS OF WOMEN

In Sikh scriptures, the role of woman is known from 1500 AD. The scriptures state that the Sikh woman is to be regarded as man's equal.

She is considered to have the same soul as man and has the equal right to grow spiritually. The Sikh woman is allowed to lead religious congregations, to take part in the Akhand Path (the continuous recitation of the Holy Scriptures), to perform Kirtan (congregational singing of hymns), to work as a Granthi and to participate in religious, traditional, social and secular activities.

Sikh history includes the role of women very prominently and portrays them as equal in service, devotion, sacrifice and bravery. Examples of their moral dignity, service and self sacrifice are a source of inspiration to the Sikhs. According to Sikhism, man and woman are two sides of the same coin of the human race. Man takes birth from a woman, and woman is born of a man. This system is interrelating and inter-dependent. Sikhism believes that man can never feel secure and complete in life without a woman: a man's success depends upon the love and support of the woman who shares her life with him, and vice versa.

Thus for Sikhs since that period, there has been an obligation to treat women as equals, and gender discrimination has not been allowed. However, high principles set by prophets and religious leaders have always been very difficult to implement and put into practice. In this respect, equality for women has been a difficult right to achieve in reality. The first woman to be remembered in Sikhism is Mata Tripta Ji, the mother of the first and founder Guru, Guru Nanak Dev Ji. She meditated while carrying the child Nanak in her womb, and she brought him up with love and tender care, trying to protect him from his father Mehta Kalu's wrath for being solitary.

Bebe Nanaki Ji, the elder and the only sister of Guru Nanak Dev Ji, was a highly intelligent, spiritually awake, and pious lady. It was she who recognized the divine light in her brother and envisaged his mission of life before anyone else could perceive it. She did not treat him just as a brother; she respected him like a Guru for the whole of her life. Throughout her life she supported her revolutionary brother, who had come to redeem people from false impression and superstitions.

With the Muslims came purdah, the veil, and zananah, confinement of womenfolk to the interior apartments. The female became a greater liability for the male of the invaded populace who, weakened economically, had not only to feed his female dependants but also to be ready to protect his honour and chastity in those troubled times. This, among other social and traditional causes, led to the practice of female infanticide, though prohibited by the Qur'an in Islam, as well as child marriage.

The state of a widow was the most pitiable. Polygamy was permissible for man, but a Hindu woman, unlike a Muslim woman, woman could not remarry even after the death of her husband. The smrtis used to enjoin upon the widow to practice sahamarana, literally simultaneous death, commonly known as sati, by burning herself on the funeral pyre of her late husband. Where concession was made and the widow allowed to live on, being pregnant or having infant children, for instance, she remained ostracized from society, submitting herself to rigorous discipline of self-denial.

With the advent of Sikhism appeared a liberating force in Indian society. Affirmation of the dignity of the human being, male as well as female, was central to Guru Nanak's teaching. His mystical vision of the immanence of the Creator in all of His creation was concertized in a forceful enunciation of the gospel of equality. Guru Nanak said that all creatures were equal before God and that to make distinctions among them on the grounds of birth or sex was sinful.

To ensure equal status for women, the Gurus made no distinction between the sexes in matters of initiation, instruction or participation in sangat, holy fellowship, and pangat, commensality. According to Sarup Das Bhalla, Mahima Prakash, Guru Amar Das disfavoured the use of veil by women. He assigned women to the responsibility of supervising the communities of disciples in certain sectors, and preached against the custom of sati. Sikh history records the names of several ladies such as Mai Bhago, Mata Sundari, Rani Sahib Kaur, Rani Sada Kaur and Maharani Jind Kaur who played a leading role in the events of their time and left their imprint on them.

Even in those days of severe trial and suffering, Sikhs were guided in their treatment of the womenfolk of enemy captured in battle by the highest standards of chivalry. They showed towards them utmost respect. In 1763, for instance, one of Ahmad Shah Durrani's generals, Jahan Khan, was defeated by the Sikhs at Sialkot and a number of his female relations and dependants fell into their hands.

Such being the respect for womanhood among the Sikhs, monogamy has been the rule for them, and polygamy a rare exception. Female infanticide is prohibited. The Rahitnamas, codes of conduct, prohibit Sikhs from having any contact or relationship with those who indulge in this practice. As for sati widow-burning, Scripture itself rejects it.

As a practical step towards discouraging the practice of sati, Sikhism permitted remarriage of widows. In the present-day democratic politics of India, women as a whole have been rid of many of their disabilities. They all enjoy political franchise and many new opportunities for advancement have opened up for them. Sikh women have shown enterprise in several fields and are among the most progressive in education and in the professions such as teaching and medicine. In the Sikh system, they are the equals of men in all respects. They can lead congregational services and participate in akhand paths, uninterrupted readings of scripture to be accomplished within forty-eight hours. They vote with men periodically to elect Sikhs' central religious body, the Shiromani Gurdwara Parbandhak Committee, which administers their places of worship.

A drastic distinction between the roles of the male and female exists in all of history's modern human societies. Women have grown to accept, not without resentment though, the male-dominated atmosphere of the world. Because people use religious doctrine to define their life styles, religious scriptures in both the East and the West seem to condone, even encourage, the unequal treatment of women. In the fifteenth century, Guru Nanak established Sikhism, the first religion to advocate emphatically the equality of all people, especially women. In a continent characterized by severe degradation of women, this bold declaration, along with others, determined to erase the impurities of the Indian society. However, prejudices and injustices based on gender linger even today.

In the dominant Western religion of Christianity, God created man, and then woman out of man's rib. Eve, the first woman persuades Adam to eat the forbidden apple, thus committing the world's first sin, a landmark recognized as the fall of mankind. The implied inferiority and corrupting influence of women in the Bible appear to justify their second rate treatment in Western society.

At the time of Guru Nanak, Indian women were severely degraded and oppressed by their society. Given no education or freedom to make decisions, their presence in religious, political, social, traditional, and economic affairs was virtually non-existent. Woman was referred to as "man's shoe, the root of all evil, a snare, a temptress. Her function was only to perpetuate the race, do household work, and serve the male members of society. Female infanticide was common and the practice of sati, the immolation of the wife on her husband's funeral pyre, was encouraged, and sometimes even forced.

Guru Nanak condemned this man-made notion of the inferiority of women, and protested against their long subjugation. The Ultimate Truth was revealed to Guru Nanak through a mystic experience, in direct communion with God. Guru Nanak conveys this Truth through the bani, Sikh Scripture.

The fundamental analogy used in the bani depicts the relationship between God and man, and proves that the physical body does not matter. Thus, according to Sikh ideology, all men and women possess equal status. All human beings, regardless of gender, caste, race, or birth, are judged only by their deeds.

With this assertion, the Sikh Gurus invited women to join the sangat (congregation), work with men in the langar (common kitchen), and participate in all other religious, social, and traditional activities of the Gurdwaras (Sikh places of worship). The Gurus redefined celibacy as marriage to one wife and taught that male and female alike need to practice conjugal fidelity.

Guru Amar Das also condemned purdah, the wearing of the veil, and female infanticide. He spoke against the custom of sati, thus permitting the remarriage of widows. Out of 146 chosen, the Guru appointed 52 women missionaries to spread the message of Sikhism, and out of 22 Manjis established by the Guru for the preaching of Sikhism, four were women. The steps the Gurus took to advocate the equality of women, revolutionized the culture of Indian society. As they began to partake in social, religious, and political affairs, their contribution and worth as equal partners of men became more obvious.

However, the Guru's teachings of equality have never been fully realized, which is clearly evident in the treatment of women even in the Sikh society today. Either because of the influence of the majority community on the Sikh minority or the Sikh male's unwillingness to give up his dominant role, women continue to suffer prejudices. A woman has never been elected as the president of Shiromani Gurdwara Prabandhak Committee (the Central Management Committee to manage the affairs of the Gurdwaras in the Punjab), or as the head of any of the five Takhats (the thrones of authority). Indian society discriminates against women in workplaces, and denies them the right to fight on the battlefield. People measure a woman's value as a bride by the size of her dowry, not necessarily by her character and integrity. Alice Basarke, a free-lance writer, sadly realizes, "After 500 years head start, Sikh Women are no better off than their counterparts in any other religion or nation."

It is against such a backdrop that the Gurus implemented reform via their missions and tackled prevalent issues in their teachings.

Guru Amar Das abolished the culture of Sati and Purdah and indeed refused to have an audience with ladies that kept Purdah. He established religious centers and women alongside men were recruited to lead and teach. Women worked alongside the men in maintaining the Guru's kitchen, performing all duties and sitting side by side the men folk in Pangat. Guru Angad strongly encouraged the education of women. Women swelled the ranks in spreading the message of the Gurus as missionaries. By the time of Guru Gobind Singh, 40% of them were women.

With the birth of the Khalsa the last of the barriers of caste and gender o 'pression had been smashed. Women though continuing their roles of mothers and wives were forever changed. They were lifted up and given the same Amrit at the side of their brothers. The same rules that applied to them to follow the Khalsa way applied to them. They were granted the same 5 K's. Guru Gobind Singh's encouragement of women to keep even shastars symbolized that he did not envision her role in society as being that of a "nice, meek housewife," but rather that of a fearless, active, independent warrior, involved in the world.

Title of Kaur: Kaur became her name. Kaur has an interesting history. Its origin can be found in the word Kanwar, literally meaning princess. Women were given Kaur to give them an identity independent of that of their husband and to uplift their spirit.

At the time of Shri Guru Gobind Singh, women who were literally and legally possessions of their husbands were now orators, teachers, warriors, and administrators and participated in the Guru's kitchen. Shri Guru Gobind Singh's wife Mata Sundri led the Khalsa Panth for many years after passing of the tenth Guru. Jathedar Sada Kaur along with Maharaja Ranjit Singh made possible the formation of the Sikh Empire. She gave her contribution to the Amrit, sweet Patashey so that the disposition of the Sikhs would be also sweet.

REFERENCES

Archer, John Calrk: "The Bible of the Sikhs. *"Punjab Past and Present*, 1977.

Bachittar Singh, Giani: ed. *Planned Attack on Aad Shri Guru Granth Sahib*. Chandigarh: International Centre of Sikh Studies, 1994.

Banerjee, A. C.: Guru Nanak to Guru Gobind Singh. Patiala, 1978

Barth, A.: Religions of India. Delhi, 1963.

Blunt, E. H. H.: The Caste Systems of Northern India.

Crooke, W.: The North-Western Provinces of India: Their History, Ethnology and Administration, 1994.

Cunningham, Joseph Davey: *A History of the Sikhs.* Delhi: S. Chand and Company, 1985.

Daljeet Singh: *Essay on the Authenticity of Kartarpuri Bi[and the Integrated Logic and Unity of Sikhism.* Patiala: Punjabi University, 1987.

Dewana, Mohan Singh: *A History of Punjabi Literature.* Jalandhar: Bharat Prakashan, 1971.

Ghurye, G. S.: Caste and Race in India. 1986.

Hutton, J. H.: Caste in India. 1980.

Ibbetson: Sir Denzil, Punjab Castes. Patiala, 1970.

Jagjit Singh: The Sikh Revolution. Delhi, 1981.

Jogendra Singh: Sikh Ceremonies. Chandigarh, 1968.

Kanwaljit Kaur: Sikh Women, Fundamental Issues in Sikh Studies, Institute of Sikh Studies, Chandigarh, 1992.

Ketkar, S. V: History of Caste System in India. 1979.

Levering, Miriam: ed. *Rethinking Scripture: Essays from a Comparative Perspective.* Albany: State University of New York Press, 1989.

Losty, Jeremiah P: *The Art of the Book in India.* London: The British Library, 1982.

Mann, Gurinder Singh: *The Goindval Pothis: The Earliest Extant Source of the Sikh Canon.* Harvard Oriental Series 51. Cambridge: Harvard University Press, 1996.

Marenco, E. K.: The Transformation of Sikh Society. Portland, Oregon, 1974.

Mohammed Marmaduke Pickthall, translator: The Meaning of Glorious Koran, Mentor Book, New American Library, New York and Scarborough, Ontario, 1924.

Narang, G. C.: Transformation of Sikhism. Delhi, 1956.

Prinsep, H. T.: Origin of the Sikh Power in the Punjab and Political Life of Maharaja Ranjit Singh. Calcutta, 1834.

$\boxed{16}$

Festivals

Sikh festivals are functions for Sikhs to dedicate themselves to the religious belief. Even martyrdoms and demise days of remembrance of the Gurus are festivals to impulse the congregation and cue them of their story and the appraise of forfeiture for a good cause. People of several religions are asked for to these celebrations to give them a view of the Sikh faith and way of life. All Sikh festivals are to be illustrious by going to a Gurdwara, paying obeisance to the Guru Granth Sahib and listening to Gurbani. There are several Sikh fairs and festivals. Some are of local importance as Maghi of Muktsar and Hola Mohalla of Anandpur.The most authoritative festivals are observed by the Sikhs wherever they are. On such occasions the whole Sikh families of a particular place accumulate in a Gurdwara. It is decently embellished and illuminated. The Granth is read perpetually. Hymns are sung in chorus or by professional Sikh singers. Prayer is said. Sweet pudding (karah prasad) is distributed in the whole congregation. In blistering brave dulcorated and iced water is served at several bases. Houses are alighted in the evening. A complimentary langar at the main Gurdwara is a moldiness for all fair and festival.

Sikh Festivals, principally the Gurpurbs, which lionise the days of remembrance of the ten Gurus (spiritual leaders) of the Sikh religion. Of these the most authoritative are the natal day* of the first and last Gurus, Guru Nanak (November 11) and Guru Gobind Singh, and the calvary days of Guru Arjan Dev, the fifth Guru and builder in 1577 of the Golden Temple (or Harimandir Sahib as it is also known) at Amritsar, who was accomplished by order of the Mughal emperor Jehangir and of Guru Tegh Bahadur, also accomplished by the reigning Mughals. Baisakhi, the day of the Sikh New Year, lionises, among other things, the establishing of the Sikh religion in its present form. These holy days are branded by ceremonies in the temples, by taking the Adi Granth, the Sikh holy book, in procession through the streets and by uninterrupted readings from the Adi Granth. Sikhs also celebrate a act of festivals in basal with Hindus, although for different reasons; Diwali, for example, lionises the release from prison of the sixth Guru, Guru Hargobind who, when he returned to Amritsar in 1620, ascertained the Golden Temple illuminated in his accolade. Today, Sikhs from far and wide accumulate at Amritsar on Diwali day and in the evening the temple is crystalised with candles, lamps, and electric lights after which firework exhibits take place. Elsewhere, as well as attending the Gurdwaras (holy places) to adoration, dwell adorn their abodes and use candles and other lights to illuminate them. The Sikhs also celebrate on the day of the Hindu festival, Holi, merely for unlike causes.

GURU NANAK JAYANTI

The faith of Sikhism prophesies that there is matchless God but that he is formless. That is why the Sikhs don't idolise idols. The festivities in the Sikh religion revolve around the anniversaries of the 10 Sikh Gurus. These Gurus were answerable for shaping the impressions of the Sikhs. Their birthdays, known as Gurpurabs, are functions for celebration and prayer among the Sikhs. Guru Nanak Dev was born on twentieth October, 1469 in Rai-Bhoi-di Talwandi in the acquaint Shekhupura District of Pakistan, now Nanakana Sahib. The Birthday of Guru Nanak Sahib falls on Kartik Puranmashi i.e. full moon day of the calendar month Kartik. In the Gregorian Calendar, the birthday of Guru Nanak commonly comes out the month of November, but its date varies from year to year, based on the conventional dates of the Indian Calendar.

The jubilation is broadly alike as all Gurpurabs; only the hymns are different. The birthday celebration usually lasts three days. Broadly two days before the birthday, Akhand Path (a forty-eight-hour around-the-clock reading of the Guru Granth Sahib, the holy book of the Sikhs) is accommodated in the Gurdwaras.

The day prior to the natal day, a advance is coordinated which is led along the Panj Pyaras (Five dearest Ones). They head the emanation acquitting the Sikh flag, known as the Nishan Sahib and the Palki (Palanquin) of Shri Guru Granth Sahib. They are accompanied by teams of singers singing verses, brass bands acting a different tunes, 'Gatka' teams (Martial Arts) exhibit their swordmanship, and buffs sing the chorus. The advancement pullulates into the streets of the town which are covered with buntings and decorated gates for this especial affair. The leaders as well banquet the message of Nanak.

On the day of the Gurpurab, the day commences early in the morning with the babbling of Asa-di-Var (morning verses) and hymns from the Sikh scriptures abided by by Katha (exposition of the scripture) collectively with lectures and recital of poems in the praise of the Guru. Following that is the Langar or special community lunch, which is arranged at the Gurdwaras by volunteers. The idea behind the free communal lunch is that people should be offered food in the spirit of seva (service) and bhakti (devotion).

Guru Nanak Jayanti is celebrated by the Sikh community all over the world and is one of the most important festivals in the Sikh calendar. The celebrations are especially colourful in Punjab and Haryana.

GURU GOBIND SINGH JAYANTI

Whether the event is Vaisakhi (Khalsa Sajna Diwas), Dewali (Bandi Chhor Diwas), or the Martyrdom of Guru Arjan Sahib (Sahidi Diwas), Sikhs assemble and commemorate their respectable Gurus and worship to pay homage to their worthy Martyrs. Gurpurabs, as they are more commonly known, are celebrated with immense devotion by the Sikh community all over the globe.

Guru Gobind Singh Jayanti, is one pious festival of the Sikhs which is celebrated with great fervour. The festival witnesses a huge convoy of Sikhs who congregate to offer extraordinary prayers at Gurdwaras. Guru Gobind Singh was born at Patna Sahib on twenty-second December. Generally, his birthday is celebrated in the month of December or in January. At times it falls twice a year as per the Hindu Bikrami Calendar. However, the birthday of Guru Gobind Singh comes on January 5 every year according to the Nanakshahi Calendar.

It is chronicled that after the death of his father Guru Tegh Bahadur, Guru Gobind Singh, the Tenth Guru felt obliged to organize a community of Sikhs into a saint-soldiers' community. In the year 1699, he assembled thousands of Sikhs together and addressed a massive audience asking his followers to sacrifice their life for him in his devotion. Not long after, five Sikhs came forward to sacrifice themselves, and the sword of Guru Gobind Singh was completely stained with their blood. To the revelation of the huge audience, Guru came out with those five followers wholly dressed in the Pure or Khalsa uniform. The demonstration given by Guru symbolizes the rebirth of the Sikh community into complete distinct identity saint-soldiers. After initiating the five sacrificed followers or 'beloved ones', into a completely new identification of Khalsa, Guru Gobind Singh requested them to initiate him. In the chronicle of human history, the absolute conversion of a solidified and distinctive community remained a defining and unique moment.

Guru Gobind Singh and his followers were engaged in many battles against several Mughal rulers during his lifetime. During that turbulent period, he lost his mother and four children in fighting for righteousness. Nevertheless, the Khalsa soldiers stood determined as a sovereign and distinct body, and could efficiently withstand their enemies.

Before his death in 1708, he added a few writings to the Sikh scriptures and requested his worshippers to take spiritual guidance out of the Guru Granth Sahib, the holy book of the Sikhs. The words enclosed in Guru Granth Sahib are from now on and will forever be present as their Guru for the Sikhs.

LOHRI

Lohri is the Indian version of an annual thanksgiving day and an extremely popular harvest festival in India, especially Northern India. Come January, and the fields of Punjab are filled with the golden harvest of wheat and farmers celebrate Lohri during this rest period before the harvesting and gathering of crops. Lohri is usually celebrated in the outdoors by friends and family who get together and have a bonfire in the evening. During the day, children go from door to door singing folk songs in praise of Dulha Bhatti, a thief in folklore who helps the poor and fights for their rights. These children are given sweets and savories, and occasionally, money. These collections are known as Lohri, and they are distributed at night during the festival. Some may be offered to the holy fire. Peanuts, popcorn and other food items are also thrown into the fire as an offering to the God of Fire, Agni.

The origin of the Lohri can be traced back to the tale of Dulla Bhatti. By the end of the first week of January, small groups of boys ring the doorbell of houses and start chanting the Lohri songs related to Dulla Bhatti. In turn, the people give them popcorn, peanuts, crystal sugar, sesame seeds (til) or gur as well as money. Turning them back empty-handed is regarded inauspicious.

Lohri marks the end of winter on the last day of Paush, and beginning of Magha (around January 12 and 13), when the sun changes its course. It is associated with the worship of the sun and fire and is observed by all communities with different names, as Lohri is an exclusively Punjabi festival. The questions like When it began and why is lost in the mists of antiquity.

The origin of Lohri is related to the central character of most Lohri songs is Dulla Bhatti, a Muslim highway robber who lived in Punjab during the reign of Emperor Akbar. Besides robbing the rich, he rescued Hindu girls being forcibly taken to be sold in slave market of the Middle East. He arranged their marriages to Hindu boys with Hindu rituals and provided them with dowries. Understandably, though a bandit, he became a hero of all Punjabis. So every other Lohri song has words to express gratitude to Dulla Bhatti.

Some believe that Lohri has derived its name from Loi, the wife of Sant Kabir, for in rural Punjab Lohri is pronounced as Lohi. Others believe that Lohri comes from the word 'loh', a thick iron sheet tawa used for baking chapattis for community feasts. Another legend says that Holika and Lohri were sisters. While the former perished in the Holi fire, the latter survived. Eating of til (sesame seeds) and rorhi (jaggery) is considered to be essential on this day. Perhaps the words til and rorhi merged to become tilorhi, which eventually got shortened to Lohri.

Ceremonies that go with the festival of Lohri usually consists of making a small image of the Lohri Goddess with gobar (cattle dung), decorating it, kindling a fire beneath it and chanting its praises. The final ceremony is to light a large bonfire at sunset, toss sesame seeds, gur, sugar-candy and rewaries in it, sit round it, sing, dance till the fire dies out. People take dying embers of the fire to their homes. In Punjabi village homes, fire is kept going round the clock by use of cow-dung cakes.

According to the Hindu calendar, Lohri falls in mid-January (13th January). The earth, farthest from the sun at this point of time, starts its journey towards the sun, thus ending the coldest month of the year and announcing the start of the summer season.

While Lohri is essentially a Punjabi festival, it is celebrated in some other states of North India as well. In cities like Delhi, which have a predominant Punjabi population, Lohri is celebrated to denote the last of the coldest days of winter. Apart from Punjab, people from other northern Indian states of Haryana, Delhi and Himachal Pradesh, become busy making preparations for Lohri. For them, Lohri is an appropriate occasion to come out of their homes and celebrate the harvesting of the Rabi (winter) crops and give in to relaxing and enjoying the cultural folk songs and dances.

In houses that have recently had a marriage or childbirth, Lohri celebrations will reach a higher pitch of excitement. Punjabis usually have private Lohri celebrations, in their houses. Lohri rituals are performed, with the accompaniment of special Lohri songs. A bonfire is made and a prayer is performed to Agni, the God of Fire, and Prasad is distributed. The prasad comprises five main foods - til, gachchak, gur, moongphali (peanuts) and phuliya or popcorn. Milk and water are also poured around the bonfire. This ritual is performed for thanking the Sun God and seeking his continued protection.

Singing and dancing form an intrinsic part of the celebrations. People wear their brightest clothes and come to dance the bhangra and gidda to the beat of the dhol. Punjabi songs are sung, and everybody rejoices. Sarson ka saag and makki ki roti is usually served as the main course at a Lohri dinner. Lohri is a great occasion that does not hold importance for farmers alone but also to those people residing in the urban area, as this festival provide the opportunity to interact with family and friends.

MAGHI

Maghi is the occassion when Sikhs commemorate the sacrifice of forty Sikhs, who fought for Gufu Gobindh Singh Ji. The day of Maghi is observed to honour the heroic fight of the Chali Mukte, or the Forty Liberated Ones, who sacrificed their own lives defending an attack by the imperial army marching in pursuit of Guru Gobind Singh. The action took place near a pool of water, Khidrane di Dhab, on 29 December 1705.

Sikhs celebrate the Maghi with recital of the holy Guru Granth Sahib and religious rituals in all the Sikh Gurdwaras. On the eve of Maghi falls the common Indian festival called the Lohri when bonfires are lighted in Hindu homes and alms are also distributed.. However the largest assembly, however, takes place at Muktsar (Punjab) where big fairs are organized and pilgrims take a holy dip in the holy waters of sarovar and also visit several shrines. A mahala or big march of pilgrims from the main shrine to Gurdwara Tibbi Sahib, holy to Guru Gobind Singh, concludes the three-day celebration.

HOLA MAHALLA

Hola Mohalla or Hola Mahalla or simply Hola is a Sikh festival that takes place on the first of the lunar month of Chet which usually falls in March. This, by a culture estabished by Guru Gobind Singh, follows the

Hindu festival of Holi by one day; Hola is the masculine form of the feminine sounding Holi. The word "Mohalla" is derived from the Arabic root hal (alighting, descending) and is a Punjabi word that implies an organized procession in the form of an army column. But unlike Holi, when people playfully sprinkle colour, dry or mixed in water, on each other, the Guru made Hola Mohalla an occasion for the Sikhs to demonstrate their martial skills in simulated battles.

Together the words "Hola Mohalla" stands for "mock fight". During this festival, processions are organized in the form of army type columns accompanied by war-drums and standard-bearers and proceeding to a given spot or moving in state from one Gurdwara to another. The custom originated in the time of Guru Gobind Singh who held the first such mock fight event at Anandpur in February 1701.

The foothills of the Shivaliks in Ropar district of Punjab's north-eastern region, especially around the historic townships of Anandpur Sahib and Kiratpur Sahib, have, since 1701 been playing host to Hola Mohalla. Recently, the Indian government accorded it the status of a national festival. The military exercise, which was personally supervised by the Guru, was carried out on the bed of the River Charan Ganga with the famous Hindu temple of Mata Naina Devi in the Shivaliks as the backdrop.

This annual festival held at Anandpur Sahib in Punjab and now replicated at other Gurdwaras worldwide was started by the tenth Sikh Guru, as a gathering of Sikhs for military exercises and mock battles on the day following the festival of Holi at Anandpur Sahib. It reminds the people of valour and defence preparedness, concepts dear to the Tenth Guru who was at that time battling the Mughal empire and the hill kings.

On this three-day grand festival, mock battles, exhibitions, display of weapons, etc., are held followed by kirtan, music and poetry competitions. The participants perform daring feats, such as Gatka (mock encounters with real weapons), tent pegging, bareback horse-riding, standing erect on two speeding horses and several other feats of bravery.

There are also a number of Darbars where the Shri Guru Granth Sahib is present and kirtan and religious lectures take place. On the last day a long procession, led by Panj Pyaras, starts from Takhat Keshgarh Sahib, one of the five Sikh religious seats, and passes through several important Gurdwaras like Qila Anandgarh, Lohgarh Sahib, Mata Jitoji and terminates at the Takhat (Keshgarh).

For people visiting Anandpur Sahib, langars (voluntary community kitchens) are organized by the local people as a part of sewa (community service). Raw materials like wheat flour, rice, vegetables, milk and sugar are provided by the villagers living nearby. Women volunteer to cook and others take part in cleaning utensils and other manual tasks that need to be carried out. Cultural cuisine is served to the pilgrims who eat while sitting in rows on the ground. (Pangat)

An enlightened person has no identification. Their values are universal and in tune with the timeless state of existence. This timeless state of existence can be given any name like Akal Purukh, God, Raam, Rahim, Hari, Parmaatma etc. But these names point to the same ultimate truth. It is useless to worship any name unless it becomes your own experience.

In our own times, developing countries like India have brought tourism into the forefront, owing to the twin advantages of employment generation and capacity to earn foreign exchange. Recent studies, however, have also pointed out the negative effects like traditional erosion, materialism, increase in crime, social conflicts, overcrowding, and environmental deterioration, which have not only proved counter productive in some cases but have also led to strong opposition, especially in case of sex-tourism in some under-developed countries, including India. The only remedial measures are strict adherence to the development of community/ religious tourism and its allied branches.

In this brief paper an attempt is made to study the prospects and impact of community/religious tourism and its potential to develop and prosper. The case study is related to the Sikh community's celebrations of Hola Mahalla at Anandpur Sahib (the birth-place of the Khalsa in 1699 AD..) in Punjab, an event that coincides with the Indian festival of Holi celebrated all over North India. This study concludes that community oriented tourism, like Hola Mahalla, can bring economic benefits apart from promoting partnership with others while protecting our traditional heritage. The paper briefly discusses the history of Hola Mahalla festival, which has been declared a State festival by the Government of Punjab. It also analyses the importance of community tourism and its impact on economic and socio-cultural environment vis-a vis the host community and tourism development.

Hola Mahalla or simply Hola is a Sikh festival, which takes place on the first of the lunar month of Chet, which usually falls in March. This follows the Hindu festival of Holi; Hola is the masculine form of the feminine sounding Holi. Mahalia, derived from the Arabic root hal (alighting, descending), is a Punjabi word that implies an organized procession in the form of an army column accompanied by war drums and standard-bearers, and proceeding to a given location or moving in state from one Gurdwara to another.

This custom originated in the time of Guru Gobind Singh (1666-1708) who held the first march at Anandpur on Chet vadi 1, 1757 Bk (twenty-second February, 1701). Unlike Holi, when people playfully sprinkle colour, dry or mixed in water, on each other the Guru made Hola Mahalla an occasion for the Sikhs to demonstrate their martial skills in simulated battles. This was probably done forestalling a grimmer struggle against the imperial power following the battle of Ninnohgarh in 1700. Holla Mahalla became an annual event held in an open ground near Holgarh Fort across the rivulet Charan Ganga, northwest to the town of Anandpur sahib.

The popularity of this festival may be judged from the fact that out of five Sikh public holidays requested by the Khalsa Diwan, Lahore in 1889, the Government approved only two - Holla Mahalla and the birth anniversary of Guru Nanak. Hola Mahalla is presently the biggest festival at Anandpur. It will be appropriate here to discuss briefly the town and the participants of this festival.

Unlike the playful sprinkling of colours as is done during Holi, the Guru made Holla an occasion to demonstrate skills in simulated battle, which is presently carried out by the Nihangs. The Nihangs assemble in thousands at Anandpur Sahib in March every year to celebrate Hola Mahalla. On this occasion they hold tournaments of military skills, including mock battles.

The most spectacular event at the Hola Mahalla is the magnificent procession of Nihangs on horses and elephants and on foot carrying a variety of cultural and modern weapons and demonstrating their skill in using them. The Hola Mahalla festival is unique and distinguishable from other festivals in that the Nihang have tried to preserve the cultural form and content as established during its inception, and strictly observed by the Akalis for more than three centuries.

The martial arts exhibited by the Nihangs provide a picture of their skills and traditions to the visitors as well as the tourist. Because of its great historical, socio-religious and military significance, the Hola Mahalla festival can impressively contribute to a greater awareness of Sikh heritage as well as foster sustainable development of community tourism.

VAISAKHI

Vaisakhi is an ancient harvest festival in Punjab, which also marks beginning of a new solar year, and new harvest season. Vaisakhi also has religious significance for Sikhs. It falls on the first day of the Vaisakh month in the solar Nanakshahi calendar, which corresponds to April 13 or April 14 in the Gregorian calendar. Vaisakhi is one of the most significant holidays in Sikh calendar, commemorating the establishment of the Khalsa in 1699. Vaisakhi is celebrated by the Khalsa as their birthday every year, the day corresponding to the event when they were created by Guru Gobind Singh in 1699.

Guru Gobind Singh, the Tenth Guru of the Sikhs founded the Khalsa (Servants of God) at the Vaisakhi gathering in 1699, at Keshgarh Sahib near Anandpur, where he had arranged for followers to meet him at the Vasakhi Fair in Anandpur. On that day Guru Gobind singh asked for a man to step forward from the congregation, who was willing to die for his cause. One man Daya Singh stepped forward, and followed Guru Ji into his tent. When Guru Ji came out of the tent, his sword was stained with blood and he asked for another volunteer. One by one Dharam Singh, Himmat Singh, Mohkam Singh and Sahib Singh came forward. One after another they entered Guru's tent, and the Guru emerged alone with his blood stained sword. The crowd was nervous, until five men then emerged from the tent, and were nominated as Panj Piares; or the five beloved ones.

The Guru put water in a bowl for sprinkling over the five in a simple initiation ceremony. He said prayers as he stirred the water with a short steel sword; symbolizing the need for strength. The Guru's wife, Mata Sundri, then came forward and placed some sugar crystals into the holy water or amrit as a reminder that strength must always be balanced by sweetness of temperament. After completing his prayers, the Guru then sprinkled the amrit over the five.

He declared them to be the first members of an old community of equals, to be called the Khalsa, meaning "belonging to the King", the King being the one God. These "saint soldiers" were to dedicate their lives to the service of others and the pursuit of justice for people of all faiths. The Panj Pyare was asked to wear five distinctive symbols of their new identity. The Five Ks.

In a move to end social divisions the Panj Pyare's surnames were removed by the Guru, mainly because surnames were associated with one's caste - the Guru then gave them (and all Sikh men) the name

Singh, meaning "lion", a reminder of the need for courage. At the same time, the Guru gave all Sikh women the name or title Kaur, meaning "princess", to emphasize dignity and complete equality. The Guru then knelt before the five and asked them to initiate him. Hence, the Khalsa became a community in which master and disciple were equal.

For Sikhs, this seasonal festival also has great importance as the founding of the Akal Khalsa (Soldiers of the Timeless One) at Anandpur Sahib. The Akal Khalsa played an important role in resistance against Mughal rule. For many centuries after that, the first male child of many Hindu families in Punjab was ordained as a Sikh in order for him to train and become a warrior and fight for the people. Other male children used to take care of the family, parents and the land.

To mark the celebrations, devotees, irrespective of their religion, throng at Gurdwaras, the Sikh place of worship. The celebrations start early as devotees, with flowers and offerings in their hands, proceed towards the Gurdwaras and temples before dawn. Processions through towns are also common. Vaisakhi is the day on which the Khalsa (The Pure Ones) was born and Sikhs were given a clear identity and a code of conduct to live by. The event was led by the last living Guru, Guru Gobind Singh Ji, who baptised the first Sikhs using sweet nectar called Amrit. Around the world at Baisakhi time, Sikhs and Punjabis reflect on the values taught to them by their Gurus and celebrate the birth of the Khalsa.

On top of this usually on this day in India, there is a huge parade/ celebration. In the United States, there is usually a parade a few days after Vaisakhi, the actually day. In Manhattan, New York City there is a huge parade where many people come out to do seva (religious work) such as giving out free food, and completing any other labour needed to be done. The local Sikh community in Surrey, British Columbia, Canada holds its annual Vaisakhi celebrations in the April long weekend, which often includes a nagar kirtan, or parade, in which an estimated 200,000 people attend.

GURU ARJAN SHAHID DIVAS

On the 16 June of every year since 1606, the Sikhs have commemorated the martyrdom of their first martyr, the fifth Guru, Guru Arjan Dev. Sikh history until then had been peaceful and non-violent. All the Sikh Gurus had taught the message of compassion, love, dedication, hard work, worship of one God and the commitment to peace and harmony for all the peoples of the world.

During the Guruship of Guru Arjan many thousands of the native people had began to follow the teachings of Sikhism and both the Hindus and Muslims were crowding to Govindwal, the centre of Sikhs during the late 1500's.

After the death of Mughal Emperor Akbar in 1605, his son Jahangir became the leader of India. Unlike his father, Jahagir was a fundamentalist Muslim, obsessed with turning the country into an Islamic state. Both Hindu and Muslim fundamentalists concerned at the rapid increase in the popularity of Guru Arjan, moved the new head of state Emperor Jahangir against the Guru. Jahangir himself was also jealous about Guru's propagation of Sikhism. He promptly obliged the enemies of Guru Sahib. Many baseless allegations were levelled against Guru Sahib, one of those was helping the rebellious Khusrau, who was Jahangir's son and the preferred choice of Akbar to be the next ruler of India rather than his son Jahangir. Jahangir was given to drinking wine and taking opium. His father thought Jahangir was unfit to rule. But in the war of succession Jahangir had won and Khusrau had managed to hold on to Punjab alone.

Accordingly in Late May 1606, Guru Arjan Dev was arrested and brought to Lahore where He was subject to severe torture. He was made to sit on a burning hot plate while hot sand was poured over his head and body. It is said that Mian Mir (a Muslim Sufi Saint and friend of Guru Sahib) tried to intercede on behalf of Guru Sahib but Guru Ji forbid him to interfere in the "Will of the Almighty". Guru Ji's body was blistered and burnt. For several days, the Guru was subjected to this unrelenting torture. Subsequently, Guru Arjan Dev was taken for a bath in the river, Ravi. As thousands watched He entered the river never to be seen again. Thus Guru Sahib embraced martyrdom on May 16, 1606. The martyrdom of Guru Sahib changed the entire character of Sikhism radically from a passive people to courageous saint soldiers.

DIWALI IN SIKHISM

The Third Sikh Teacher, Guru Amar Das institutionalized this as one of the special days when all Sikhs would gather to receive the Gurus blessings at Goindwal. In 1577 the foundation stone of The Golden Temple was laid on Diwali. The Diwali festival took place during the life of the sixth Sikh Guru Hargobind Sahib. The Muslim Emperor Jahengir imprisoned the Guru and 52 Kings. The Emperor ruled India at this time. The Asian Indians begged the Emperor to release the Guru and the Emperor agreed but the Gurus said also release the kings. Guru Ji had a gown made with 52 string pieces for the Hindus to hold. The Guru and the Hindu kings were also freed at Diwali, Sikhs were very happy when their leader was released. Guru Hargobind Sahib went to the Golden Temple Amritsar in the Punjab. Sikh Diwali is recalled throughout India and in many countries; each year to remember Guru Ji's release. At Diwali we worship the religious freedom for Sikhs and this is why Diwali is called the Light Festival. As Guru's Mother was full of happiness that her son was released she ordered food and sweets and gave them to everyone. The worshippers float multi-coloured light candles on the water at the Golden Temple. The Gurdwara, hold a grand fireworks display.

GURU TEGH BAHADUR SHAHID DIVAS

It is an extremely important event in Sikh history that had a profound impact on the future direction of Sikhism, the religion of the Sikhs. Guru Tegh Bahadar undertook the supreme sacrifice for the protection of the most fundamental of human rights - the right of a person to freely practice his or her religion without interference or hindrance. In the modern day we tend to take this freedom for granted - but in 1675, millions of people were denied this basic right.

However, what is even more astonishing is the fact that the Guru was not protecting the right of the Sikhs to practice their religion but instead the rights of non-Sikh peace-loving people from Kashmir. These people from Kashmir were very respected Hindus who were being converted to Islam under the threat of death by the "Muslim" Emperor, Aurangzeb. In 1669, the Mughal ruler Aurangzeb departed from the policy of tolerance practiced by his predecessors and unleashed instead a policy of religious persecution against non-Muslims. This caused large-scale demoralisation, fear and panic among the people.

The commitment by the Sikh Guru to protect and support the liberty of all the people of a country is unprecedented. This type of supreme sacrifice has never previously been recorded in human history. On May 25, 1675 upon the appeal by an elite group of Kashmiri Pandits, Guru Tegh Bahadar made the momentous decision that has forever changed the level of moral commitment, dedication and sacrifice required by followers of the path to God. The Guru made this critical decision to lay down his life to protect the right of the Hindu people to follow their religion freely without interference or duress.

The Guru by this act has set a yardstick by which the Sikh must gauge their devotion to their religion. This does not even get near the level of awareness required for the followers of Sikhism. The Guru has by his example taught the followers to maintain a high level of morality.

It should be remembered that the Gurus did not believe in the practices of the Hindu religion and had issued several holy Shabads denouncing several Hindu practices like Sati, Purdah, Idol worship, etc. However, this had no bearing when it came to the decision to protect these Kashmiri Hindus - for the right of a person to freely practice their religion was considered to be predominant over their own personal beliefs and preferences.

To bring to the attention of all human beings in greater India and to record in world history the barbaric ways of the Mughal Empire, Guru Tegh Bahadar escalated the consciousness of the Sikh psyche to a newer level. It was now not acceptable for a God loving people to protect just their own kind, but it was the duty of all God loving people to protect the rights of all the people of God, no matter what their chosen religion may be. Guru Tegh Bahadar put into practice the profound message of Gurbani that had been existant ever since Guru Nanak Dev's time.

Emperor Aurangzeb was a barbaric ruler of the Mughal Dynasty who came to power in 1658 and ruled for 49 painful years until his death in 1707. When he came to power in 1658, he killed all his three brothers, imprisoned his father, and forcibly converted 100,000 of Hindus to Islam. He is commonly considered the last of the "grand" Mughal emperors. After his death the Mughal Empire lost its strong-hold on the sub-continent.

The Kashmiri Pandits were Hindus renowned for their high intellect and education. They had a good relationship with the Sikhs and their Gurus. Guru Nanak Dev met Pandit Brahm Das who was an ancestor of Pandit Kripa Ram in Mattan. Kripa Ram had known the Ninth Guru and also taught Sanskrit classics to the young Gobind Rai. During the reign of Jehangir, Guru Hargobind came to Srinagar and met Kashmiri saintess Mata Bagh Bari, who lived at Rainawari. It is interesting to note that Mata Bagya Bari's spiritual interaction with the sixth Sikh Guru is incredibly well-preserved in the Sikh religious culture. In Pandit culture Mata Bagya Bari is a person renowned for her high spiritual merits.

In early 1675, the Kashmiri Pandits approached Guru Tegh Bahadar to seek his assistance in their acute hour of need. These Hindus from Kashmir had been given a deadline by Emperor Aurangzeb to convert to Islam or be killed. Pandit Kripa Ram with his large delegation met Guru Tegh Bahadar at Chak Nanki, Kahlur (now known as Anandpur Sahib).

He explained their dilemma to the Guru in the open Sangat at the place where today stands Gurdwara Manji Sahib, in Anandpur Sahib.

In the summer of 1675, the Guru, along with some of his companions were finally brought to Delhi and asked to convert to Islam or else face the penalty of death. Guru Ji was also asked to perform a miracle. Guru Tegh Bahadur averred that he would rather sacrifice his life than give up his faith and his freedom or belief or perform a miracle. Thus, under Aurangzeb's orders, Guru Ji and his companions were tortured. The Guru was chained and imprisoned in a cage and was tortured in the cruellest and the most inhuman ways for five long days. In order to terrorise him further into submission, one of his distinguished devotees (Bhai Mati Das) was sawn alive, another (Bhai Dyal Das) was boiled in the cauldron and the third (Bhai Sati Das) was roasted alive before the Guru.

Finally, the Guru himself was beheaded, under imperial warrant, in broad daylight, in the middle of a public square, the most prominent public place in India, called Chandni Chowk, of Delhi, on the charge that he was a stumbling block preventing the spread of Islam in the Indian subcontinent. The exact location of the beheading is marked by Gurdwara Sis Ganj in Delhi. His martyrdom was yet another challenge to the Sikh conscience. It was then realized that there could be no understanding between an insensate power imbrued with blood and a proud people wedded to a life of peace with honour. The sacrifice roused the Hindus from their passive silence and gave them the fortitude to understand the power that comes from self-respect and sacrifice. Guru Tegh Bahadur thus earned the affectionate title of "Hind-di-Chadar" or the Shield of India.

REFERENCES

G. B. Singh: *Shri Guru Granth Sahib dian Prachin Bi[an.* Lahore: Modern Publications, 1944.

Ganda Singh: ed, ed. *Hukamname.* Patiala: Punjabi University, 1985.

Ganda Singh: ed. *Punjab, 1849–1960 Bhai Jodh Singh Abhinandan Granth,* Ludhiana: Punjabi Sahitt Academy, 1962.

Grewal, J. S.: *Sikh Ideology Polity and Social Order.* New Delhi: Manohar, 1996.

Hans, Surjit: *A Reconstruction of Sikh History from Sikh Literature.* Jalandhar: ABS Publications, 1988.

Harbans Singh: *The Heritage of the Sikhs*. New Delhi: Manohar, 1983.

Jodh Singh, Bhai: *Bhai Jodh Singh Gadd Saurabh*. Ed. Piar Singh. Patiala: Punjabi University, 1986.

Joginder Singh: *Japji de like*. Jalandhar: Hindi Press, 1981.

Kalal, Koer Singh: *Gurbilas Patishahi 10*. Ed. Shamsher Singh Ashok. Patiala: Punjabi University, 1986.

Mishra, Bhagavatsvarup: ed. *Kabir Granthavali*. Agra: Vinod Pustak, 1969.

Nahar Singh: "Some Documents regarding Sacred Sikh Relics in England. " *Punjab Past and Present*, 1974.

Nikki-Guninder Kaur Singh: *The Name of My Beloved*. San Francisco: Harper SanFrancisco, 1995.

Nirankari, Surinder Singh: ed. *Nirankari Gurmati Prarambhata*. Amritsar: Young Men's Association, 1951.

Pritam Singh: ed. *Sikh Concept of the Divine*. Amritsar: Guru Nanak Dev University, 1985.

Qaiser, Iqbal: *Historical Sikh Shrines in Pakistan*. Lahore: Punjabi History Board, 1998.

Santokh Singh, Bhai: *Shri Gurpratap Suraj Granth*. Vol. 6. Ed. Bhai Vir Singh. Amritsar: Khalsa Samachar, 1963.

Seva Singh: *Shahid Bilas*. Ed. Giani Garja Singh. Ludhiana: Punjabi Sahitt Academy, 1961.

Sevadas: *Parchi Patishahi Dasvin ki*. Ed. Piara Singh Padam. Patiala: Kalam Mandir, 1988.

Shan, Harnam Singh: *Guru Granth Sahib di Koshkari*. Patiala: Punjab Language Department, 1994.

Sikh Itihas Research Board: Shiromani Gurdwara Prabandhak Committee, 1982.

Suri, Sohan Lal: *Umdat-ut-Tvarikh*, daftar III. Trans. V. S. Suri. Delhi: S. Chand and Company, 1961.

Suri, Sohan Lal: *Umda-ut-Tvarikh*, daftar IV. Trans. V. S. Suri. Chandigarh: Punjab Itihas Prakashan, 1972.

Religious Places

It is often stated by Sikhs and proudly so, that where ever there are two Sikhs, they will establish a Gurdwara or a religious place of their own. Given the work schedules, work ethics and the distances many amongst them do not get time or make efforts to go to their religious place on daily basis. On weekend however, especially on Sundays the Sikh religious places usually get full with devotees primarily due to this being a free day for many. In almost all the Sikh Gurdwaras, a free kitchen commonly known as Langar is run where devotees regardless of their faith are served full meals without any charge. At the end of the religious ceremony, Sikh congregation is requested to eat together sitting on the floor in the form of rows regardless of caste, creed and social status. This free kitchen is supported by the devotees and members who in keeping with the cardinal features of their faith always chip in and try to maintain this service selflessly. The food that is served at Langar in the Gurdwaras is no less than an elabourate feast including salads, chuttani, pickles and desserts besides usual two vegetarian dishes, chapattis and rice.

RELIGIOUS PLACES IN INDIA

Harmandir Sahib

The Harmandir Sahib or Darbar Sahib informally referred to as The Golden Temple or Temple of God, is culturally the most significant shrine of the Sikhs and one of the oldest Sikh Gurdwara. It is located in the city of Amritsar, which was established by Guru Ram Das, the fourth Guru of the Sikhs and the city that it was built in, is also due to the shrine, known as "Guru Di Nagri" meaning city of the Sikh Guru.

The Harmandir Sahib is considered holy by Sikhs because the eternal Guru of Sikhism, the Shri Guru Granth Sahib, is always present inside in it and its construction was mainly intended to build a place of worship for men and women from all walks of life and all religion to come and worship God equally. The Shri Guru Granth Sahib is the holiest literature in the Sikh religion, the tenth Guru of Sikhism, Guru Gobind Singh on seventh October 1708 made it the eternal Sikh Guru and the leader of Sikhism. Anywhere in the world where the Guru Granth Sahib is present is equally holy and precious to Sikhs. Amritsar is the location of Harmandir Sahib.

Its name literally meaning, House of God. The fourth Guru of Sikhism, Guru Ram Das, excavated a tank in 1577 AD which subsequently became known as Amritsar (Pool of the Nectar of Immortality), giving its name to the city that grew around it. In due course, a splendid Sikh edifice, Harmandir Sahib (The abode of God), rose in the middle of this tank and became the supreme centre of Sikhism. Its sanctum came to house the Adi Granth comprising compositions of Sikhi Gurus and other saints considered to have Sikh values and philosophies e.g. Baba Farid, Kabir, etc. The compilation of the Adi Granth was started by the fifth Guru of Sikhism, Guru Arjan Dev.

Amritsar is located in the Majha region of the Punjab. Majha is also known as the Bari Doab, since it is the Doab tract of land which lies between two of the five great rivers of the state, the Ravi and the Beas. As such, Majha lies in the heart of the ancient Punjab region, comprised of Gurdaspur, Batala and Tarn Taran Sahib as well as Amritsar.

Originally built during 1574 AD, the site of the temple was surrounded by a small lake in a thin forest. The third of the six grand Mughals, emperor Akbar, who visited the third Sikh Guru, Guru Amar Das, at the neighbouring town of Goindval was so impressed by the way of life in the town that he gave a jagir (the land and the revenues of several villages in the vicinity) to the Guru's daughter Bhani as a gift on her marriage to Bhai Jetha, who later became the fourth Sikh Guru, Guru Ram Das. Guru Ram Das enlarged the lake and built a small township around it. The town was named after Guru Ram Das as "Guru Ka Chak", "Chak Ram Das" or "Ram Das Pura".

During the leadership of the fifth Guru, Guru Arjan Dev (1581-1606), the full-fledged Temple was built. In December 1588 the great Muslim Sufi saint of Lahore, Hazrat Mian Mir, who was a close friend of Guru Arjan Dev Ji, initiated the construction of the temple by laying the first foundation stone (December 1588 AD). A mason then straightened the stone but Guru Arjan Dev told him that, as he had undone the work just completed by the holy man, a disaster might come to the Harmandir Sahib. It was later attacked by the Mughals.

The temple was completed in 1604. Guru Arjan Dev, installed the Guru Granth Sahib in it and appointed Baba Buddha Ji as the first Granthi (Reader) of it on August 1604 AD. In the mid eighteenth century it was attacked by the Afghans, by one of Ahmed Shah Abdali's Generals, Jahan Khan, and had to be substantially rebuilt in the 1760s. However, in response a Sikh Army was sent to hunt down the Afghan force. They were under orders to show no mercy and historical evidence suggests none was shown. Both forces met each other 5 miles outside Amritsar; Jahan Khan's army was destroyed. He himself was decapitated by commander Sardar Dayal Singh.

The temple is surrounded by a large lake of water, known as the Sarovar which consists of Amrit (Holy Water or Immortal Nectar). There are four entrances to the temple, signifying the importance of acceptance and openness; ostensibly, this concept is reminiscent of the tent of Abraham in the Old Testament — his tent was open on all four sides in order to be able to welcome travelers from all directions. Inside the temple complex there are many shrines to past Sikh Gurus, Saints and martyrs. There are three holy trees (Bers) each signifiying a historical event or Sikh saint. Inside the temple there many memorial plaques that commemorate past Sikh historical events, saints, martyrs and includes commemorative inscriptions of all the Sikh soldiers who died fighting in World wars one and two. For a new visitor the first recommended place to visit is the information Office highlighted in the map and followed by visiting the Sikh Central museum near the main entrance and clock tower. Anyone who wants to enter the Harmandir Sahib may do so, irrespective of religion, colour, creed or sex. The only restrictions are that the person must not drink alcohol, eat meat or smoke cigarettes or other drugs while in the shrine. Visitors are, as well, expected to dress appropriately and everyone must cover their heads as a sign of respect, remove their shoes and wash their feet in the small pool of water as they enter the Harmandir Sahib premises. Head scarves are provided. All Sikh temples (Gurdwaras) in the world follow this cultural rule that everyone is welcome to enter. There are four doors to get into the Harmandir Sahib, meaning that Harmandir sahib is open to anyone.

Much of the present decorative gilding and marblework dates from the early 1800s. All the gold and exquisite marble work were conducted under the patronage of Hukam Singh Chimni and Emperor Ranjit Singh, Maharaja of the Sikh Empire of the Punjab. The Darshani Deorhi Arch stands at the beginning of the causeway to the Harmandir Sahib; it is 202 feet (62 m) high and 21 feet (6 m) in width. The gold plating on the Harmandir Sahib was begun by Emperor Ranjit Singh and was finished in 1830 AD. The Sher-e-Punjab (Lion of the Punjab), was a heavy donor of wealth and materials for the shrine and is remembered with much affection by the Punjabi people in general and the Sikh community in particular. Maharaja Ranjit Singh also built two of the other most holy temples in Sikhism. This was due to Maharaja Ranjit Singh having a deep love for the tenth Guru of Sikhism Guru Gobind Singh. The other two most holy temples in Sikhism, which he built, are Takht Shri Patna Sahib (intiation or birth place of Guru Gobind Singh) and Takht Shri Hazur Sahib the place of Guru Gobind Singh's Sikh ascension into heaven.

Shri Akal Takht Sahib

Akal Takht is the primary seat of Sikh religious authority and central altar for Sikh political assembly. Through hukamnamas edicts or writs, it may issue decretals providing guidance or clarification on any point of Sikh doctrine or practice referred to it, may lay under penance personages charged with violation of religious discipline or with activity prejudicial to Sikh interests or solidarity and may place on record its appreciation of outstanding services rendered or acrifices made by individuals espousing the cause of Sikhism or of the Sikhs. The edifice stands in the Darbar sahib precincts in Amritsar facing Harimandar, now famous as the Golden Temple. The word Akal, a negative of kal(time), is the equivalent of timeless, beyond time, everlasting, and takht, in Persian, that of royal throne or chair of state. Akal Takht would thus mean "timeless or everlasting throne" or throne of the Timeless One, i.e. God." In the Sikh system, God is postulated as Formless (Nirankar), yet to proclaim His sovereignty over His creation, He is sometimes referred to as sultan, patshah, sacha Patshah, or the True King; His seat is referred to as sachcha Takht. the True Throne, sitting on which he dispenses sachcha niao, true justice. it also became common for Sikhs, at least by the time of Guru Arjan (1563-1606), to refer to the Guru as sachcha patshah and to his gaddi or spiritual seat as Takht and the congregation he led as darbar or court. Panegyrizing the Gurus, The bards, Nalya and Mathura, in their verses included in the Guru Granth Sahib, use the word takht in this very sense. Formally, to proclaim Sikh faith's common concern for the spiritual and the worldly, synthesis of miri and piri, Guru Hargobind (1595-1644), son and successor of Guru Arjan adopted royal style. For the ceremonies of succession, he had a platform constructed opposite the Harimandar, naming it Akal Takht.

The Guru laid the cornerstone and Bhai Buddha and Bhai Gurdas completed the construction, no third person being allowed to lend a helping hand. Guru Hargobind used the takht for the accession ceremonies which, according to the source quoted, took place on 26 Har suds 10, 1663 sk/ 24 June 1606. From here, he conducted the secular affairs of the community. From here he is said to have issued the first hukamnama (q.v.) to far flung sangats or Sikh centers announcing the creation of Akal Takht and asking them to include in their offerings thenceforth gifts of weapons and horses. Bhai Gurdas was named of officiant in charge of the Akal Takht. A building subsequently raised over the Takht was called Akal Bunga (house) so that the Takht is now officially known as Takht Shri Akal Bunga although its popular name Akal Takht is more in common use.

The Sikhs recognize four other holy places as takhts, namely Takht Shri Kesgarh Sahib, Anandpur; Takht Shri Harimandar Sahib, Patna; Takht Sachkhand Hazur Sahib, Abchalnagar, Nanded; and Takht Shri Damdama Sahib, Talvandi Sabo. All four are connected with the life of Guru Gobind Singh (1666 - 1708). All five Takhts are equally venerated, but the Akal Takht at Amritsar enjoys a special status. Historically, this is the oldest of the takhts and along with Harimandar, across the yard, constitutes the capital of Sikhism. Meetings of the Sarbatt Khalsa or general assembly represent native of the entire Panth are traditionally summoned at Akal Takht and it is only there that cases connected with serious religious offenses committed by prominent Sikhs are heard and decided. Hukamnamas or decrees issued by the Akal Takht are universally applicable to all Sikhs and all institutions.

After Guru Hargobind's migration to Kiratpur early in 1635, the shrines at Amritsar, including the Akal Takht fell in the hands of the descendants of Prithi Chand, elder brother of Guru Arjan, his grandson, Hariji (d. 1696), remaining in charge for over fifty-five years. Soon after the creation of the Khalsa in March 1699, Guru Gobind Singh sent Bhai Mani Singh to Amritsar to assume control of the Harimandar and the Akal Takht. Later, After Guru Gobind Singh's death, his wife Mata Sundari Ji, sent Bhai Mani Singh again to Amritsar on behalf of the Khalsa panth During the troublous period following the martyrdom of Banda Singh Bahadur. The holy samovars or holy tank, at Amritsar, the Harimandar and the Akal Takht continued a source of inspiration and Spirit and veneration for the Sikhs when circumstances permitted, and usually on Baisakhi and Diwali, their scattered bands defying all hazards converged upon Akal Takht to hold sarbatt khalsa assemblies and discuss matters of policy and strategy, for instance, through a gurmata, sarbatt Khalsa at the Akal Takht resolved on 14 October 1745 to reorganize their scattered fighting force into 25 jathas or bands of about 100 warriors each. By another gurmata on Baisakhi, 29 March 1748 the sarbatt khalsa meeting, again, at Akal Takht, formed the Dal Khalsa or the army of the Khalsa consisting of 11 mists or divisions.

On Diwali, 7 November 1760, the sarbatt khalsa resolved to attack and occupy Lahore (till then Sikhs had not occupied any territory, their only possession being the small fortress of Ram Rauni or Ramgarh they had built at Amritsar in 1746). Akal Takht was again the venue of the sarbatt khalsa on Baisakhi day, 10 April 1763, when through gurmata it was decided to go out to the help of a Brahman who had brought the complaint that his wife had been forcibly abducted by the Afghan chief of Kasur.

Even after the Punjab had been parceled into Several Sikh independencies or kingdoms. Amritsar remained the common capital where all sardars or chiefs had built their bungas and stationed their vamps or agents. But as the need for a common strategy and action decreased and rivalries among the mist chiefs raised their head, sarbatt khalsa and correspondingly the Akal Takht lost their political pre-eminence. Maharaja Ranjit Singh felt little need for sarbatt khalsa assemblies after 1805 when it was summoned to consider the question whether or not the fugitive Maratha prince Jasvant Rao Holkar be assisted against the British. The religious authority of the Akal Takht, however, remained intact and the State never challenged it in any manner.

There are in fact instances of the State showing subservience as in the case of Maharaja Ranjit Singh himself responding to the summons from the Akal Takht and accepting for a moral misdemeanor penalty imposed by its custodian, Akal Phula Singh, who had fought as a loyal soldier in several of the Maharaja's military campaigns. In spite of its supremacy in the matter of enforcing religious discipline, Akal Takht discharges no divine dispensation. It remits no sins, nor does it invoke God's wrath upon anyone.

On several occasions during the eighteenth century, Akal Takht shared with the Harimandar desecration and destruction at the hands of Mughal satraps and Afghan invaders. Ahmad Shah Durrani, who had razed the Harimandar in 1762, again attacked Amritsar in December 1764. On this occasion a small band of 30 Sikhs under their leader, Nihang Gurbakhsh Singh stationed there to serve and protect the Akal Takht, came out to dare the invading horde and fell fighting to the last man. Ahmad Shah had the Akal Bunga completely demolished. Sikhs, however, continued to hold the sarbatt khalsa in front of the ruins and decided at one such gathering on Baisakhi, 10 April 1765, to rebuild the Akal Bunga as well as the Harimandar. Funds for this purpose had already been set apart from the pillage of Sirhind in January 1764. The work was entrusted to Bhai Des Raj, who was also furnished with Guru ki Mohar or the Guru's seal to enable him to raise more funds. The construction of the ground floor of the Akal Bunga was completed by 1774.

The rest of the five - storeyed domed edifice was completed during the reign of Maharaja Ranjit Singh. The gilded dome atop the building was built by Hari Singh Nalva at his own expense. The facade of the first four storeys including the basement (originally ground floor but rendered partly below ground level because of the raising of the level of the circumambulatory terrace in front) had a semi-circular orientation. The ground door was a large hall With an attached pillared marble portico. The facades of the next two floors had projected eaves supported on decorative brackets. The facade of the third floor, a large hall with galleries on the sides, had cupped arched openings, nine in number. The exterior of the fourth floor, covering the central hall of the lower floor, was decorated with projected ornamental eaves and a domed kiosk at each corner. The Guru Granth Sahib was seated on the first floor, where the jathedar of the Akal Takht also took his seat. The second floor was used for important meetings and also for amrit prachar, administration of the initiation of the Khalsa. The hall on the third floor was used especially for the meetings of the Shiromani Gurdwara Parbandhak Committee until a separate office block, called Teja Singh Samundari Hall, was constructed for the purpose during the 1930's.

Takht Shri Damdama Sahib

The Takht Shri Darbar Sahib Damdama Sahib, one of the Five Takhts or Seat of Temporal Authority of Sikhism, Takht Shri Damdama Sahib is situated at Bathinda in Punjab, India and is the place where Guru Gobind Singh, the tenth Sikh Guru, prepared the full version of the Sikh Scriptures called Shri Guru Granth Sahib in 1705. The other four Takhts are the Akal Takht, Takht Shri Keshgarh Sahib, Takht Shri Patna Sahib and Takht Shri Hazur Sahib.

The Takht is located at village Talwandi Sabo, 28 km Southeast of Bathinda. Literally, Damdama means breathing place. Guru Gobind Singh stayed here after fighting battles against the Mughals. Before his arrival at

Talwandi Sabo, two of the Guru's younger sons, Zorawar Singh and Fateh Singh, aged 9 and 7 respectively, were bricked alive by Wazir Khan,the Nawab of Sirhind(Today, the place is known as Fatehgarh Sahib). His two elder sons, Ajit Singh and Jujhar Singh, laid down their lives while fighting Mughal forces at Chamkaur Sahib. After writing the Zafarnama, Guru Gobind Singh fought a successful battle at Muktsar and then moved towards Talwandi Sabo.

Kashi means a great learning centre.(Kashi is also another name of the Hindu holy city of Varanasi, which was a great centre for Learning in ancient India). This title was given because of the intense literary activities that Guru Gobind Singh engaged in during his stay here(the compilation of Sikh Scriptures).It is said that one day Guru Gobind flung a handful of reed pens over the heads of the congregation('Sangat'), saying: "Here we will create a pool of literature. No one of my Sikhs should remain illiterate." The Damdame Wali Bir as it is sometimes called was completed here by the Guru. It was transcribed by Bhai Mani Singh. The hymns of Guru Tegh Bahadur Sahib, the ninth Guru and father of Guru Gobind Singh were added into the Bir.

This Takht was officially recognized as the fifth Takht of Sikhism on Novemver 18, 1966. On a demand from the Sikhs, a sub-committee was appointed by the Shiromani Gurdwara Prabandhak Committee, Amritsar by a General Meeting Resolution No: 789 on July 30, 1960. A report of the sub-committee containing 183 pages was received to declare Damdama Sahib or Guru Ki Kashi as the fifth Takht of the Sikhs. A general body meeting of the Shiromani Gurdwara Prabandhak Committee at Amritsar approved the recommendations through resolution number 32 on November 18, 1966. It has been declared as the fifth Sikh Takht by the Government of India in April 1999 during tricentennial celebrations of the formation of the Khalsa.

Takht Shri Keshgarh Sahib

Takht Shri Kesgarh Sahib is situated in the central place of city Anandpur Sahib After the establishment of Anandpur Sahib, Guru Gobind Singh Ji used to hold congregations on this hill. Revelation of Khalsa and first inititation (Khande Di Pahul) took place here. At that time the hill of Kesgarh Sahib was at least 10-15 feat higher than its present height. By the side of this hill there stood another hill. It was known as "Tambu (tent) Wali Pahari" because a special tent was set up here on the day of revelation of Khalsa. This hill does not exist any more. Similarly, there was a long range of small hills extending from Kesgarh Sahib to Anandpur fort.

Kesgarh Sahib fort was built in 1699. The hill armies attacked Anandpur Sahib several times between 1700 and 1705 but never could the invading armies reach Kesgarh Sahib because it was a very strong fort and before reaching the gates of this fort the armies had to capture the fort at Taragarh, Agamgarh, Fatehgarh and Anandgarh. This could not happen even once in the history of Anandpur Sahib. It was only on December 6, 1705, when Guru Sahib abandoned the town, the hill armies entered this fort and demolished it. The Sikhs could not enter Anandpur Sahib till Baba Banda Singh Bahadur subjugated the ruler of Bilaspur. The Sikhs had to face another wave of persecution after the fall of Baba Banda Singh.

Within the next ten years most of the Sikh homeland was under the rule of Maharaja Ranjit Singh, the Sikh Misls and the Patiala dynasty and this meant peace in the Punjab; hence Anandpur Sahib was most safe place for the Sikhs. Takht Shri Keshgarh Sahib is the main shrine at Anandpur Sahib. At Anandpur Sahib there are lying many historical Relics which belong to Shri Guru Gobind Singh Ji, Khanda (Double Edged Sword) Guru Ji used to prepare amrit on the revelation of Khalsa Day. Kataa,r It was Shri Guru Gobind Singh's personal Dagger he used to carry it with him. Saif, It is double egded Weapon presented to Guru Sahib by Mughal Empror Bahadur Shah. Gun was presented to Guru Sahib by one of Sikhs from Lahore. One of the Five Takhats or Seat of Authority of the Sikhs. This takhat is situated at Anandpur Sahib which is where Guru Gobind Singh, the tenth Guru of the Sikhs performed the first Amrit Sanchar (Initiation Ceremony) in 1699 to form the Khalsa.

Takht Shri Hazur Sahib

Nanded, is one of the important centres of Sikh pilgrimage situated on the left bank of River Godavari, is a district town in Maharashtra (India). It is a railway station on the Manmad-Kachiguda section of the south central railway, and is also connected by road with other major towns of the region. The Sikhs generally refer to it as Hazur Sahib or Abichal Nagar. Both of these names apply, in fact, to the principal shrine, but are extended in common usage to refer to the town itself. Hazur Sahib is a title of reverence, meaning Exalted Presence; Abichal Nagar: Abichal= Immortal,everlasting and Nagar Town or City. The town ranks as one of the takhts, or seat of religious authority and legislation for the Sikhs. Nanded, which was visited both by Guru Gobind Singh, claims several Sikh shrines of historical importance.

Around 1823, Raja Chandu Lal, Diwan of Hyderabad state, had the management of the shrine made over to the Udasis. He also secured for the shrine an endowment of about 525 acres of land. In 1832 Maharaja Ranjit Singh built on the site a two-storeyed Gurdwara, with a golden dome. During this time, Sikh artisans and workmen came to Nanded in large numbers, and many of them settled here permanently. Additionally, the Nizam enlisted a troop of Sikhs in his army. With this influx of Sikh population, the Udasi influence receded. Sikhs assumed the responsibility for religious services in the shrine at Nanded, whereas the administration was taken over by the Nizam's government.

The control of the main shrine and other Gurdwaras at Nanded was transferred to a 17-member Gurdwara Board, with a 5-member Managing Committee constituted under the Nanded Sikh Gurdwaras Act passed on 20 September 1956 by Hyderabad state legislature. A chakra (quoit), a broad sword, a steel bow, a steel arrow, a gurz (heavy club with a large spherical knob), a small gilded kirpan and five gilded swords are on display in the sanctum of Takht Sachkhand as Guru Gobind's relics.

Takht Shri Patna Sahib

Patna, ancient Patliputra, now capital of Bihar State is reverently called Patna Sahib by the Sikhs because of its consecration by Guru Nanak Dev, Guru Tegh Bahadur and Guru Gobind Singh. The latter was born here during Guru Tegh Bahadur's tour of eastern Bihar, Bengal and Assam from 1666 to 1670. Patna Sahib is situated on the right bank of the River Ganges. This City has following Sikh Gurdwaras:

Gurdwarā Pahilā Bari (lit, the first and larger), commonly known as Gurdwārā Gāe Ghāt, is dedicated to Guru Nanak Dev, who during his visit to Patna stayed here with Bhāi Jaita, a pious man, confectioner by trade, who became the Guru's follower and later converted his house into a dharmsala.

Takht Shri Harimandir Sahib, the principal shrine at Patna Sahib and one of the five Takhts or the highest seats of religious authority for the Sikhs, marks the site of the Chhoti Sangat. Guru Tegh Bahadur had first alighted at Ban Sangat at Gae Ghat from where he was brought in procession to this place which had once been the commodious mansion of Salas Rai, the jeweller, and where Raja Fateh Chand Maim now built a new house to accommodate the holy family.

Gurdwara Bal Lila Maini Sangat, in a narrow lane dose to Takht the house where Raja Fateh Chand Maini lived. His childless rani had developed special fondness for the young Gobind Das, who, too often, came to sit in the Rani's lap giving her immense delight and spiritual solace. She fed the Sahibzada and his playmates, at his demand, with salted and boiled gram. Even now boiled and salted gram is served as Prasad in this Gurdwara, which, unlike the other shrines is served by nirmala Sikhs.

Gurdwara Shri Guru Gobind Singh Ghãt is where the child Gobind Das used to play with his playmates on the bank of the Ganges. Gurdwara Guru ka Bagh is about three kilometres east of Takht Harimandir Sahib where Guru Tegh Bahadur first alighted in a garden belonging To Nawabs Rahim Baksh and Karim Baksh, nobles of Patna, and where sangat of Patna came to receive him back from his four year long odyssey.

Gurdwara Sheeshganj

The ninth Sikh Guru Shri Tegh Bahadur, was beheaded in the heart of the city in 1675 AD.. by the order of Mughal King Aurangzeb, for espousing the cause of freedom of worship of the Hindus, against whom the Emperor had unleashed a war of extermination. Guru Tegh Bahadur opposed it and paid heavy price by sacrificing his life. At the place of his martyrdom, stands Gurdwara SisGanj,as a symbol of unique sacrifice made by the sage Prophet. Adjoining the Gurdwara Sis Ganj is the Kotwali (police station), where the faithful disciples of the Great Guru Bhai Mati Das, Bhai Dyala and Bhai Sati Das were tortured to death.

Hemkund Sahib

One of the most revered of all Sikh Shrines, the Hemkund Sahib Gurdwara, the Worlds Highest Gurdwara, situated at an altitude of 4,329 mts above sea level, on the bank of a glacial lake Hemkund (Lok Pal), marks the place where Guru Gobind Singh the 10th and the last Guru unified with God after prolonged meditation. The shrine is encircled by seven snow clad peaks and their associated glaciers. Streams from Hati Parvat and Sapt Rishi Peaks feed the lake and a small stream called Himganga flows out of his lake. According to the Holy Granth Sahib, it is believed that Guru Gobind Singh, the 10th Guru of the Sikhs recounts that in a previous life he had meditated on the shores of a lake surrounded by seven snowcapped mountains. Hemkund Sahib, Sikh pilgrims have decided, is that holy lake where there 10th Guru has meditated. The Hemkund Sahib Gurdwara is an imposing star shaped structure of stone and masonry at the edge of lake Lok Pal 2 km. in circumference whose cristal clear water mirrors the image of snow clad Sapt Shring Peaks (5500 mts).

Ponta Sahib

Ponta Sahib is situated on the river Yamuna, on the Border with Uttrakhand. It is linked with Guru Gobind Singh the 10th Sikh Guru who lived here. At Bhangani, 23 Km. away, he achieved a great military victory when his forces defeated the combined might of 22 hill-country kingdom. His weapons are displayed in the town and his Gurdwara still overlooks the river.

Nanakmatta

Nanakmatta, a place of great religious intrest for the Sikhs, lies on the Khatima - Tanakpur road. It is believed that Guru Nanak Dev, the first Guru had visited this place on his way to Kailash Parvat in 1515 AD.. Nearby is a Gurdwara and the lake called Nanak Sagar.

RELIGIOUS PLACES OUTSIDE INDIA

Nankana Sahib

Sikh history originates from Nankana Sahib. Guru Nanak Dev, the founder of Sikh faith, was born here in 1469. The name of the place at that time was Rai Bhoi di Talwandi. The landlord contemporary of Guru Nanak Dev was Rai Bular, who himself became a devotee of the Guru. It was renamed Nankana after the Guru. It is located in what is called Niliarwali Bar (forest where nilgais abound), and is about 75 kilometres west-southwest of Lahore. Nankana Sahib is in Sheikhupura district and is connected to the district town by rail and road. There are several shrines connected with the memory of Guru Nanak Dee's childhood and early youth here. Later Guru Arjan dev and Guru Hargobird also visited Nankana Sahib and a Gurdwara was also raised subsequently in their honor. During the Sikh rule, these Gurdwaras were richly endowed with liberal land grants (over 7,000 hectares).

The management was in the hands of Udasi and Nirmala priests until the Shiromani Gurdwara Parbandhak Committee took over during the Gurdwara Reform Movement of 1920-25. The Gurdwaras had to be abandoned in the aftermath of the Partition in 1947. They are now looked after by the Government of Pakistan. Nankana Sahib is one of the three places which can be visited periodically by bands of Sikh pilgrims with the approval of the Government of Pakistan, the other two being Panja Sahib near Hasan Abdal and Lahore. In these simple words the community, a minute minority in the populous Indian sub-continent, expresses its loss, its grief, its pangs of separation from its venerable, holy, historical shrines left behind when they left their homes and hearths in circumstances beyond their control. Following are the historical Gurdwaras at Nankana Sahib; Gurdwara Janam Asthan, Gurdwara Bal Lila, Gurdwara Patti Sahib, Gurudwar Kiara sahib, Gurdwara Mal Ji Sahib, Gurdwara Tambu Sahib and   Gurdwara Chhevin Patshahi

Gurdwara Panja Sahib

Some 45 km from Rawalpindi on the main G.T road is the Attock District in which Hasan Abdal is a small flourishing town. Hasan Abdal's running waters and springs have always helped it stay as a traditional nucleus in a populous region. The Gurdwara of Panja Sahib at Hasan Abdal is the famous Sikh pilgrimage center and Sikh pilgrims from all over the world flocked here every year in the month of April for the Baisakhi Festival. The temple situated in the center of the town depicts typical Sikh architecture and stands in the middle of a large stone water tank beside the huge stone with the large hand print of Guru Nanak.

The dera had a specific significance for giving boon to the man of the faith and punishing the non-believers. Guru Nanak along with Bhai Mardana reached Hasan Abdal in Baisakh Samwat 1578 B.K. corresponding to 1521 AD.. in the summer season. Under a shady cool tree, Guru Nanak and Bhai Mardana started reciting Kirtan, the devotees gathered together which annoyed Wali Qandhari but he was helpless. According to a legend, Bhai Mardana was sent three times to Wali Qandhari so that the former might quench his thirst. Wali Qandhari refused and even used harsh words for him. Despite all of this, Mardana still very politely stuck to his demand. The Wali ironically remarked : Why don't you ask your Master whom you serve? Mardana reached the holy presence of Guru in a miserable state and qouthed. "Oh lord ! I prefer to death to thirst but will not approach the Wali, the egoist." The true Lord said smilingly," Oh Bhai Mardana ! Repeat the Name of God, the Almighty; and drink the water to your heart's content." The Guru put aside a big piece of stone lying nearby, Where a pure fountain of water sprang up and began to flow endlessly. Bhai Mardana quenched his thirst and felt grateful to the Creater. On the other hand, the fountain of Wali Qandhari got dried up like vanishing of comforts and conveniences of an unfortunate fellow. On witnessing the wondrous act, the Wali in rage, threw a part of a mountain towards the Guru from the top of the hill. The true Lord halted the hurled stone with his hand. An indelibe mark of Guru's hand was inserted in the stone. Observing that miracle, the ego of Wali vanished and he became the Guru's fast devotee. Several attempts were made to deface the impression of the hand of the Guru but all of non avial and the mark remained for ever and ever. This holy and revered place is now known as Panja Sahib.

Gurdwara Dera Sahib

Gurdwara Dera Sahib is situated opposite Lahore Fort near Badshahi Mosque. This is the place where Sat Gur Arjun Dev Ji was martyred in the River Ravi facing the tortures inflicted by Chandu on 30th May 1606 AD.The Gurdwara was built by Maharaja Ranjit Singh in the memory of Guru Arjan Dev, the fifth Sikh Guru who complied the Adi Granth, the principal part of Sikh scriptures. This shrine has a highly gilded attractive dome. The followers of Guru Arjan Singh assert that it is the same spot where Guru Arjan Dev miraculously disappeared in 1606 AD.. in the waters of river Ravi. The site where Guru Arjun Dev was martyred a Thara (platform) Sahib was built at by Guru Hargobind Ji in Samvat 1919 when he came to Lahore visiting Gur Asthans.

REFERENCES

Badan Singh, Giani: ed. *Adi Shri Guru Granth Sahib Ji Samik (Faridkot valalika).* 4 vols. Patiala,

Dil, Balbir Singh: *Amar Kavi Guru Amardas.* Patiala: Punjab Language Department, 1975.

G. B. Singh: *Shri Guru Granth Sahib dian Prachin Bi[an.* Lahore: Modern Publications, 1944.

Ganda Singh: ed, ed. *Hukamname.* Patiala: Punjabi University, 1985.

Ganda Singh: ed. *Punjab, 1849–1960 Bhai Jodh Singh Abhinandan Granth,* Ludhiana: Punjabi Sahitt Academy, 1962.

Grewal, J. S.: *Sikh Ideology Polity and Social Order.* New Delhi: Manohar, 1996.

Hans, Surjit: *A Reconstruction of Sikh History from Sikh Literature.* Jalandhar: ABS Publications, 1988.

Harbans Singh: *The Heritage of the Sikhs.* New Delhi: Manohar, 1983.

Jodh Singh, Bhai: *Bhai Jodh Singh Gadd Saurabh.* Ed. Piar Singh. Patiala: Punjabi University, 1986.

Joginder Singh: *Japji de like.* Jalandhar: Hindi Press, 1981.

Kalal, Koer Singh: *Gurbilas Patishahi 10.* Ed. Shamsher Singh Ashok. Patiala: Punjabi University, 1986.

McLeod, W. H.: *Sikhism*. New York: Penguin, 1997.

Mishra, Bhagirath, and Rajnarayan Maurya: eds. *Sant Namdev ki Hindi Padavali*. Pune: Pune University, 1964.

Nahar Singh: "Some Documents regarding Sacred Sikh Relics in England. " *Punjab Past and Present*, 1974.

Nikki-Guninder Kaur Singh: *The Name of My Beloved*. San Francisco: Harper SanFrancisco, 1995.

Nirankari, Surinder Singh: ed. *Nirankari Gurmati Prarambhata*. Amritsar: Young Men's Association, 1951.

Pritam Singh: ed. *Sikh Concept of the Divine*. Amritsar: Guru Nanak Dev University, 1985.

Qaiser, Iqbal: *Historical Sikh Shrines in Pakistan*. Lahore: Punjabi History Board, 1998.

Sevadas: *Parchi Patishahi Dasvin ki*. Ed. Piara Singh Padam. Patiala: Kalam Mandir, 1988.

Shan, Harnam Singh: *Guru Granth Sahib di Koshkari*. Patiala: Punjab Language Department, 1994.

Sikh Itihas Research Board: Shiromani Gurdwara Prabandhak Committee, 1982.

Suri, Sohan Lal: *Umdat-ut-Tvarikh*, daftar III. Trans. V. S. Suri. Delhi: S. Chand and Company, 1961.

Suri, Sohan Lal: *Umda-ut-Tvarikh*, daftar IV. Trans. V. S. Suri. Chandigarh: Punjab Itihas Prakashan, 1972.

Teja Singh, and Ganda Singh: *A Short History of the Sikhs*. Patiala: Punjabi University, 1989.

Van Nooten, Barend A. and Gary B. Holland: eds. *Rig Veda*. Cambridge: Harvard Oriental Series 50. Cambridge: Harvard University Press, 1994.

Vaudeville, Charlotte: *A Weaver Named Kabir*. Delhi: Oxford University Press, 1993.

Art and Iconography

Sikhism is the fifth largest organized religion in the world, with around twenty-three million disciples. Sikh History is around five hundred years old and in that time the Sikhs have formulated unequalled expressions of art and culture which is influenced by their faith and synthesizes that culture from many other traditions. Sikhism is Punjab's only indigenous religion with all other religions coming from outside Punjab. All the Sikh gurus, saints and majority of the martyrs in Sikh history were from Punjab and from the Punjabi people. Punjabi culture and Sikhism are considered inseparably interlaced.

HISTORY

Sikh temple is called a Gurudwara. Outside there is a flagpole, called a nishan sahib, flying a triangular flag with the Sikh insignia. There is no special requirement for the design of the building. Sikhs worship only one god and are opposed to idol worship. You'll probably see pictures of the Gurus (the spiritual leaders who founded Sikhism), especially the first, fifth and tenth (last) Gurus. The wisdom of the Gurus is contained in the Guru Granth Sahib, a book written by Arjun, the fifth Guru, in the early 17th century. It has become an object of veneration in itself and is regarded as the 'living' Guru.

The Golden Temple in Amritsar, Punjab, is the paragon of Sikh Temples. The holiest shrine of Sikhism, also known as the Hari Mandir, blends Hindu and Muslim styles of architecture.

The holiest shrine of the Sikh religion also known as Hari Mandir Sahib, is located in the old part of Amritsar. The temple itself is surrounded by the pool, which gave the town its name, and is reached by a causeway. Open to all, it's a beautiful place, especially early in the morning. Hari Mandir standing in the middle of the sacred pool, the Golden Temple is a two storey marble structure reached by a causeway known as the Guru's Bridge. The lower parts of the marble walls are decorated with inlaid flower and animal motifs in the pietra dura style of Taj Mahal. Once inside the temple, pilgrims offer sweet doughy prasaad to the attendants, who take half to distribute to everyone as they leave the temple.

The architecture of the Golden Temple is a blend of Hindu and Muslim styles. The golden dome said to be glided with hundred kg of pure gold is supposed to represent an inverted lotus flower. It is inverted, turning back to the earth, to symbolise the Sikh's concern with the problems of this world.

ARCHITECTURE

Sikh architecture, is a style of architecture that is characterized with values of progressiveness, exquisite intricacy, austere beauty and logical flowing lines. Due to its progressive style, it is constantly evolving into many newly developing branches with new contemporary styles. Although Sikh architecture was initially developed within Sikhism its style is used in many non-religious building due its beauty. Three hundred years ago, Sikh architecture was distinguished for its many curves and straight lines, Shri Keshgarh Sahib and the Golden Temple are prime examples and history of a gurdwara.

The study of the art and architecture of the Golden Temple has remained a subject of unconcern for art historians and critics. Even scholars of Indian temple architecture have bypassed it and references, whenever made, were mere courtesies. According to the official list of buildings of interest, published by the Punjab Government in 1875, the design of the temple, as reconstructed by Ranjit Singh, was borrowed from the shrine of Saint Mian Mir, near Lahore. The architectural prototype of the Golden Temple came into being as an idea combining the dharamshala and the tank envisaged by Guru Arjan, the son and successor of Guru Ram Das. Instead of building the temple on a high plinth in the Hindu style, Guru Arjan had it built in a depression so that worshippers had to go down the steps in order to enter it. Also it had four entrances, symbolic of the new faith which made no distinction between the four Hindu castes. Although there is no written record or contemporary sketch giving the concept of the prototype, it appears to have been, more or less, similar to the present structure dating from 1764, with the greater part of its decoration added in the early years of the nineteenth century.

The main structure rises from the centre of the sacred pool, 150 metres square, approached by a causeway about 60 metres long. An archway on the western side of the pool opens on to the causeway, bordered with balustrades of fretted marble, and, at close intervals, there are standard lamps, their great lanterns set upon marble columns. The 52-metre square-based Hari Mandir, to which the causeway leads, stands on a 20-metre square platform. Its lower parts are of white marble, but the upper parts are covered with plates of gilded copper. In the interior, on the ground floor, is the Guru Granth Sahib, placed under a gorgeous canopy, studded with jewels. On the second storey is a pavilion known as Shish Mahal or Mirror Room, so designed as to have a square opening in the centre to view from there the ground floor, with the further provision of a narrow circumambulatory around the square opening.

Further examples of Sikh architecture can be found in India, Pakistan, Afghanistan, Bangladesh, Saudi Arabia, Iraq and Turkey- these examples are mostly memorials of the places the Sikh gurus visited. Modern examples can be found world-wide: America, Australia, United Kingdom, Europe and Asia.

SCULPTURE

Around fifteen miles away from Jagraon in a small village of Manuke, is Gurdwara Mehdiana Sahib which is famous for its architecture and monuments depicting important events in Sikh history. The Gurdwara is also commonly known as the School of Sikh History. A beautiful Sarovar and greenery all around with birds chirping on the tall trees have made this place a heavenly abode for pilgrims. The Gurdwara is built in the memory of Guru Gobind Singh. During the reign of the Mughal dynasty, the Guru travelled on horseback through Roykot, Jatpure and Manuke and reached Mehdiana. Impressed by the beauty of that place and the pure water of its pond he decided to rest there for a few days.

A few years ago the Mehdiana complex looked like a forest with dense trees and bushes growing all around the place of worship. The Gurdwara was not developed and maintained properly and there was no habitation within a distance of two to three miles. Later Jathedar Jora Singh Lakha took the responsibility for its development and made Mehdiana Sahib a popular destination for pilgrims. In 1972, when Lakha started the work, only a few acres were attached to the Gurdwara but slowly the Gurdwara complex covered 25 acres.

In the vicinity of this Gurdwara are the sculptures and statues of Sikh warriors who not only laid their lives for the sake of the religion but also endured torture at the hands of the Mughals. These statues depict soldiers, women and children being cut to pieces. Some sculptures show Bahi Kanya, one of the soldiers of Guru Gobind Singh, serving water not only to the wounded soldiers in their own army but also to wounded enemy soldiers. Through these sculptures Lakha not only aimed to depict history but also to educate people that religion was more important than their lives. e felt it was better to sacrifice one's life than to accept injustice and cruelty and lose one's self-respect.

The Gurdwara is a fine specimen of Sikh architecture. Crores of rupees have been spent on its construction. Exquisite Meenakari work can be seen here. On the door of the eighth floor of the building is engraved the picture of Bhai Gurdas who is dictating the bagtan di bani to the fifth guru. On the walls of the Gurdwara are engraved the pictures of Guru Gobind Singh's miracles along with his hymns and on the main door is shown Bhai Daya Singh Hura holding the horse of the Guru. Inside the main building of Gurdwara a beautifully decorated Guru Granth Sahib is kept.

Other beautiful examples of Sikh sculptures can be widely seen in other places specially in the Gurdwaras situated at various places. One of the most famous and living example is the Golden temple of Amritsar.

CALLIGRAPHY

Calligraphy is a form of ornamental handwriting found in various cultures throughout the world and whose origins date back to ancient times. A contemporary definition of calligraphic practice would be the art of giving form to signs in an expressive, harmonious and skilful manner. Calligraphic works range from functional inscriptions and hand lettering to fine art pieces where the artistic manifestation may take precedence over the legibility of the letters. Well-crafted calligraphy differs from typography and non-classical hand-lettering in that characters are disciplined yet fluid and spontaneous. Often they are improvised at the moment of writing.

Calligraphy has played a significant role in the history of many cultures and their languages. Muslims were among those who valued calligraphy not only as art but also used it as the ultimate expression of God's words. Ancient and holy books of many religions have been handwritten in illuminated calligraphic script. In present times, calligraphy continues to flourish in the form of wedding and event invitations, typography, original hand-lettered logo design, commissioned calligraphic art, maps, and other works involving writing. Persian and Arabic script is thought to have influenced Indian calligraphy, although the scripts used are somewhat different. The flowing Persian script was thought to have influenced the writing style of Indian epics. Calligraphy in India was especially influenced by Sikhism whose holy book has been traditionally handwritten and illuminated. In ancient times the lack of modern printing technology resulted in a rich heritage of calligraphy in many Indian languages.

There have been many great calligraphers of Gurmukhi in the past. Some of them were mural painters. The wall of shrines and Royal mansions they embellished have now disappeared. The surviving calligraphy and art of wall paintings is either in a pathetic condition or in most of cases it is subject to our awful negligence. The concrete and marble is rapidly consuming our art relics. Right at the turn of the century Maharaja Ranjit Singh's summer palace at Ram Titwali has been acquired for creating a new dam. The unique art on the walls and ceilings of this temple and the palace will be submerged under the rainy season streams of the Kandhi. There is no movement to save these most important cultural treasures.

PRESENT DAY EXAMPLES

- Golden Temple, Amritsar.
- The Royal Punjabi Palaces and monuments of Patiala.
- Purana Quilla in Bathinda.
- Wagha Border.
- Bhakra Nangal Dam across the Sutlej River.
- Mehdiana Sahib Gurudwara.
- The Gurudwaras and historic monuments at Anandpur Sahib.
- Hussaini Wala Border, Ferozpur.
- Chandigarh, the modern city designed by French architect Le Corbusier.
- The Royal Punjabi Palaces of Faridkot.
- Historic monuments in Fatehgarh Saheb, Chamkaur Saheb and Sirhind, which saw a lot of action during Guru Gobind Singh's time as the 10th Guru of Sikhism.
- Historic monuments in Nabha and Sangrur.
- Ancient Fort at Bathinda, in Bathinda.
- The Gurudwara Bhabour Sahib, a Sikh place of worship, as well as several other holy places and an Ashram are located at Nangal.

- Shahpur kandi fort and Madhopur headworks near Pathankot.
- Ancient Buddhist and Hindu archeological sites at Sanghol in Fatehgarh Sahib and Dholbaha in Hoshiarpur district respectively.
- Indus Valley civilization site at Ropar
- Gurdwara Nanaksar and Gurdwara Mehdiana Sahib at Jagraon
- Fazilka India Pakistan Border Town Fazilka, Asafwala War Memorial, Fazilka

REFERENCES

Avtar Singh: *Ethics of the Sikhs*. Patiala: Punjabi University, 1983.

Bachittar Singh, Giani: *Planned Attack on Aadi Sri Guru Granth Sahib*. Chandigarh: International Centre of Sikh Studies, 1994.

Callewaert, Winand M, and Bart Op de Beeck: eds. *Devotional Hindi Literature*. Vol. 1. New Delhi: Manohar, 1991.

Duggal, Kartar Singh: *Philosophy and Faith of Sikhism*. Himalayan Institute Press, 1998.

Fauja Singh: *Guru Amardas: Life and Teachings*. Delhi: Sterling, 1979.

Ganeri, Anita: *Guru Granth Sahib and Sikhism*. Black Rabbit Books, 2003.

Kharak Singh: Philosophy of Sikhism and History. Chandigarh: Institute of Sikh Studies, 1999.

Mann, Gurinder Singh: *The making of Sikh Scripture*. Oxford University Press, 2001.

Marenco, E. K.: The Transformation of Sikh Society. Portland, Oregon, 1974.

Prajnanananda, Swami: *A Historical Study of Indian Music*. Delhi: Munshiram Manoharlal, 1981.

Robert O. Ballou: The Portable World Bible, Penguin Books, 1976.

Sahib Singh: *Bhagat Bagi Samik*. Amritsar: Singh Brothers, 1974.

Teja Singh: *Sikhism: Its Ideals and Institutions*. Bombay, 1938.

Vaudeville, Charlotte: *A Weaver Named Kabir*. Delhi: Oxford University Press, 1993.

19

Sikhism in Modern World

The chronicle of Sikhs is one of the most significant episodes in the account of India. Guru Nanak Dev grounded Sikhism in the 15 century and he was accompanied by nine Gurus. Guru Angad acquired the Gurumukhi script. Guru Ram Das placed the grounding for the city of Amritsar. Guru Arjan Dev accumulated the Adi Granth, the religious text of Sikhs (a.k.a. Siri Guru Granth Sahib).

But it was Guru Gobind Singh who applied Sikhism a reincarnated vigor and aggregate following in the seventeenth century. The rule of Sikhism is that there was simply one God, and altogether people are servants of God and Guru, and are attached collectively in a holy brother-sisterhood called the Khalsa. He announced that he was the end of the Gurus, and demanded his followers to idolise only the Guru-Word afterward his end.

Guru Gobind Singh likewise constructed the instauration of Akalis. The Akalis were spiritual warriors; soldiers of God. Late in the twentieth century (1970s and 1980s), the Akalis were to wage a all-fired battle against the Indian authorities, which moderated to monumental built up nauseating against them.

Nowadays, people of Sikh faith can be detected all over the cosmos, due to years of persecution in their fatherland (in 1738 along Nadir Shah, in 1748 to 1751 by Ahmed Shah Abdadi and by the British in 1849 as well as due to their enterprising sprightliness. The Sikhs have been bully sponsors of art, faith and scholarship. Along with Rajputs, they are the called the most audacious dwell in India, and their adult female*, amongst India's most beautiful. The Sikhs have entered in India's nation constructing for hundreds of years, agitating the British, functioning in the armed forces (the Sikh regiment is the most decorated regiment of the Indian ground forces) and surpassing in sports, and they have even served as the President (Gianni Zail Singh, 1916-1994, President of India, 1982-87, and a veteran freedom fighter) and PM (Manmohan Singh) of India.

DIASPORA

The circumstance Diaspora is an old word, etymologically inferred from the Greek Diasperien, from dia specifying "over" and sperien "to sow or scatter germs". The Greek translations of Hebrew Scriptures, expressly destined it for the Hellenic Jewish communities in Alexandria to account the Jews being in expat from the fatherland of Palestine. The "Diaspora" accepted, consequently, a certain religious partial tone in the knightly rabbinical writings to delineate the pledge of Jews dwelling exterior of Palestine. The perceptions and ecumenical beliefs began basal falsifying some time in 70s and early 80s with the achiever chronicles of many Indians domiciliating abroad. It comprised called for whether their achievements beyond the sea can be repeated back home in particular when India was embarking on the twenty-first century below the vernal leadership of Rajiv Gandhi, who converted a in-person icon of India aiming to constitute a hearty cosmos player, supercharged by science and applied science. The coming to ability of the Bartiya Janata company below the leadership of Shri A.B. Vajpai began the blossoming of the long developed agendum of the party to attract the Indian Diaspora to comprise a mate in the total development programmes of the nation.

The particular area of Sikh Diaspora would postulate carefully analysing and arrangement for the homocentric circle in the curving over greater circles of the Indian Diaspora and the Punjabi Diaspora respectively. There is, of course, no declining the info that the 'Kesdhari Sikhs', asserting the symbolizations of the five K's have been cladding additional obstructers in their master person and personal lifespan. In conditions of country-wise analytic thinking, it would come along to comprise appropriate to begin with the Indian Diaspora community in Britain, which could be considered representing the diversity of India and the alone diachronic gene linkage between the two countries. The spiritual break down of the Indian universe, though disputable to account, is an authoritative expression emphasizing the tradition and the language of the assorted groups. Apparently, those categorised, as Hindus are the greatest group abided by by the Sikhs- it is pointed out that although the Sikh population in India comprises fewer than 2% approximates of Sikhs because a ratio of Indians in Britain are cast at more than a third. The Sikhs accepting no qualifications are accounted to be 20% while the anatomies for Hindus is 15% and for Muslims 33%. The anatomies for ownership of domiciliating are indeed assuring for the Sikhs, who are U.K's top house-owner; 8 out of 10 Sikhs are likely to own a house, conceived the canonic symbol of prosperity. The Sikh Gurdwaras - since the curtain raising of the first in 1911, the number has accomplished more than 200 - are expand in length and breadth of Britain and have convert the centres of many positive and some arguable activities of the community. In what could be named a total contradiction in conditions of the instructions of the Sikh Gurus, there are caste-oriented Gurdwaras and a important number of them are controlled along the components rejected by the thought Sikh community.

There are almost twenty-six million Sikhs in the cosmos. 3 million live away South Asia, chiefly in three countries. Over 700,000 dwell in Great Britain, with about one-half a million each in the United States and Canada. Northward American civilisation has a young recorded history of just over 200 years of immigrants and settlers from across the world. In this short time span, Sikhs have been an important and integral part for over a century. Early Sikh settlers arrived in Canada in 1897. The San Francisco Chronicle of April 6, 1899 reported the arrival of four Sikhs in California. In 1906, Sikhs had established their first Gurdwara - Sikh place of worship - in Stockton. Less than a hundred years later, now there are over 100 Gurdwaras that dot the landscape of North America. Sikh workers helped construct the Panama Canal at the turn of the twentieth century.

In 1913 the Sikhs of California bore to the Ghadr Party, dedicated to oust the British from India. (Decades later, from the United States the Irish were to wage a similar struggle versus the British presence in Ireland.) A hundred years ago, the laws of the United States were repressing, regressive and discriminative. Asian immigrants could not become citizens; they could not own land, nor could they sponsor their family members from their several native countries. These rights were not seized and won until 1946, after the Second World War.

If there were to be a Sikh poster boy from those days it would have to be Dalip Singh Saund. He arrived in California in 1920, earned a PhD in mathematics from Berkeley but could not land a job as a schoolteacher. Rather he became a potato farmer. He also became active in local politics struggling for the rights of Asian immigrants, and when the laws exchanged, served as a judge. He also turned the first Sikh and the first Asian to become a US Congressman where he served for two terms.

Given the preferential laws of the United States at that time, the number of Sikhs that came at the turn of the century stayed small.

The communities that they established in and around Yuba City and Stockton in California and in Victoria and Vancouver in Canada even exist as vivacious, thriving salutes to multiculturalism. Second Wave (1960 - 1984) The second wave of Sikh migrants to this country started as students who came for advanced studies, often funded by fellowships and scholarships, and expanded geometrically after the mid 1960's when President Lyndon Johnson set immigration confinements aside. Sikh immigrants provided highly skilled professionals for this country's needs and continue to do so. The clamber for this most basic and fundamental of civil rights goes forward to be waged. The corporate world had also been reluctant to admit Sikhs into its world because of their distinct appearing, to wit, the turban, long hair and beard. Such discriminatory, though clearly illegal policies, hearken back to the days when no one but a WASP male was deemed eligible for admission into society. Less than 30 years ago, Sikhs fought a long and bitter struggle with the New York Telephone Company, which was leaving to hire Sikhs but not with turbans. The kirpan of the Sikhs has also attracted unwarranted negative care and been the subject of legal action. Fortunately better sense prevailed, as it also did in many engineering firms that needed Sikhs to replace their pillboxes with hard hats.

Over the past 30 years, many potbellies have revised their code to be non-preferential; other employers remain obdurate and will need continuous legal and federal persuasion. Although the United States armed services remain closed to general enlisting of Sikhs at this time, nevertheless, uniformed Sikh officers do serve at high ranks in the US army dental and aesculapian corps. Now the American born and reared young children of migrant Sikhs face their own hard choices. Their raises have to go to their schools to educate their teachers as well as their schoolmates of who we are and how we live and pray. These immature people want the same opportunities as their non-Sikh friends on the football field or in the classroom.

Many milestones deserve mentioning in these never ending battles. After a extended struggle, in 1995 Sikhs won the right to serve in the Royal Canadian Mounted Police without compromising their religious articles of faith. And now several officers in the Canadian Police are Sikh. Sikhs also serve in the Canadian armed services, as they do in the armed services and police (including Scotland Yard) of Great Britain Holland, Singapore, Malaysia, Kenya, Tanzania, and, of course, India

The police services in California and in the capital district have just this year revised their administratively codes to allow Sikhs to serve without hindrance of any sort; similar battles continue to be waged in other jurisdictions across the country. Sikh-Americans remain concerned about the denial of rights to their people in India that have been relentlessly authenticated over many years. Such feelings are natural in an immigrant community, as are most clearly seen in the American immigrant engaged and pertained about the Arab-Israeli conflict and the Irish-American longing for justice in Ireland.

MODERN RELIGIOUS MOVEMENTS

Though there is no deviation in belief between the Gurus there is significant elabouration, expansion and development. Guru Tegh Bahadur believed that life was short and that time past away without individuals seizing the opportunities given to them. He reiterated the idea of liberation in life by saying that there should be engagement but without entanglement. This ideal led to his teaching that this was only possible by conquering the fear of death. As Sikhs were becoming warriors this was seen as of paramount importance. Guru Tegh Bahadur, like the early Gurus, also refute the belief that occult powers were a sign of one's spiritual achievement.

The terminology of the Gurus also changes in time. This is most evident with the tenth Guru Gobind Singh, who called Akal Purakh, Sarab Loh 'All Steel'. Gobind believed that God commissions particular individuals to fight evil, and that he had been chosen to defend his people and fight against Mughal and Afghan persecution. Thus he developed his Grandfather Hargobind's teaching in the unity of the socio-political and the religious realms (miri-piri) into the Saint-Soldier (sant-sipahi) who fights only for righteousness (dharam) at Akal's calling. The affairs of the temporal world and the spiritual world are believed to be coterminous. Gobind believed that it is righteous to pick up arms when all other means fail, providing it is the will of Akal Purakh/Sarab Loh. The warrior Singhs abided by a code of conduct (rahit) given to them by Gobind. Before Guru Gobind died he sanctified the scripture as the next Guru, thus the Adi Granth became the textual Guru Granth Sahib for the Khalsa Singh. And with the inauguration of the Khalsa the Sikh Panth were transformed into the Guru Panth. Now decisions made in the presence of the Guru Granth Sahib by the Guru Panth were (and are today) seen with equal authority as that of the Gurus' decisions amongst his Sikhs and Singhs in the past. This logically followed from the previous Gurus' equation of the Word (sabad) with the true Guru (satGuru).

SPIRITUAL REVOLUTION

According to the Sikh Gurus, religious, moral and spiritual activity covers the totality of life of the individual as well as of the society. For, life is one whole and cannot be arbitrarily split up into separate religious, social and political spheres. Nor can it be ignored of left to take care of itself. For them, religion has to meet all the problems and challenges thrown up by life. Each and every activity of man is either God-oriented or self-oriented - viz. it is either for the uplift of man and his society or it is destructive. There cannot be a neutral position.

FUTURE

Since times old the human beings have been in a hasten to get ahead of their peers. In order to achieve their personal short-sighted objectives; some will not even hesitate in treading over the established values of certain important aspects of life. This is especially true in the kingdom of religions for it is here that deliberate attempts are often made to meddle with the original codes of demonstrated religions to suit individual needs. Such actions indirectly belittle those who remain steadfast against any diversion or pollution of the true concepts of their faiths no matter of the hurdles in their way and the subtle pressure that is often exerted upon them. The proponents for changes on the other hand justify their stand by arguing that rules, regulations and codes of established religions are incomplete up to date nor in synch with modern world. They wish to reinvent the wheel under the garb of regenerates and justify their actions as the natural extension of the modern world labeling it as a need of the hour. Such development is not only prevalent in Judeo-Christian faiths but is rapidly taking hold amongst the migrant people of eastern heritage, thanks to the prevalent tradition of so-called innovative society that tries to encourage freedom of what it indicates as a "new thought and action" in each and every facet of our lives, faiths admitted.

The Sikhs in the today world are no immunity. In fact they seem to have been in particular affected by this phenomenon. This could be explained in part due to natural relaxation of religious restraints in the multicultural and multi-religious society of the west. This is brought unto them by a pseudo-feeling of liberation from the back home societal web that kept them below the folds of true dictums of Sikh faith in the past ordaining its followers to maintain a singular identity with uncut hair and turban as a pre-requisite for being and becoming a true Sikh. The incidence of 9-11 and its negative reverberations upon Sikh identity in the today's world caused further harm by providing a ready made excuse to those on the edge to shun this fundamental code. The doctrine that "Every thing goes here" led several Sikhs in the today's world to make personal choices contrary the norms of their religion.

Presently Sikhs with whiskers and turbans living in the today's world find themselves in a pull that is oppositely directed. On one hand they have this strong good sense of asserting their full identity with beards and turbans. Equally strong is the difficulty that they find on daily basis as a result of a widely prevalent unawareness and peculiarity about Sikh faith and its identity in foreign cultures. Often times harsh verbal comments, hateful frowns and queer looks create many troubles including obtaining and maintaining their jobs. The subtle but continuous ongoing pressure exerted by their admirers and relatives who had already bid farewell to the Sikh identity element adds fuel to the fire. Had it been simply an element of curiosity or ignorance, one could have reasoned it out but when it turns into hatred erupting into physical violence as it did times and again after 9-11, this becomes an issue of grave fear that simply can not be lost sight of and requires measured analysis.

Sikh Americans, contempt not having any role in the atrocious crime against America on that day, ended up paying heavily in the form of furiousness against them including loss of a few lives. Such physical incidences of hate against turbans and beards allowed for ready made justification of saying good bye to Sikh identity in the minds of those who were already on shaky grounds making them unsuitably question the very rationale of following the pronouncements of their Gurus under such environments. Those who firmly believed that the articles of Sikh identity blessed to them by Guru Gobind Singh were to be maintained under all consideration; happened to be the ones who ended up facing such issues single-handedly. It was here that the leadership of Sikh community in India failed miserable for they could have intervened by exerting their political pressure in helping Sikhs living abroad but unfortunately their own petty inner opposing and mud casting battle with each other kept them entangled into their own enwraps.

Individuals dismiss the fact that acculturation does not and need not have to be mechanically interpreted into de-identification. In their opinion the outbound show of purity without purity of heart and deeds is not worth the effort. True, but it also should not have led them to assume that having outward Sikh identity will somehow lead to the pollution of the internal pureness. It is no denying the fact that either kind of individuals both with and without Sikh identity exist in good deal in this universe-some pure at heart and others not. The fact of the matter is that to live a true Sikh way of life one has to believe and live with a full belief in outward appearance of Sikh faith while maintaining total inner purity. Sikhism comes in a package deal. How could one ask a Sikh to be pure at heart and in deeds yet dismiss the first and fundamental step of preserving a visible distinct Sikh identity? Sikhs are enacted to have certain codes; both moral and external, which are not contradictory. To justify certain elements that may suite one while dismissing others is to twist the facts of the history and lead astray the youth.

SIKHISM AS A GLOBAL RELIGION

Sikhs transmigrated in small numbers to the West in the last years of the ninteenth century and the early twentieth century. Mass scale inmigration to Great Britain happened after World War II, when men were called for to run British industries. Having a strong work ethic, Sikhs made a good living and received their relatives to settle there. Now, Sikhs are bringing a significant role in British social, political, and economic fields. The children of immigrant Sikhs are well demonstrated in several professional fields. They have proven themselves as top-class doctors, engineers, industrialists, and businessmen. Sikhs also spread extensive throughout southeast Asia, and some Sikhs reached as far as Africa. Early visitors to North America settled mainly on the Pacific coast, in California, USA, and British Columbia, Canada. They demonstrated Gurdwaras in Stockton, Vancouver, and former cities.

They faced stiff opposition to their comportment. During those days, the United States refused to grant citizenship to anybody who was not white. In a landmark Supreme Court case, United States vs. Bhagat Singh Thind, the Supreme Court ruled that Bhagat Singh could not become a naturalized citizen even though anthropologists had defined him as a extremity of the Caucasian race. According to the U.S. Supreme Court, Bhagat Singh, despite technically being Caucasian, was not a white person as used in "common speech, to be interpreted in accordance with the agreement of the common man". The opinion, written by Associate Justice George Sutherland, found that while Bhagat Singh was technically Caucasian, "the average man knows perfectly well that there are apparent and profound differences", so he was denied citizenship. There are several facts which make the above ruling appalling, three of which will be mentioned here. First, Bhagat Singh Thind was a World War I combat veteran in the United States Army. Obviously this was not important enough for him to be granted behavior.

Second, the same Court had prevailed antecedently in United States vs. Takao Ozawa that Mr. Ozawa could not become an American citizen, even though he was undistinguishable from whites in show and mannerisms, because technical he was not Caucasian. Hence, many people felt that the Court had contradicted itself in the two cases with opposite rulings. Third, this ruling allowed the retroactive stripping of citizenship from Sikhs who were already Americans. Many Sikhs were forced to leave their country and their land was seized. The above rendering of the law remained in effect until July 2, 1946, when President Truman signed the Luce-Celler Act, which reversed the Thind decision. This opened the door to Sikh immigration, and after further protective laws were reversed, tens of thousands of Sikhs took advantage of the opportunity to become American citizens. Sikhs faced similar problems in Canada. Laws there were equally harsh. Sikhs were not allowed to marry, to become professional person such as doctors or lawyers, or even to travel on interstate highways. Anti-Asiatic rioters stoned Sikh businesses and assaulted Sikhs. Permits for the building of Gurdwaras, the foundations of Sikh life, were made as difficult to obtain as possible. But ultimately, after a long and hard struggle, these laws too came tumbling down. One of the most instrumental Sikh leaders in reversing this secernment was Teja Singh, who later was to become Professor Sant Teja Singh of Mastuana. He was a graduate of Harvard University and president of the Pacific Coast Society of Sikhs. He explicated Sikhism to the Canadian religious leaders, politicians, and other members of society who resented the Sikh presence. He told them that Sikhism is a faith for all humanity, and that Sikhs were tireless, patriotic, and meriting people. impression

This made a vast impact in turning popular opinion in favour of the Sikhs. Today, it is guessed there are over a million Sikhs in Britain, Canada, the United States, and other European countries. Sikh leaders like Sant Teja Singh Ji had the due date to understand that every person immigrating to a new social, traditional, or geographic environment will face problems, and thus they took steps to educate the local populace, promote strong citizenship, and ultimately, earn the grace and trust of those who once resented them. Visionary leaders foretold the potency of Sikhism in Western countries, and now those predictions are coming true. A Sikh served in the United States Congress, a Sikh was constituted to the Canadian Supreme Court, Sikhs have become prominent elected politicos in both Canada and Great Britain, and now, a Sikh has become the Prime Minister of India. In addition, Sikhs have begun to formulate extensive community support networks in their newly adopted Western countries.

There are now Sikh lobbyers to the United States Congress, Sikh newspapers and media outlets, Sikh affirm and civil rights groups, and more. These curves should extend and intensify. Sikhism has gone global, both geographic and in mindset.

REFERENCES

Callewaert, Winand M, and Bart Op de Beeck: eds. *Devotional Hindi Literature*. Vol. 1. New Delhi: Manohar, 1991.

Callewaert, Winand M.: and Mukund Lath, eds. *The Hindi Padavali of Namdev*. Delhi: Motilal Banarsidass, 1989.

Chahil, Pritam Singh: *Shri Guru Granth Sahib*. New Delhi: Crescent Printing, 1995.

Chaturvedi, Parashuram: *Kabir Sahitya ki Parakh*. Alahabad: Bharati Bhandar, 1964

Coward, Harold: *Sacred Word and Sacred Text: Scripture in World Religion*. New York: Orbis Books, 1988.

Crooke, W.: The North-Western Provinces of India: Their History, Ethnology and Administration, 1994.

Cunningham, Joseph Davey: *A History of the Sikhs*. Delhi: S. Chand and Company, 1985.

Daljeet Singh: Sikhism. Chandigarh, 1979.

Daljeet Singh: *Essay on the Authenticity of Kartarpuri Bi[and the Integrated Logic and Unity of Sikhism*. Patiala: Punjabi University, 1987.

Dewana, Mohan Singh: *A History of Punjabi Literature*. Jalandhar: Bharat Prakashan, 1971.

Ghurye, G. S.: Caste and Race in India. 1986.

Hutton, J. H.: Caste in India. 1980.

Ibbetson: Sir Denzil, Punjab Castes. Patiala, 1970.

Jagjit Singh: The Sikh Revolution. Delhi, 1981.

Jogendra Singh: Sikh Ceremonies. Chandigarh, 1968.

Kanwaljit Kaur: Sikh Women, Fundamental Issues in Sikh Studies, Institute of Sikh Studies, Chandigarh, 1992.

Randhir Singh. Jalandhar: *Prem Sumarag Granth,* New Book Company, 2000.

Shackle, Christopher; Mandair, Arvind-Pal Singh: *Teachings of the Sikh Gurus: Selections from the Sikh Scriptures.* United Kingdom: Routledge, 2005.

Shri Guru Granth Sahib by Dr Gopal Singh M.A Ph.D.: Published by World Book Centre in 1960

Taran Singh: "Shri Guru Granth Sahib vich Kavita te Rag da Sambandh. " In *M. S. Randhawa Abhinandan Granth.* Delhi: Navyug, 1969.

Taran Singh: *GurbaGi dian Viakhia PraGalian.* Patiala: Punjabi University, 1980.

Teja Singh: ed. *Shabadarth Shri Guru Granth Sahib Ji.* 4 vols. Amritsar: Shiromani Gurdwara Prabandhak Committee, 1969.

Bibliography

Abnash Kaur: *Professor Sahib Singh: Jivan te Rachna*. Patiala: Punjabi University, 1983.

Akali Kaur Singh: *Guru Shabad Ratan Prakash*. Patiala: Punjab Language Department, 1986.

Album Central Sikh Museum: Amritsar: Sri Darbar Sahib, 1996.

Amol, S. S.: *Professor Teja Singh*, Patiala: Punjabi University, 1977.

Anant, L. B. Ram: *Kabir Granthavali*. Delhi: Regal Book Depot, 1968.

Archer, John Calrk: "The Bible of the Sikhs. *Punjab Past and Present*, 1977.

Ashok, Shamsher Singh: *Punjabi Hamhlikhatan di Suchi*. Patiala: Punjab Language Department, 1963.

Attar Singh: *Socio-Cultural Impact of Islam on India*. Chandigarh: Panjab University, 1976.

Avtar Singh: *Ethics of the Sikhs*. Patiala: Punjabi University, 1983.

Avtar Singh: Philosophical Perspectives of Sikhism. ed. Gurnam Kaur. Patiala: Punjabi University, 1998.

Bachittar Singh, Giani: *Planned Attack on Aadi Sri Guru Granth Sahib*. Chandigarh: International Centre of Sikh Studies, 1994.

Bahura, Gopal Narayan: ed. *The Padas of Surdas*. Jaipur: Maharaja Savai Man Singh II Museum, 1982.

Bal, Giani Rajinder Singh: *Bhai Banno DarpaG ate Khare vali Bi[*. Jalandhar: Central Town, 1989.

Balbir Singh: *Ragmala da Saval te Jodh Kavi ate Aiam*. Amritsar: Khalsa Samachar, 1969.

Banerjee, A. C.: Guru Nanak to Guru Gobind Singh. Patiala, 1978

Barque, A. M.: *Eminent Sikhs of Today*. Lahore: Barque and Company, 1942.

Barrier, N. G., and V. A. Dusenbery: eds. *The Sikh Diaspora: Migration and Experience beyond Punjab*. Columbia, Mo.: South Asia Books, 1989.

Barth, A.: Religions of India. Delhi, 1963.

Bhagat Singh Heera, Giani: Gurmat Vichardhara. New Delhi: National Book Shop, 1969.

Bhagat Singh: *Maharaja Ranjit Singh and His Times.* New Delhi: Sehgal Publishers Service, 1990.

Bhalla, Sarupdas: *Mahima Prakash, Bhag Duja.* Ed. Gobind Singh Lamba and Khazan Singh. Patiala: Punjab Language Department, 1971.

Bhandari, Sujan Rai: *Khulastut Tvarikh.* Trans. Ranjit Singh Gill, ed. Fauja Singh. Patiala: Punjabi University, 1972.

Bosch, Gulnar K., John Carswell, and Guy Petherbridge: *Islamic Bindings and Book Making.* Chicago: Oriental Institute, University of Chicago, 1981.

Brown, Kerry: ed. *Sikh Art and Literature.* New York: Routledge, 1999.

Callewaert, Winand M, and Bart Op de Beeck: eds. *Devotional Hindi Literature.* Vol. 1. New Delhi: Manohar, 1991.

Callewaert, Winand M. and Pater G. Friedlander: *The Life and Works of Raidas.* New Delhi: Manohar, 1992.

Callewaert, Winand M.: and Mukund Lath, eds. *The Hindi Padavali of Namdev.* Delhi: Motilal Banarsidass, 1989.

Chahil, Pritam Singh: *Sri Guru Granth Sahib.* New Delhi: Crescent Printing, 1995.

Chandar, Satish: "Jizayah and the State in India during the 17th Century. " *Journal of the Economic and Social History of the Orient* 12. 1969.

Charan Singh: *Sri Guru Granth BaGi Biaura.* Amritsar: Khalsa Tract Society, 1945.

Chaturvedi, Parashuram: *Kabir Sahitya ki Parakh.* Alahabad: Bharati Bhandar, 1964

Chaupa Singh: *The Chaupa Singh Rahit-nama.* Ed. W. H. McLeod. Otago: University of Otago Press, 1987.

Cole, W. Owen, and Piara Singh Sambhi: *The Sikhs: Their Religious Beliefs and Practices.* Brighton: Sussex Academic Press, 1995.

Coward, Harold, and David Goa: *Mantra: Hearing the Divine in India* Chambersburg, Pa.: Anima Books, 1991.

Coward, Harold: *Sacred Word and Sacred Text: Scripture in World Religion.* New York: Orbis Books, 1988.

Crooke, W.: The North-Western Provinces of India: Their History, Ethnology and Administration, 1994.

Cunningham, Joseph Davey: *A History of the Sikhs*. Delhi: S. Chand and Company, 1985.

Daljeet Singh: Sikhism: A Comparative Study of its Theology and Mysticism. New Delhi: Sterling Publishers, 1979.

Darshan Singh: *A Study of Bhakta Ravidasa*. Patiala: Punjabi University, 1981.

Dass, Nirmal: *Songs of Kabir from the Adi Granth*. Albany: State University of New York Press, 1992.

Denny, Frederick M., and R. L. Taylor: *The Holy Book in Comparative Perspective*. Columbia: University of South Carolina Press, 1993.

Deol, Harnik: *Religion and Nationalism in India*. Routledge, 2000.

Dewana, Mohan Singh: *A History of Punjabi Literature*. Jalandhar: Bharat Prakashan, 1971.

Dil, Balbir Singh: *Amar Kavi Guru Amardas*. Patiala: Punjab Language Department, 1975.

Duggal, Kartar Singh: *Philosophy and Faith of Sikhism*. Himalayan Institute Press, 1998.

Fauja Singh and Gurbachan Singh Talib: *Guru Tegh Bahadur: Martyr and Teacher*. Patiala: Punjabi University, 1975.

Fauja Singh: *Guru Amardas: Life and Teachings*. Delhi: Sterling, 1979.

Foley- Garces, Kathleen: *Death and Religion in a changing World*. M.E Sharpe, 2005.

Fowler, Jeaneane: *World Religions:An Introduction for Students*. Sussex Academic, 1997.

Ganda Singh: ed, ed. *Hukamname*. Patiala: Punjabi University, 1985.

Ganda Singh: ed. *Punjab, 1849–1960 Bhai Jodh Singh Abhinandan Granth*, Ludhiana: Punjabi Sahitt Academy, 1962.

Gandhi, Surjit Singh: *Perspectives on Sikh Gurdwara Legislation*. New Delhi: Atlantic Publishers, 1993.

Ganeri, Anita: *Guru Granth Sahib and Sikhism*. Black Rabbit Books, 2003.

Gangoly, O. C.: *Rags and Raginis*. Bombay: Nalanda Publications, 1935.

Ghurye, G .S.: Caste and Race in India. 1986.

Gonda, J.: *Mantra Interpretation in the Satpatha-Brahmana*. Leiden: E. J. Brill, 1988.

Gopal Singh: *Sri Guru Granth Sahib*. 4 vols. Delhi: Gurdas Kapur and Sons, 1960–1962.

Grewal, J. S. and S. S. Bal.: *Guru Gobind Singh*. Chandigarh: Panjab University, 1987.

Grewal, J. S.: *Contesting Interpretations of the Sikh Tradition*. New Delhi: Manohar, 1998.

Grewal, J. S.: *Guru Nanak in History*. Chandigarh: Panjab University, 1979.

Grewal, J. S.: *Sikh Ideology Polity and Social Order*. New Delhi: Manohar, 1996.

Grewal, J. S.: *The Sikhs of the Punjab*. New York: Cambridge University Press, 1990.

Grewal, J. S: *Contesting Interpretations of the Sikh Tradition*. New Delhi: Manohar, 1998.

Griffin, Lepel H., and Charles Francis Massy: *Chiefs and Families of Note in the Punjab*. Lahore: Punjab Government Press, 1939.

Guninder Kaur: The Guru Granth Sahib: Its Physics and Metaphysics. New Delhi: Sterling Publishers, 1981.

Gupta, Hari Ram: *History of the Sikhs Vol.1; The Sikh Gurus, 1469-1708*. Munshiram Manoharlal Publishers, 2000.

Gupta, Mataprasad: ed. *Kabir Granthavali*. Alahabad: Lokbharati, 1969.

Gurdas, Bhai: *Kabbitt Savaiye*. Ed. Onkar Singh. Patiala: Punjabi University, 1993.

Gurdas, Bhai: *Varan*. Ed. Gursharan Kaur Jaggi. Patiala: Punjabi University, 1987.

Gurdit Singh, Giani: "Adi Bir da Rachna Kal, "*Prakash*, June 30, 1952,

Hans, Surjit: *A Reconstruction of Sikh History from Sikh Literature*. Jalandhar: ABS Publications, 1988.

Harbans Singh: *The Heritage of the Sikhs*. New Delhi: Manohar, 1983.

Harvey, Alper: *Understanding Mantras*. Albany: State University of New York Press, 1989.

Hawley, John Stratton, and Mark Juergensmeyer: *Songs of the Saints of India*. New York: Oxford University Press, 1988.

Hawley, John Stratton: "Author and Authority in the *Bhakti* Poetry of North India. "*Journal of Asian Studies*, 1988.

Hawley, John Stratton: "The Music in Faith and Morality. " *Journal of the American Academy of Religion,* 1984.

Hoiberg, Dale; Indu Ramchandani: *Students' Britannica India*. Popular Prakashan, 2000.

Hutton, J. H.: Caste in India. 1980.

Ibbetson: Sir Denzil, Punjab Castes. Patiala, 1970.

Jagjit Singh: The Sikh Revolution. Delhi, 1981.

Jarnail Singh: *Sri Gourou Granth Sahib*. 4 vols. Providenciales, West Indies: Intellectual Services International, 1998.

Jodh Singh, Bhai: *Bhai Jodh Singh Gadd Saurabh*. Ed. Piar Singh. Patiala: Punjabi University, 1986.

Jodh Singh, Bhai: Gurmat Nirnai. 3rd ed. Patiala: Language Department, 1980.

Jogendra Singh: Sikh Ceremonies. Chandigarh, 1968.

Joginder Singh: *Japji de like*. Jalandhar: Hindi Press, 1981.

Kalal, Koer Singh: *Gurbilas Patishahi 10*. Ed. Shamsher Singh Ashok. Patiala: Punjabi University, 1986.

Kanwaljit Kaur: Sikh Women, Fundamental Issues in Sikh Studies, Institute of Sikh Studies, Chandigarh, 1992.

Kashmir, Singh: "Sri Guru Granth Sahib - A juristic Person"., Global Sikh Studies.

Keene, Michael: *New Steps in Religious Education*. Nelson thomes, 2002.

Ketkar, S. V: History of Caste System in India. 1979.

Khalsa, S. S. Shanti Kaur: ed. *The History of Sikh Dharma of the Western Hemisphere*. Espanola, NM: Sikh Dharma Publications, 1995.

Kharak Singh: Philosophy of Sikhism and History. Chandigarh: Institute of Sikh Studies, 1999.

Khazan Singh, Sardar: History and Philosophy of Sikhism. 1914.

Khushwant Singh: *A History of the Sikhs*. 2 vols. Princeton: Princeton University Press, 1984.

Kohli, Surinder Singh: *A Critical Study of Adi Granth*. Delhi: Motilal Banarsidass, 1976.

Kohli, Surinder Singh: *Sikhism and Guru Granth Sahib*. Delhi: National Book Shop, 1990.

LaRocca, Donald J.: *The Gods of War: Sacred Imagery and the Decoration of Arms and Armor*. New York: Metropolitan Museum of Art, 1996.

Leitner, G. W. : *Indigenous Education in the Punjab Since Annexation*. Patiala: Punjab Language Department, 1970.

Levering, Miriam: ed. *Rethinking Scripture: Essays from a Comparative Perspective*. Albany: State University of New York Press, 1989.

Losty, Jeremiah P: *The Art of the Book in India*. London: The British Library, 1982.

Mahendranath, Shri Gurudev: The Pathless Path to Immortality. 2004.

Manmohan Singh: *Sri Guru Granth Sahib*. 8 vols. Amritsar: Shiromani Gurdwara Prabandhak Committee, 1962.

Mann, Gurinder Singh: *The Goindval Pothis: The Earliest Extant Source of the Sikh Canon*. Harvard Oriental Series 51. Cambridge: Harvard University Press, 1996.

Mann, Gurinder Singh: *The making of Sikh Scripture*. Oxford University Press, 2001.

Marenco, E. K.: The Transformation of Sikh Society. Portland, Oregon, 1974.

McLeod, W. H.: "Guru Nanak and Kabir. " *Proceedings of the Punjab History Conference*. Patiala: Punjabi University, 1965.

McLeod, W. H.: *Guru Nanak and the Sikh Religion*. Oxford: Clarendon Press, 1968.

McLeod, W. H.: *Historical Dictionary of Sikhism*. Lanham, Md.: The Scarecrow Press, 1995.

McLeod, W. H.: *Sikhism*. New York: Penguin, 1997.

McLeod, W. H.: *The Evolution of the Sikh Community: Five Essays*. Oxford: Clarendon Press, 1996.

McLeod, W. H.: *The Sikhs: History, Religion and Society*. New York: Columbia University Press, 1989.

Mishra, Bhagavatsvarup: ed. *Kabir Granthavali*. Agra: Vinod Pustak, 1969.

Mishra, Bhagirath, and Rajnarayan Maurya: eds. *Sant Namdev ki Hindi Padavali*. Pune: Pune University, 1964.

Mohammed Marmaduke Pickthall: *The Meaning of Glorious Koran, Mentor Book*, New American Library, New York and Scarborough, Ontario, 1924.

Nahar Singh: "Some Documents regarding Sacred Sikh Relics in England. " *Panjab Past and Present*, 1974.

Narang, G. C.: Transformation of Sikhism. Delhi, 1956.

Nayar, Kamala Elizabeth; Jaswinder Singh Sandhu:*The Socially Involved Renunciate: Guru Nanak's Discourse to the Nath*, 2007.

Neki, J.S: "Sahaja: an Indian ideal of mental health", *Psychiatry*, vol.38, 1975,

Nikki-Guninder Kaur Singh: *The Name of My Beloved*. San Francisco: Harper SanFrancisco, 1995.

Nirankari, Surinder Singh: ed. *Nirankari Gurmati Prarambhata.* Amritsar: Young Men's Association, 1951.

Nirbhai Singh: *Bhagata Namadeva in the Guru Grantha.* Patiala: Punjabi University, 1981.

Nirbhai Singh: *Sikh Dynamic Vision.* New Delhi: Harnam Publications, 2003.

Nizami, Khaliq Ahmad: *Some Aspects of Religion and Politics in India during the Thirteenth Century.* Delhi: Idarah-i Adabiyat-i Delli, 1974.

Nripinder Singh: *The Sikh Moral Tradition.* Columbia, Mo.: South Asia Publications, 1990.

O'Connell, Joseph T., et al.: *Sikh History and Religion in the Twentieth Century.* Toronto: University of Toronto, 1988.

Partridge, Christopher Hugh: *Introduction to World Religions,* 2005.

Pashaura Singh: "Scriptural Adaptation in the Adi Granth. " *Journal of American Academy of Religion,* 1996.

Pashaura Singh: "Scriptural Adaptation in the Adi Granth. " *Journal of American Academy of Religion,* 1996.

Pashaura Singh: "Sikh Self-Defintion and the Bhagat Ba0i. "M. A. diss., University of Calgary, 1987.

Pashaura Singh: "The Text and Meaning of the Adi Granth. " Ph. D. diss., University of Toronto, 1991.

Piar Singh: *Gatha Sri Adi Granth.* Amritsar: Guru Nanak Dev University, 1992.

Prajnanananda, Swami: *A Historical Study of Indian Music.* Delhi: Munshiram Manoharlal, 1981.

Prinsep, H. T.: Origin of the Sikh Power in the Punjab and Political Life of Maharaja Ranjit Singh. Calcutta, 1834.

Pritam Singh: "Keertana and the Sikhs. " *Journal of Sikh Studies,* 1976.

Pritam Singh: "The Translation of the Guru Granth Sahib into Devanagari Script. " *Journal of Sikh Studies,* 1977.

Pritam Singh: ed. *Sikh Concept of the Divine.* Amritsar: Guru Nanak Dev University, 1985.

Qaiser, Iqbal: *Historical Sikh Shrines in Pakistan.* Lahore: Punjabi History Board, 1998.

Randhawa, Harveen Kaur: "Early Printing History of *Guru Granth Sahib.* " M. Phil. term paper, Guru Nanak Dev University, 1985.

Randhir Singh. Jalandhar: *Prem Sumarag Granth,* New Book Company, 2000.

Randhir Singh: ed., Prem Sumarag Granth.Jalandhar, 1965.

Robert O. Ballou: The Portable World Bible, Penguin Books, 1976.

Sahib Singh: *Bhagat Bagi Samik.* Amritsar: Singh Brothers, 1974.

Sainapati: *Sri Gur Sobha.* Ed. Ganda Singh. Patiala: Punjabi University, 1988.

Santokh Singh, Bhai: *Sri Gurpratap Suraj Granth.* Vol. 6. Ed. Bhai Vir Singh. Amritsar: Khalsa Samachar, 1963.

Santokh Singh: *Philosophical Foundations of the Sikh Value System.* New Delhi: Munshi Ram Manohar Lal Publishers, 1983.

Sardool Singh Kavishar: *Sikh Dharam Darshan.* ed. Dr. Wazir Singh, Patiala: Punjabi University, 1969.

Schomer, Karine, and W. H. McLeod: eds. *The Sants: Studies in a Devotional Tradition of India.* Delhi: Motilal Banarasidass, 1987.

Seva Singh: *Shahid Bilas.* Ed. Giani Garja Singh. Ludhiana: Punjabi Sahitt Academy, 1961.

Sevadas: *Parchi Patishahi Dasvin ki.* Ed. Piara Singh Padam. Patiala: Kalam Mandir, 1988.

Shackle, Christopher: *A Guru Nanak Glossary.* London: School of Oriental and African Studies, 1981.

Shackle, Christopher: *An Introduction to the Sacred Language of the Sikhs.* London: School of Oriental and African Studies, 1983.

Shackle, Christopher: *Catalogue of the Punjabi and Sindhi Manuscripts in the India Office Library.* London: India Office Library and Records, 1977.

Shackle, Christopher; Mandair, Arvind-Pal Singh: *Teachings of the Sikh Gurus: Selections from the Sikh Scriptures.* United Kingdom: Routledge, 2005.

Shan, Harnam Singh: *Guru Granth Sahib di Koshkari.* Patiala: Punjab Language Department, 1994.

Sher Singh: Philosophy of Sikhism. Ludhiana: Chardi Kala Publications, 1966.

Singh, G.B.: *Gandhi: Behind the Mask of Divinity.* Prometheus Books, 2004.

Singh, Ganda, Gurdev Singh: *Perspectives on the Sikh Tradition.* Singh Brothers, Amritsar (India), 1996.

Singh, Gurbachan, Sondeep Shankar: *The Sikhs: Faith, Philosophy and Folks.* Roli & Janssen, 1998.

Smith, Wilfred Cantwell: *What Is Scripture: A Comparative Approach.* Minneapolis: Fortress Press, 1993.

Sri Guru Granth Sahib by Dr Gopal Singh M.A Ph.D.: Published by World Book Centre in 1960

Suri, Sohan Lal: *Umdat-ut-Tvarikh*, daftar III. Trans. V. S. Suri. Delhi: S. Chand and Company, 1961.

Talib, Gurbachan Singh: *Bani of Sri Guru Amar Das*. New Delhi: Sterling Publishers, 1979.

Taran Singh: "Sri Guru Granth Sahib vich Kavita te Rag da Sambandh. " In *M. S. Randhawa Abhinandan Granth*. Delhi: Navyug, 1969.

Teja Singh, and Ganda Singh: *A Short History of the Sikhs*. Patiala: Punjabi University, 1989.

Teja Singh: ed. *Shabadarth Sri Guru Granth Sahib Ji*. 4 vols. Amritsar: Shiromani Gurdwara Prabandhak Committee, 1969.

Teja Singh: *Sikhism: Its Ideals and Institutions*. Bombay, 1938.

Vaudeville, Charlotte: *A Weaver Named Kabir*. Delhi: Oxford University Press, 1993.

Index

H

I

J

S

Sahib, 1, 2, 3, 4, 6, 7, 9, 13, 14, 15, 16,
17, 21, 22, 25, 28, 29, 30, 33, 35, 38,
39, 44, 45, 46, 51, 56, 57, 60, 61, 62,
63, 64, 65, 66, 67, 68, 69, 70, 71, 72,
73, 74, 77, 78, 83, 84, 85, 86, 87, 88,
89, 90, 91, 93, 94, 95, 96, 98, 104,
108, 109, 111, 112, 113, 117, 122,
123, 124, 125, 126, 127, 133, 134,
140, 142, 145, 147, 148, 156, 157,
158, 160, 161, 162, 165, 166, 170,
171, 172, 173, 174, 178, 179, 180,
181, 183, 187, 188, 191, 192, 193,
194, 198, 201, 211, 212, 214, 215,
216, 217, 218, 220, 221, 222, 223,
225, 226, 229, 230, 231, 232, 233,
237, 239, 240, 246, 248, 249, 255,
258, 262, 264, 265, 266, 267, 269,
270, 271, 272, 273, 274, 275, 276,
278, 280, 281, 282, 283, 284, 285,
287, 288, 289, 290, 291, 292, 293,
294, 295, 298

Sain, 46

Sanatan Singh Sabha, 184

Sanskara, 59

Sanskrit, 1, 11, 45, 46, 47, 49, 73, 91,
94, 98, 162, 193, 231, 233, 236, 248,
277

Sant Sohan Singh, 167, 168

Scripture, 1, 8, 13, 14, 16, 17, 25, 29, 37,
46, 63, 72, 83, 84, 86, 87, 91, 111,
141, 185, 187, 188, 212, 213, 233,
234, 237, 259, 260, 262

Shabad Hazare, 96, 98

Shastar Nam Mala, 96, 98

Shiromani Akali Dal, 17, 24, 151

Shiromani Gurdwara Prabandhak
Committee, 17, 21, 83, 126, 158,
173, 212, 220, 221, 235, 288

Sikh Dharma, 1, 83, 187, 212

Sikhism, 1, 2, 3, 4, 7, 8, 9, 10, 13, 17, 25,
27, 28, 29, 30, 31, 32, 33, 34, 35, 37,
38, 39, 42, 43, 44, 45, 46, 47, 48, 49,
57, 61, 62, 68, 73, 78, 82, 83, 84, 85,
86, 91, 96, 113, 114, 116, 117, 120,
121, 122, 123, 124, 125, 127, 128,
129, 130, 132, 133, 135, 138, 143,
144, 146, 157, 158, 160, 162, 163,
166, 170, 173, 174, 176, 181, 184,
185, 187, 190, 191, 192, 194, 197,
199, 201, 203, 204, 211, 214, 219,
220, 221, 223, 228, 230, 231, 233,
236, 237, 244, 245, 246, 247, 252,
254, 255, 256, 257, 258, 259, 260,
262, 263, 264, 265, 275, 276, 277,
281, 282, 284, 285, 287, 288, 295,
298

Simran, 43, 128, 138, 214, 236, 237, 244,
245, 247

Singapore, 167, 168, 201

Singh Sabha Movement, 143, 149, 194

Singh, Sobha, 81, 82

Social Conduct, 244

Sohan Lal Suri, 169, 170

Sohni, 81

Steel Bracelet, 123, 182

Sultanpur, 4, 62, 67, 100, 102, 162, 191

Surasagara, 109

Svami, 46

Swayyae, 98

Sword, 6, 11, 12, 15, 32, 65, 147, 177,
180, 182, 206, 217, 218, 223, 266,
273, 289, 290

T

Talvandi, 4, 9, 67, 68, 69, 74, 100, 285